ACCLAIM FOR JOSEPH J. ELLIS'S

AMERICAN SPHINX

"Beautifully written . . . shows us how a first-class mind grapples with major historical issues. . . . A brilliant account." —*Chicago Tribune*

"Mr. Ellis . . . is a remarkably clear writer. . . . *American Sphinx* is fresh and uncluttered but rich in historical context."
—*The New York Times Book Review*

"A superbly written, brilliantly wrought portrait. . . . Jefferson's flaws and contradictions are dealt with plausibly and perceptively."
—*Forbes* magazine

"Finely wrought, well-balanced . . . a cogent, common-sense character sketch of a complex, important man." —*Philadelphia Inquirer*

"Perceptive and persuasive . . . we have long needed the kind of book that Ellis has written." —*Los Angeles Times*

"Lively and provocative, Joseph Ellis has taken a fresh look at that large, varied, often puzzling, often surprising, and all-important territory known as the mind of Thomas Jefferson, and the result is first-rate." —David McCullough

"An admirable command of the sources and a vivid prose style . . . a first-rate guide to the internal logic of Jeffersonian positions."
—*Wall Street Journal*

JOSEPH J. ELLIS

AMERICAN SPHINX

Joseph J. Ellis is the author of several books of American history, among them *Passionate Sage: The Character and Legacy of John Adams* and *Founding Brothers: The Revolutionary Generation*, which won the 2001 Pulitzer Prize. He was educated at the College of William and Mary and Yale University and lives in Amherst, Massachusetts, with his wife, Ellen, and three sons.

ALSO BY JOSEPH J. ELLIS

Founding Brothers:
The Revolutionary Generation

Passionate Sage:
The Character and Legacy of John Adams

After the Revolution:
Profiles of Early American Culture

School for Soldiers:
West Point and the Profession of Arms
(with Robert Moore)

The New England Mind in Transition

AMERICAN SPHINX

AMERICAN SPHINX

(handwritten: 閱 12, 146)

The Character
of Thomas Jefferson

JOSEPH J. ELLIS

VINTAGE BOOKS

A Division of Random House, Inc.

New York

FIRST VINTAGE EDITION, APRIL 1998

Copyright © 1996 by Joseph J. Ellis

All rights reserved under International and Pan-American Copyright
Conventions. Published in the United States of America by Vintage Books,
a division of Random House, Inc., New York, and simultaneously
in Canada by Random House of Canada Limited, Toronto.
Originally published in hardcover in the United States by
Alfred A. Knopf, Inc., New York, in 1997.

The Library of Congress has catalogued the Knopf edition as follows:

Library of Congress Cataloging-in-Publication Data
Ellis, Joseph J.
American sphinx : the character of Thomas Jefferson /
by Joseph J. Ellis.—1st ed.
p.   cm.
Includes index.
ISBN 0-679-44490-4
1. Jefferson, Thomas, 1743–1826—Psychology. I. Title.
E332.2E45   1997
973.4′6′092—dc20   96-26171
CIP

Vintage ISBN: 0-679-76441-0

www.randomhouse.com

Book design by Mia Risberg

Printed in the United States of America

20 19 18 17

For Edmund S. Morgan

CONTENTS

PREFACE AND

ACKNOWLEDGMENTS

A NY ASPIRING BIOGRAPHER of Jefferson, recognizing the ink already spilled and the libraries already filled, might do well to recall the young Virginian's famous words of 1776. Which is to say that no one should undertake yet another book on Thomas Jefferson for "light and transient causes." In fact "prudence dictates" and "a decent respect of the opinions of mankind requires" that the publication of all new books about that man from Monticello be accompanied by a formal declaration of the causes that have impelled the author to undertake the effort.

My own defense would begin over thirty years ago, when I entered graduate school at Yale to study early American history. It is impossible to avoid Jefferson while attempting to master the story of the American Revolution, since his career crisscrosses the major events of the era.

And his ideas, or at least the ideas for which he became the most eloquent spokesman, define the central themes of the story of the emerging American republic. Moreover, I was a native Virginian who, like Jefferson, had graduated from the College of William and Mary. I even had reddish blond hair like Jefferson and had learned how to disguise my insecurities behind a mask of enigmatic silence. It was therefore natural for me, once ensconced in the former cradle of New England Puritanism and Federalism, to identify with Jefferson's edgy doubts about the arrogant austerities and quasi-Arctic climate of New England.

My eventual mentor in graduate school, Edmund S. Morgan, even had a huge Jefferson portrait on his office wall, the luminous Rembrandt Peale likeness of 1800, which looked down on our seminar sessions with otherworldly authority that I found oddly reassuring. Jefferson and I were kindred spirits, I told myself, allies in this alien world where a southern accent seemed inversely correlated with one's seriousness of purpose. This youthful infatuation for Jefferson eventually went the way of my southern accent, never completely gone altogether but relegated to the blurry margins, where it lost its distinctive character. Like any young love, however, it became a permanent part of my emotional inventory.

Not that I actually knew very much about Jefferson's life or thought. My affinity for Jefferson was more personal than scholarly. Only once, when I was scouting about for a dissertation topic, did I consider working on Jefferson. My recollection is that C. Vann Woodward, a fellow southerner also recently arrived in New Haven—though as a mature and not just budding historian—alerted me to the dangers. One should not attempt biography until a bit further down the trail of life, he suggested. As for Jefferson, he was such a sprawling and famously elusive subject that any young historian who sallied forth after him was like the agile youth sent forward against impossible odds in a story about the tragic casualties of war. This excellent advice had the immediate sound of truth. I did not give Jefferson any serious scholarly consideration for another twenty-five years.

As a college teacher I assigned books about Jefferson in my courses, and I developed formal lectures on the Declaration of Independence and Jefferson's paradoxical stance on slavery. But it was not until I began research for a book on John Adams that I probed beneath the surface of the Jefferson correspondence. It was an odd way for a Virginian to come home again, arriving at Monticello by way of Quincy, but that is how it happened.

Adams had a truly special relationship with Jefferson that developed out of their common cause against English imperial rule and their different roots in the regional cultures of New England and Virginia. As a result, Adams admired, even loved Jefferson; they sustained a fifty-year friendship that culminated in an exchange of letters in their twilight years that most historians regard as the intellectual capstone to the achievements of the revolutionary generation. But Adams also disagreed profoundly with Jefferson's version of the American Revolution. Indeed he thought that Jefferson's entire political vision rested on a seductive set of attractive illusions. The more I read, the more I concluded that Adams was right. For the first time I began to see Jefferson critically and ironically.

My clinching commitment to a book-length study of Jefferson came in the process of writing an essay for the inaugural issue of *Civilization* about Jefferson's somewhat problematic place in contemporary American culture. If my work on Adams had given me a new perspective, my essay for *Civilization* gave me a fresh appreciation of Jefferson's resonance as an American icon. One could work for several years on Adams and enjoy splendid isolation. But working on Jefferson was like entering a crowded room in which there were always several ongoing conversations, and the constant buzz suggested that more was at stake than the resolution of merely historical questions. Jefferson was electromagnetic. He symbolized the most cherished and most contested values in modern American culture. He was one of those dead white males who still mattered.

These evolving thoughts became not just the reasons for writing a book about Jefferson but also the decisive influences on the shape of the book itself. The vast literature on Jefferson has a decidedly hyperbolic character, as if one had to declare one's allegiance at the start for or against the godlike version of Jefferson depicted in Jean-Antoine Houdon's marble bust or at least Rembrandt Peale's saintly portrait. This overdramatized atmosphere actually reproduces the polarized and highly politicized climate of opinion in Jefferson's own lifetime, when you were either with him or against him, loved him or hated him. True enough, most biographers take the sides of their subjects. But in Jefferson's case the sides are more sharply drawn and the choices less negotiable. It seems impossible to steer an honorable course between idolatry and evisceration.

That is precisely the course I have tried to pursue in the pages below, inspired by the example of John Adams to believe that affection and criticism toward Jefferson are not mutually exclusive postures, rooted in the assumption that no authentically human creature who ever walked the earth could bear the mythological burden imposed on Jefferson, convinced in my own mind that youthful infatuations must go the way of youth, that all mature appraisals of mythical figures are destined to leave their most ardent admirers somewhat disappointed. The best and the worst of American history are inextricably tangled together in Jefferson, and anyone who confines his search to one side of the moral equation is destined to miss a significant portion of the story.

My approach is selective—one early reader even called it cinematic—but maintains a traditional commitment to chronology. Another full-scale, multivolume narrative of Jefferson's life and times is clearly unnecessary. My goal is to catch Jefferson at propitious moments in his life, to zoom in on his thoughts and actions during those extended moments, to focus on the values and convictions that reveal themselves in these specific historical contexts, all the while providing the reader with sufficient background on what has transpired between sightings to follow the outline of Jefferson's life from birth to death. This approach requires that choices be made all up and down the line, and I can only concur with the inevitable critics who conclude that the crucial years as secretary of state or the exasperating experience of his second term as president cry out for fuller treatment. My only defense is to cite the extensive scholarship that already exists, to reaffirm my belief that Jefferson's story needs to fit between two covers and to admit my self-protective desire to avoid the fate of so many predecessors: a free fall into the Jeffersonian abyss.

Our chief quarry, after all, is Jefferson's character, the animating principles that informed his public and private life and made him the significant statesman and distinctive man he was. As I have found him, there really is a core of convictions and apprehensions at his center. Although he was endlessly elusive and extraordinarily adroit at covering his tracks, there were bedrock Jeffersonian values that determined the shape of the political vision he projected so successfully onto his world and that remain such a potent influence on ours. Moreover, again as I have found him, Jefferson consistently and tenaciously sustained his allegiance to those core convictions from the time he first appeared on the national stage in 1775 until his exquisitely timed death on July 4, 1826. Jefferson's much-touted contradictions and inconsistencies were quite real, to be sure, but his psychological agility, his capacity to play hide-and-seek within himself, was a protective device he developed to prevent his truly radical and highly romantic personal vision from colliding with reality. As I try to show in chapter 1, subsequent generations, including our own, have certainly discovered multiple meanings in the Jeffersonian vision, which naturally lends itself to diverse interpretations, but Jefferson himself knew what he meant and meant what he believed.

What I have tried to do is to recover that man and that meaning within the late-eighteenth-century context in which they congealed and to do so in language that embraces the Jeffersonian belief in the intelligence of the common American. This means that the specialized language of scholarly discourse has been translated into ordinary English and the resonant meanings of such loaded terms as "republicanism," "Whig," "liberal" and "political party" have not been assumed to be self-evident. While I certainly hope my fellow scholars will read the book, and even find the interpretation fresh and the inevitable blunders few, the audience I had in my mind's eye was that larger congregation of ordinary people with a general but genuine interest in Thomas Jefferson.

My scholarly debts conjure up comparisons with Jefferson's massive financial shortfall at the end, which I can only hope to repay in the currency of gratitude. All students of Jefferson owe an unpayable debt to the late Dumas Malone and to Merrill D. Peterson, whose heroic efforts to tell the story of the man and his time start from different assumptions and therefore reach different conclusions from the story I try to tell here, but who have set the biographical standard against which all the rest of us must be judged. The late Julian P. Boyd and his editorial successors at The Papers of Thomas Jefferson project at Princeton have sustained a similarly high standard for assembling the primary sources on which all our stories depend. Finally, the superb staff at the Thomas Jefferson Memorial Foundation were unfailingly helpful during my several visits to Monticello. Indeed, a special note of thanks is owed to Daniel P. Jordan, director of the foundation, and Douglas Wilson, director of the International Center for Jefferson Studies, who not only put me up at Kenwood and arranged several public occasions at which I could share my work in progress but also sustained the highest levels of civility and support even as it became clear that God had not given me the grace to see Jefferson as they did.

Individual draft chapters or chapter-sized chunks of the manuscript were read by Howard Adams, Joann Freeman, Ann Lucas, Pauline Maier, Lucia Stanton and Mary Jo Salter. Most or all of the manuscript benefited from the criticism of Catherine Allgor, Andrew Burstein, Eric McKitrick, Peter Onuf, Stephen Smith and Douglas Wilson. The customary caveats apply, meaning that none of these generous colleagues should be held responsible for my interpretive prejudices. Coming to terms with Thomas Jefferson is an inherently argumentative process, and the quality of the advice I received accurately reflected the serious disagreements about his legacy.

Special thanks are due Stephen Smith, the editor of *Civilization*, who let me try out early versions of my argument in his magazine. The prologue here first appeared in *Civilization*'s November-December 1994 issue; my discussion of Jefferson's drafting of the Declaration of Independence in the issue of June-July 1995; my interpretation of Jefferson and slavery in the issue of November-December 1996.

My agent, Gerry McCauley, held my hand and took me to lunch at the appropriate moments. At Knopf my editor, Ashbel Green, along with his assistant, Jennifer Bernstein, ushered the book along with civility and grace.

The entire manuscript was handwritten, then transcribed onto a disk by Helen Canney, whose ability to decipher the slant of my scrawl approached pure art. My three children, Peter, Scott and Alexander, developed a full repertoire of jokes about falling into the Jeffersonian abyss. My wife, Ellen, read each draft chapter as it dribbled out and invariably had stylistic suggestions that I could not afford to ignore.

The dedication at the start is to the historian who, both personally and professionally, embodies the values that my own work strives to emulate.

The appearance of the Vintage edition of *American Sphinx* in April 1998 permitted me to make several silent revisions to the Knopf hardback edition. These were the kind of minor corrections that careful readers catch after authors and copy editors have done their best to avoid such embarrassments.

Now, however, the Vintage edition requires more extensive revisions in light of the publication of a DNA study by Dr. Eugene Foster that significantly changes the terms of the long-standing debate over Jefferson's relationship with Sally Hemings. Genuinely new evidence seldom arrives to influence a historical controversy as old and much-studied as this one. But such is the case with the Foster study.

The revisions prompted by this new evidence are too substantial to be made silently. I have made four significant changes: first, added the story of the Foster study to my account of Jefferson's contemporary relevance (Prologue, **24–26**); second, revised my account of the scandal when it first emerged on the national scene in 1802 (chapter 4, **258–61**); third, added a paragraph on the Jefferson-Hemings relationship at the very end of Jefferson's life (chapter 5, **347**); fourth, inserted a discussion of the Foster study into my account of the history of the controversy (Appendix, **366–67**).

I have changed my mind on the Sally Question, but not on Jefferson. He emerges in this revised edition as more of an American sphinx than ever before, more complicated and inscrutable, more comfortable in his contradictions.

> Joseph J. Ellis
> Amherst, Mass.
> November 1998

AMERICAN SPHINX

JEFFERSONIAN SURGE:
AMERICA, 1992–93

If Jefferson was wrong, America is wrong.
If America is right, Jefferson was right.
—JAMES PARTON (1874)

YOU COULD REACH into your pocket, pull out a nickel and find him gazing into the middle distance—as my liberal friends noted, always looking left. You could go to Charlottesville, Virginia, and see full-length statues of him on the campus he designed, then travel a few miles up his mountaintop and visit his spirit and mansion at Monticello. As of 1993, you could follow the James River down to Williamsburg, a route he took many times as a young man, and see another full-length statue of him on the campus of the College of William and Mary, a recent gift from the college he founded to the college from which he graduated, there looking off to the right—as my conservative friends noted—apparently studying the comings and goings at the adjacent women's dormitory. You could head north out of the Tidewater region, past Civil War battle sites—Cold Harbor, Chancellorsville,

Fredricksburg—where both Union and Confederate soldiers believed they fought in behalf of his legacy. And you could cross over the Potomac from Virginia to the District of Columbia and find him in his own memorial on the Tidal Basin, looking straight ahead in this rendition, with plaques on the marble walls around him reproducing several of his most inspirational declarations of personal freedom. Or if you shared his romance with the American West, you could catch him in his most mammoth and naturalistic version on Mount Rushmore.

But these were all mere replicas. In November 1993 a reincarnated Thomas Jefferson promised to make a public appearance in the unlikely location of a large brick church in Worcester, Massachusetts. On this raw New England evening an impersonator named Clay Jenkinson had come to portray the flesh-and-blood Jefferson, alive among us in the late twentieth century. My own sense was that forty or fifty hardy souls would brave the weather and show up. This, after all, was a semischolarly affair, designed to recover Jefferson without much media hoopla or patriotic pageantry. As it turned out, however, about four hundred enthusiastic New Englanders crowded into the church. Despite the long-standing regional suspicion of southerners, especially Virginians (John Adams had said that "in Virginia, all geese are swans"), the appearance of Jefferson was obviously a major attraction.

The American Antiquarian Society hosted a dinner before the event. All the community leaders, including the superintendent of schools, the heads of local insurance and computing companies and a small delegation from the Massachusetts legislature, seemed to have turned out. What's more, representatives from the Library of Congress and the National Endowment for the Humanities had flown in from Washington. Also present were two filmmaking groups. From Florentine Films came Camilla Rockwell, who told me that Ken Burns of *Civil War* fame was planning a major documentary on Jefferson for public television. And from the Jefferson Legacy Foundation came Bud Leeds and Chip Stokes, who had just announced a campaign to raise funds for a big-budget commercial film on Jefferson. (From Leeds and Stokes I first learned that another major film, on Jefferson in Paris, was already planned, starring Nick Nolte in the title role.) Their entourage included an Iranian millionaire who said that he had fallen in love with Jefferson soon after escaping persecution by the Islamic fundamentalists in Iran, an experience that gave him unique access to Jefferson's genius in insisting upon the separation of church and state.

It was during the dinner that the germ of the idea made its first appearance in my mind, initially in the form of a question: What was it about Jefferson? Granted, 1993 was the 250th anniversary of Jefferson's birth, so a momentary surge in his reputation was to be expected. But were there any other prominent figures from the American past who could generate this much contemporary interest? There were only two possible contenders, so it seemed to me, both of whom also occupied sacred space on the Mall in the nation's capital, the American version of Mount Olympus. There was George Washington, the "Father of Our Country," who had the largest monument to patriarchal achievement in the world, dwarfing the memorials of the other American icons. Then there was Abraham Lincoln, who had a bigger memorial on the Tidal Basin than Jefferson and was usually the winner whenever pollsters tried to rate the greatest American presidents.

But Washington usually lost out to Jefferson; he seemed too distant and silent. There were no words etched on the walls of the Washington Monument. He was the Delphic oracle who never spoke, more like an Old Testament Jehovah who would never come down to earth as Jefferson was doing tonight. Lincoln was a more formidable contender. Like Jefferson, he was accessible and had also spoken magic words. Ordinary citizens tended to know about the Gettysburg Address nearly as much as the Declaration of Independence. But Lincoln's magic was more somber and burdened; he was a martyr and his magic had a tragic dimension. Jefferson was light, inspiring, optimistic. Although Lincoln was more respected, Jefferson was more loved.

These were my thoughts as we walked across the street to the church where Jenkinson was scheduled to re-create Jefferson. He appeared on the sanctuary steps in authentic eighteenth-century costume and began talking in measured cadences about his early days as a student at the College of William and Mary, his thoughts on the American Revolution, his love of French wine and French ideas, his achievements and frustrations as a political leader and president, his obsession with architecture and education, his elegiac correspondence with John Adams during the twilight years of his life, his bottomless sense of faith in America's prospects as the primal force for democracy in the world.

Jenkinson obviously knew his Jefferson. As a historian familiar with the scholarly literature I was aware of several tricky areas where a slight misstep could carry one down a hallway of half-truths, places where a little knowledge could lead one astray in a big way. But Jenkinson never faltered. He was giving us an elegantly disguised lecture on American history that drew deftly on the modern Jefferson scholarship.

Two things he did *not* do were also impressive. He did not try to speak with a southern or Virginian accent. He obviously realized that no one really knows how Jefferson talked or sounded, whether the accent was more southern or English or some unique combination. So Jenkinson spoke American. He also did not pretend to be in the eighteenth century. His Jefferson had materialized in our world and our time. He could not be accused of committing the sin of "presentism" because he was not making any claims about being oblivious to the fact that it was now, not then.

Indeed, most of the questions from the audience were about current affairs: What would you do about the health care problem, Mr. Jefferson? What do you think of President Clinton? Do you have any wisdom to offer on the Bosnian crisis? Would you have committed American troops to the Gulf War? Sprinkled into this mixture were several questions about American history and Jefferson's role in its making: Why did you never remarry? What did you mean by "the pursuit of happiness" in the Declaration of Independence? Why did you own slaves?

This last question had a sharp edge, and Jenkinson handled it carefully. Slavery was a moral travesty, he said, an institution clearly at odds with the values of the American Revolution. He had tried his best to persuade his countrymen to end the slave trade and gradually end slavery itself. But he had failed. As for his own slaves, he had treated them benevolently, as the fellow human beings they were. He concluded with a question of his own: What else would you have wanted me to do? A follow-up question at this point could have ignited some intellectual fireworks, but no one asked it. The audience had not come to witness an argument so much as to pay its respects to an icon. If Jefferson was America's Mona Lisa, they had come to see him smiling.

Despite the obviously respectful mood, it still surprised me that no one asked "the Sally question." My own experience as a college teacher suggested that most students could be counted on to know two things about Jefferson: that he had written the Declaration of Independence and that he had been accused of an illicit affair with Sally Hemings, a mulatto slave at Monticello. This piece of scandal had first surfaced when Jefferson was president, in 1802, and had subsequently affixed itself to his reputation like a tin can that rattled through the ages and pages of history. I subsequently learned that Jenkinson had a standard response to "the Sally question," which was that the story had originated with a disappointed office seeker named James Callender who had a long-standing reputation for scandalmongering (true enough) and that Jefferson had denied the charge on one occasion but otherwise refused to comment on it (also true). A few months after I saw him at Worcester, Jenkinson was the main attraction at a gala Jefferson celebration at the White House, where he won the hearts of the Clinton people by saying that Jefferson would dismiss the entire Whitewater investigation as "absolutely nobody's business."

Jenkinson's bravura performance that November night stuck in my mind, but what became an even more obsessive memory was the audience. Here, in the heart of New England (surely Adams country), Jefferson was their favorite Founding Father, indeed their all-time American hero. In its own way their apparently unconditional love for Jefferson was every bit as mysterious as the enigmatic character of the man himself. Like a splendid sunset or a woman's beauty, it was simply there. Jefferson did not just get the benefit of every doubt; he seemed to provide a rallying point where ordinary Americans from different backgrounds could congregate to dispel the very possibility of doubt itself.

In a sense it had always been this way. Soon after his death in 1826 Jefferson became a touchstone for wildly divergent political movements that continued to compete for his name and the claim on his legacy. Southern secessionists cited him on behalf of states' rights; northern abolitionists quoted his words in the Declaration of Independence against slavery. The so-called Robber Barons of the Gilded Age echoed his warnings against the encroaching powers of the federal government; liberal reformers and radical Populists referred to his strictures against corrupt businessmen and trumpeted his tributes to the superiority of agrarian values. In the Scopes trial both William Jennings Bryan and Clarence Darrow were sure that Jefferson agreed with their position on evolution. Herbert Hoover and Franklin Roosevelt both claimed him as their guide to the problems of the Great Depression. The chief chronicler of the multiple Jeffersonian legacy, Merrill Peterson, gave it the name "protean," which provided a respectably classical sound to what some critics described as Jefferson's disarming ideological promiscuity. He was America's Everyman.[1]

But at least until the New Deal era of Franklin Roosevelt there *were* critics. The main story line of American history, in fact, cast Jefferson and Alexander Hamilton in the lead roles of a dramatic contest between the forces of democracy (or liberalism) and the forces of aristocracy (or conservatism). While this formulation had the suspiciously melodramatic odor of a political soap opera, it also had the advantage of reducing the bedeviling complexities of American history to a comprehensible scheme: It was the people against the elites, the West against the East, agrarians against industrialists, Democrats against Republicans. Jefferson was only one side of the American political dialogue, often the privileged side to be sure, the voice of "the many" holding forth against "the few."

To repeat, this version of American history always had the semifictional quality of an imposed plot line—the very categories were Jeffersonian and therefore prejudicial—but it ceased making any sense at all by the 1930s, when Franklin Roosevelt invoked Hamiltonian methods (i.e., government intervention) to achieve Jeffersonian goals (i.e., economic equality). After the New Deal most historians abandoned the Jefferson-Hamilton distinction altogether and most politicians stopped yearning for a Jeffersonian utopia free of government influence. No serious scholar any longer believed that the Jeffersonian belief in a minimalist federal government was relevant in an urban, industrialized American society. The disintegration of the old categories meant the demise of Jefferson as the symbolic leader of liberal partisans fighting valiantly against the entrenched elites.[2]

What happened next defined the new paradigm for the Jefferson image and set the stage for the phenomenon I witnessed in that Worcester church. Jefferson ceased to function as the liberal half of the American political dialogue and became instead the presiding presence who transcended *all* political conflicts and parties. As Peterson put it, "the disintegration of the Jeffersonian philosophy of government heralded the ultimate canonization of Jefferson." The moment of Jefferson's ascent into the American version of political heaven can be dated precisely: April 13, 1943, the day that Franklin Roosevelt dedicated the Jefferson Memorial on the Tidal Basin. "Today, in the midst of a great war for freedom," Roosevelt declared, "we dedicate a shrine to freedom." Jefferson was now an American saint, our "Apostle of Freedom," as Roosevelt put it; he concluded by quoting the words inscribed around the inside of the Jefferson Memorial's dome: "For I have sworn on the altar of God eternal hostility against every form of tyranny over the mind of man." Jefferson was no longer just an essential ingredient in the American political tradition; he was the essence itself, a kind of free-floating icon who hovered over the American political scene like one of those dirigibles cruising above a crowded football stadium, flashing words of inspiration to both teams.[3]

The more I thought about it, the clearer it seemed to me that the audience at Worcester offered a nice illustration of what we might call grass roots Jeffersonianism. Scholars and biographers of Jefferson seldom pay much attention to this phenomenon, since it has almost nothing to do with who the historical Jefferson really was, and the mental process at work, at least on the face of it, appears to resemble a blend of mindless hero worship and political fundamentalism. But it seemed to me that lots of ordinary Americans carried around expectations and assumptions about what Jefferson symbolized that were infinitely more powerful than any set of historical facts. America's greatest historians and Jefferson scholars could labor for decades to produce the most authoritative and sophisticated studies—several had done precisely that—and they would bounce off the popular image of Jefferson without making a dent. This was the Jefferson magic, but how did the magic work?

The obvious place to look was the shrine on the Tidal Basin. According to the National Park Service, about a million visitors pay their respects to Jefferson in his memorial each year.[4] On the March day in 1993 that I visited, several hundred tourists walked up the marble steps, then proceeded to spend a few minutes studying the dignified statue of Jefferson and snapping pictures. Then most of them looked up to the four inscribed panels on the walls and read the words, often moving their lips and murmuring the famous phrases to themselves. The first panel, which attracted more attention than the others, contained the most famous and familiar words in American history: "We hold these truths to be self-evident, that all men are created equal, that they are endowed by their Creator with certain inalienable Rights, that among these are Life, Liberty and the pursuit of Happiness."

Actually, these are not quite the words Jefferson composed in June 1776. Before editorial changes were made by the Continental Congress, Jefferson's early draft made it even clearer that his intention was to express a spiritual vision: "We hold these truths to be sacred & undeniable; that all men are created equal & independent, that from that equal creation they derive rights inherent & unalienable, among which are the preservation of life, & liberty, & the pursuit of happiness." These are the core articles of faith in the American Creed. Jefferson's authorship of these words is the core of his seductive appeal across the ages, his central claim, on posterity's affection. What, then, do they mean? How do they make magic?

Merely to ask the question is to risk being accused of some combination of treason and sacrilege, since self-evident truths are not meant to be analyzed; that is what being self-evident is all about. But when these words are stripped of the patriotic haze, read straightaway and literally, two monumental claims are being made here. The explicit claim is that the individual is the sovereign unit in society; his natural state is freedom from and equality with all other individuals; this is the natural order of things. The implicit claim is that all restrictions on this natural order are immoral transgressions, violations of what God intended; individuals liberated from such restrictions will interact with their fellows in a harmonious scheme requiring no external discipline and producing maximum human happiness.

This is a wildly idealistic message, the kind of good news simply too good to be true. It is, truth be told, a recipe for anarchy. Any national government that seriously attempted to operate in accord with these principles would be committing suicide. But, of course, the words were not intended to serve as an operational political blueprint. Jefferson was not a profound political thinker. He was, however, an utterly brilliant political rhetorician and visionary. The genius of his vision is to propose that our deepest yearnings for personal freedom are in fact attainable. The genius of his rhetoric is to articulate irreconcilable human urges at a sufficiently abstract level to mask their mutual exclusiveness. Jefferson guards the American Creed at this inspirational level, which is inherently immune to scholarly skepticism and a place where ordinary Americans can congregate to speak the magic words together. The Jeffersonian magic works because we permit it to function at a rarefied region where real-life choices do not have to be made.

And so, for example, in that Worcester church or in the hallowed space of the Jefferson Memorial, American citizens can come together in Jefferson's presence and simultaneously embrace the following propositions: that abortion is a woman's right and that an unborn child cannot be killed; that health care and a clean environment for all Americans are natural rights and that the federal bureaucracies and taxes required to implement medical and environmental programs violate individual independence; that women and blacks must not be denied their rights as citizens and that affirmative action programs violate the principle of equality. The primal source of Jefferson's modern-day appeal is that he provides the sacred space—not really common ground but more a midair location floating above all the political battle lines—where all Americans can come together and, at least for that moment, become a chorus instead of a cacophony.

As a practicing professional historian who had recently decided to make Jefferson his next scholarly project, I found this a rather disconcerting insight, full of ominous implications. Jefferson was not like most other historical figures—dead, forgotten and nonchalantly entrusted to historians, who presumably serve as the grave keepers for those buried memories no one really cares about anymore. Jefferson had risen from the dead. Or rather the myth of Jefferson had taken on a life of its own. Lots of Americans cared deeply about the meaning of his memory. He had become the Great Sphinx of American history, the enigmatic and elusive touchstone for the most cherished convictions and contested truths in American culture. It was as if a pathologist, just about to begin an autopsy, had discovered that the body on the operating table was still breathing.

Not just any man can become Everyman. During the preceding five years, while I was working on a book about the life and thought of John Adams, only a few scholarly friends ever asked me what I was doing or, once apprised, felt any urge to follow up with inquiries that indicated Adams touched their lives in any way. (The most common response from my nonacademic friends was that they knew the Adams face because it appeared on their favorite beer, but they were mistaking John for his cousin Sam.) Working on Jefferson, on the other hand, was like entering an electromagnetic field where lots of friends and neighbors—businessmen, secretaries, journalists, janitors—already resonated with excitement. When my furnace stopped working in the dead of the winter, the local repairman noticed the books on Jefferson piled up in my study. As I held the flashlight for him in the basement while he lay on his back replacing worn-out parts of the heat pump, he talked for a full hour about how critics had maligned Jefferson as an atheist. The repairman was a devout Christian and had read somewhere about Jefferson's keen interest in the Bible. No, sir, Jefferson was a good Christian gentleman, and he hoped I would get *that* right in my book.

A neighbor who taught in the local high school, upon learning that I was working on Jefferson, promised to send me a book that he had found extremely helpful in distilling the Jeffersonian message for his students. A package then arrived in the mail that contained three copies of *Revolution Song,* which was not written but "assembled" by one Jim Strupp in order to "provide young people with a contemporary look into the beliefs, ideals and radical thought of Thomas Jefferson." The blurb on the cover went on: "In our country today, true democratic government is betrayed at all levels. As democracies emerge around the world, they are also subtly being destroyed." The hyperventilating tone of *Revolution Song* was reminiscent of those full-page newspaper ads in which Asian gurus or self-proclaimed prophets lay out their twelve-step programs to avert the looming apocalypse. Actually, the propagandistic model for *Revolution Song* was even more provocative: "This little book attempts to serve as a democratic alternative to the works of Chairman Mao and other non-democratic leaders." It was designed as a succinct catechism of Jeffersonian thought, a "little blue book" to counter Mao's "little red book." No matter that Mao was in disgrace, even in China, and that communism since 1989 was an ideological lost cause, loitering on the world stage only as an object lesson in political and economic catastrophe. The global battle for the souls of humankind was never-ending, and Jefferson remained the inspirational source, the chosen beacon of the chosen people, still throwing out its light from Monticello, his own personal City on a Hill. Silly stuff, to be sure, but another example of how hauntingly powerful Jefferson's legacy remained at the popular level.[5]

Soon after I had received my complimentary copies of *Revolution Song,* another piece of mail arrived from someone also exploring the Jefferson trail. The letter came from Paris, and the sender was Mary Jo Salter, a good friend who also happened to be one of America's most respected poets. She and her husband, the writer Brad Leithauser, were spending a sabbatical year in Paris, where Mary Jo was continuing to perform her duties as poetry editor of the *New Republic* and completing a volume of new poems. The longest poem in the collection, it turned out, would focus on the ubiquitous Mr. Jefferson. Although she explained that "98 percent of the facts and 92 percent of the interpretations historians can provide about Jefferson will never get into my poem at all," Mary Jo wondered if I might help with the history, explaining that it would be "a crime to get my substantive fact wrong if one can possibly avoid it."[6]

For a poet of Mary Jo's stature and sensibility, Jefferson was certainly not a political choice, at least in the customary sense of the term. She had no ideological axes to grind, no patriotic hymns to sing. And it made no sense to think that propagandists and poets were plugged into the same cultural grid, which had its main power source buried beneath the mountains around Monticello. So I asked her: Why Jefferson?

That question provoked a spirited exchange of letters over several months. Part of Jefferson's poetic appeal, it turned out, was his lifelong concern with language. He had also been the subject of several distinguished poets of the past; Robert Frost, Ezra Pound and Robert Penn Warren had taken him on. But mostly, Mary Jo explained, "poets are seized by images," and in Jefferson's case two specific incidents struck her as poetic occasions: The first was his death on July 4, 1826, fifty years to the day after the acceptance of the Declaration of Independence by the Continental Congress and the same day John Adams died; the second was another eerie coincidence—his purchase of a thermometer on July 4, 1776, and his recording a peak temperature of seventy-six degrees Fahrenheit that special day. These were "poignant and eminently visual events," she explained, that captured a poet's imagination. They were the kinds of historical facts that poets usually were required to invent. Whether it was a certain knack or sheer fate, Jefferson's life possessed the stuff of poetry.[7]

The thirty-page poem that Mary Jo eventually produced, entitled "The Hand of Thomas Jefferson," was a meditation on the hand that wrote the Declaration of Independence, was broken in Paris during a romantic frolic with Maria Cosway, then crafted those elegiac last letters to Adams and finally reached across the ages to pull us toward him. When I asked what about Jefferson pulled *her*, Mary Jo said it was his "accessible mysteriousness," the fact that there appeared to be a seductive bundle of personae or selves inside Jefferson that did not talk to one another but could and did talk to us. This was a bit different from Peterson's "protean" Jefferson, which suggested a multidimensional Renaissance Man. Mary Jo's Jefferson was more like Postmodern Man, a series of disjointed identities that beckoned to our contemporary sense of incoherence and that could be made whole only in our imagination, the place where poets live.[8]

I was not sure where that left historians, who were not, to be sure, obliged to disavow the use of their imaginations but were duty-bound to keep them on a tight tether tied to the available evidence. Watching Mary Jo work made me wonder whether Jefferson's enigmatic character might not require the imaginative leeway provided by fiction or poetry to leap across those interior gaps of silence for which he was so famous. Did that mean that any historian who took on Jefferson needed to apply for a poetic license? It was absolutely clear to me that the apparently bottomless and unconditional love for Jefferson at the grass roots level was virtually impervious to historical argument or evidence. It even seemed possible that the quest for the historical Jefferson, like the quest for the historical Jesus, was an inherently futile exercise. No less a source than Merrill Peterson, the best Jefferson biographer alive, seemed to endorse such doubts when he made what he called the "mortifying confession" that after over thirty years of work, "Jefferson remains for me, finally, an impenetrable man."[9]

Anyone who paused too long to contemplate the wisdom of the quest was likely to be trampled by the crowds, who harbored no doubts. Upwards of six hundred thousand Jefferson lovers were attracted to a major exhibit on "The Worlds of Thomas Jefferson at Monticello," which ran from April to December 1993. Susan Stein, Monticello's curator of art, had made a heroic effort to reassemble most of the furnishings that had been dispersed starting in 1827, when Jefferson's crushing debts forced his descendants to auction off the estate. The result was a faithful replication of what Monticello's interior spaces actually looked like during Jefferson's lifetime. If the rooms of the mansion were in any reliable sense an accurate reflection of his many-chambered personality, they suggested wildly extravagant clutter and a principle of selection guided only by a luxuriously idiosyncratic temperament: Houdon busts next to Indian headdresses, mahogany tables brimming over with multiple sets of porcelain and silver candlesticks, wall-to-wall portraits and prints and damask hangings and full-length gilt-framed mirrors.[10]

Perhaps all our lives would look just as random and jumbled if our most precious material possessions, gathered over a lifetime, were reassembled in one place. By any measure, however, chockablock Monticello resembled a trophy case belonging to one of America's most self-indulgent and wildly eclectic collectors. How did one square this massive treasure trove of expensive collectibles with a life at least nominally committed to agrarian simplicity and Ciceronian austerity? The exhibit suggested that Jefferson lived in a crowded museum filled with the kinds of expensive objects one normally associates with a late-nineteenth-century Robber Baron whose exorbitant wealth permitted him to indulge all his acquisitive instincts. The one discernible reminder of Jefferson's preference for what he called "republican simplicity" was the most valued item in the exhibit: the portable writing desk on which he had composed the Declaration of Independence. It was on loan from the Smithsonian, where it had resided since 1880, and the only other time it had been permitted to travel was in 1943, when Franklin Roosevelt took it with him the day he dedicated the Jefferson Memorial. The Smithsonian recognized that the writing desk was a sacred relic of American history and insisted on posting a twenty-four-hour guard during the month it was on loan to Monticello. In part because of the sacred desk, the only private dwelling in America to attract more visitors than Monticello that year was Elvis Presley's Graceland.[11]

The phenomenon deserved a name or title, so I began to call it the Jeffersonian Surge. Nothing like it had accompanied the 250th birthday of George Washington, Benjamin Franklin or John Adams. Nor had Lincoln's 150th birthday generated anything like this popular outpouring. The Jeffersonian Surge was not a movement led or controlled by professional historians. Jefferson was part of the public domain with drawing power independent of his status in the academic world. The folks who ran publishing houses (seventeen new books with Jefferson's name in the title appeared in 1993), the producers and directors of films (Florentine Films was now in production, and James Ivory and Ismail Merchant had begun filming in Paris), as well as museum curators and foundation directors, all obviously regarded Jefferson as a sure thing. Compared with the belongings of all other historical figures, things Jeffersonian had a broad, deep and diverse market. It was as if one had attended a Fourth of July fireworks display and, instead of the usual rockets and sparklers, had born witness to the detonation of a modest-sized nuclear bomb.[12]

In the academic world the winds were gusting in a different direction. Not that scholars had ignored Jefferson or consigned him to some second tier of historical significance. The number of scholarly books and articles focusing on Jefferson or some aspect of his long life continued to grow at a geometric rate; two full volumes were required merely to list all the Jefferson scholarship, much of it coming in the last quarter century.[13] The central scholarly project, *The Papers of Thomas Jefferson*, continued to emerge from Princeton University Press at the stately pace of one volume every two years or so (twenty-five volumes had appeared by 1993), though at the current rate no adult was likely to be alive when the editors ushered Jefferson off to the hereafter.

The problem, then, was not lack of interest so much as lack of consensus about what the man stood for and what his career had accomplished. The love affair that continued to flourish in the public domain had encountered some rough patches in the academic world; indeed, in some scholarly precincts it had turned quite sour. Once the symbol of all that was right with America, Jefferson had become the touchstone for much that was wrong.

You could look back and, with the advantage of hindsight, locate the moment when the tide began to turn in the 1960s. In 1963 Leonard Levy published *Jefferson and Civil Liberties: The Darker Side*, which, as its title announced, found Jefferson's record as a liberal defender of minority rights less than inspiring and his rhetoric about freedom of speech and freedom of the press often at odds with his actions. But an even bigger blow fell in 1968 with the publication of Winthrop Jordan's *White over Black*, a magisterial reappraisal of race relations in early America featuring a long section on Jefferson. While hardly a heavy-handed indictment of Jefferson, Jordan's book argued that racism had infiltrated the American soul very early in our history and that Jefferson provided the most resonant illustration of the way deep-seated racist values were buried within the folds of the white man's personality.[14]

Jordan adopted an agnostic attitude toward the allegations of a sexual liaison with Sally Hemings but, while not endorsing the Sally stories, depicted a Jefferson whose deepest feelings toward blacks had their origins in primal urges that, like the sex drive, came from deep within his subconscious. Many other scholarly books soon took up related themes, but *White over Black* set the terms of the debate about the centrality of race and slavery in any appraisal of Jefferson. Once that became a chief measure of Jefferson's character, his stock was fated to fall in the scholarly world.

Another symptom of imminent decline—again, all this in retrospect—was an essay in 1970 by Eric McKitrick reviewing the recent biographies of Jefferson by Dumas Malone and Merrill Peterson. McKitrick had the temerity to ask whether it might not be time to declare a moratorium on the celebratory approach toward Jefferson. McKitrick asked: "What about those traits of character that aren't heroic from any angle?"—traits that went beyond the obvious complicity with slavery. What about his very un-Churchillian performance as governor of Virginia during the American Revolution, when he failed to mobilize the militia and had to flee Monticello on horseback ahead of the marauding British Army? What about the fiasco of his American Embargo of 1807, when he clung to the illusion that economic sanctions would keep us out of war even after it was abundantly clear that they only devastated the American economy?[15]

From the perspective at Charlottesville, these were impertinent, if not downright hostile, questions. Dumas Malone, the quintessential grand old man of Jefferson scholarship, had toiled for most of his long life, much of that time on the campus at the University of Virginia, to create his authoritative six-volume biography *Jefferson and His Time*, one of the great labors of love in American scholarship. Merrill Peterson's scholarly renderings of Jefferson were only slightly less heroic. Now McKitrick was saying that the insights available from the Charlottesville perspective, what he called "the view from Jefferson's camp," had just about exhausted their explanatory power.

Rather amazingly it was in Charlottesville that the scholarly reappraisal of Jefferson that McKitrick had called for reached a crescendo. It happened in October 1992, when the Thomas Jefferson Memorial Foundation convened a conference under the apparently reverential rubric "Jeffersonian Legacies." The result was a spirited exchange—one reporter called it "an intellectual free-for-all"—that went on for six days. The conference spawned a collection of fifteen essays published in record time by the University Press of Virginia, an hour-long videotape of the proceedings shown on public television and a series of newspaper stories in the Richmond papers and the *Washington Post*. Advertised as the scholarly version of a birthday party (Jefferson's 250th was coming up in April), the conference assumed the character of a public trial, with Jefferson cast in the role of defendant.

The chief argument for the prosecution came from Paul Finkelman, a historian then teaching at Virginia Tech, and the chief charge was hypocrisy. "Because he was the author of the Declaration of Independence," said Finkelman, "the test of Jefferson's position on slavery is not whether he was better than the worst of his generation, but whether he was the leader of the best." The answer had the clear ring of an indictment: "Jefferson fails the test." According to Finkelman, Jefferson was an out-and-out racist who rejected even the possibility that blacks and whites could ever live together on an equal basis. Moreover, his several attempts to end the slave trade or restrict the expansion of slavery beyond the South were halfhearted, as was his contemplation of a program of gradual emancipation. His beloved Monticello and personal extravagances were possible only because of slave labor. Finkelman thought it was misguided—worse, it was positively sickening—to celebrate Jefferson as the father of freedom.[16]

If Finkelman was the chief prosecutor, the star witness for the prosecution was Robert Cooley, a middle-aged black man who claimed to be a direct descendant of Jefferson and Sally Hemings. Cooley stood up in the audience during a question-and-answer session to offer himself as "living proof" that the story of Jefferson's liaison with Sally Hemings was true. No matter what the scholarly experts had concluded, there were several generations of African-Americans living in Ohio and Illinois who *knew* they had Jefferson's blood in their veins. Scholars could talk till doomsday about the absence of hard evidence or documentation. But the evidence did not exist for a good reason. "We couldn't write back then," Cooley explained. "We were slaves." And Jefferson's white children had probably destroyed all written records of the relationship soon after his death. Cooley essentially pitted the oral tradition of the black community against the written tradition of the scholarly world. His version of history might not have had the hard evidence on its side, but it clearly had the political leverage. When he sat down, the applause from the audience rang throughout the auditorium. The *Washington Post* reporter covering the conference caught the mood: "Jefferson's defenders are on the defensive. What tough times these are for icons."[17]

Actually, neither Finkelman's sledgehammer blows nor Cooley's dramatic personal testimony were accurate reflections of the conference as a whole, though press accounts tended to focus on these presentations because they were the most colorful and controversial occasions. A more balanced assessment of the current state of Jeffersonian scholarship came from Peter Onuf, the successor to Merrill Peterson as Thomas Jefferson Memorial Foundation Professor at the University of Virginia and the chief organizer of the Charlottesville conference. In an article entitled "The Scholars' Jefferson" published in the October 1993 issue of the *William and Mary Quarterly,* the leading scholarly journal in the field, Onuf suggested that Jefferson's stock was definitely going down but that only a few historians were willing to follow Finkelman all the way and transform Jefferson from the ultimate American hero to the ultimate American villain. Scholars were not quite ready to raze the Jefferson Memorial or chip his face off Mount Rushmore. On the other hand, the mindless devotion to the mythical Jefferson that still dominated the popular culture clearly drove serious students of Jefferson to the edge of sanity. And the filio-pietistic tradition represented by Malone and Peterson was certainly dead in the scholarly world.[18]

Onuf suggested two sensible ways to understand the somewhat problematic character of the current scholarly situation. First, the democratic revolution that Jefferson had helped launch in America had now expanded to include forms of human equality—especially racial and sexual equality—that Jefferson could never have countenanced or even imagined. He was, for that reason, a large and obvious target for those ideologically inspired historians and political pundits who went charging back into the American past in search of monstrous examples of racism, sexism and patriarchy to slay, then drag back into the present as trophies emblematic of how bad it was back then. And he was the perfect target for such raiding parties precisely because so many ordinary Americans had so much invested in him. He was a contested prize in the ongoing culture wars. If history was any kind of reliable guide, the more wild-eyed critics were unlikely to win the war, but the growing emphasis on Jefferson as a slave-owning white racist had the potential to erode his heroic reputation, as the critical judgment of scholars seeped into popular culture. The scholarship on Jefferson, then, was probably a preview of coming attractions in the broader public world.

Second, Onuf suggested that the fascination with Jefferson's vaunted psychological complexity was gradually giving way to frustration. The famous paradoxes that so intrigued poets and devotees of "protean Jefferson" were beginning to look more like outright contradictions. Onuf described the emerging scholarly portrait of Jefferson as "a monster of self-deception," a man whose felicitous style was a bit too felicitous, dressing up platitudes as pieces of political wisdom that, as Onuf put it, "now circulate as the debased coin of our democratic culture." The multiple personalities of Jefferson were looking less like different facets of a Renaissance man and more like the artful disguises of a confidence man.[19]

The final word came from Gordon Wood, generally regarded as the leading historian of the revolutionary era, who was asked to review the published collection of essays that came out of the Charlottesville conference. Wood argued that the core of the Jefferson problem was not his inevitable flaws but our unrealistic expectations. "We Americans make a great mistake in idolizing . . . and making symbols of authentic figures," Wood warned, "who cannot and should not be ripped out of their time and place." No real-life historical figure could ever prove a satisfactory hero because his human weaknesses would always undercut his saintly status. "By turning Jefferson into the kind of transcendent moral hero that no authentic historically situated human being could ever be," Wood wrote, "we leave ourselves demoralized by the time-bound weaknesses of this eighteenth-century slaveholder."[20]

It seemed to me that Wood's point was true enough; in fact, just the kind of sober assessment of the Jefferson problem one wanted to hear amid all the shrill pronouncements. But it also seemed abundantly clear that it would make absolutely no practical difference. Yes, perhaps we all would be better served if Americans were allowed to select their heroes (and villains) only from fictional characters, who would therefore never disappoint us. But we won't and can't. We would be even better served if we discarded our need for heroes altogether. But no people in recorded history have ever been able to do that, and there was no reason to believe that modern Americans would prove an exception. Moreover, the scholarly instinct to establish a secure checkpoint between the past and the present in order to prevent the flow of traffic back and forth, while it had the advantage of deterring those ideologically motivated raiding parties that wanted to go back to capture heroes and villains to suit their own political agenda, also had the disadvantage of making history an irrelevant, cloistered, indeed dead place, populated only by historians.

The Jefferson genie had long since escaped from the historical bottle anyway. There was no putting him back. Evidence of Jefferson's natural tendency to surge out of the past and into the present kept popping up in the press even as the 250th anniversary celebrations died down. The *New York Times* reported a special mock-trial session organized by the New York City Bar Association, presided over by Chief Justice William Rehnquist, designed to try Jefferson on three charges: that he subverted the independence of the federal judiciary, that he lived in the lavish manner of Louis XIV (the Monticello exhibit), and that he frequently violated the Bill of Rights. Though the prosecution possessed a hefty load of evidence for conviction, Jefferson was found not guilty on all charges; the lawyers for both sides toasted his name.[21]

Meanwhile, down in northern Virginia the *Washington Post* reported a new development in the escalating protest against the plan to locate a new Walt Disney theme park in the historic region around several Civil War battlegrounds. A wealthy Iranian real estate owner named Bahman Batmaughelidj had gone over to the opposition. Called Batman in the press, he turned out to be the same Iranian philanthropist I had met that night in Worcester. He had learned that the Walt Disney Corporation was the producer and main distributor of the Merchant and Ivory film *Jefferson in Paris,* which endorsed the story of Jefferson's sexual liaison with Sally Hemings. He had now decided to throw his considerable weight against the Disney theme park scheme because of Disney's complicity in the reinvigoration of the Sally scandal. "Americans don't realize," Batmaughelidj warned, "how profoundly Jefferson and his ideas live on in the hopes and dreams of people in other countries. This movie will undercut all that. People all around the world will view it as the defining truth about Jefferson. And of course it is a lie."[22]

RESURGENCE, 1998

WELL, THE DEFINING TRUTH about the Sally Hemings story was that the available evidence on each side of the controversy was sufficient to sustain the debate but insufficient to resolve it one way or the other. Anyone who claimed to have a clear answer to this most titillating question about the historical Jefferson was engaging in massive self-deception or outright lying. On two occasions I had made presentations before the staff and tour guides at Monticello in which I suggested that we exhume Jefferson's remains in order to obtain genetic material that would permit DNA comparisons with the Hemings descendants. That, so it seemed to me, was the only way the mystery could be solved. The folks at Monticello listened attentively, concurred with my assessment of the situation, but shook their heads in horror at the ghoulish thought of desecrating the Jefferson grave. Besides, several argued, there probably wasn't enough physical evidence remaining to obtain the DNA material required for a reliable scientific study anyway.

Unbeknownst to me, modern science was racing to the rescue with a new technique that permitted DNA comparisons without obtaining genetic material from Jefferson himself. Because the Y chromosome is passed intact on the male side of the family, and because more sophisticated laboratory methods for identifying the genetic markers on specific Y chromosomes were now scientifically feasible, one did not have to dig Jefferson up. A research team headed by Dr. Eugene Foster, a retired pathologist at the University of Virginia, obtained blood samples containing Jefferson's Y chromosome from a living descendant and from several descendants in the Hemings line. The results, published in the prestigious scientific magazine *Nature* and released to the press on Halloween Day, 1998, showed a match between Jefferson and Eston Hemings, Sally's last child. The chances of such a match occurring randomly were less than one in a thousand. This constituted conclusive evidence that Jefferson fathered at least one of Sally's children and, in conjunction with the preexistent circumstantial evidence, made it highly probable that a long-term sexual relationship existed between them. If the Tom and Sally story was the longest-running soap opera in American history, it had at last reached its final episode.[23]

The scholarly response to this revelation is virtually certain to extend and deepen the critical consensus that Peter Onuf had summarized five years earlier. We already knew that Jefferson was an inherently elusive character who lived the central contradiction in American history, which is to say that he crafted the most inspiring egalitarian promise in modern history while living his entire life among two hundred slaves. Now we also know that he fathered several children by one of those slaves while claiming to regard racial amalgamation as a horrific prospect and a central reason why slavery itself could not be easily ended. Prior to the DNA evidence, one might have reasonably concluded that Jefferson was living a paradox. Now it was difficult to avoid the conclusion that he was living a lie.

All the major newspapers, magazines and television networks covered the story as a front-page item; a revitalized version of the culture wars broke out in the op-ed pages. Because I had coauthored the essay that accompanied the DNA study in *Nature*, and was also on record as opposing the ongoing impeachment hearings on President Clinton's sexual indiscretions, William Safire of *The New York Times* accused me of timing the release of the study to undermine the case against Clinton, presumably by demonstrating that illicit liaisons with younger women had a distinguished presidential pedigree. Several black scholars and journalists used the occasion to ask why so many white historians, including yours truly, had failed to get this right and had paid insufficient attention to the oral tradition within the Hemings family, which had always regarded the existence of a sexual relationship between Tom and Sally as a self-evident truth. The clear implication was that racism was at work, along with the collateral urge to protect Jefferson from complicity in the secret sexual history between blacks and whites in the American South.[24]

At the level of popular opinion, however, neither the scholarly critique of Jefferson's exalted status nor the journalistic craving to make him a double-edged weapon in the culture wars seemed to make much difference at all. Rather like a stock market that had already anticipated a stirring piece of fresh financial information, mainstream Americans took the news in stride, which only confirmed my impression that the Fawn Brodie version of the Sally and Tom story had long since triumphed in the marketplace of public opinion. Tourists at the Jefferson Memorial and at Monticello, when asked to offer their reaction to the recent revelations, expressed casual indifference, claiming to have known it all along. (In retrospect, it would seem that the only folks who had resisted the truth were the white descendants in the Jefferson family and the majority of professional historians.) A positive spin on the story could also be detected in the calls pouring into the talk shows. Jefferson was now more resolutely human than ever before, the American Everyman for our more permissive era, the word made flesh who dwelt amongst us. In yet another stunning metamorphosis, his most unattractive feature—his deep convictions that blacks were inherently inferior and could never live alongside whites in peace and harmony—was now subject to reconsideration. No matter what Jefferson had publicly said or written, he had lived a biracial private life. In that sense he was our long-lost multicultural hero.

Such interpretive excesses only reinforced my realization that Jefferson was the most potent and promiscuous icon in American history. More than any other figure in the American pantheon, he embodied our will to believe. No matter what we learn about the historical Jefferson, that real man who walked the earth between 1743 and 1826, the mythological Jefferson will survive and flourish. The Jefferson Memorial is enduringly situated on the Tidal Basin, the mansion at Monticello is impeccably restored, the face on Mount Rushmore is forever. It is safe to get to know him as he really was.

The Jefferson who emerges in the pages that follow is a flawed creature, a man who combined massive learning with extraordinary naiveté, piercing insights into others with daunting powers of self-deception, utter devotion to great principles with a highly indulged presumption that his own conduct was not answerable to them. While offering an early version of this warts-and-all portrait before an audience in Richmond, an elderly woman rose to scold me for my irreverence. "My good man," she complained, "you are a mere pigeon on the great statue of Thomas Jefferson." All I can say in my defense is that the subject of the chapters that follow, while great, is not a statue.

I

PHILADELPHIA: 1775–76

It is easier to reach a confident opinion about the sort of man he was in 1776 than to do so for 1793 or 1800.
— DUMAS MALONE (1948)

IT WAS A PROVINCIAL version of the grand entrance. On June 20, 1775, Thomas Jefferson arrived in Philadelphia in an ornate carriage, called a phaeton, along with four horses and three slaves. The roughly three-hundred-mile trip from Williamsburg had taken him ten days, in part because the roads were poor and poorly marked—twice he had been forced to hire guides to recover the route—and in part because he had dawdled in Fredericksburg and Annapolis to purchase extra equipment for his entourage. As the newest and youngest member of Virginia's delegation to the Continental Congress, he obviously intended to uphold the stylish standard of the Virginia gentry, which the Philadelphia newspapers had recently described, with a mixture of admiration and apprehension, as those "haughty sultans of the South. . . ."[1]

So he had outfitted Jesse, Jupiter and Richard, his black servants, in formal attire befitting the regalia of a proper Virginia gentleman, to include a postilion's whip for Jesse, who rode the lead horse in the team. Richard sat inside the phaeton with his master; Jupiter, who had been Jefferson's personal servant and companion ever since student days at the College of William and Mary, trailed behind with the two extra horses. (Jupiter, as it turned out, was to accompany Jefferson throughout most of the early ride into history; he died in 1800 just before Jefferson ascended to the presidency, after drinking a medicinal potion prepared by the "witch doctor" within the slave quarters at Monticello.) No contemporary record survives of the impression this elegant entourage made upon the more austere Quaker residents of Philadelphia, but the jarring juxtapositions that lie at the center of Jefferson's character and career had already begun to reveal themselves. The man who, precisely a year later, was to draft the most famous and eloquent statement of human rights in American—and perhaps world— history entered national affairs as a conspicuously aristocratic slave-owner.[2]

So much that we know about young Jefferson derives from later recollections, when memories were clouded by the golden haze surrounding the mythology of the Declaration of Independence and remembered anecdotes were realigned to fit various personal and political agenda. Moreover, there is the nearly insurmountable difficulty posed by what Jefferson specialists have come to call the problem of the Shadwell fire, which destroyed most of Jefferson's personal papers in 1770, making the recovery of his formative years an exercise in inspired guesswork. Given the paucity of early evidence and the veritable flood of material that begins to flow after 1776, the temptation to read the young revolutionary through the elder statesman is nearly irresistible and, in some ways, unavoidable.

Take, for example, the matter of young Jefferson's physical appearance. What did the thirty-two-year-old delegate from Virginia look like? All agree that he was tall, six feet two inches, perhaps a quarter inch taller. After that, however, the picture begins to blur. Edmund

Bacon, Jefferson's overseer at Monticello during the presidential years and then into his retirement, recalled that "his skin was very clear and pure—just like he was in principle." But most other reports, and most of the later portraits, describe him as red-faced and heavily freckled, with a complexion that was either scorched or radiant, depending on the viewer's predilections. The only contemporary picture of young Jefferson, a pen-and-ink drawing done by Pierre du Simitière in 1776, shows a somewhat padded face with a vacant stare. And there are reasons to doubt the drawing is really Jefferson at all. But most descriptions of the older Jefferson emphasize his "scranny" or thin face. Bacon said he "had no surplus flesh"—and bright, luminous eyes. The color of his eyes is also controversial. Virtually all the later reports indicate they were clear blue; the earlier descriptions, and most of the portraits, have them hazel or green. Perhaps they changed color in different light.③

One of his ex-slaves, Isaac, emphasized his erect posture. "Mr. Jefferson was a tall, straight-bodied man as ever you see," he recalled. "Nary a man in this town walked so straight." Bacon agreed that Jefferson was "straight as a gun barrell." But others, mostly enemies, described him as loosely jointed and seemingly collapsible, all wrists, elbows and ankles. The discrepancy might have been a function of different postures. On his feet he was square-shouldered and formal. He bowed to everyone he met and tended to stand with his arms folded across his chest, defining his own private space and warding off intruders. When seated, however, he seemed to melt into the upholstery with a kind of contorted grace, one hip high, the other low, shoulders slouched and uneven, his torso folded in several places, part jackknife and part accordion.

His two most distinctive characteristics were his hair and his incessant singing. Disagreements about the color of his hair, unlike disagreements about his eyes, seem susceptible to reconciliation. It was reddish blond or sandy red. Those few commentators who described it as gray came from a later period, when aging had reduced the reddish hues but made no inroads into his naturally full and thick complement, which was seldom dressed and even less frequently powdered or wigged. He tended to tie it behind his neck much as he sat, loosely and with an air of disheveled informality.

He sang whenever he was walking or riding, sometimes when he was reading. His former slave Isaac reported that one could "hardly see him anywhar outdoors, but that he was a-singin'." Bacon confirmed that "when he was not talking he was nearly always humming some tune, or singing in a low voice to himself." Apparently this constant singing was a long-standing habit. So, if we are prepared to take a few leaps of faith, we can plausibly envision him riding into Philadelphia in 1775 in his phaeton, with his horses and his slaves, a tall and slim young Virginian, with reddish blond hair and a self-consciously diffident air, lounging nonchalantly in his seat, singing to himself.⁴

YOUNG JEFFERSON

THE ELEMENTAL facts of his earlier life, at least the most basic pieces of biographical information, are less fuzzy than a picture of his physical appearance. Jefferson was born in Shadwell, in Albemarle County, Virginia, in the foothills of the Blue Ridge Mountains in 1743. Family legend has it that his earliest memory, when he was only about three years old, "was of being carried on a pillow by a mounted slave on the journey from Shadwell to Tuckahoe," perhaps a kind of early premonition of his Philadelphia entry. His father, Peter Jefferson, was a moderately successful planter with a local reputation for physical strength and a flair for adventure as an explorer and surveyor of western lands. When he died in 1757, he left behind two hundred hogs, seventy head of cattle, twenty-five horses, sixty slaves, six daughters, two sons and his widow, Jane Randolph Jefferson.

Little is known of her (the problem of the Shadwell fire again), except that as a Randolph she was descended from one of the most prominent families in Virginia. There is reason to believe that Jefferson's relationship with his mother was strained, especially after his father's death, when, as the eldest son, he did everything he could to remove himself from her supervision. But all inspired speculation on this point is really pure guesswork; no explicit evidence exists. After boarding with the local schoolmaster to learn his Latin and Greek, he went off to the College of William and Mary in 1760. There he gained a reputation among his classmates as an obsessive student, sometimes spending fifteen hours with his books, three hours practicing his violin and the remaining six hours eating and sleeping. He was an extremely serious young man.⁵

After graduating in 1762, he brought his highly disciplined regime to the study of the law in Williamsburg under the tutelage of George Wythe (pronounced *with*). Then, after a long, five-year apprenticeship, he began to practice on his own, mostly representing small-scale planters from the western counties in cases involving land claims and titles. Although he broke no legal ground and handled no landmark cases, he gained a reputation in the Williamsburg court as an extremely well-prepared barrister, an indifferent speaker before the bench but a formidable legal scholar.[6]

In 1768 he made two important decisions: first, to build his own home atop an 867-foot-high mountain on land that he had inherited from his father; second, to offer himself as a candidate for the House of Burgesses. The first decision reflected what was to become his life-long urge to withdraw into his own very private world. The name he first picked for his prospective home was The Hermitage, a retreat that soon became Monticello, his mansion on a mountain and lifetime architectural project. The second decision reflected his political ambition and growing reputation within the transmontane region of the Old Dominion, as well as his emerging stature within the planter elite of the Tidewater. He took his seat in the House of Burgesses in May 1769, then quickly became a protégé of two established Tidewater grandees: Peyton Randolph, an uncle on his mother's side as well as the most powerful figure in the legislature, and Edmund Pendleton, the shrewd and famously agile apologist for the planter aristocracy.⁷

On New Year's Day of 1772 he completed his self-image as an aspiring "paterfamilias" by marrying Martha Wales Skelton, an attractive and delicate young widow whose dowry more than doubled his holdings in land and slaves. Marriage seemed to steady him. Up until the early 1770s the various account and commonplace books that he kept for recording his dealings and readings seemed to have been written by a series of different people. The handwriting varies wildly with wholly different slants, penmanship styles and spacing. Around the time of his marriage this unconscious experimentation stopped; his writing settled into the clear, unpretentious form that it retained until old age and that is now enshrined in the original draft of the Declaration of Independence.[8]

His political identity, on the other hand, remained shadowy and marginal. The first vivid image of Jefferson in the House of Burgesses proved emblematic. As a young law student in Williamsburg he stood in the hallway of the House, listening to Patrick Henry toss off his extempore oratorical thunderbolts against the Stamp Act in 1765. Jefferson was a listener and observer, distinctly uncomfortable in the spotlight, shy and nervous in a distracted manner that was sometimes mistaken for arrogance.[9]

From his earliest days in the House he opposed all forms of parliamentary taxation and supported nonimportation resolutions against British trade regulations. But so did most other members of the House, along with the entire Tidewater leadership. (In 1771 his political radicalism collided with his domestic agenda when he ordered an expensive piano from London, "of fine mahogany, solid, not veneered," in anticipation of his marriage to Martha. Even though this violated the nonimportation resolution, he ordered it sent anyway, saying he would store it until the embargo was lifted. The same thing happened three years later on an order of "sashed windows" for Monticello.) He seemed to most of his political contemporaries a hovering and ever-silent presence, like one of those foreigners at a dinner party who nod politely as they move from group to group but never reveal whether or not they can speak the language. He had a deep-seated aversion to the inherent contentions and routinized hurly-burly of a political career and was forever telling his friends that life on the public stage was not for him. Just as his political career was getting started, he seemed poised for retirement.[10]

Given his subsequent role in the Continental Congress and then in shaping the course of the American Revolution, his selection to serve on the Virginia delegation in Philadelphia was a fortunate accident. Jefferson was not elected to the original delegation in 1774; he was not considered a sufficiently prominent figure to be included with the likes of George Washington, Patrick Henry, Edmund Pendleton and Peyton Randolph. In 1775, however, he was chosen as a potential substitute for Randolph—Jefferson was regarded as Randolph's political godson—in anticipation of Randolph's decision to abandon his post at Philadelphia in order to assume leadership of what was regarded as the more important business back in Virginia. It would be fair to say that Jefferson made the list of acknowledged political leaders in the Old Dominion, but just barely, and largely because of his ties by blood and patronage with the Randolph circle. If his arrival in Philadelphia in June 1775 marked his entry into national affairs, he entered by the side door.[11]

WHIG PRINCIPLES

THERE WAS ONE significant exception to this dominant pattern of reticence and marginality, but it happened to be the one item that delegates from the other colonies knew about the young Jefferson. "I have not been in Company with him yet," reported Samuel Ward the day after Jefferson arrived, but "he looks like a very sensible spirited, fine Fellow and by the Pamphlet which he wrote last Summer he certainly is one." Likewise John Adams recalled that Jefferson entered the Continental Congress carrying "the reputation of a masterly pen . . . , in consequence of a very handsome public paper which he had written for the House of Burgesses, which had given him the character of a fine writer."[12]

The reference was to a pamphlet that Jefferson had somewhat inad-vertently published the previous year. In July 1774 he had taken it upon himself to draft a set of instructions for the first Virginia delegation to the Continental Congress. In a typical act of avoidance he had come up sick for the debate in the Virginia Convention, but friends had arranged for the publication of his draft by a press in Williamsburg. From there printers and newspaper editors throughout the colonies had picked up the pamphlet under the title of *A Summary View of the Rights of British America.* The audience at whom Jefferson had actually aimed his instructions, the Virginia legislators, chose not to follow them, preferring to recommend that its delegates adopt a moderate posture toward Great Britain. What Jefferson had recommended, and what became the basis of his political reputation outside Virginia, was decidedly more radical. Indeed, if the arguments of *Summary View* were to be believed, they put him in the vanguard of the revolutionary movement in America.[13]

The style of *Summary View* was simple and emphatic, with a dra-matic flair that previewed certain passages in the Declaration of Inde-pendence (e.g., "Single acts of tyranny may be ascribed to the accidental opinion of the day; but a series of oppressions, begun at a distinguished period, and pursued unalterably thro' every change of ministers, too plainly prove a deliberate, systematical plan of reducing us to slavery"). What most readers noticed, however, and Jefferson later claimed was his chief contribution, was the constitutional argument that Parliament had no right *whatsoever* to exercise authority over the colonies. While this position had been implicit in the colonial protest literature ever since the Stamp Act crisis in 1765, the clarity of the colo-nial case had fallen afoul of several complicating distinctions. Granted, Parliament had no right to *tax* the colonists without their consent, but did it not have the power to *regulate* trade? Well, yes, it did, but not when the intent of the trade regulation was to raise revenue. But, then, how was intent to be gauged? And what about Parliament's other leg-islative actions, like quartering troops in colonial cities and closing Boston's port? These nagging questions made for a somewhat convoluted constitutional problem. Could Parliament do some of these things but not others? If so, how did one decide which was which? The core appeal of *Summary View* was that Jefferson cut through the tangle with one sharp thrust: "[T]he British parliament has no right to exercise authority over us."[14]

The timing of the pamphlet was also exquisite. Several other colonial dissenters—John Adams in Massachusetts and James Wilson in Pennsylvania—were simultaneously reaching the same conclusion about Parliament's lack of authority in the colonies. It was, as mentioned earlier, the logical implication of the entire colonial protest movement that had begun in 1765. But Jefferson staked out the constitutional ground just as it was becoming the only tenable position for the opponents of British imperial policy to stand on. And he did it in a pamphlet that combined the concision and matter-of-factness of a legal brief with the epigrammatic force of a political sermon.[15]

Two other salient features of *Summary View* received little attention at the time but were destined to loom large in the debates within the Continental Congress over the ensuing months. The first was Jefferson's treatment of George III and his attitude toward the British monarchy. The dominant public reaction to *Summary View* focused on its repudiation of parliamentary authority, because that was the pressing constitutional issue then being faced throughout the various colonial legislatures. What went largely unnoticed was that Jefferson had already moved forward to the next target, the monarchy, which was in fact the only remaining obstacle to the assertion of American independence. To put it somewhat differently, the lengthy indictments against the king that take up two-thirds of the Declaration of Independence were already present in embryo in *Summary View*.

Jefferson's posture toward the monarch throughout *Summary View* is declaratory rather than plaintive, and the tone toward George III ranges between the disrespectful and the accusatory. The king is not some specially endowed ruler but merely "the chief officer of the people, appointed by the laws, and circumscribed with definite powers, to assist in working the great machine of government erected for their use, and consequently subject to their superintendence." Rather than blame the entire mismanagement of imperial policy toward America on Parliament or "the evil ministers to the king," still the accepted approach within even the radical camp, Jefferson made the king complicitous in the crimes against colonial rights. He accused George III of negligence: permitting colonial assemblies to be dissolved; refusing to hear appeals from aggrieved petitioners; delaying the passage of land reforms. But he also charged the king with outright acts of illegality on his own: sending armed troops into colonial cities to put down lawful demonstrations; prohibiting the natural migration of colonial settlers beyond the Appalachian Mountains. He even introduced the charge that provoked such spirited debate when included in his original draft of the Declaration of Independence—namely, that George III had perpetuated the existence of chattel slavery by repeatedly blocking colonial efforts to end the African slave trade. In effect, with the advantage of hindsight, it is possible to see *Summary View* as a preliminary draft of the bill of indictment against George III contained in the Declaration, written a full two years before the more famous document and before Jefferson had even taken his seat in the Continental Congress.[16]

The second latent feature in *Summary View* that went unnoticed at the time is of even greater significance in exposing Jefferson's cast of mind at the dawn of his public career. It is an elaborate and largely mythological version of English history. In the midst of his litany against monarchical abuses of power, Jefferson inserted a long paragraph in which he traced the origin of such abuses back to the Norman Conquest. The source of the colonial problem with British authority did not date from the Stamp Act crisis of 1765; the problem really began in 1066, when the Normans defeated the Saxons at the Battle of Hastings. This was the origin of what Jefferson called "the fictitious principle that all lands belong originally to the king. . . ." All of English history since the Norman Conquest had been an unfortunate aberration, known under the name of feudalism, which then flared up in a most virulent form in the recent royal exercise of arbitrary power in the colonies. Jefferson indulged his own "fictitious principle" by purporting to discover in the Saxon past of pre-Norman England, and before that in the forests of Germany, a set of people who lived freely and harmoniously, without kings or lords to rule over them, working and owning their land as sovereign agents.[17]

The "once upon a time" character of Jefferson's interpretation, which has also come to be known as the Whig interpretation of history, deserves studied attention as a crucial clue to Jefferson's deepest intellectual instincts. He had been exposed to the central story line of Whig history in several books that he read as a young man, chiefly Paul de Rapin's multivolume *History of England* and Sir John Dalrymple's *History of Feudal Property in Great Britain*. He had also read in translation Tacitus's *Germania*, the key source for the Whig historians because of its description of the Saxon model of representative government before contamination by feudal monarchs. So Jefferson's youthful reading in standard works of Whig history unquestionably helped shape his political thinking before 1776 and was one reason he consistently referred to "the ancient Whig principles" as the wellspring for the values underlying the movement for American independence. But the appeal of the Whig histories derived from something more than their rhetorical or logic power. They were influential precisely because they told a story that fitted perfectly with the way his mind worked. Their romantic endorsement of a pristine past, a long-lost time and place where men had lived together in perfect harmony without coercive laws or predatory rulers, gave narrative shape to his fondest imaginings and to utopian expectations with deep roots in his personality. The Whig histories did not create his romantic expectations. They put into words the visionary prospects he already carried around in his mind and heart.

During the initial months in Philadelphia Jefferson was less concerned with plumbing the depths of his Whig principles than with sharing their practical implications with his fellow delegates. The key term was "expatriation." The core idea was that America was the refuge for the original Saxon values. Throughout the fall and winter of 1775 Jefferson did extensive research in Richard Hakluyt's *Voyages* with the aim of documenting the claim that the earliest migrants from England to America came over at their own expense "unassisted by the wealth or the strength of Great Britain" and, most significantly, regarded their migration as a clean break with the mother country. If true, this was revisionist history with the most revolutionary consequences, for it suggested that independence from England was not some future prospect that he and his fellow delegates in the Continental Congress were seriously contemplating; it was an event that had already happened in the misty past.[18]

The theory of expatriation was utterly groundless as history. (Jefferson clung to the theory with nearly obsessive tenacity throughout his life, though even he admitted that "I had never been able to get any one to agree with me but Mr. Wythe," his old law teacher.) John Adams had only recently published his own survey of colonial history, entitled *Novanglus,* in which he too searched for the sources of American claims to independence from royal and parliamentary authority. But instead of a mystical Saxon past, Adams discovered a complex web of overlapping precedents and contested jurisdictions. This was truer to the inherent messiness of English and colonial history, which had witnessed several major changes in the relationship between royal and parliamentary power during the colonial era, fundamental differences among charters contingent on when different colonies were founded, and only the most gradual realization on the part of English authorities that they in fact were overseeing an empire. Jefferson's theory of expatriation bore the same relation to colonial history as a nursery rhyme does to a Jamesian novel. That undoubtedly was part of its appeal.[19]

The Jeffersonian impulse to invent and then embrace such seductive fictions was not a deliberate effort at propaganda. Jefferson believed what he wrote. True, he could consciously play fast and loose with the historical evidence on behalf of a greater cause. Jefferson's intellectual dexterity in assigning blame for the slave trade on George III, for example, could be explained as a clever ploy. No one in his right mind believed it, but it could be endorsed as a politically useful misrepresentation. The same thing could be said for his spiffied-up version of the Boston Tea Party in *Summary View*. In Jefferson's account, a dedicated group of loyal Bostonians risked arrest and persecution to destroy a cargo of the contraband. Samuel Adams, a major figure in the Continental Congress and the chief organizer of the Tea Party, must have chuckled in satisfaction, knowing as he did that the "loyal Bostonians" were really a group of hooligans and vandals who had disguised themselves as Indians in order to avoid being identified and who had enjoyed the tacit support of the Boston merchants, many of whom had made their fortunes in smuggling. Sam Adams realized that the Tea Party was an orchestrated act of revolutionary theater. Jefferson described it as a spontaneous act of patriotism conducted according to the etiquette of, well, a tea party. But then again, perhaps Jefferson's version was itself a propagandistic manipulation, just as self-consciously orchestrated as the Tea Party itself.[20]

The Saxon myth and the doctrine of expatriation, however, were a different matter. They were not clever and willful distortions. They were complete fabrications. And Jefferson clearly believed they were true. Their distinguishing feature was an otherworldly, almost fairy-tale quality. History is full of wise and great figures whose greatness derived from the will to believe in what eventually proved to be a set of illusions. But Jefferson's illusions possess a sentimental and almost juvenile character that strains credulity. Since this affinity for idealized or idyllic visions, and the parallel capacity to deny evidence that exposed them as illusory, proved a central feature of Jefferson's mature thought and character, it seems necessary to ask where it all came from.

The explanation lies buried in the inner folds of Jefferson's personality, beyond the reach of traditional historical methods and canons of evidence. What we can discern is a reclusive pattern of behavior with distinctive psychological implications. The youthful Jefferson had already shown himself to be an extremely private temperament. Monticello offers the most graphic illustration of Jefferson's need to withdraw from the rest of the world, filled as it was with human conflicts and coercions, and create a refuge where the perfect Palladian architec-

ture established the ideal environment for his vision of domestic harmony. And he tended to talk about his craving for a safe haven from
the messiness and disorder of the world in decidedly melodramatic
terms. "There may be people to whose tempers and dispositions Contention may be pleasing," he wrote to John Randolph in 1775, "but to
me it is of all states, but one, the most horrid." He much preferred "to
withdraw myself totally from the public stage and pass the rest of my
days in domestic ease and tranquillity, banishing every desire of afterwards even hearing what passes in the world." The most astute student
of Jefferson's lifelong compulsion to make and then remake Monticello into a perfect palace and a "magical mystery tour of architectural
legerdemain" has concluded that Jefferson's obsessive "putting up and
pulling down" are best understood as a form of "childhood play
adapted to an adult world." Both the expectations that Jefferson harbored for his private life in his mansion on the mountain, as well as his
way of trying to design and construct it, suggested a level of indulged
sentimentality that one normally associates with an adolescent.[21]

The very few personal letters from his early years that have survived
reflect a similar pattern of juvenile romanticism. At the age of twenty,
soon after he had graduated from William and Mary, Jefferson wrote
his best friend, John Page: "I verily beleive [sic] Page that I shall die
soon, and yet I can give no other reason for it but that I am tired with
living. At this moment when I am writing I am scarcely sensible that I
exist. Adieu Dear Page." A few months later he reported to Page his
mortification at discovering that his infatuation with Rebecca Burwell,
a coquettish beauty then turning heads in Williamsburg, was a hopeless cause. Jefferson had approached her at a dance in the Apollo
Room of Raleigh Tavern, only to find himself tongue-tied and Rebecca
uninterested. "I had dressed up in my own mind, such thoughts as
occurred to me, in as moving language as I knew how, and expected to
have performed in a tolerably creditable manner," he explained. "But,
good God!"[22]

In one sense such fragments of evidence only document that Jefferson was the epitome of the painfully self-conscious teenager (though in fact he was twenty at the time of the Rebecca Burwell fiasco). In another sense, however, they offer glimpses of a very vulnerable young man accustomed to constructing interior worlds of great imaginative appeal that inevitably collided with the more mundane realities. Rather than adjust his expectations in the face of disappointment, he tended to bury them deeper inside himself and regard the disjunction between his ideals and worldly imperfections as the world's problem rather than his own.

Jefferson's strange attachment, then, to the myth of the Saxon past was an early ideological manifestation of a characteristically Jeffersonian cast of mind. It represented his discovery—in truth, his invention—of an idyllic time and place that accorded with his powerful sense of the way things were meant to be. And any compromise of that seductive vision was a betrayal of one's personal principles. Back there in the faraway world of pre-Norman England, prior to the feudal corruptions, men and women had found it possible to combine individual independence and social harmony, personal freedom and the rule of law, the need to work and the urge to play. Throughout his life Jefferson was haunted by the prospects of such a paradise and eager to find it in bucolic pastoral scenes, distant Indian tribes, well-ordered gardens, local communities (he later called them ward-republics) or new and therefore uncorrupted generations. At the private level the young man who was taking his seat in the Continental Congress had already begun to build his personal version of utopia at Monticello. At the public level he was preparing to release his formidable energies against a British government that, as he saw it, was threatening to disrupt and destroy the patch of potential perfection that was forming on the western edge of the British Empire. Whatever weaknesses this Jeffersonian perspective harbored as a mature and realistic appraisal of the Anglo-American crisis, it possessed all the compensating advantages of an unequivocal moral commitment driven by an unsullied sense of righteous indignation.[23]

PROSE ORATIONS

SUCH ASSETS were not immediately visible to his colleagues in the
Continental Congress. We know, with the advantage of hindsight, that
Jefferson was destined to emerge in the history books as the most
famous figure in Philadelphia in 1776. In the summer of 1775, however,
while his authorship of *Summary View* provided a measure of status
and his membership in the Virginia delegation assured that his opinions mattered, no one could have predicted that his contribution over
the course of the next year would earn him a permanent place in posterity. Not only was he a thoroughly marginal player within Virginia's
cast of stars, he lacked precisely those qualities that the members of
Congress considered most essential. His most glaring deficiency was
the talent most valued in Philadelphia: He could not speak in public.

This was a major liability because the Continental Congress was
regarded by most observers as an arena for orators. John Adams, who
has left the fullest personal account of the debates and deliberations,
had come to Philadelphia the previous year wondering who would be
the American Cicero or Demosthenes (and hoping the fates had
selected him for both roles). His diary entries convey something of the
sense that pervaded the debates, the sense that as each man rose to
speak, he was being judged by his colleagues as a contestant in a game
of conspicuous eloquence. Adams observed that Edward Rutledge of
South Carolina was "sprightly but not deep" and had the distracting
habit of speaking through his nose. Benjamin Rush of Pennsylvania
was dismissed as "too much of a talker. . . . Elegant but not deep."
Roger Sherman of Connecticut was a perfect model of awkwardness:
"There cannot be a more striking contrast to beautiful Action, than the
Motions of his Hands. Generally, he stands upright with his Hands
before him. . . . But when he moves a Hand, in any thing like Action,
Hogarth's Genius could not have invented a Motion more opposite to
grace. It is Stiffness, and Awkwardness itself. Awkward as a Junior Bach-

elor, or a Sophomore." By the time Jefferson arrived in Philadelphia Adams himself had begun to emerge as one of the most effective public speakers in the Congress, a man whose own throbbing ego had lashed itself to the cause of independence and whose combination of legal learning and sheer oratorical energy had overwhelmed more moderate delegates in a powerful style that seemed part bulldog and part volcano.[24]

Meanwhile the elevated status of the Virginia delegation derived primarily from its reputation for oratorical brilliance. Edmund Pendleton was the silver-haired and silver-tongued master of the elegant style. Jefferson later described him as the "ablest man in debate I have ever met with." Pendleton's specialty was the cool and low-key peroration that hypnotized the audience, while his arguments waged a silent guerrilla war against its better judgment, until the matter at issue came around to his way of thinking almost inadvertently, like a natural aristocrat winning a race without ever appearing to exert himself.[25]

Richard Henry Lee was more inflammable and ostentatious. If Pendleton's technique suggested a peaceful occupation, Lee was a proponent of the all-out invasion. Opponents winced whenever he rose to speak, knowing as they did that their arguments were about to be carried off to oblivion in a whirlwind of words. Lee's theatricality was somewhat contrived; he liked to wrap his hand in a silk handkerchief as he spoke, explaining that he wished to shield onlookers from the unsightly appearance of his mangled hand, missing several fingers because of a hunting accident. Or was it a duel? Lee was to Pendleton as a bomb was to a pistol. But both men were famous on their feet.[26]

The undisputed oratorical champion of Virginia of course was Patrick Henry, whose presence in the Virginia delegation generated more public attention than anyone else except George Washington. Henry's speech against the Stamp Act had been widely publicized throughout the colonies, so he already carried a national reputation for incandescence. As Edmund Randolph put it, "for grand impressions in the defense of liberty, the Western world has not yet been able to exhibit a rival." If Pendleton was the suave aristocrat and Lee the mannered dramatist, Henry was the evangelical preacher, who came at an audience in waves of emotional inspiration, each separated by exaggerated pauses that seemed to most listeners like the silence preceding divine judgment.

All of Jefferson's surviving observations on Henry date from a later time, when their friendship had turned sour (Jefferson claimed that Henry was "avaritious & rotten hearted" and always spoke "without logic, without arrangement . . ."). But even Jefferson's criticisms betrayed a certain admiration for Henry's capacity to sway a crowd by emotional appeals unencumbered with any learning or evidence. In 1784 he warned James Madison that Henry's opposition to constitutional reforms in Virginia must not be taken lightly since one of his spellbinders could undo weeks of careful work behind the scenes. There was no way to account for his mysterious influence over others or to deal with him in full flight. "What we have to do," lamented Jefferson to Madison, "is devoutly pray for his death." In the Continental Congress, of course, Henry's oratorical brilliance was still a priceless asset rather than a formidable liability. Like Jefferson, Henry was a product of Virginia's western frontier who had won acceptance from the Tidewater elite, but unlike Jefferson, he always retained the primal quality of a natural force, like the Natural Bridge that Jefferson so admired, one of those spontaneous creations of the gods spawned in the western mountains.[27]

Compared with Henry, Jefferson epitomized the diametrically different sensibility of the refined and disciplined scholar. As far as we know, he never rose to deliver a single speech in the Continental Congress. Even within the more intimate atmosphere of committees, he preferred to let others do the talking. John Adams recalled, with a mingled sense of admiration and astonishment, that "during the whole Time I sat with him in Congress, I never heard him utter three sentences together." No one, however, including the ever-skeptical Adams, ever doubted his radical credentials. His clear denunciation of British authority in *Summary View* put him on record as an opponent of moderation. But he was utterly useless in situations that demanded the projection of a public presence. He was almost as inadequate in behind-the-scenes arm twisting and cajoling, which were the specialty of John's cousin Sam Adams. He was simply too shy and withdrawn to interact easily in the corridors.[28]

By disposition and habit, Jefferson's most comfortable arena was the study and his most natural podium was the writing desk. Ever since his college days at William and Mary, continuing through his study and eventual practice of the law, Jefferson spent an inordinate amount of his time alone, reading and taking extensive notes on what he read. He called this practice "commonplacing," referring to the copying over of passages from Coke or Pufendorf on the law, Milton or Shakespeare on the human condition, Kames or Hutcheson on man's moral sense. But Jefferson made copying a creative act, often revising a passage to suit his own taste or, more often, blending his own thoughts on the subject into his notes. He was a young man who very much liked to be in control. Solitary study allowed him to work out his private perspectives without interference and without the unpredictability of an improvisational debate.[29]

His first act after settling into his quarters on Chestnut Street was to undertake a solitary assessment of how much a war against England might cost the colonies, not in terms of deaths but in terms of dollars. He seemed to believe that an all-out military conflict would not last long. "One bloody campaign," he wrote a friend, "will probably decide everlastingly our future course." So his calculations of cost were based on the assumption of a six-month war, which he estimated would require about three million dollars in new taxes.[30]

At some point during the summer he commissioned his landlord, Benjamin Randolph, who was a relative on his mother's side as well as a skilled cabinetmaker, to design a writing desk. He also acquired a new Windsor chair as a comfortable seat. These implements, which eventually became sacred relics because of their subsequent association with the Declaration of Independence, defined the space within which his creative energies could best express themselves. Within a short time his accountlike estimates of military costs were put aside for the more serious business of explaining, in words, why the American colonies must take up arms in the first place.

The leadership in Congress selected him to draft an address eventually entitled *Declaration of the Causes and Necessity for Taking Up Arms*. This was a significant assignment. The address was regarded as a major statement of current thinking in Congress; an earlier effort had floundered over disagreements about language. The selection of Jefferson reflected his reputation as a literary craftsman and the practical recognition that he could make his greatest contribution as a writer rather than a speaker.

The assignment also forces us to notice an awkward and easily forgotten fact—namely, that although an official declaration of American independence was a year away, the war itself had already started. By the time Jefferson arrived in Philadelphia the battles of Lexington, Concord and Bunker Hill had already occurred and George Washington had headed off to command an army outside Boston. While the moderates within the Continental Congress continued to hold open the hope of reconciliation with England, by the summer of 1775 the initiative had passed over to the radicals, led by John and Sam Adams, who regarded independence as inevitable. And every action by the British ministry seemed calculated to undercut the moderate faction and make the radicals appear prescient. From the beginning Jefferson identified himself, as did the Virginia delegation, with the radicals. His personal correspondence at this time reflects no doubt that the time for compromise had passed. In June 1775, for example, he wrote relatives in Virginia that "the war is now heartily entered into, without a prospect of accommodation but thro' the effectual interposition of arms." A month later he was writing John Randolph that rather than agree to English terms for reconciliation, he "would lend my hand to sink the whole island in the ocean." The question as Jefferson saw it was no longer whether the American colonies would declare independence, but when and how.[31]

This is crucial to understand, for it served to shape in subtle but important ways Jefferson's stylistic agenda throughout the next year as the chief draftsman for the revolutionary cause. On the one hand, the delegates in the Continental Congress were busy raising an army, instructing colonial legislatures on ways to draw up new state constitutions, investigating foreign alliances, overseeing an ongoing war. On the other hand, they were insisting they wished to avoid an open rupture with the mother country and pledging their undying loyalty to George III. Somehow these incompatible political postures, which reflected the split between radicals and moderates in the Congress, had to be stitched together rhetorically. And although the official audience was the English ministry, the actual audience was the American people, or at least the different colonial legislatures that needed to be provided with a way of explaining to themselves why the formerly unthinkable had now become inevitable.

At the purely constitutional level Jefferson's argument in *Causes and Necessity* represented a slight retreat from the position advanced in *Summary View*. Instead of denying Parliament any legitimate authority in the colonies, Jefferson conceded that "some occasional assumptions of power by the parliament of Great Britain, however unacknowledged by the constitution of our governments, were finally acquiesced in thro' warmth of affection." This was undoubtedly a concession to the moderates in the Congress and a reflection of Jefferson's realization that he needed to accommodate perspectives different from his own. The expatriation theme was also presented in muted form. "Our forefathers . . . left their native land," he wrote, "to seek on these shores a residence for civil and religious freedom." But there was no invocation of the Saxon myth or of the Norman captivity of traditional English rights. Jefferson was bending over backward to avoid alienating the undecided.[32]

Jefferson's main contribution in *Causes and Necessities* was to provide a story line that brought all American colonists together as innocent victims. Earlier American critics of British policy—men like John Adams, John Dickinson and Daniel Dulany—had made the legal argument that Parliament's intrusion into colonial affairs after the end of the French and Indian War (1763) was unprecedented. In England

Edmund Burke had referred to the period prior to the war as an era of "salutary neglect." Jefferson's version of the Anglo-American conflict simply enhanced the dramatic implications of the shift in British policy. Before 1763 the empire was harmonious and healthy, an American version of his earlier descriptions of serenity in the Saxon forests. Then, all of a sudden, "the ministry, finding all the foes of Britain subdued, took up the unfortunate idea of subduing her friends also." Jefferson showed a flair for, and an intuitive attraction toward, a narrative structure built around moralistic dichotomies. The empire "then and now" set the theme. The story became a clash between British tyranny and colonial liberty, scheming British officials and supplicating colonists, all culminating in the clash at Lexington and Concord between General Thomas Gage's "ministerial army" and "the unsuspecting inhabitants" of Massachusetts. All this was conveyed in what we might call the sentimental style of the innocent victim.[33]

It is impossible to know how much of this cartoonlike version of the imperial crisis Jefferson actually believed and how much was a stylistic affectation. William Livingston, the delegate from New York, observed that Jefferson's prose in *Causes and Necessities* reminded him of the oratorical style of the other Virginians: "Much fault-finding and declamation, with little sense of dignity. They seem to think a reiteration of tyranny, despotism, bloody, etc., all that is needed to unite us at home. . . ." Perhaps Jefferson's draft represented his attempt to achieve in prose what his Virginian colleagues like Henry were creating in set-piece orations. Within that self-consciously melodramatic tradition, one was allowed to speak of "the unsuspecting inhabitants" of Lexington and Concord, all the while knowing perfectly well that they were lined up in military formation when the British troops arrived.[34]

Specific factual extravagances are less important to note than Jefferson's overall narrative scheme. The colonists are innocent bystanders being acted on by an aggressive British government. The political conflict invariably takes the form of a moral dichotomy that leaves no room for shaded meanings or ambivalent loyalties. The bitterness and confusion of the present are contrasted with the "once upon a time" version of the past. And most effectively, the real revolutionaries are not American colonists but British officials, who are just as unmitigatedly corrupt as the colonists are virtuous.

The rhetorical excess of *Causes and Necessities* merits additional meditation, in part because it was a preview of coming attractions in the Declaration and in part because its message was conveyed in coded language familiar to Jefferson and his contemporaries but strange to our modern ears and sensibilities. The key feature was the apparent extremism of the contrast between American virtue and British corruption, which itself depended upon an implicit presumption that sinister forces were conspiring in London's faraway corridors of power to deprive unsuspecting colonists of their liberties. Like the Saxon myth, this way of thinking and talking about politics had deep roots in the Whig tradition in England, dating back to the Puritan dissenters during the English Civil War in the 1640s. The chief eighteenth-century proponents of this dissenting tradition, who called themselves Real Whigs or the Country Party, were Englishmen: Henry St. John Bolingbroke, John Trenchard and Thomas Gordon (writing under the pseudonym of Cato) and James Burgh. They had created a language, and indeed an ideology, of opposition to the arbitrary and abusive exercise of power by the British ministry, often described as the Court Party, distinctive for its neurotic suspicion of government's motives and its stark moral contrasts between popular virtue and official corruption.

Jefferson's library contained copies of the major writings of Bolingbroke, "Cato" and Burgh, and he along with his colleagues in the Continental Congress were well versed in the arguments and the idiom of English Whiggery. What strikes our modern ears as hyperbolic and melodramatic both in its tone and its posture toward political authority—virtually any expression of governmental power is stigmatized—was in fact part of a venerable Whig tradition of opposition. It was an acceptable and familiar style of political argumentation that had proved extremely useful in the previous decade of protest against British taxation. It had enormous polemic potential in simplifying the bewildering constitutional complexities facing both the colonists and the British ministry. Even its quasi-paranoid attitude toward the motives of decision-makers in London and Whitehall enjoyed at least the appearance of cool reason during the spring of 1776, as George III and his ministers seemed bent on behaving like villains in the Whig script.

What deserves special attention, however, is that Jefferson's embrace of the Whig rhetoric and the Whig story line was utterly sincere. His draft of *Causes and Necessities*, then his subsequent draft of the Declaration, were not undertaken as self-conscious polemics or exaggerated pieces of propaganda. What he wrote actually reflected his understanding of the forces swirling through Anglo-America. What some delegates in the Congress regarded as a conveniently useful distortion that would help mobilize colonial opinion in the direction that destiny required, Jefferson regarded as an accurate characterization of the essential elements of the political situation. Whether or not he had acquired the primal categories of his political thinking from the Whig historians and Country Party theorists, by the spring of 1776 he had thoroughly absorbed their style and substance into his own personality, where they only served to buttress his extreme aversion to explicit expressions of authority and his instinctive tendency to think in terms of moralistic dichotomies. Jefferson was, then, a quintessential Whig, but the Whig values were so appealing because they blended so nicely with his own quintessentially Jeffersonian character.

He also showed himself extremely sensitive to any criticism of his prose. This led to Jefferson's first political battle in the Continental Congress, when John Dickinson questioned the tone and wording of several sections of the Jefferson draft of *Causes and Necessities*. Dickinson was a delegate from Pennsylvania and the acknowledged leader of the moderate faction in the Congress. He had been put on the committee to draft *Causes and Necessities* in order to assure bipartisan support for the document. Jefferson's late-in-life recollection of Dickinson's objections therefore sounded quite plausible: "I prepared a Draught of the Declaration committed to us. It was too strong for Mr. Dickinson. He still retained the hope of reconciliation with the mother country, and was unwilling it should be lessened by offensive statements."

After much editorial detective work in the twentieth century, however, Jefferson's wholly plausible recollection has been discredited. Dickinson's suggested revisions did not represent a watering down of Jefferson's message. In fact Dickinson inserted the strongest and most quotable words in the entire document: "Our cause is just. Our union is perfect. Our internal resources are great, and, if necessary, foreign assistance is attainable." Jefferson's objections were essentially stylistic and temperamental. Dickinson's revisions injected a more matter-of-fact tone that offset Jefferson's dramatic dichotomies. Mostly, however, Jefferson could not abide any tampering with his verbal creations. He had worked out his arrangement of words in isolation. In the give-and-take of the drafting committee, he regarded all critical suggestions as unwelcome and misguided corruptions. The purity of his prose, like the purity of the colonial cause, did not permit compromise.[35]

The Continental Congress resolved the impasse by approving a final draft that included most of Dickinson's changes. Despite the revisions, it retained Jeffersonian intonations that, a year later in slightly altered form, were to echo through the ages: "So to Slight Justice and the Opinion of Mankind, we esteem ourselves bound by Obligations of Respect to the Rest of the World, to make known the Justice of our Cause." His composition of *Causes and Necessities,* like *Summary View,* proved a dress rehearsal for the drafting of the Declaration of Independence.[36]

By the end of the summer of 1775, then, the pattern was set. Jefferson played no role in the public debates, but he was appointed to several committees and often charged with the responsibility of drafting the reports. He was asked, for instance, to draft the Resolutions of Congress on Lord North's Proposal, a spirited rejection of the English government's halfhearted offer of compromise. He was asked to draft the Declaration on the British Treatment of Ethan Allen, a protest against trying Allen for treason. Despite his public silence, as well as his reticence during committee debates and his thin-skinned attitude toward criticisms of his literary craftsmanship, the leadership of the radical faction in the Congress counted him as a staunch and valuable ally. More than fifty years later John Adams remembered Jefferson as "a silent member in Congress," but "so prompt, frank, explicit and decisive . . . that he soon won my heart." Though only eight years older than Jefferson, Adams claimed that he initially regarded him as a son.[37]

The gravitational pull of Monticello remained a constant seduction. Indeed, if there were a fundamental rule of emotional physics for Jefferson, it was an attraction for isolation and an aversion to the public arena: He hated the debates in Congress; could barely tolerate the bickerings on committees; preferred to read and work alone in his quarters, but longed to escape the "cockpit of revolution" altogether and retire to his mountaintop. In December 1775 he did just that. Throughout the winter and spring, while the governor of Virginia, Lord Dunmore, declared martial law and infuriated the Tidewater leadership by inviting all slaves to join him as free men in war against the planter class, and while the political tempo in Philadelphia quickened, especially after the publication of Tom Paine's *Common Sense*, Jefferson remained secluded at Monticello. He focused his attention on Martha, who was ill, probably because of a difficult pregnancy. And he indulged his private cravings. He stocked his cellar with Madeira (vintage 1770), his private park with domesticated deer, his stable with a new line of thoroughbred foals and his soul with a much needed dose of serenity.[38]

He planned, albeit reluctantly, to return to Philadelphia in April but was struck by a "mysterious malady" that left him incapacitated for more than a month. The ailment turned out to be a migraine headache, the first recorded occurrence of what proved a lifelong affliction that flared up whenever he felt unduly pressured. The immediate sources of the pressure he felt in the spring of 1776 were probably twofold: First, his public duties in the Continental Congress were at odds with his private preferences to remain at home; second, his mother had died on the last day of March. His estrangement from her in all likelihood prompted complicated feelings of guilt and relief. In any event his only mention of the event was characteristically cold and curt. "The death of my mother you have probably not heard of," he wrote to William Randolph: "This happened on the last day of March after an illness of not more than an hour. We suppose it to have been apoplectic. Be pleased to tender my affectionate wishes to Mrs. Randolph and my unknown cousins. . . ." Save for a brief mention in his autobiography, it was the last time Jefferson acknowledged her existence.[39]

He arrived back in Philadelphia on May 14. Not only did he lack any inkling of the historic events that were about to transpire—he confessed that he was completely out of touch with the evolving situation in Congress—but he even tried to persuade friends in Virginia to have him recalled. The Virginia legislature was meeting in convention at Williamsburg to draft a state constitution, and Jefferson, like a good many other delegates in Philadelphia, presumed that the most crucial political business was now occurring at the state rather than national level. The act of drafting new state constitutions, he noted, "is the whole object of the present controversy." He meant that the establishment of state governments was the most discernible way to declare American independence, indicating as it did the assumption of political responsibility for the management of American domestic affairs. (John Adams agreed with this perspective and, leaving nothing to chance, had spent the spring designing model constitutions for several states.) Peyton Randolph, Edmund Pendleton and Patrick Henry all had opted to remain back home in the Old Dominion, either to oversee the drafting of Virginia's constitution or to take the field against Dunmore's ragtag army of former slaves and loyalists. George Washington was in the field organizing the Continental Army. Philadelphia, or so it seemed, had become a mere sideshow.[40]

But Philadelphia was where duty demanded that Jefferson place himself. Anticipating the imminent arrival of a hot and humid summer, he decided to shift his lodgings to the outskirts of the city in order to "have the benefits of a freely circulating air." On May 23 he moved his Windsor chair and writing desk into new quarters on the second floor of a three-story brick house at the corner of Market and Seventh streets. The chair, the desk and the entire dwelling were about to become sacred relics of what history was to record as America's most miraculous moment.[41]

TEXTS AND CONTEXTS

DURING THE NEXT six weeks, from mid-May to early July 1776, Jefferson wrote the words that made him famous and that, over the course of the next two centuries, associated him with the most visionary version of the American dream. As a result, this historical ground has been trampled over by hordes of historians, and the air surrounding it is perpetually full of an incandescent mixture of incense and smoke. His authorship of the Declaration of Independence is regarded as one of those few quasi-religious episodes in American history, that moment when, at least according to the most romantic explanations, a solitary Jefferson was allowed a glimpse of the eternal truths and then offered the literary inspiration to inscribe them on the American soul.

Given this supercharged context, it is the beginning of all genuine wisdom to recognize that neither Jefferson nor any other of the participants foresaw the historical significance of what they were doing at the time. What's more, within the context of Philadelphia in the summer of 1776, the writing of the Declaration of Independence did not seem nearly so important as other priorities, including the constitution-making of the states and the prospect of foreign alliances with France or Spain. The golden haze around the Declaration had not yet formed. The sense of history we bring to the subject did not exist for those making it.

One man, John Adams, has left a record that suggests he *was* conscious of being "present at the creation." In May he wrote to his beloved Abigail in a prophetic mood: "When I consider the great Events which are passed, and those greater which are rapidly advancing, and that I may have been instrumental in touching some Springs, and turning some small Wheels, which have had and will have such Effects, I feel an Awe upon my Mind, which is not easily described." Two weeks later he announced to Abigail that he had begun to make copies of all his letters, a clear sign that he was sending them to posterity. But Adams was hardly typical. His neurotic sensitivity to his own place in history became legendary. And his remarks at the time referred to actions in the Continental Congress requiring the states to draft new constitutions, not to the drafting of the Declaration, which he considered a merely ornamental afterthought.[42]

Jefferson, for his part, remained focused on events back in Virginia. Throughout the weeks of late May and early June he devoted the bulk of his energies to producing three different drafts of a new constitution for his home state. Clearly influenced by the John Adams pamphlet *Thoughts on Government,* Jefferson emphasized the separation of powers, an independent judiciary and a bicameral legislature, with a weak executive (called the Administrator in order to signify his lack of governing power). Every political paper that Jefferson had written up to this point in his life had been a protest statement against some aspect of British policy. Therefore it is interesting to note that his initial effort at a positive and practical vision of government recommended a constitutional structure that adopted the general form of the old colonial governments, the exception being the diminution of executive authority, clearly a lesson rooted in the colonial resistance to gubernatorial claims of royal prerogative.[43]

Anyone on the lookout for more avowedly progressive features in Jefferson's thinking could have found them. Although he required a property qualification for all voters, he also proposed a land distribution policy that would provide fifty acres for each resident. He quietly inserted a radical provision for complete religious freedom. And he urged that the new constitution be ratified by a special convention called exclusively for that purpose rather than by the sitting legislature, a democratic idea that John Adams had also proposed as a way of implementing the principle of popular sovereignty. All in all, Jefferson's prescriptions for the new Virginian republic were an impressive

blend of traditional forms and selective reforms. They establish the historically correct, if unorthodox, context for answering the proverbial
question: What was Jefferson thinking about on the eve of his authorship of the Declaration of Independence? The answer is indisputable.
He was not thinking, as some historians have claimed, about John
Locke's theory of natural rights or Scottish commonsense philosophy.
He was thinking about Virginia's new constitution.[44]

An aspect of his thinking proved directly relevant for the task he
was about to assume. In his preamble to the first and third drafts of the
Virginia constitution, he composed a bill of indictment against George
III. One could see glimmerings of these charges against the British
monarch in *Summary View,* then even more explicit accusations in
Causes and Necessities. But the lengthy condemnation of the king in his
draft constitution extended the list of crimes against colonial rights. It
was in effect his penultimate draft for the list of grievances that became
the longest section of the Declaration of Independence.

One of the grievances stands out, in part because it dealt with what
soon proved to be the most controversial issue during the debate in
Congress over the wording of the Declaration, in part because of the
difference between what Jefferson wrote for the Virginia constitution
in May and what he wrote for the Declaration in June. This is the passage in the Declaration in which Jefferson blamed George III for insti-
gating and perpetuating the slave trade, thereby implying that slavery
was an evil institution imposed on the colonists by a corrupt monarch.
In the earlier draft for the Virginia constitution, however, he charged
George III with "prompting our negroes to rise in arms against us;
those very negroes who by an inhuman use of his negative he hath
refused us permission to exclude by law." Here one can see Jefferson
juggling two incompatible formulations: One is to blame the king for
slavery; the other is to blame him for emancipating the slaves (i.e.,
Lord Dunmore's proclamation). It was symptomatic of a deep disjunction in his thinking about slavery that he never reconciled.[45]

Another one of the proverbial questions—how or why was Jefferson
selected to draft the Declaration?—is also answerable with a recovery of

the immediate context. The short answer is that he was the obvious choice on the basis of his past work in the Congress as a draftsman. That was his specialty. The longer answer emerges clearly from the situation that existed in the Congress in June 1776.

Virginia had taken the lead by instructing its delegates on May 15 to propose total and complete American independence from Great Britain. On June 7 Richard Henry Lee moved the resolution "that these United Colonies are, and of right ought to be, free and independent States. . . ." A debate then ensued over when the vote on Lee's resolution should occur. The Congress decided to delay a vote until July 1, in deference to delegations that were still divided (i.e., Pennsylvania) and to delegations that lacked clear instructions from their state legislatures (i.e., New York). In the meantime a committee could be working on a document that implemented the Lee resolution. A Virginian presence on the committee was essential, and Jefferson was the most appropriate Virginian, both because of his reputation as a writer and because Lee, the other possible choice, was the author of the resolution before the Congress and presumably would lead the debate in its behalf.[46]

The committee convened shortly after it was appointed on June 11. (Besides Adams and Jefferson, it included Benjamin Franklin, Robert Livingston and Roger Sherman.) The rest of the committee delegated the drafting to Adams and Jefferson. At this point one can reasonably ask why Adams did not write it himself. This was a question Adams raised with himself countless times over the ensuing years, as the significance of the Declaration grew in the popular imagination and Jefferson's authorship became his major ticket into the American pantheon. In his autobiography Adams recalled that he delegated the task to Jefferson for several reasons, among them his sense that his own prominence as a leader of the radical faction in Congress for the past two years would subject the draft to greater scrutiny and criticism. But such latter-day recollections only tend to obscure the more elemental fact that no one at the time regarded the drafting of the Declaration as a major responsibility or honor. Adams, like Lee, would be needed to lead the debate on the floor. That was considered the crucial arena. Jefferson was asked to draft the Declaration of Independence, then, in great part because the other eligible authors had more important things to do.(47)

Context is absolutely crucial. For all intents and purposes, the decision to declare independence had already been made. Thomas Paine's *Common Sense,* published in January, had swept through the colonies like a firestorm, destroying any final vestige of loyalty to the British crown. In May the Congress had charged each colony to draft new state constitutions, an explicit act of political independence that Adams always regarded as the decisive move. Most important, the war itself had been raging for more than a year. The bulk of the Congress's time in fact was occupied with wartime planning and military decisions, as the British fleet was sighted off the coasts of New York and South Carolina and an American expeditionary force to Canada met with humiliating defeat. (One more debacle or major military blunder, and the American war for independence might have been over before the delegates in Philadelphia got around to declaring it started.) Nothing about the scene permitted much confidence or the opportunity to be contemplative. It did not seem to be a propitious moment for literary craftsmanship.

But whether they knew it or not—and there was no earthly way they could have known—the members of the Continental Congress had placed the ideal instrument in the perfect position at precisely the right moment. Throughout the remainder of his long career Jefferson never again experienced a challenge better suited to call forth his best creative energies. The work had to be done alone, isolated from the public debates. It needed to possess an elevated quality that linked American independence to grand and great forces that transcended the immediate political crisis and swept the imagination upward toward a purer and more principled world. Finally, it needed to paint the scene in bright, contrasting colors of truth and falsehood, right and wrong, "ought" and "is" without any of the intermediate hues or lingering doubts. It is difficult to imagine anyone in America better equipped, by disposition and experience, to perform the task as well.

Jefferson wrote the Declaration of Independence in a matter of a few days—Adams later remembered it took him only "a day or two"—and then showed the draft to Adams and Franklin, later recalling that "they were the two members of whose judgments and amendments I wished most to have the benefit." They suggested a few minor revisions (i.e., replacing "sacred & undeniable truths" with "self-evident truths"); then the committee placed the document before the Continental Congress on June 28. After Lee's resolution was debated and passed (July 1–2), the Congress took up the wording of the Declaration; it made several major changes and excised about one-quarter of the text. During the debate Jefferson sat silently and sullenly, regarding each proposed revision as another defacement. Franklin sat next to him and tried to soothe his obvious pain with the story of a sign painter commissioned by a hatter, who kept requesting more concise language for his sign until nothing was left on the sign but a picture of a hat. On July 4 the Congress approved its revised version and the Declaration of Independence was sent to the printer for publication. Jefferson later recalled that it was signed by the members of Congress on that day, but that is almost surely not correct. The parchment copy was signed by most members on August 2.[48]

Most of the debate in the Congress and most of the revisions of Jefferson's draft of the Declaration focused on the long bill of indictment against George III, the section that modern readers care about least. When Jefferson much later insisted that he was not striving for "originality of principle or sentiment" but was seeking only to provide an "expression of the American mind," he was probably referring to this section, which was intended to sum up the past twelve years of colonial opposition to British policy in language designed to make the king responsible for all the trouble. Jefferson had been practicing this list of grievances for more than two years, first in *Summary View*, then in *Causes and Necessities* and then in his drafts of the Virginia constitution.

"I expected you had . . . exhausted the Subject of Complaint against Geo. 3d. and was at a loss to discover what the Congress would do for one to their Declaration of Independence without copying," wrote Edmund Pendleton when he first saw the official version, "but find that you have acquitted yourselves very well on that score."[49]

As an elegant, if decidedly one-sided, version of recent Anglo-American history, this section of the Declaration has certainly stood the test of time, providing students of the American Revolution with a concise summary of the constitutional crisis from the colonists' perspective at the propitious moment. As a reflection of Jefferson's thinking, however, it is missing three distinctive and distinctively Jeffersonian perspectives on the conflict. When Jefferson wrote back to friends in Virginia, complaining that critics in the Congress had, as one friend put it, "mangled . . . the Manuscript," these were the three major revisions he most regretted.[50]

First, as we noticed earlier, the Congress deleted the long passage blaming George III for waging "cruel war against human nature itself" by establishing slavery in North America; Jefferson also accused the king of blocking colonial efforts to end the slave trade, then "exciting those very people to rise in arms against us . . . by murdering the people on whom he has also obtruded them." Several complicated and even tortured ideas are struggling for supremacy here. One can surmise that the members of Congress decided to delete it out of sheer bewilderment, since the passage mixes together an implicit moral condemnation of slavery with an explicit condemnation of the British monarch for both starting it and trying to end it.

In his own notes on the debate in Congress Jefferson claimed that the opposition was wholly political. Several southern delegations, especially those of South Carolina and Georgia, opposed any restraint on the importation of slaves, he reported, adding that their "Northern brethren also I believe felt a little tender under those censures; for tho' their people have very few slaves themselves, yet they had been pretty considerable carriers of them to others." Jefferson's clear implication is that he was trying to take a principled stand against both slavery and the slave trade but that a majority of delegates were unprepared to go along with him.[51]

The truth was much messier. With regard to the trade, Jefferson knew from his experience in the House of Burgesses that many established slaveowners in the Tidewater region favored an end of imports because their own plantations were already well stocked and new arrivals only reduced the value of their own slave populations. Ending the trade in Virginia, in short, was not at all synonymous with ending slavery. With regard to slavery itself, Jefferson's formulation made great polemic sense but historical and intellectual nonsense. It absolved slaveowners like himself from any responsibility or complicity in the establishment of an institution that was clearly at odds with the values on which the newly independent America was based. Slavery was another one of those vestiges of feudalism foisted upon the liberty-loving colonists by the evil heir to the Norman Conquest. This was complete fiction, of course, but also completely in accord with Jefferson's urge to preserve the purity of his moral dichotomies and his romantic view of America's uncontaminated origins. Slavery was the serpent in the garden sent there by a satanic king. But the moral message conveyed by this depiction was not emancipation so much as commiseration. Since the colonists had nothing to do with establishing slavery—they were the unfortunate victims of English barbarism—they could not be blamed for its continuance. This was less a clarion call to end slavery than an invitation to wash one's hands of the matter.[52]

Second, Jefferson tried once again, as he had tried before in *Causes and Necessities,* to insert his favorite theory of expatriation, claiming that the first settlers came over at their own expense and initiative "unassisted by the wealth or the strength of Great Britain." His obsessive insistence on this theme derived from his devotion to the Saxon myth, which allowed for the neat separation of Whiggish colonists and feudal or absolutist English ministers. The tangled history of imperial relations did not fit very well into these political categories, but Jefferson found it much easier to revise the history (i.e., claiming there had never been any colonial recognition of royal or parliamentary authority) than give up his moral dichotomies. Once again his colleagues in the Continental Congress found his argument excessive.[53]

Third, the last excision came toward the very end of Jefferson's draft. It was a rousingly emotional passage with decidedly sentimental overtones that condemned "our British brethren" for sending over "not only souldiers of our common blood, but Scotch & foreign mercenaries to invade and destroy us." It went on: "These facts have given the last stab to agonizing affection, and manly spirit bids us to renounce for ever these unfeeling brethren. We must endeavor to forget our former love for them, and to hold them as we hold the rest of mankind, enemies in war, in peace friends; but a communication of grandeur & of freedom it seems is below their dignity. Be it so, since they will have it. The road to happiness & to glory is open to us too. We will tread it apart from them. . . ." This was a remarkable piece of rhetoric that Jefferson apparently regarded as one of his better creations. Even at the end of his life he was bitter about its deletion. "The pusillanimous idea that we had friends in England worth keeping terms with, still haunted the minds of many," he recalled, and therefore "those passages which conveyed censures on the people of England were struck out, lest they should give them offence."[54]

What strikes the modern reader is not the timidity of the Continental Congress for excising the passage so much as the melodramatic sentimentalism of Jefferson in composing it. As with the expatriation theory, Jefferson was anxious to depict the separation of the colonies from the British Empire as a decision forced upon the colonists, who are passive victims rather than active agents of revolution. But here the broken bonds are more affective than political. A relationship based on love and trust has been violated, and the betrayed partner, the colonists, is bravely moving forward in life, wounded by the rejection but ready to face alone a glorious future that might otherwise have been shared together. This is a highly idealized and starkly sentimental rendering of how and why emotional separations happen, a projection onto the imperial crisis of the romantic innocence Jefferson had displayed in his adolescent encounters with young women, an all-or-nothing-at-all mentality that the other delegates found inappropriate for a state paper purporting to convey more sense than sensibility.

AMERICAN CREED, AMERICAN DREAM

THE MOST FAMOUS section of the Declaration, which has become the most quoted statement of human rights in recorded history as well as the most eloquent justification of revolution on behalf of them, went through the Continental Congress without comment and with only one very minor change. These are, in all probability, the best-known fifty-eight words in American history: "We hold these truths to be self evident; that all men are created equal; that they are endowed by their Creator with certain [inherent and] inalienable Rights; that among these are life, liberty & the pursuit of happiness; that to secure these rights, governments are instituted among men, deriving their just powers from the consent of the governed." This is the seminal statement of the American Creed, the closest approximation to political poetry every produced in American culture. In the nineteenth century Abraham Lincoln, who also knew how to change history with words, articulated with characteristic eloquence the quasi-religious view of Jefferson as the original American oracle: "All honor to Jefferson—to the man who, in the concrete pressure of a struggle for national independence by a single people, had the coolness, forecaste, and capacity to introduce into a merely revolutionary document, an abstract truth, and so to embalm it there, that today and in all coming days, it shall be a rebuke and a stumbling block to the very harbingers of reappearing tyranny and oppression." The entire history of liberal reform in America can be written as a process of discovery, within Jefferson's words, of a spiritually sanctioned mandate for ending slavery, providing the rights of citizenship to blacks and women, justifying welfare programs for the poor and expanding individual freedoms.[55]

No serious student of either Jefferson or the Declaration of Independence has ever claimed that he foresaw all or even most of the ideological consequences of what he wrote. But the effort to explain what *was* in his head has spawned almost as many interpretations as the words themselves have generated political movements. Jefferson himself was accused of plagiarism by enemies or jealous friends on so many occasions throughout his career that he developed a standard reply. "Neither aiming at originality of principle or sentiment, nor yet copied from any particular and previous writing," he explained, he drew his ideas from "the harmonizing sentiments of the day, whether expressed in letters, printed essays or in the elementary books of public right, as Aristotle, Cicero, Locke, Sidney, etc."[56]

This is an ingeniously double-edged explanation, for it simultaneously disavows any claims to originality and yet insists that he depended upon no specific texts or sources. The image it conjures up is that of a medium, sitting alone at the writing desk and making himself into an instrument for the accumulated wisdom and "harmonizing sentiments" of the ages. It is only a short step from this image to Lincoln's vision of Jefferson as oracle or prophet, receiving the message from the gods and sending it on to us and then to the ages. Given the creedal character of the natural rights section of the Declaration, several generations of American interpreters have felt the irresistible impulse to bathe the scene in speckled light and cloudy mist, thereby implying that efforts to dispel the veil of mystery represent some vague combination of sacrilege and treason.

Any serious attempt to pierce through this veil must begin by recovering the specific conditions inside that room on Market and Seventh streets in June 1776. Even if we take Jefferson at his word, that he did not copy sections of the Declaration from any particular books, he almost surely had with him copies of his own previous writings, to include *Summary View, Causes and Necessities* and his three drafts of the Virginia constitution. This is not to accuse him of plagiarism, unless one wishes to argue that an author can plagiarize himself. It is to say that virtually all the ideas found in the Declaration and much of the specific language, especially the grievances against George III, had already found expression in those earlier writings.

Recall the context. The Congress is being overwhelmed with military reports of imminent American defeat in New York and Canada. The full Congress is in session six days a week, and committees are meeting throughout the evenings. The obvious practical course for Jefferson to take was to rework his previous drafts on the same general theme. While it seems almost sacrilegious to suggest that the creative process that produced the Declaration was a cut-and-paste job, it strains credulity and common sense to the breaking point to believe that Jefferson did not have these items at his elbow and draw liberally from them when drafting the Declaration.

His obvious preoccupation with the ongoing events at the Virginia convention, which was drafting the Virginia constitution at just this time, is also crucial to remember. Throughout late May and early June couriers moved back and forth between Williamsburg and Philadelphia, carrying Jefferson's drafts for a new constitution to the convention and reports on the debate there to the Continental Congress. On June 12 the Virginians unanimously adopted a preamble drafted by George Mason that contained these words: "All men are created equally free and independent and have certain inherent and natural rights . . . , among which are the enjoyment of life and liberty, with the means of acquiring and possessing property, and pursuing and obtaining happiness and safety." The *Pennsylvania Gazette* published Mason's words the same day they were adopted in Williamsburg. Since Jefferson's version of the same thought was drafted sometime that following week, and since we know that he regarded the unfolding events in Virginia as more significant than what was occurring in Philadelphia and that he was being kept abreast by courier, it also strains credulity to deny the influence of Mason's language on his own.[57]

While that explains the felicitous phrase "pursuit of happiness," which Mason himself could have picked up from several English and American sources, it does not explain Jefferson's much-debated deletion of "property," the conventional third right memorialized in Locke's *Second Treatise on Government*. He made that choice on his own. He was probably aware that Mason's language had generated spirited

opposition from a segment of the planter class in Virginia who worried
that it implied a repudiation of slavery; they insisted on an amendment that excluded slaves by adding the qualifying clause "when they
enter into a state of society." All this suggests that Jefferson was probably aware of the contradiction between his own version of the natural
rights philosophy and the institution of slavery. By dropping any reference to "property" he blurred that contradiction. This helps answer the
intriguing question of why no debate over the issue occurred in the
Continental Congress, as it did in the Virginia convention. Perhaps
the debate over the slave trade provision also served that purpose.[58]

Beyond the question of immediate influences on Jefferson's choice
of words and his way of framing the case for independence, however,
lies the more murky question of the long-term influences on his political thinking. Granted that his own earlier writings and drafts of the Virginia constitution almost certainly lay strewn across his lap and writing
desk, where did the ideas contained in those documents come from?
Granted that we know beyond a reasonable doubt what Jefferson was
looking at, that he and the other delegates in the Congress were under
enormous pressure to manage the ongoing war as military disaster
loomed in Canada and New York, so he had little time to do more
than recycle his previous writings, what core of ideas was already fixed
in his head?

The available answers fall into two primary headings, each argued
persuasively by prominent scholars and each finding the seminal
source of Jefferson's political thought in particular books. The older
and still more venerable interpretation locates the intellectual wellspring in John Locke. Even during Jefferson's lifetime several commentators, usually intending to question his originality, noted that the
doctrine of natural rights and the corollary endorsement of rightful
revolution came straight out of Locke's *Second Treatise.* Richard Henry
Lee, for example, claimed that Jefferson had merely "copied from
Locke's treatise on government." Several conclusions followed naturally from the Lockean premise, the chief ones being that Jeffersonian
thought was inherently liberal and individualistic and, despite the sub-

stitution of "pursuit of happiness" for "property," fundamentally compatible with America's emerging capitalistic mentality.[59]

The second and more recent interpretive tradition locates the source of Jefferson's thinking in the Scottish Enlightenment, especially the moral philosophy of Francis Hutcheson. The key insight here is that Jefferson's belief in the natural equality of man derived primarily from Hutcheson's doctrine of the "moral sense," a faculty inherent in all human beings that no mere government could violate. Moreover, the Scottish school of thought linked Jefferson to a more communal or collectivistic tradition that was at odds with Lockean liberalism and therefore incompatible with unbridled individualism, especially the sort of individualism associated with predatory behavior in the marketplace.[60]

There is, in fact, a third most recent and most novel interpretation, at once brilliant and bizarre, that operates from the premise that Jefferson intended the Declaration to be read aloud or performed. This claim is based on the discovery that his final draft was punctuated by a series of quotation marks designed to guide the reading of the document in order to enhance its dramatic effect. This discovery has led to the conclusion that Jefferson was influenced by the new books on rhetoric by such English authors as James Burgh and Thomas Sheridan, in which spoken language was thought to derive its power by playing on the unconscious emotions of the audience. The secret power of the Declaration, so this argument goes, derives from Jefferson's self-conscious orchestration of language, informed by the new rhetoric, which overrides all contradictions (i.e., slavery and human equality; individualism and community) in a kind of verbal symphony that still plays on within American political culture.[61]

Each of these interpretations offers valuable insights into the intellectual sources of Jefferson's thinking as he sat down to write the Declaration. Clearly, he knew his Locke, though his favorite Lockean treatise was not the one on government but the *Essay on Human Understanding*. That said, the fundamental claim that revolution is justified if the existent rulers demonstrate systematic disregard for the rights of their subjects certainly originated with Locke. Jefferson may have gotten his specific language from George Mason, but both men knew whom they were paraphrasing. Just as clearly, Jefferson believed that the distinguishing feature that made human beings fully human, and in that sense equal, was the moral sense. Whether he developed that belief by reading Hutcheson or any of the other members of the Scottish school or from his own personal observation of human behavior is ultimately unknowable and not terribly important.

The claim that Jefferson meant the Declaration to be read aloud is more difficult to swallow. A simpler explanation of his unusual punctuation marks would be that he was worried that he might be required to read the document aloud when the committee presented it to the Congress on June 28, so he inserted oratorical guides for his delivery, not trusting his own famously inadequate speaking ability. (We really don't know whether he himself read it or whether it was read by the secretary of the Congress.) But the recognition that the Declaration plays on the sentiments of readers and listeners, that its underlying tones and rhythms operate in mysterious ways to win assent despite logical contradictions and disjunctions, is a key insight very much worth pondering.

The central problem with all these explanations, however, is that they make Jefferson's thinking an exclusive function of books. True, he read voraciously as a young man, took notes on his reading and left a comprehensive list of the books in his library. Since we know so much about his reading habits, and so little about other aspects of his early life (the Shadwell fire, again), the temptation to make an implicit connection between his ideas and his books is irresistible. Then once the connection is made with, say, Locke or Hutcheson, one can conveniently talk about particular texts as if one were talking about Jefferson's mind. This is a long-standing scholarly tradition—one might call it the scholarly version of poetic license—that depends on the unspoken assumption that what one thinks is largely or entirely a product of what one reads.[62]

In Jefferson's case, it is a very questionable assumption. In the specific case of the natural rights section of the Declaration, it sends us baying down literary trails after false scents of English or Scottish authors, while the object of the hunt sits squarely before us. In all his previous publications the young Thomas Jefferson had demonstrated a strong affinity for and deep attachment to visions of the ideal society. He found it in various locations "back there" in the past: the forests of Saxony; England before the Norman Conquest; the American colonies before the French and Indian War. (Here his previous reading clearly *did* have a discernible influence, though the relevant books were the Whig histories and the Real Whig writings, but they had been so thoroughly digested that their themes and categories blended imperceptibly into Jefferson's cast of mind.) His several arguments for American independence all were shaped around a central motif, in which the imperfect and inadequate present was contrasted with a perfect and pure future, achievable once the sources of corruption were eliminated. His mind instinctively created dichotomies and derived its moral energy from juxtaposing the privileged side of any case or cause with the contaminated side. While his language was often colorful, the underlying message was nearly always painted in black and white.

The vision he projected in the natural rights section of the Declaration, then, represented yet another formulation of the Jeffersonian imagination. The specific form of the vision undoubtedly drew upon language Locke had used to describe the putative conditions of society before governments were established. But the urge to embrace such an ideal society came from deep inside Jefferson himself. It was the vision of a young man projecting his personal cravings for a world in which all behavior was voluntary and therefore all coercion unnecessary, where independence and equality never collided, where the sources of all authority were invisible because they had already been internalized. Efforts on the part of scholars to determine whether Jefferson's prescriptive society was fundamentally individualistic or communal can never reach closure, because within the Jeffersonian utopia such choices do not need to be made. They reconcile themselves naturally.

Though indebted to Locke, Jefferson's political vision was more radical than liberal, driven as it was by a youthful romanticism unwilling to negotiate its high standards with an imperfect world. One of the reasons why European commentators on American politics have found American expectations so excessive and American political thinking in general so beguilingly innocent is that Jefferson provided a sanction for youthful hopes and illusions, planted squarely in what turned out to be the founding document of the American republic. The American dream, then, is just that, the Jeffersonian dream writ large.

ESCAPE

Soon after he had finished drafting the Declaration, but before the debate on it began in the Continental Congress, Jefferson expressed the strong desire to escape from Philadelphia. "I am sorry," he wrote Edmund Pendleton, that "the situation of my domestic affairs renders it indispensably necessary that I should sollicit the substitution of some other person here," explaining in his indirect way that the "delicacy of the house will not require me to enter minutely into the private causes which render this necessary." The "private causes" were unquestionably related to Martha's health; she was pregnant for the third time in six years and miscarried that summer. "For god's sake, for your country's sake, and for my sake," he wrote to Richard Henry Lee, "I am under a sacred obligation to go home." It would have been perfectly in keeping with his character to draft the Declaration, then absent himself from the debate over its content, especially when the center of his private world at Monticello was in danger.[63]

But he was needed in Philadelphia to preserve a quorum for the Virginia delegation, which was filled with men who preferred to attend the constitutional debates in Williamsburg. So Jefferson did his duty, remaining at his post throughout the summer. He made no contribution to the debates in the Congress over prospective foreign alliances or the shape of the national government under the Articles of Confederation, but he took extensive notes on what others said that became the fullest historical record of those exchanges. Within the context of the moment these issues loomed larger than the passage of the Declaration, which was signed on parchment by all members present on August 2. One of the many ironies of the signing is that Jefferson was available to affix his name to the document that became the basis for his fame only because he had been forced, against his will, to sustain Virginia's official presence in the Congress.

For his part, Jefferson went out of his way to disavow responsibility for the version of the Declaration passed by the Congress. His own version, he explained to friends back in Virginia, had been badly treated (the operative word was "mangled"); he devoted considerable energy to copying out his own draft, with the revisions made by the Congress inserted in the margins and the deleted sections restored. He needed to differentiate between his language and the published version being circulated throughout the country, claiming that the Congress had watered down the purity of his message in order to appease the faint of heart, who still hoped for reconciliation with England. Although this was hardly the case—the revisions of his draft were driven less by any desire to compromise than to clarify—Jefferson maintained a wounded sense of betrayal by the Congress throughout the remainder of his life.[64]

His friends in Virginia, perhaps recognizing he needed reassurance, wrote back to him in a commiserative tone. "I am also obliged by your Original Declaration of Independence," explained Edmund Pendleton, "which I find your brethren have treated as they did your Manifesto last summer [i.e., *Causes and Necessities*], altered it much for the worse; their hopes of a Reconciliation might restrain them from plain truths then, but what could cramp them now?" Richard Henry Lee also tried to soothe his young friend's wounded pride by agreeing that the Jeffersonian draft was much better but concluded that "the *Thing* is in its nature so good, that no Cookery can spoil the Dish for the palates of Freemen." Jefferson's hypersensitivity to criticism precluded the possibility of a more detached perspective like Lee's. He contented himself with the preservation, for the historical record, of the difference between his own words and the official version.[65]

His sensitivity extended to matters beyond drafts of the Declaration. Word reached him in July about rumors circulating in Williamsburg that his support for independence was only lukewarm, a misguided charge that was probably a function of his seclusion at Monticello in the spring when other Virginian leaders were taking the field against Dunmore. "It is a painful situation to be 300 miles from one's country," he complained to his old friend William Fleming, "and thereby open to secret assassination without a possibility of self-defence." Then, later in the month, he heard that reports were circulating within the Virginia leadership that he harbored dangerously radical ideas about the inherent wisdom of the people-at-large, reports that were possibly based on second thoughts within the planter class of his language in the natural rights section of the Declaration. He tried to quash such rumors by writing Edmund Pendleton, who had succeeded the recently deceased Peyton Randolph as the presiding presence of the Tidewater elite, assuring him that "the fantastical idea of virtue and the public good being a sufficient security of the state . . . , which you have heard insisted upon by some, I assure you was never mine." He reminded Pendleton that none of his drafts of the Virginia constitution called for direct election of the upper house or senate: "I have ever observed that a choice by the people themselves is not generally distinguished for its wisdom" and that the "first secretion from them is usually crude and heterogeneous."[66]

Then there was the charge that he had no stomach for war and had gone soft on the question of military action against the Indians allied with the British. He wrote home to assure friends this too was slander. He favored an all-out campaign against the Indians pursued without mercy: "Nothing will reduce those wretches so soon as pushing the war into the heart of their country. But I would not stop there. I would never cease pursuing them while one of them remained on this side the Mississippi."[67]

These were emphatic overstatements of his own considerably less belligerent and more trusting convictions. He felt forced into making them in order to answer his critics. His statements are less a measure of what he really thought than a symptom of how vulnerable he felt. He saw himself as an honorable young man who had grudgingly but voluntarily agreed to do his duty by remaining in Philadelphia despite compelling personal reasons to return home. Listening to the delegates in the Continental Congress while they questioned and revised and deleted his wording of the Declaration was bad enough. But then to be whipsawed by rumormongering enemies back in Virginia, accused of being either a tepid or excessive supporter of the revolutionary cause, this was unbearable.

Later in his career Jefferson learned to suffer in silence and to present a placid, impenetrable facade to his critics. John Adams commented admiringly on the mature Jefferson's capacity to remain silent and unperturbed whenever he was the target of innuendo or of the inevitable jealousies generated by ambitious men playing politics. (Adams lamented his own failure to perfect the technique, which he called "the wisdom of taciturnity," admitting that his own inveterate tendency was to erupt like a volcano and fondly hope to eliminate his critics in a lava flow.) But young Jefferson had not yet perfected the technique either. The enigmatic masks he eventually learned to wear were essential additions to his public personality precisely because he was by nature thin-skinned and took all criticism personally. Fate had selected him to play a prominent role in what posterity came to regard as the most propitious moment in American history. But for a young man of his tender and vulnerable disposition, making history came at an unacceptable personal cost.[68]

In September 1776 Jefferson's prayers were answered when Richard Henry Lee came up from Virginia to replace him in Philadelphia. His exit was less grand but more speedy than his entrance more than a year earlier. Only Jupiter accompanied him this time, and if Jefferson followed his customary habit whenever in a hurry, he drove the horses of his phaeton himself. He could not wait to get back to Martha and Monticello. A month later, when John Hancock wrote in behalf of the

Continental Congress asking him to join Benjamin Franklin and Silas
Deane as a member of the American commission to France, Jefferson
sent his regrets, explaining that personal considerations "compel me to
ask leave to decline a service so honorable and at the same time so
important to the American cause." He was played out. Both his pride
and his vulnerable core of personal feelings had been wounded. He
needed time to heal.[69]

2

Paris: 1784–89

I am much pleased with the people of this country. The roughness of the human mind are so thoroughly rubbed off with them that it seems as one might glide thro' a whole life among them without a justle.

—JEFFERSON TO ELIZA HOUSE TRIST
PARIS, AUGUST 18, 1785

I am savage enough to prefer the woods, the wilds, and the independence of Monticello, to all the brilliant pleasure of this gay capital.

—JEFFERSON TO BARON GEISMAR
PARIS, SEPTEMBER 6, 1785

THE MAN ENTERING Paris in August 1784 was older and more complicated than the young Virginian who had ridden into history nine years earlier at Philadelphia. He was traveling in a phaeton again, but this one was a larger, sturdier carriage, handcrafted by his slaves at Monticello, with glass on four sides to protect the passengers. He was accompanied by his twelve-year-old daughter Martha, named after her mother but best known as Patsy, an uncommonly tall and long-limbed girl with her father's bright eyes and angular bone structure. His other companion was James Hemings, a nineteen-year-old mulatto slave who had replaced Jupiter as a favorite servant. Hemings was also along to learn the fine art of French cooking.[1]

The party required a full week to make the trip from Le Havre to Paris, following the Seine River through Rouen, where centuries ago

Joan of Arc had been burned at the stake. "I understand the French so imperfectly as to be uncertain whether those to whom I speak and myself mean the same thing," Jefferson confessed. The language problem meant that he was "roundly cheated" by porters at several stops. But nothing could spoil the wonder of the French countryside at the start of the harvest season. When they crossed the Seine at the Pont de Neuilly—Jefferson proclaimed it "the most beautiful bridge in the world"—then rolled onto the Champs-Élysées, he was clearly starting a new chapter in his career as America's minister plenipotentiary to France.[2]

We have a much clearer sense of how he looked because his ascending fame made him the subject of several portraits, engravings and busts during his five years in France. The skin on his face was now taut and tight, with a permanently reddish hue that made him always appear as if he had just finished exercising. His hair was now more sandy than red, but just as thick and full as ever, cut so that it covered his ears, then tied in the back so as to fall just below his collar. His frame remained angular but was now more muscled and less gangly, the product of daily four-mile walks and a vigorous regimen that included soaking his feet in cold water each morning.

In general, he had grown more handsome with age, like one of those gawky and slightly awkward young men who eventually inhabit their features more comfortably with the years. Time had also allowed him to occupy his height in more proper proportions and carry it with more natural grace. He remained a very tall man for his time. We know that when he made his first official appearance with John Adams and Benjamin Franklin at the French court at Versailles, the physical contrast struck several observers as almost comical, like watching a cannonball, a teapot and a candlestick announce themselves as the American trinity.[3]

If aging had served him well physically—perhaps here was an underlying reason why Jefferson always thought that the future was on his side—it had also seasoned him psychologically. Many American lives had been caught up in the turmoil of the war for independence, then deposited on the other side of the historic conflict with scars and wounds that never went away. Though Jefferson never commanded troops or fired a shot in anger, his personal experience during and immediately following the war included two traumatic episodes that toughened him on the inside even more than his marathon walks and cold-water baths toughened his body.

The first incident occurred during his two-year term as governor of Virginia from 1779 to 1781. It was the worst possible time for a man who preferred the rarefied atmosphere of scholarship and the study to assume the duties of governor, since wartime exigencies generated massive economic, logistical and political problems that even the most adroit executive would have found daunting. Despite his best efforts, Virginia's economy became a shambles and the state failed to meet its quota of men for the Continental Army. Then Jefferson approved an expedition that carried off Virginia's best troops to a futile campaign against Detroit, just before a British invasion force under the command of Benedict Arnold swept in from the Chesapeake Bay and burned the capital at Richmond to the ground. To make matters worse, cavalry detachments from General Cornwallis's army moved against Charlottesville and nearly captured Jefferson himself at Monticello.[4]

Stories spread throughout the state of Jefferson's ignominious last-minute escape on horseback, implying rather unfairly that he had behaved in a cowardly fashion or that he was derelict in his duty by allowing the state to become so vulnerable to British military occupation. The Virginia Assembly even passed a resolution calling for an investigation into his conduct. This was eventually dropped; a final resolution officially absolved him of any wrongdoing. But even though the wartime mishaps were probably beyond his or anybody's control, they had happened on his watch. The stain of failure as an executive never wholly disappeared—all the stories resurfaced when he ran for the presidency in 1796 and again in 1800—and Jefferson himself learned that his refined sensibility was ill suited for the rigors of leadership during times of crisis. As for the emotional effects, Jefferson confided to a friend that the experience had "inflicted a wound on my spirit that will only be cured by the all-healing grave."[5]

The second incident came straight on the heels of the first and unquestionably constituted the most traumatic experience of his entire life. In May 1782 his wife Martha gave birth for the seventh time in their ten-year marriage. The daughter, named Lucy Elizabeth, was only the third child to survive, and Martha herself fell desperately ill after the delivery. Her delicate disposition had obviously been destroyed by the never-ending pregnancies. She lingered on through the summer, with Jefferson at her bedside nearly around the clock. Family lore, reinforced by reminiscences within the slave community at Monticello, described a melodramatic deathbed scene in which Martha extracted a promise from Jefferson that he would never marry again, allegedly because she did not want her surviving children raised by a stepmother. He never did. She died on September 6, 1782.[6]

Jefferson was inconsolable for six weeks, sobbing throughout the nights, breaking down whenever he tried to talk. Word of his extended grieving leaked out from Monticello and caused some friends to worry that he was losing his mind. "I ever thought him to rank domestic happiness in the first class of the chief good," wrote Edmund Randolph, "but scarcely supposed that his grief would be so violent as to justify the circulating report of his swooning away whenever he sees his children." When he eventually emerged from seclusion to take long rides through the local woods, Patsy became his constant companion in what she later called "those melancholy rambles."[7]

He agreed to accept the diplomatic post in Paris as part of the effort to move past this tragedy and to escape from his memories of Martha at Monticello. But he was scarred in a place that never completely healed. God had seen fit to reach down into the domestic utopia that he had constructed so carefully and snatch away its centerpiece. (Jefferson did not seem to possess any sense of complicity in causing her pregnancies or any sense of warning as her health deteriorated after each new miscarriage or birth.) We cannot know for sure whether, as family tradition tells the story, he promised his dying wife that he would never remarry. The promise he made to himself undoubtedly had the same effect: He would never expose his soul to such pain again; he would rather be lonely than vulnerable.

If this, then, was how he looked and—as much as we can ever know—how he felt upon his arrival in Paris in the late summer of 1784, there remains the question of what he thought. His reputation as a political thinker, which did not yet benefit from his authorship of the Declaration of Independence since that achievement was not yet widely known, was based primarily on his legislative work in the Virginia Assembly and the federal Congress. From 1776 to 1779 he had almost single-handedly attempted the root-and-branch reform of the Virginia legal code, calling for the abolition of primogeniture and entail as the last vestiges of English feudalism, the reform of the criminal law so as to limit the use of the death penalty, the expansion of the suffrage to include more of the independent yeomen from the western counties, the expansion of the public school system of the state and, most important, the elimination of the Anglican establishment in favor of a complete separation of church and state.

This phenomenal effort at legislative reform proved too visionary for his colleagues in the Virginia Assembly, who defeated all his proposals save the abolition of primogeniture and entail, which was on the verge of dying a natural death anyway. But the thrust of his political thinking was clear: to remove all legal and political barriers to individual initiative and thereby create what he called "an opening for the aristocracy of virtue and talent." It was in effect an attempt to implement the ideals articulated in the natural rights section of the Declaration. Just as clearly, his favorite ideas were several steps ahead of public opinion. He was more a prophet than a politician.[8]

The same pattern held true in the federal Congress at Philadelphia. Throughout the winter and spring of 1784 he threw himself into the reform of the coinage system, successfully urging the dollar and decimal units in lieu of the English pound and shilling. He also tried but failed to replace the English system of weights and measures with metric standards. He wrote the Ordinance of 1784, which established the principles on which all new states would be admitted to the Union on an equal basis with existing states. The final provision required the end of slavery in all newly created states by 1800. But it lost by one vote, prompting Jefferson to remark later that "the fate of millions unborn [was] hanging on the tongue of one man, and Heaven was silent in that awful moment!" It was the most far-reaching proposal to end slavery that Jefferson ever wrote but also the high-water mark of his anti-slavery efforts, which receded afterward to lower levels of caution and procrastination.[9]

Throughout the spring of 1784 he expressed frustration with the paralyzing combination of indolence and garrulousness that afflicted the Congress. (It was barely possible to muster a quorum to approve the peace treaty ending the war with England.) Given his subsequent hostility to consolidated federal power in virtually every form, his impatience at this time with what he called "the petty justlings of states" stands out as an indication of his temporary willingness to accept federal power as a corrective to local and regional bickering. He confided to friends his conviction that the Articles of Confederation, in giving the federal government power over foreign affairs, had implicitly given it power over all trade and commerce. (This endorsement of the doctrine of implied powers came back to haunt him a decade later.) He wanted to see treaties of amity and commerce negotiated with European nations, in part for the economic benefits they would generate but mostly because, as he put it, "the moment these treaties are concluded the jurisdiction of Congress over the commerce of the states springs into existence, and that of the particular states is superseded. . . ."[10]

To sum up, then, the man riding into Paris as America's minister plenipotentiary was not the same young Virginian who had drafted the Declaration of Independence. He was more famous, more physically impressive, a more confident carrier of his natural assets and abilities. He was more seasoned as a legislator, though still and always an idealist with greater talent at envisioning what ought to be than skill at leading others toward the future he imagined. He was also more seasoned as a man, less vulnerable and sensitive because more adroit at protecting his interior regions from intruders by layering his internal defenses in ways that denied access at all check points. (This psychological dexterity was to serve him well as a diplomat.) Finally, he had managed to combine his utopian vision of an American society of liberated individuals, freely pursuing happiness once the burden of English corruption and European feudalism had been removed, with a more practical recognition that an independent America required some kind of federal government to coordinate its burgeoning energies and excesses. Without surrendering his youthful radicalism, he had also become a dedicated nationalist.

FRIENDS AND PIRATES

Settling himself and his entourage took much longer than he had expected. First there was the problem of his health, which, except for his recurrent migraine headaches, had always been excellent. But within a few weeks he came down with a severe cold that he could not shake for six months. "I have had a very bad winter," he explained to his friend James Monroe back in Virginia, "having been confined the greatest part of it. A seasoning as they call it is the lot of most strangers: and none I believe have experienced a more severe one than myself. The air is extremely damp, and the waters very unwholesome. We have had for three weeks past a warm visit from the Sun (my almighty physician) and I find myself almost reestablished." Though he eventually fell in love with the people, the wine and the architecture of France, the weather was another matter, causing him to speculate that there was a nearly permanent cloud bank over this section of western Europe that produced pale and anemic human constitutions.[11]

Then there was the problem of the language. Jefferson was justifiably renowned for his facility with foreign languages, which included Latin, Greek, French and Italian. He even claimed that he had taught himself Spanish on the voyage to France by reading *Don Quixote* with the aid of a grammar book. (Years later, when he was president, Jefferson recalled the incident over dinner. John Quincy Adams, who was present at the dinner party with the president, recorded the claim in his memoirs, then added: "But Mr. Jefferson tells large stories.") The truth seems to be that Jefferson was adept at learning how to read foreign languages but not to speak or write them. Even after five years in France his spoken French never reached a sufficient level of fluency to permit comfortable conversation, and he never trusted his written French sufficiently to dispense with a translator for his formal correspondence.[12]

Finally there was the problem of where to live. He shuttled among a series of hotels for the first few months, then, in October 1784, signed a lease for a villa at Cul-de-sac Taitbout on the Right Bank. But this proved inadequate and inconvenient, so he moved the following year to the Hôtel de Langeac on the Champs-Élysées near the present-day Arc de Triomphe, then on the outskirts of the city. He rented the entire building, a fashionable and spacious three-story dwelling originally built for the mistress of a French nobleman. This became his Parisian Monticello, complete with several salons, three separate suites, stables, a garden and a full staff of servants, maids, cooks, plus a coachman and gardener. It was lavish and expensive—the rent and furniture exceeded his annual salary of nine thousand dollars—but what he required to feel at home abroad.[13]

When all the arrangements were finally completed, Jefferson had constructed an extensive support system of servants, secretaries and acolytes that afforded him the same kind of physical and emotional protection that he had enjoyed on his Virginia plantation. At the center of the household stood Jefferson himself. (Patsy had been placed in a convent school, the Abbaye Royale de Panthemont, which Jefferson was assured—and frequently felt the need to reassure himself—was renowned for its liberal attitude toward non-Catholic students. She was home only on special weekends.) The inner circle of defense was manned by James Hemings, who was Jefferson's personal servant when not attending culinary classes, and Adrien Petit, the supremely competent overseer of all household affairs and employees. The next ring of protection handled political and diplomatic issues. It was managed by two secretaries: David Humphreys, the thirty-two-year-old Connecticut poet who had served on George Washington's staff during the war and had now attached himself to Jefferson as the fastest-rising star in American statecraft, and William Short, a twenty-five-year-old law student, a graduate of William and Mary, Jefferson's in-law, protégé and all-purpose political handyman.[14]

The outer perimeter of counsel and comfort lay back in America, in effect a series of listening posts in Virginia and the Congress at Philadelphia from which James Madison and James Monroe delivered regular reports, often using a ciphered code to conceal sensitive information. Taken together, Madison, Monroe and Short represented that segment of the younger generation of political talent in Virginia that had come to regard Jefferson as its titular leader; each was almost old enough to be his younger brother and almost young enough to be his son. The correspondence with Madison proved to be the start of a fifty-year partnership, perhaps unique in American history, in which Madison was the ever-loyal junior member. (Madison succeeded Jefferson in the presidency; then Monroe succeeded Madison, thereby occupying the office with Jeffersonians for the first twenty-four years of the nineteenth century.) Jefferson cultivated all three of these young Virginians as his protégés, even envisioning the day when they would live next to him at Monticello. In February 1784 he shared the dream with Madison: "Monroe is buying land almost adjoining me. Short will do the same. What would I not give you could fall into the circle. With such a society I could once more venture home and lay myself up for the residue of life, quitting all contentions which grow daily more and more insupportable. Think of it. To render it practicable only requires you to think it so." Part praetorian guard, part quasi-members of his extended family, these younger Virginians had already identified Jefferson as the heir apparent to Washington in the line of succession to state and national leadership. Much of Jefferson's first year in France was spent establishing the communications network of this looming Virginia dynasty.[15]

The settling process during that first year included one final variable of long-term historical significance, Jefferson's relationship with the Adams family. When news reached John Adams of Jefferson's appointment, he let out word that he was pleased: "Jefferson is an excellent hand," he noted to friends back in New England. "You could not have sent better." When some members of Congress expressed concern about Jefferson's excessive idealism, Adams would have none of it: "My Fellow Labourer in Congress, eight or nine years ago, upon many arduous Tryals, particularly in the draught of our Declaration of Independence . . . , I have found him uniformily the same wise and prudent Man and Steady Patriot." Adams's wife, Abigail, and their daughter, called Nabby, had joined him and their son John Quincy the same week that Jefferson had arrived in France. For nine months, until Adams was dispatched to London as America's first ambassador to the Court of St. James's, the Adams quarters at Auteuil became Jefferson's second home.[16]

More than fifty years later, and after a phase of bitter political disagreements that seriously frayed their friendship, Adams still recalled this time with fondness. Upon John Quincy's election as president in 1824, for example, Adams reminded Jefferson that "our John" had won. "I call him our John," he explained, "because when you was at Cul de sac at Paris, he appeared to be almost as much your boy as mine." The special relationship between Adams and Jefferson had its origins in their political partnership of 1776, but the deep emotional bonding between the two men occurred in France in 1784–85.[17]

Abigail Adams played a crucial role. Jefferson's first winter in Paris was one long and nearly debilitating illness. His recovery during the spring occurred under her watchful eye and then with the whole Adams family in their parlor, swapping anecdotes and opinions about the whole range of diplomatic and domestic subjects. Abigail was the link between questions of foreign policy and family priorities, probably the first woman Jefferson came to know well who combined the traditional virtues of a wife and mother with the sharp mind and tongue of a fully empowered accomplice in her husband's career. Jefferson had always regarded these different assets as inhabiting distinct and separate spheres that God or nature had somehow seen fit to keep apart. In Abigail, however, they came together. She was Martha with a mind of her own. Transcripts of those afternoon conversations, needless to say, do not exist. But the character and quality of the free-flowing banter survive in the playful letters exchanged after the Adams family moved to London.

First there was the bond of mutual admiration and jocular courting. Abigail asked Jefferson to purchase several small replicas of classical beauty. Jefferson responded: "With respect to the figures I could only find three of those you named, matched in size. These were Minerva, Diana, and Apollo. I was obliged to add a fourth, unguided by your choice. They offered me a fine Venus; but I thought it out of taste to have two at table at the same time." Or Abigail requested Jefferson to survey the Parisian shops for black lace and evening shoes, apologizing at the end for "troubling you with such trifling matters," which was "a little like putting Hercules to the distaff."[18]

Then there was the running joke about the inherent depravity of the English monarch and nation. Jefferson reported "a blind story here of somebody attempting to assassinate your king [i.e., George III]. No man upon earth has my prayers for his continuance in life more sincerely than him. He is truly the American Messias. . . ." Abigail observed that all stories originating in the English newspapers were lies: "The account is as false—if it was not too rough a term for a Lady to use, I would say false as Hell, but I would substitute one not less expressive and say false as English." Jefferson asked her if there was anything he could do, in his official capacity, to improve English manners. Abigail informed him that "there is a want of many French commodities, Good Sense, Good Nature, Political Wisdom and benevolence"; Jefferson would "render essential service to his Britanick Majesty if he would permit Cargoes of this kind to be exported into this kingdom."[19]

Finally there was the matter of Jefferson's parental responsibilities. The Adamses were still in Paris when Jefferson received word that Lucy, his youngest child and the daughter whose birth had led to Martha's fatal illness, had herself died of whooping cough back in Virginia. Abigail helped console Jefferson—he went into a deep despondency—and they developed a special affinity as parents. When her own daughter, Nabby, announced her intention to marry Colonel Stephen Smith, the personal secretary to husband John, Abigail proposed a unique arrangement to Jefferson: "Now I have been thinking of an exchange with you Sir. Suppose you give me Miss Jefferson [Patsy], and in some [fu]ture day take a Son [her grandson] in lieu of her. I am for Strengthening [the] federal union."[20] But most of Abigail's maternal advice concerned Jefferson's middle daughter, Maria, called Polly. Jefferson had left her with relatives back in Virginia—she was only four years old—and in part because of Abigail's prodding, he decided to risk the Atlantic voyage and have her sent over to Paris to consolidate his family. Abigail was at the wharf in London when Polly arrived and immediately began to initiate Jefferson in the time-honored Adams tradition of brutal honesty.

Polly herself was an absolute charmer. "I never saw so intelligent a countenance in a child before," Abigail wrote, "and the pleasure she has given me is an ample compensation for any little services I have been able to render her." But Jefferson needed to face his failures as a father: "I show her your picture. She says she cannot know it, how could she when she could not know you." When Jefferson wrote to say that official duties prevented him from crossing the Channel to fetch Polly, so he was sending Petit, his chief household servant, Abigail felt obliged to insist that Jefferson contemplate Polly's reaction to this news: "Tho she says she does not remember you, yet she has been taught to consider you with affection and fondness, and depended upon your coming for her. She told me this morning, that as she had left all her friends in virginia to come over the ocean to see you, she did think you would have taken the pains to have come here for her, and not have sent a man [Petit] whom she cannot understand. I express her own words."[21] As if this were not enough, Abigail wondered out loud how a man who professed to feel such affection for his children could then commit them to the care of Catholic nuns. The decision to place Patsy in the convent at Panthemont had always mystified her. Now that Polly had finally joined her father, "I hope that she will not lose her fine spirits within the walls of a convent too, to which I own I have many, perhaps false prejudices."[22]

Jefferson's relationship with John Adams also mingled deep and mutual affection with a level of bracing honesty from the Adams side that frequently forced Jefferson to face the persistent gap between his ideals and the messier realities of the real world. Jefferson, for his part, provided Adams with an extremely thoughtful and hardworking partner in the business of representing America's interest in Europe. Abigail claimed that Jefferson was "the only person with whom my Companion could associate with perfect freedom, and unreserve. . . ." Taken together, the two men were the proverbial opposites that attracted: the stout, candid-to-a-fault New Englander with the effusive temperament and the pugilistic disposition, and the lean, ever-elusive Virginian with the glacial exterior and almost eerie serenity. Each man seemed to sense in the other the compensating qualities missing in his own personality. In the amiable atmosphere created by Abigail at Auteuil, they found the leisured conditions that allowed them to appreciate the attractiveness of their respective other sides, "completing" each other, if you will, and creating a truly formidable diplomatic team in the process.[23]

As distinctive products of the war for independence, they shared a bottomless commitment to the prospects for an independent American nation and an equally limitless mistrust of English policy toward its former colonies. Jefferson claimed that he had "an infallible rule for deciding what that nation [England] would do on every occasion." It was a simple rule—namely, "to consider what they ought to do, and to take the reverse of that as what they would assuredly do. . . ." He claimed that, by adopting this formula, he "was never deceived." Adams concurred completely. "If John Bull don't see . . . a Thing at first," he observed to Jefferson, "You know it is a rule with him ever afterwards to swear that it don't exist, even when he does both see it and feel it." Adams believed that the loss of the war with America, and with it a substantial portion of their overseas empire, had rendered most Englishmen incapable of fair-mindedness toward their former colonies. "They care no more for us," he concluded, "than they do about the Seminole Indians." There was even a dramatic, almost melo-dramatic moment, when their mutual Anglophobia was sealed in a symbolic blood oath. When Jefferson visited Adams in England in the spring of 1786, the two former revolutionaries were presented at court and George III ostentatiously turned his back on them both. Neither man ever forgot the insult or the friend standing next to him when it happened.[24]

In addition to their mutual animosities toward England and their common sense of indignation at the insufferable arrogance of the king, the friendship worked because Jefferson deferred to Adams. After all, Adams was his senior and had been negotiating with the French and English for five years. Jefferson's deferential pattern began as soon as he arrived in France: "What would you think of the enclosed Draught to be proposed to the courts of London and Versailles?" Jefferson inquired. "I know it goes beyond our powers; and beyond the powers of Congress too. But it is so evidently for the good of the states that I should not be afraid to risk myself on it if you are of the same opin-ion." The proposal envisioned reciprocal rights for citizens of all nations, complete freedom of trade and a reformed system of interna-tional law. Yes, Adams replied, it was a "beau ideal" proposal, but unfortunately it was also completely irrelevant to the current, and cut-throat, European context: "We must not, my Friend, be the Bubbles of our own Liberal Sentiments. If we cannot obtain reciprocal Liberality, We must adopt reciprocal Prohibitions, Exclusions, Monopolies, and Imposts. Our offers have been fair, more than fair. If they are rejected, we must not be Dupes."[25]

The same pattern repeated itself in the dialogue over American pol-icy toward the vexing problem of the Barbary pirates. Several Muslim countries along the North African coast had established the tradition of plundering the ships of European and American merchants in the western Mediterranean and eastern Atlantic, capturing the crews and then demanding ransom from the respective governments for their release. In a joint message to their superiors in Congress, Adams and Jefferson described the audacity of these terrorist attacks, pirates leaping onto defenseless ships with daggers clenched in their teeth. They had asked the ambassador from Tripoli, Adams and Jefferson explained, on what grounds these outrageous acts of unbridled savagery could be justified: "The Ambassador answered us that it was founded on the Laws of the Prophet, that it was written in their Koran, that all nations who should not have acknowledged their authority were sinners, that it was their right and duty to make war upon them wherever they could be found, and to make slaves of all they could take as Prisoners. . . ."[26] Jefferson found such unmitigated blackmail beyond his comprehension and beyond any recognized principle of law or justice. He initially proposed that the United States refuse to pay ransoms and instead dispatch a naval force to the Mediterranean to teach these outlaws of the sea a lesson. Later he supplemented his proposal with a comprehensive scheme whereby the United States would organize an international task force comprised of all European nations whose shipping was being victimized. "Justice and Honor favor this course," he exclaimed to Adams, and it would probably cost less in the long run to boot.[27]

Adams agreed that it was impossible to negotiate with the Barbary pirates; as he put it, "Avarice and Fear are the only Agents at Algiers. . . ." But Jefferson's accounting, Adams observed, grossly underestimated the cost. It would require at least £500,000 annually to sustain a naval force in the region. The Congress would never authorize such a sum. And the United States had nothing in the way of a navy to send over anyway. "From these Premises," he apprised Jefferson, "I conclude it to be wisest for us to negotiate and pay the necessary Sum, without loss of Time. . . ." Adams insisted that Jefferson's solution, while bold and wholly honorable in its own terms, was an idea whose time had not

come. "Congress will never, or at least not for years, take any such Resolution," he reminded Jefferson, "and in the mean time our Trade and
Honour suffers beyond Calculation. We ought not to fight them at all
unless we determine to fight them forever." Jefferson remained uncon-
vinced but agreed that Adams's opinion should be the basis for the official American position: "You make the result differently from what I
do," he wrote to Adams in London, but "it is of no consequence; as I
have nothing to say in the decision."[28]

It is possible to detect in Jefferson an early undertone of resentment
toward Adams's realism, which consistently undercut his own grander
vision. Jefferson even tried to go over Adams's head by having his own
proposal for an international naval force presented to Congress by a
third party, a ploy that failed when Congress rejected the scheme outright, as Adams had predicted it would. If one were looking for early
signs of the eventual clash between these longtime colleagues, one
could find them in embryo here. But Jefferson's momentary duplici-
ties were more than overbalanced by his genuine admiration for
Adams. The admiration went even deeper, to the recognition that
Adams possessed a mental toughness, a capacity to flourish in the
midst of innuendo and invective and high-stakes decisions. "Indeed
the man must be a rock," Jefferson wrote to Abigail, "who can stand all
this." He went on to confess his own sense of inadequacy in embattled
situations and to hold up Adams as a mentor: "I do not love difficulties. I am fond of quiet, willing to do my duty, but irritable by slander,
and apt to be forced by it from my post. These are weaknesses from
which reason and your counsels will preserve Mr. adams."[29]

DIPLOMATIC FUTILITIES

THERE WAS OF course a third American minister in France, more
famous by far than the other two. Benjamin Franklin had been representing American interests abroad longer than any other diplomat, and
his reputation in France had reached epic proportions. He was the visi-

ble embodiment of American values in their most seductively simple form. When Franklin and Voltaire had embraced before the multitudes of Paris, it created a sensation in the French press, the union of the two greatest champions of human enlightenment in history's most enlightened century. Jefferson himself regarded Franklin as second only to Washington as the greatest American of the revolutionary generation, going so far as to observe that there was a discernible gap between Franklin and the next tier of American revolutionary heroes, a group in which he included Adams but modestly excluded himself.[30]

Unofficial rumors had it that Jefferson had been appointed Franklin's eventual replacement. (Franklin, who was nearing eighty, had let it be known that he wished to return to America in the near future.) When Jefferson was presented to the French court soon after his arrival, legend has it that Vergennes, the French foreign minister, asked him if he was intended to serve as Franklin's replacement, to which Jefferson allegedly replied: "No one can replace him, Sir; I am only his successor." Adams, for his part, was far from saddened to see Franklin leave. The two men had quarreled incessantly throughout the negotiations that produced the Treaty of Paris (1783) ending the war, Adams contending that Franklin left the bulk of the work for him, shared American negotiating secrets too freely with Vergennes and too often mistook flirtatious evenings with admiring French ladies for his main diplomatic duties. Franklin in turn regarded Adams as the kind of neurotic Yankee who gave hard work a bad name and who failed to appreciate the benefits of informal associations with France's salon society, especially the sort of harmless flirtations of an old man with the lovely and once-lovely women who helped shape the values of Parisian culture. No one, not even Jefferson, could turn a phrase as deftly as Franklin; his characterization of Adams became famous in its own day, then with posterity, as the ultimate one-sentence evisceration: "Always an honest Man, often a wise one, but sometimes, and in some things, absolutely out of his senses."[31]

For the brief time that they were together as a ministerial team, Jefferson served as a valuable buffer between the two senior members, both of whom found him likable and dedicated. Indeed, it is possible to argue, without much fear of contradiction, that during the nine months Adams, Franklin and Jefferson represented American interests in France the United States enjoyed the greatest assemblage of sheer intellectual talent in the whole subsequent history of American diplomacy. Their chief problem, then, was hardly a lack of wisdom or skill; it was simply that there was very little for them to accomplish.

When all was said and done, there were very few European countries with much interest in signing treaties of amity and commerce with the recently established American republic. Franklin possessed the most exquisite sense of timing of any member of the revolutionary era; his departure in the summer of 1785 signaled the end of prospects for the American cause in Europe. (He arrived back in Philadelphia in plenty of time to participate in the deliberations of the Constitutional Convention.) Adams complained that there was little for him to do in Paris or London. He spent the bulk of his time composing a massive three-volume study of political theory entitled *A Defence of the Constitutions of the United States*. Although Jefferson was fully engaged by routine diplomatic duties throughout his years in France, the strategic situation in which fate and the American Congress had placed him virtually precluded any significant foreign policy achievements on his watch.

Although there were, in fact, several overlapping layers of insurmountable difficulty, the chief problem lay back in Philadelphia. To put it most concisely, the federal Congress created under the Articles of Confederation lacked sufficient authority to oversee American foreign policy. A typical letter from John Jay, who had responsibility for foreign affairs, reported the chronic condition of gridlock. "It has happened from various Circumstances," Jay wrote to Jefferson, "that several Reports on foreign Affairs still lay before Congress undecided upon. The want of an adequate Representation for long Intervals . . . has occasioned Delays and Omissions which however unavoidable are much to be regretted." Jefferson was particularly incensed when the Congress dismissed his plan for a naval force to destroy the Barbary pirates as impossibly expensive. "It will be said," he wrote to Monroe, "there is no money in the treasury. There never will be money in the treasury till the confederacy shows its teeth. The states must see the rod." But Madison informed him that the will to pass revenue bills was simply nonexistent. The current revenue in the treasury amounted to less than $400,000, which was not enough to pay off old debts, much less take on new ones. Madison agreed that it was a lamentable situation that would "confirm . . . all the world in the belief that we are not to be respected, nor apprehended as a nation in matters of Commerce." The outstanding debt to France particularly grated on Jefferson, since he was constantly besieged by French veterans of the American Revolution for the back pay owed them. But apart from shaking his head in a gesture of consolation and disbelief, there was absolutely nothing he could do about it.[32]

Then there was the intractable problem of English arrogance. David Hartley, an English diplomat more disposed toward America than his colleagues, put the matter squarely to Jefferson: "An English proverb says Losers have a right to complain," wrote Hartley. "After a storm the waves will continue to roll for some time." In short, having lost half its empire in a long and unsuccessful war, England was not about to render one iota of economic assistance to its former colonies. During his visit with Adams in London in the spring of 1786 Jefferson confirmed this prevailing attitude: "With this nation nothing is done; and it is now decided that they intend to do nothing with us. The king is against a change of measures; his ministers are against it . . . ; and the merchants and people are against it. They sufficiently value our commerce; but they are quite persuaded they shall enjoy it on their own terms." Sadly enough, English presumption was proving correct, since the British continued to control more than 80 percent of America's foreign trade. Why should they negotiate new commercial treaties with the Americans when they already enjoyed a monopoly on their own terms? To make matters worse, the English were fond of raising awkward questions about the power of American diplomats to negotiate on behalf of the United States, asking rhetorically and mischievously if the federal government actually possessed sovereign power over the respective states. Meanwhile the English press kept up a steady stream of anti-American sentiment, suggesting that the former colonies were in a condition of near anarchy. (Jefferson was especially amused by false reports in the London papers that Franklin had either been captured by Algerian pirates on his return voyage or had been stoned by mobs upon landing in Philadelphia.) The dominant opinion among the English aristocracy in their private clubs, Jefferson observed cynically, was that America was poised to petition for readmission into the British Empire. One could hardly expect any cooperation from this quarter.[33]

By all accounts, and certainly by Jefferson's initial reckoning, France should have been different. France, after all, was America's major European ally, its source of salvation in the war for independence, the inveterate enemy of England, and home for philosophes who shared Jefferson's liberal faith in open markets and free trade. Jefferson drafted many lengthy memoranda designed to persuade the French ministry that if the United States and France could reach reciprocal agreements whereby all tariffs and duties were abolished between their respective countries, the net result would be a bonanza of cheaper raw materials for France and an equivalent cornucopia of cheaper manufactured goods for America. Moreover, the chief victim of this new arrangement would be their common enemy, England. But once again the theoretical beauty of Jefferson's liberal vision ran afoul of mundane realities, this time in the court politics of Paris and Versailles and the entrenched bureaucracies of French provincial governments. Despite the rational appeal of Jefferson's vision of open markets, he was forced to acknowledge that "it seems to walk before us like our shadows, always appearing in reach, yet never overtaken."[34]

The best example of the problem was the tobacco monopoly maintained by the highly organized and deeply entrenched agricultural lobby known as the Farmers-General, which insisted on high duties for foreign imports in order to protect its own domestic products, as well as line the pockets of its many customs officers. "The abolition of the *monopoly* of our *tobacco* in the hands of the *Farmers General* will be pushed *by us* with all *our* force," Jefferson wrote in coded language to Monroe, "but it is so interwoven with the very formulations of *their* system of *finance* that it is of *doubtful* event." John Jay wrote from Philadelphia to commiserate with Jefferson, recalling that during his own service in France he had heard the system of complex regulations and clandestine payoffs "censured by almost every Gentleman Whom I heard speak of it, and yet it seems so firmly fixed, perhaps by golden Rivlets, even of Sovereignty itself, as that the speedy Destruction of it seems rather to be wished for than expected."[35]

Even when Jefferson was able to persuade the French ministry to agree to modest reductions in the duties on tobacco, the political power of the Farmers-General blocked implementation. "I am unable to answer those agents," Jefferson complained, "Who inform me that the officers of the customs and farms do not yet consider themselves bound to the new regulations." The bureaucracy, not the government, seemed to be in charge. Throughout his tenure in Paris Jefferson continued to draft lengthy and elaborate proposals condemning the inherent irrationality of the established system and describing in considerable detail the mutual advantages of a free trade policy. But like a Socratic argument for justice made to representatives of the Mafia, it all came to nothing. His only success after five years of relentless effort was a slight reduction in the tariff on American whale oil.[36]

The major diplomatic achievement of his stay in France was a $400,000 loan from Dutch bankers, done in collusion with Adams in the spring of 1787. The loan was significant because it allowed the American government to consolidate its European debts, thereby creating a source of funding to ransom American captives in Algiers and make regular payments to French veterans of the American Revolution. Jefferson took considerable pleasure in the deal, since it provided a semblance of fiscal responsibility for America's European creditors. But he acknowledged that he was a passive accomplice in the negotiations, which were handled primarily by Adams. In fact Jefferson confessed that the intricacies of high finance, involving floating bond rates and multiple interest charges, left him feeling confused and uncomfortable. He trusted Adams's judgment on such matters more than his own.[37]

When Adams prepared to depart London for America, he passed along to Jefferson responsibility for the Dutch loan, warning him to be on guard against "the unmeasurable avarice of Amsterdam." At just that moment the Dutch bankers threatened to increase the interest rates on the loan, and Adams worried out loud to Jefferson that they were doing so because they sensed that the American minister to France did not really understand the intricacies of the financing agreement: "I pity you, in your situation," Adams wrote to Jefferson, "dunned and teazed as you will be, all your Philosophy will be wanting to support you." Just remember one thing, Adams advised: "[T]he Amsterdammers love Money too well to execute their threats." Jefferson listened to this advice; the loan was not renegotiated, and American credit in the capitals and markets of Europe improved. All the forward-looking Jeffersonian visions of a liberal international community, comprised of open markets and national cooperation, had foundered on the rocks of European intransigence. From a historical perspective, his lifelong recognition that American foreign policy was the one area requiring a strong federal government congealed at this time. It was also becoming clear that his own idealistic instincts worked best when surrounded by more realistic and tough-minded colleagues. Ironically, the major substantive success of his tenure was a hardheaded financial arrangement with the Amsterdam bankers that, as he freely admitted, he never fully understood.[38]

VOICE OF AMERICA

OF COURSE diplomacy entailed much more than negotiating treaties. The departure of Franklin for America in the summer of 1785 left Jefferson as the ranking American minister at the court of Versailles. Like Franklin, Jefferson was the beneficiary of France's apparently irresistible urge to project onto its premier American resident the Gallic

version of the American essence. Jefferson's reputation as a younger
Franklin with a southern accent received a boost when the Marquis de
Chastellux published an account of his travels in America that featured
a romantic sketch of Jefferson at Monticello. "It seemed as if from his
youth," Chastellux wrote, Jefferson "had placed his mind, as he had
done his house, on an elevated situation, from which he might contemplate the universe." Back in America he was only beginning to be
known beyond the borders of Virginia. The American Philosophical
Society in Philadelphia seemed to confirm Chastellux's estimate by
electing Jefferson one of its members in 1786; Yale College followed
suit by awarding him an honorary Doctor of Laws degree the same
year. American visitors to Paris further reinforced his emerging reputation by describing Jefferson's infinite composure and aristocratic bear-
ing at court sessions in Versailles.[39]

Whereas Franklin's fame in France merely intensified his established reputation in America, Jefferson's budding prominence in Paris
served to create his image as a great American, which then migrated
back to America with all the prestige of European recognition. He
became the primary conduit for the Franco-American cultural
exchange. The French had never seen wild honeysuckle or swamp lau-
rel, so seeds should be sent over from Virginia for planting in French
soil. The Americans, for their part, needed to know of French experi-
ments in the new science of air travel or "ballooning," to include the
several calamitous failures when "at the height of about 6000 feet,
some accident happened" and the unfortunate aviators "fell from that
height, and were crushed to atoms." Meanwhile the French reading
public, which was so deprived of news from America that, as Jefferson
put it, "we might as well be on the moon," received the benefit of Jefferson's editorial additions to the *Encyclopédie Méthodique*. There he
corrected several factual errors in the French accounts of the American
Revolution, predicted that the unfortunate institution of slavery was
slowly but surely dying out, that emancipation "will take place there at
some point not very distant" and envisioned the entire North American continent occupied by American settlers within forty years.[40]

He saw to it that France's premier sculptor, Jean-Antoine Houdon, was dispatched to Mount Vernon to do the casts for the definitive sculpture of George Washington. He requested, in fact ordered, that all work cease on the new Virginia capitol at Richmond, so that the builders could work from an architectural model he was sending over. It was based on the Maison Corrée at Nîmes in southern France, what he called "the best morsel of antient architecture now remaining." (When it came to architectural matters, Jefferson was utterly unambiguous.) The Richmond builders needed to tear down what they had constructed and start again, using the designs he was providing: "They are simple and sublime. More cannot be said. They are not the brat of whimsical conception never before brought to light, but copied from the most precious, the most perfect model of antient architecture remaining on earth." The Virginia Assembly, acknowledging his discerning architectural eye and uncompromising tone, did precisely as it was told.[41]

Finally, and rather comically, Jefferson decided to refute the leading French naturalist of the day, Georges de Buffon, who had argued that the mammals and plants of North America were inferior in size, health and variety to those of Europe. Buffon's theory, silly as it sounds today, benefited from his reputation as France's premier natural scientist; it also had the disarming implication of rendering the entire American environment as fatally degenerate, a kind of laboratory for the corruptive process. Jefferson launched an all-out campaign to gather specimens of American animals that were larger than anything in Europe. Sparing no expense, he commissioned an expedition into the White Mountains of New Hampshire to obtain "the skin, the skeleton, and the horns of the Moose, the Caribou, and the Original or Elk." The hunters were ordered to "leave the hoof on, to leave the bones of the legs and of the thighs if possible in the skin with the horns on, so that by sewing up the neck and belly of the skin we should have the true form and size of the animal." The expedition produced the desired specimens, but Jefferson was disappointed in their lack of size, especially the moose, which he had counted on as the trump card to play against Buffon's puny European deer.

So another hunting party went out, another moose was killed, another carcass was shipped over to Paris, where Jefferson put it on display in the entry hall of his hotel, still somewhat frustrated that the moose was only seven feet tall and that its hair kept falling out. Buffon, who was himself a minuscule man less than five feet tall, was invited to observe the smelly and somewhat imperfect trophy but concluded it was insufficient evidence to force a revision of his anti-American theory. It was one of the few occasions when Jefferson failed to enhance mutual understanding along the Franco-American axis.[42]

His unqualified success as the most visible American in Paris derived in great part from his outspoken affection for all things French. His abiding awkwardness with spoken French could be forgiven as the single stain on an otherwise spotless record of Francophilia. French wine, French food, French architecture and the discreet charms of French society were all obvious sources of pleasure for the American minister to the court at Versailles—his equally obvious hatred of England also helped the cause—and he let it be known throughout Parisian society that though he had been born a Virginian, France was his adopted home, just as the French people were his brethren in spirit, if not in blood. "I am much pleased with the people of this country," he wrote in a typical expression of endearment, noting that their inherent civility and sophistication allowed one to "glide thro' a whole life among them without a justle."[43]

This was a sincere sentiment, an authentic expression of genuine affinity between the urbane and cosmopolitan side of his character and the almost sensual seductions of the cultural capital of Europe. But it coexisted alongside its diametric opposite. In letters to friends and colleagues back in America, or in advisory notes to Americans traveling in Europe, Jefferson described France, and Europe more generally, as a hopeless sinkhole of avarice, ignorance and abject poverty. Indeed, what Buffon had said about the inherently degenerative conditions of

America, Jefferson turned against Europe and, inverting Buffon's prejudices, developed a formulaic argument about European inferiority.

The argument tended to take the familiar Jeffersonian form of a dichotomy between moral polarities. "The comparison of our governments [in America] with those of Europe," he wrote typically, "are like a comparison of heaven to hell"; England served as a kind of limbo or "intermediate station." When George Wythe wrote him in 1786 to report the good news that the Virginia Assembly had finally passed his bill guaranteeing religious freedom, Jefferson reacted by contrasting what was possible in America with European hopelessness: "If all the sovereigns of Europe were to set themselves to work to emancipate the minds of their subjects from their present ignorance and prejudices . . . , a thousand years would not place them on the high ground on which our common people are now setting out. . . . If any body thinks that kings, nobles, or priests are good conservators of the public happiness, send them here." This became a common theme in his letters to American correspondents. "If any of our countrymen wish for a king," he wrote to David Ramsay in South Carolina, "give them Aesop's fable of the frogs who asked for a king; if this does not cure them, send them to Europe." "The Europeans are governments of kites over pidgeons," he reported to John Rutledge, adding cynically that "the best schools for republicanism are London, Versailles, Madrid, Vienna, Berlin, &c."[44]

In a privately circulated document entitled "Hints to Americans Travelling in Europe," he criticized those tourists who were overly impressed with the art and monuments of European capitals, concluding that "they are worth seeing, but not studying" because they tended to distract attention from the real and deep social corruption of urban life throughout Europe. He urged young men who were embarking on some version of the grand tour to beware of the temptations and sexual traps they would encounter. (His own secretary, William Short, was engaged in a passionate affair with the beautiful young wife of the Duc de La Rochefoucauld-Liancourt.) The typical young traveler "is led by the strongest of all the human passions into a spirit for female intrigue destructive of his own and others happiness, or a passion for whores destructive of his health. . . ." Paris, he warned, was one huge fleshpot.[45]

The psychological agility required to sustain a sincere and highly visible affection for all things French, especially while simultaneously denouncing European decadence with equivalent sincerity, depended upon mysterious mechanisms inside Jefferson that prevented his different voices from hearing one another. In his letters he could modulate his message to fit his different audiences. The publication of his *Notes on the State of Virginia* created some intriguing problems on this score because, unlike private letters, one could not control its distribution; it could be read by anybody and everybody. Part travel guide, part scientific treatise and part philosophical meditation, *Notes* had been written in the fall of 1781, just after his unfortunate experience as governor of Virginia and just before the tragic death of his wife. He permitted publication of a French translation, albeit without his name on the cover and in a limited edition of two hundred copies, in order to enhance French knowledge of America, and this only after he had learned that an unauthorized version was already in press. Indeed, despite his effort at anonymity, the fact that the American minister to France was the author of *Notes* quickly became an open secret throughout Parisian society and contributed significantly to his growing reputation as the dominant voice of America in Europe. Abigail and John Adams read it in their coach riding to Calais on the way to their new post in London: "I thank you kindly for your Book," Adams noted, adding that "it is our Meditation all the Day long. I cannot now say much about it, but I think it will do its Author and his Country great Honour. The Passages upon slavery are worth Diamonds. They will have more effect than Volumes written by mere Philosophers."[46]

But Jefferson in fact was deeply worried about the effect his remarks on slavery might have on his reputation back in America, especially in Virginia. He confided to Madison that "there are sentiments on some subjects which I apprehend ought be displeasing to the country [and] perhaps to the [Virginia] assembly or to some who lead it. I do not wish to be exposed to their censure. . . ." Madison wrote back with a

cautiously optimistic message and in a highly elliptical style designed
to prevent snoopers at the respective postal offices, even if they managed to decode his cipher, from understanding what he was talking
about: "I have found the copy of your notes . . . , looked them over
carefully myself and consulted several judicious friends in confidence.
We are all sensible that the *freedom of your* strictures on some *particular
measures* and *opinions* will displease their respective abbetors. But we
equally concur in thinking that this consideration ought not to be
weighed against the *utility of your plan.*"47

Actually, Jefferson's personal belief that slavery was morally incompatible with the principles of the American Revolution was not cause
for worry. He had made his position on that controversial subject
known on several occasions in the Virginia Assembly and the federal
Congress. What did merit worry was his insinuation that the planters
of Virginia and the Chesapeake region were already moving inexorably
toward emancipation. This was a piece of wishful thinking that defied
the unattractive political realities. True, he had said much the same
thing in his discussion of slavery in the *Encyclopédie Méthodique,* but
those remarks were aimed at a French audience and were designed to
put an optimistic gloss on a potentially damaging topic.

Most worrisome of all were those dramatic passages in *Notes* proph-
esying racial war in America and "convulsions which will probably
never end but in the extermination of the one or the other race."
Indeed Jefferson seemed to say that if racial war should come, God was
on the side of the blacks: "Indeed I tremble for my country. When I
reflect that God is just: that his justice cannot sleep for ever: that considering numbers, nature and natural means only, a revolution of the
wheel of fortune, an exchange of situation, is among possible events;
that it may become probable by supernatural interference! The
Almighty has no attribute which can take sides with us in such a contest." Jefferson was justifiably concerned that such apocalyptic sentiments would enjoy no supportive audience at all. French readers
would be shocked; Virginians would be enraged.48

As it happened, all the letters he received commenting on the antislavery passages of *Notes* were strongly supportive. David Ramsay, the South Carolina historian, even lectured him on not going far enough. Ramsay claimed that "in a few centuries the negroes will lose their black color. I think now they are less black in Jersey than Carolina." So instead of racial conflict, one could look forward to the gradual assimilation of all blacks, who would achieve this worthy goal by actually becoming white. The Reverend James Madison, president of William and Mary, disagreed, saying that Jefferson's formulation in *Notes* was being borne out by experience. The Indian population, Reverend Madison predicted, would eventually be integrated into American society. There were even reports of an Indian near Albany who had become almost fully white in a matter of only a few years. But there were no reliable reports of any black man changing color. "It seems," observed Reverend Madison sadly, "as if Nature had absolutely denied to him the Possibility of ever acquiring the Complexion of the Whites." Reverend Madison congratulated Jefferson for forcing his fellow Virginia slaveowners to recognize that unless something were done about slavery, their children or grandchildren would die in a genocidal war between the races. While indicative of the prevalent and deeprooted racism present even within the more progressive circles of American society, the remarks of Ramsay and Madison also showed that Jefferson's treatment of the forbidden subject had not isolated him as fully as he had initially feared.⁽⁴⁹⁾

Nevertheless, the worrying he did about the public response to *Notes* exposed his intense discomfort with any expression of his personal thoughts that he could not orchestrate or control. This is the likely reason why *Notes* became the first and last book he ever published. More significantly, the experience had a lasting effect on his posture toward the slavery question. From this time onward the characteristically Jeffersonian position emphasized the need to wait for public opinion to catch up with the moral imperative of emancipation. Instead of a crusading advocate, he became a cautious diplomat. "You know that nobody wishes more ardently to see an abolition not only of the trade but of the condition of slavery," he wrote to a French friend in 1788. "But . . . I am here as a public servant; and those whom I serve having not yet been able to give their voice against this practice, it is decent for me to avoid too public a demonstration of my wishes to see it abolished. Without serving the cause here, it might render me less able to serve it beyond the water." He began to develop the argument—it became the centerpiece of his public position on slavery throughout his mature years until the end of his life—that the problem should be passed along to the next generation of American statesmen. These were the leaders born during the American Revolution and therefore "suckled in the principles of liberty as it were with their mother's milk." And so "it is to them," he now claimed, that "I look with anxiety to turn the fate of this question." Here was a political posture that possessed several strategic advantages, the chief one being that it allowed him to retain his moral principles while justifying inaction on the grounds of seasoned wisdom and practical savvy. He thereby kept his principles pure and intact by placing them in a time capsule; there they could stay until that appropriate moment in the future when the world was ready for them.[50]

Meanwhile there were also capsules or compartments inside his own mind or soul that were being constructed at this time to keep certain incompatible thoughts from encountering one another. Perhaps the most graphic example of this capacity to keep secrets from himself dates from August 1786. A fellow American slaveowner traveling to France inquired about the French law prohibiting slavery and allowing any slave brought into the country to claim his freedom. "I have made enquiries," Jefferson explained, "on the subject of the negro boy you brought, and find that the laws of France give him freedom if he claims it, and that it will be difficult, if not impossible, to interrupt the course of the law." But there was a way around or perhaps over the law: "I have known an instance," Jefferson observed discreetly, "where a person bringing in a slave, and saying nothing about it, has not been disturbed in his possession." If one simply avoids mentioning the subject, "the young negro will not probably . . . think of claiming his freedom." The instance Jefferson was referring to almost certainly involved his own black servant James Hemings. It is almost equally certain that Jefferson felt no twinge of conscience about recommending a policy of secrecy, which merely mirrored the deeper secrecies he routinely practiced inside himself.[51]

In sum, the considerable diplomatic experience Jefferson acquired during his years in France was accompanied by what we might call a diplomacy of the interior regions. Or perhaps the psychological dexterity he had always possessed became fully visible during his French phase. At the most obvious and well-intentioned level, this internal diplomacy derived from his genuine desire to tell different correspondents what they wanted to hear. Jefferson always regarded candor and courtesy as incompatible, and when forced to choose, he invariably picked courtesy, thereby avoiding unpleasant confrontations. This was what he meant by "taking the handle by the smooth end." Letter writing was a perfect instrument for this diplomatic skill, in part because of Jefferson's mastery of the written word and in part because different audiences could be independently targeted. A Frenchman would have been disconcerted to read the advice he was offering to young Americans about the snares and pitfalls of decadent Paris and might have plausibly concluded that Jefferson was a hypocrite. But Jefferson saw himself as modulating his message to suit his audience, adjusting his own views to accord better with the attitudes of his correspondents. This was not so much duplicity as politeness.

Pushed a bit further, however, and the harmless urge to avoid conflict could assume more sinister implications. Unlike Adams, whose heart and mind were wired together in a single network that carried ideas and urges along lines that linked them to a common power source, Jefferson had created separate lines of communication inside himself that were designed to prevent one set of signals from interfering with the other. Adams, as a result, could be most dangerous when most honest. Honesty for Jefferson, on the other hand, was a more complicated internal negotiation. He was most disarming when a morally resonant subject like slavery drove a wedge between his incompatible convictions, and he remained serenely oblivious of the disjunction.

What his critics took to be hypocrisy was not really that at all. In some cases it was the desire to please different constituencies, to avoid conflict with colleagues. In other cases it was an orchestration of his internal voices, to avoid conflict with himself. Both the external and internal diplomacy grew out of his deep distaste for sharp disagreement and his bedrock belief that harmony was nature's way of signaling the arrival of truth. More self-deception than calculated hypocrisy, it was nonetheless a disconcerting form of psychological agility that would make it possible for Jefferson to walk past the slave quarters on Mulberry Row at Monticello thinking about mankind's brilliant prospects without any sense of contradiction. Though it made him deaf to most forms of irony, it had the decided political advantage of banishing doubt or disabling ambiguity from his mental process. He had the kind of duplicity possible only in the pure of heart.

SENTIMENTAL JOURNEYS

ONE OF JEFFERSON'S most distinctive voices, which became fully audible during his French years, was the voice he assumed toward women. As we have seen, Abigail Adams played a major role in helping him settle in Paris. She also provided him with what was probably his first exposure to a wife who was a full partner in her husband's career, as well as a woman capable of conversation that moved naturally from questions of parental responsibility to matters of European statecraft. But even Abigail felt most comfortable offering Jefferson her sharpest-edged advice about his obligations as a father. In that sense she implicitly recognized the legitimacy of the borders separating the domestic domain of women and the traditional male province of politics. In effect Abigail provided Jefferson with a gentle introduction to an entire gallery of Frenchwomen who crossed the sexual borders with an impunity that seemed to cast doubt on all his traditional presumptions about gender.

One can conjure up some sense of what Jefferson experienced in an observation that John Adams made many years later, when he recalled his own initial encounter with the "learned Ladies" of the Parisian salons. "I have such a consciousness of Inferiority to them," Adams remembered in his best self-effacing style, "that I can scarcely speak in their presence. . . . Very few of these Ladies have ever had the conde-scention to allow me to talk. And when it has so happened, I have always come off mortified at the discovery of my Inferiority."[52]

Adams was referring to the conspicuously cavalier style of the lead-ing ladies of France's salon society. Jefferson was more adept than Adams at negotiating such elegant obstacles. What distressed him was what occurred after the parties were over. He explained to George Washington that the informal but highly influential authority that wives and mistresses had over the decisions of government was the sin-gle most worrisome feature of French society: "The manners of the nation allow them to visit, alone, all persons in office, to sollicit the affairs of the husband, family, or friends, and their sollicitations bid defiance to laws and regulations. . . . [Few Americans] can possibly understand the desperate state to which things are reduced in this country from the omnipotence of an influence which, fortunately for the happiness of the sex itself, does not endeavor to extend itself in our country beyond the domestic line." Especially when writing to Ameri-can women, he liked to document his contrast of American virtue with European decadence by congratulating American women, "who have the good sense to value domestic happiness above all other," with Frenchwomen, "who wrinkle their heads with politics." It was, he con-cluded, "a comparison of Amazons and Angels."[53]

Jefferson was on the side of the angels. One of the reasons he went against Abigail's advice and placed both his daughters in a convent school was that the arrangement, or so he thought, provided insulation from the vicissitudes of Parisian society. He was hard pressed to assure friends that Patsy and Polly were not being protected from the world at the risk of being indoctrinated in the values of Catholicism. He insisted that "not a word is ever said to them on the subject of religion. . . . It is a house of education only." And Panthemont offered the kind of education appropriate for the fairer sex—that is, courses in drawing or painting, dancing, music, etiquette and Italian.[54]

Though always eager to please her father, Patsy proceeded to demonstrate that neither the ladylike curriculum nor the high walls of the convent afforded the insulation Jefferson wanted for her. She reported that, while her French was nearly native, she was losing the ability to speak, write or even think in English. Then she revealed that not even the nuns could prevent adolescent girls from sharing stories of sexual scandal. "There was a gentleman," she wrote her father, "that killed himself because he thought his wife did not love him. They had been married ten years. I believe that if every husband in Paris was to do as much, there would be nothing but widows left." Then came the final straw, when Patsy announced that she had decided to become a nun. Family legend has it that Jefferson drove up to the gates of Panthemont the following day, said not a word to the nuns or to Patsy, escorted her into his carriage, then drove her home in silence. This happened in April 1789, and Jefferson immediately began to make plans for returning to America, in part to assure that his daughters would be raised in a safer, more domestically inclined environment.[55]

It is possible to get glimpses of Jefferson's interactions with his daughters that support the image of a loving and devoted father. One visitor to Jefferson's quarters, for example, described an intimate family scene in which Patsy was playing the harpsichord while a doting father helped Polly write a letter to friends back in Virginia. This is the kind of sentimental scene that Jefferson always idealized. And it allows us to visualize the domestic sphere not just as a special place that women inhabit but also as the innermost chamber of Jefferson's private utopia. In that sense his tendency to consign women to a more rarefied and less contentious domain was not an alienating act but rather an endorsement of feminine values and virtues as central fixtures in the Jeffersonian paradise.[56]

But most of the available evidence about Jefferson's relationship with his daughters comes from letters. And the letters exist because Jefferson chose to keep his daughters separate from his household throughout the vast bulk of his time in France. Moreover, both the major message and the abiding tone of the letters conveyed a willful distancing of parent from child, what might be called arm's-length parenting in the patriarchal style. For example, Patsy had wanted to accompany her father on his tour of southern France in the spring of 1787. Jefferson declined the request, then sent back sermons: "Determine never to be idle. No person will ever have occasion to complain of the want of time, who never loses any. It is wonderful how much may be done, if we are always doing. And that you may always be doing good, my dear, is the ardent prayer of yours affectionately."

From Aix-en-Provence he apologized for his infrequent letters, then continued in the moralistic mode: "No laborious person was ever yet hysterical. . . . It is part of the American character to consider nothing as desperate; to surmount every difficulty by resolutions and contrivance. . . . You ask me to write you long letters. I will do it my dear, on condition that you will read them from time to time, and practice what they inculcate."

An earlier letter to Polly strung together the same homilies on hard work and then, in a particularly insensitive passage, seemed to say that his own love was conditional upon her measuring up. You must apply yourself, Jefferson lectured, "to play on the harpsichord, to draw, to dance, to read and talk French and such things as will make you more worthy of the love of your friends. . . . Remember too as a constant charge not to go out without your bonnet because it will make you very ugly and then we should not love you so much."[57]

It is difficult to avoid the conclusion that Jefferson, who was so remarkably adept at crafting his literary persona to suit the audience, simply lacked the ability to convey affection to his own children. This does not mean that he was an unloving or uncaring father. His idealization of domestic bliss as the ultimate source of his personal happiness was certainly sincere, and his children were integral parts of that protected space where the ideal lived in his imagination. But in real life, in the day-by-day interactions with his flesh-and-blood daughters, he was incapable of sustained intimacy.

His relationships with mature women were decidedly different. If Jefferson tended to place women on a pedestal and then place that pedestal in the most cherished chamber of his mental Monticello, his letters to women friends combined conspicuous gallantry with a flirtatious, playfully intimate style. If his letters to his daughters have a lecturish, almost wooden tone and seem hurried and obligatory, his correspondence with women his own age is highly personal, soft to the point of sentimentality and carefully crafted.

For example, his letters to Angelica Schuyler Church, a renowned beauty and accomplished artist whose daughter was attending Panthemont with Patsy, suggest a kind of male coquette. "When you come again," he apprised Church after her visit in Paris, "I will employ myself solely in finding or fancying that you have some faults, and I will draw a veil over all your good qualities, if I can find one large enough." He then imagined Church visiting him at Monticello, the two of them gazing appreciatively all afternoon at the majesty of the Natural Bridge. He affected the same swooning style in correspondence with Madame de Tessé, an aunt of the Marquise de Lafayette's whose estate at Chaville featured gardens in which Jefferson loved to stroll: "Here I am, Madam," he wrote from Nîmes, "gazing whole hours at the Maison quarrée, like a lover at his mistress. The stock-weavers and silk spinners around it consider me as an hypochondriac Englishman, about to write with a pistol the last chapter of his history. This is the second time I have been in love since I left Paris." The first, he noted, was occasioned by a statue of Diana he viewed in Beaujolais.[58]

Actually, the statue of Diana had been preceded by a quite living and equally lovely woman by the name of Maria Cosway, the wife of the prominent miniaturist Richard Cosway. (Almost all of Jefferson's female friends were married or widowed.) If ever Jefferson encountered the essence of femininity as he imagined it, Cosway personified the ideal perfectly. She was described by contemporaries as "a golden-haired, languishing Anglo-Italian, graceful to affectation, and highly accomplished, especially in music," and the various portraits that survive depict a set of deep blue eyes, a tumble of blond curls, a beguiling blend of hauteur and vulnerability. When these were combined with an almost imperious pouting posture and the soft trace of a foreign accent—Italian was her native language—the total effect was usually devastating on men. Jefferson proved no exception. They met in early August 1786, introduced by the young American artist John Trumbull, who had accepted Jefferson's invitation to join his household in Paris while he worked on his painting "The Declaration of Independence." Within days Jefferson was head over heels in love.[59]

For the next six weeks Jefferson and Cosway were together almost daily, touring every garden, viewing every distinctive building, statue, painting or ancient ruin in Paris and its environs. For Jefferson, the luxuriant beauty of a work of art activated the same deep pool of passion that a beautiful woman also tapped—aesthetic appreciation and femininity were closely associated primal urges within his soul—and the commingling of Parisian art and architecture with the seductive attractions of a beautiful young woman (Cosway was twenty-seven) generated an explosive combination that left him utterly infatuated. He ignored his diplomatic chores, often dispatching Petit to make his excuses for missed appointments.

The rhapsodic adventure reached a climax on September 18, 1786, when Jefferson, still very much under the spell of emotional exuberance, broke his right wrist while trying to vault over a large kettle or fountain—there is disagreement over which it was. Just where the accident occurred and whether Cosway was even with him at the time are not known. Jefferson's most revealing comment on the incident came a month later: "How the right hand became disabled would be a long story for the left to tell," he wrote to William Stephens Smith. "It was by one of those follies from which good cannot come, but ill may." The injury incapacitated Jefferson for several weeks and put an effective end to the romantic frolics with Cosway. "It is with infinite regret," he wrote her with his left hand, "that I must relinquish your charming company for that of the surgeon." But two different French physicians botched the treatment—the wrist gave him trouble for the rest of his life—and Cosway left for London with her husband before another rendezvous could be arranged. He did manage to see her off, claiming that he turned away as she disappeared on the horizon, feeling "more dead than alive."[60]

We can never know with any certainty what transpired between Jefferson and Cosway during the fall of 1786. Historians, biographers and even filmmakers have lingered over the episode in loving detail and reached different answers to the "did-they-or-didn't-they?" question. What is indisputable is that Jefferson spent several months in a romantic haze, which he described in terms reminiscent of the young lover in *The Sorrows of Young Werther:* "Living from day to day, without a plan for four and twenty hours to come," he confessed to another woman friend, "I form no catalogue of impossible events. Laid up in port, for life as I thought myself at one time, I am thrown out to sea, and an unknown one to me." Indeed, the Cosway affair is significant not because of the titillating questions it poses about a sexual liaison with a gorgeous young married woman but because of the window it opens into Jefferson's deeply sentimental soul and the highly romantic role he assigned to women who touched him there.[61]

The most self-revealing letter he ever wrote was sent to Cosway in October 1786, while he was still under the spell of their whirlwind infatuation and still recovering from the injured wrist, which itself served as a perfect metaphor for his wounded condition. Twelve pages and more than four thousand words long, Jefferson labored over the letter with the same intensity he had brought to the Declaration of Independence. The famous letter—it has been endlessly interpreted by several generations of scholars—takes the classic if somewhat contrived form of "a dialogue between the Head and the Heart." Though the announced intention of the letter is to offer Cosway a problematic picture of the internal battle within Jefferson between reason and emotion, it is a love letter, and therefore the powers of the heart are privileged. The heart has the last word as well as the best lines (i.e., "Had they [philosophers] ever felt the solid pleasure of one generous spasm of the heart, they would exchange for it all the frigid speculations of their lives . . ."). Jefferson even enlists the American Revolution in behalf of the heart's side of the argument, claiming that victory in the war for independence was a matter of "enthusiasm against numbers" because it defied any rational measure of probability. So at one level the heart is the unequivocal winner of the debate. Despite the agony he felt at Cosway's departure, the ecstasy of their time together was worth the pain. But at another level it is Jefferson's head that is orchestrating the arguments and words of the dialogue. The act of crafting the letter allowed him to recover control over the powerful emotions that the relationship with Cosway had released. He kept a letterpress copy of the letter to record the emotions of the moment for posterity. In the long run the head prevails.[62]

Jefferson's subsequent correspondence with Cosway charts the gradual and perhaps inevitable cooling of the infatuation. It also bears witness to his urge to transport his palpable feelings for a real woman to a more imaginary region where perfect love could be more easily and safely experienced. In December 1786, still suffering from the wrist injury and the pain of separation, he recalled a magic cap he had read about as a child that enabled its wearer to fly wherever he wished. "I should wish myself with you, and not wish myself away again," he wrote. "If I cannot be with you in reality, I will in imagination." He reported his dream of the two of them in Virginia, visiting the Natural Bridge: "I shall meet you there, and visit with you all the grand scenes. I had rather be deceived than live without hope. It is so sweet! It makes us ride so smoothly over the roughness of life."[63]

In her early letters Cosway was able to match him with her own romantic imaginings. "Are you to be painted in future ages," she wrote in February 1787, "sitting solitary and sad, on the beautiful Monticello tormented by the shadow of a woman who will present you a deform'd rod [presumably his wrist], twisted and broken, instead of the emblematic instrument belonging to the Muses. . . ."[64]

But by the summer of 1787 Jefferson's letters had become less frequent. Cosway fell back on her pouting and petulant poses, complaining about his lack of attention and threatening to cease writing until the number of Jefferson's letters matched hers. She was now, however, locked into a war of words with one of the virtuoso prose stylists of the age. His long silence, he explained, was the result of a trip to southern France and northern Italy, where he "took a peep into Elysium" and realized that "I am born to lose everything I loved." But the references were not to Cosway, at least explicitly; they were to the architecture of Italy and his failure to see Rome. "Your long silence is unpardonable," she replied, then admitted that she did not know what else to say: "My war against you is of such a Nature that I cannot even find terms to express it. . . . But I begin to run on and my intention was only to say *nothing;* send a blank paper. . . ."[65]

Jefferson's response to Cosway's impatience only increased her frustration: "I do not think I was in arrears in my epistolary account when I left Paris. In affection I am sure you were greatly my debtor. I often determined during my journey to write you; but sometimes the fatigue of exercise and sometimes a fatigued attention hindered me." She had by now become a lovely memory that he could summon up and appreciate in the privacy of his imagination: "At Heidelberg I wished for you too. In fact I led you by the hand thro' the whole garden. . . . At Strasbourg I sat down to write you. But for my soul I could think of nothing at Strasbourg but the promontory of noses. . . . Had I written to you from thence it would have been a continuation of Sterne upon noses. . . ." This last reference was to a passage in Laurence Sterne's *Tristram Shandy* that describes an elongating nose, an unmistakable piece of sexual innuendo intended to be provocative. But the reference eluded Cosway, who was accustomed to leaving her male admirers in various European capitals wondering and wandering in her wake. (No less than James Boswell said she treated men like dogs.) Now, however, she herself was dangling, the femme fatale who had more than met her match. She was incensed: "At last I receive a letter from you, am I to be angry or not. . . . lett me tell you I am not your debtor in the least. . . . how could you lead me by the hand all the way, think of me, have Many things to say, and not find One word to write, *but on Noses?*"[66]

During Cosway's return visit to Paris the two former lovers managed to see each other only briefly and always in large social gatherings.

During Jefferson's return trip to America, he lay over in England for ten days while waiting for a ship but chose not to make the effort to visit her before sailing. She reciprocated by claiming that a bad cold made a trip to him impossible. In one of her last letters she acknowledged defeat in the verbal jousting match, along with a pervasive sense of personal inadequacy: "I wish always to converse with you longer. But when I read your letters they are so well wrote, so full of a thousand pretty things that it is not possible for me to answer such charming letters. I could say many things if my pen could write exactly My sentiments and feelings, but my letters must appear sad scrawls to you." Jefferson, for his part, said good-bye in terms that recognized how the sizzling infatuation and then quarrelsome coquetry had now congealed into a cooler but more comfortable friendship. The more unmanageable emotions had long since been consigned to a cherished and safely insulated chamber of his soul. "Adieu my very dear friend," he wrote. "Be our affections unchangeable, and if our little history is to last beyond the grave, be the longest chapter in it that which shall record their purity, warmth and duration." While his customary discretion makes it impossible to know whether the affair with Cosway had an active and not just a suggestive sexual dimension, the abiding character of their lengthy correspondence makes it abundantly clear that Jefferson preferred to meet his lovers in the rarefied region of his mind rather than the physical world of his bedchamber.[67]

MADISONIAN ADVICE

By THE MID-POINT of his time in France, then, Paris had come to mean many things to Jefferson: It was the diplomatic capital of Europe in which the political and commercial stature of the new American nation he represented remained marginal at best; the epitome of the Old World's civilized seductions, as well as its urban corruptions; and the perfect place to fall in love. Paris also proved to be the ideal perch from which to observe two of the most significant political events in

Western history. From afar it afforded Jefferson a conveniently
detached perspective on the debate surrounding the creation and ratification of the new Constitution of the United States, a debate in which
the combination of his distance and the quality of his chief source—
James Madison—allowed him to accommodate himself to political
ideas that violated his deepest ideological instincts. From close up it
provided him with the unique opportunity to witness the coming of
the French Revolution and, in the crucible of conversations with several of its staunchest supporters and ultimate victims, to work out the
full implications of his truly radical vision of politics. As both a bird's-
eye observer of American developments and a ringside witness of
French convulsions, in short, he fashioned what were to become
enduringly Jeffersonian convictions about mankind's tenuous relationship with government.

His ongoing correspondence with Madison and Monroe had kept
him abreast of the growing dissatisfaction with the inherent weakness
of the federal Congress in Philadelphia. "The politics of Europe render
it indispensably necessary that with respect to every thing external we
be one nation only, firmly held together," he informed Madison,
adding, "Interior government is what each state should keep to himself." He wanted it known back home in Virginia and in Philadelphia
that he favored reform of the Articles of Confederation to enlarge federal jurisdiction over foreign trade and foreign policy but preferred
leaving control over all domestic concerns, including taxation, to the
particular states. "To make us one nation as to foreign concerns, and
keep us distinct in Domestic ones," he wrote to Madison, "gives the
outline of the proper division of powers between the general and particular governments."[68]

By 1786 Madison was already contemplating much more drastic
changes in the structure of the federal government. Jefferson had inadvertently contributed to such thoughts by sending over two trunks of
books, including the collected works of David Hume, which Madison
then proceeded to study in preparation for the Constitutional Convention. (The historian Douglass Adair has called Madison's intensive

reading of Hume perhaps the most productive and consequential act of scholarship in American history.) But Madison did not initially share his more critical assessment of the American government with Jefferson. The established pattern of their political alliance was for Madison or Monroe to provide the information about congressional debates and for Jefferson then to dictate the directions to be taken. For example, when Monroe reported a congressional proposal to move the national capital from Philadelphia to New York, Jefferson told him to join with Madison to block the move since the interest of Virginia demanded a location on the Potomac. "It is evident that when a sufficient number of the Western states come in," he apprised Monroe, "they will move it to George town. In the meantime it is our interest that it should remain where it is, and give no new pretensions to any other place." Given the deference that Madison customarily displayed toward Jefferson's commands, it is not surprising that Jefferson remained unaware of the root-and-branch reforms Madison believed essential until after the Constitutional Convention had completed its work. In this one all-important instance their roles were reversed; Madison was in the lead.[69]

Meanwhile Jefferson was receiving reports from other quarters about an insurrection in western Massachusetts led by a veteran of the American Revolution named Daniel Shays to protest new taxes imposed by Boston. In the grand scheme of things Shays's Rebellion was a tempest in a teapot, but prominent figures throughout the country interpreted it as a harbinger of incipient anarchy and a clarion call for a more vigorous and fully empowered federal government: "In short, my Dr. Sir," John Jay wrote from Philadelphia, "we are in a very unpleasant Situation. Changes are Necessary, but what they Ought to be, what they will be, and how and when to be produced, are arduous questions." From London Abigail Adams summoned up the scene of a looming apocalypse. "Ignorant, wrestless desperadoes, without conscience or principles," she informed Jefferson, "have led a deluded multitude to follow their standard, under pretence of grievances which have no existence but in their own immaginations."[70]

In retrospect it is clear that both the Shaysites' fear of tyranny and the corresponding fear of observers like Jay and Abigail Adams that America was on the verge of social disintegration were mutually reinforcing overreactions of near-paranoid proportions. Jefferson's response to the entire display was especially revealing both for its clearsighted and even serene endorsement of popular resistance to government in almost any form and for its eventually famous phrasing: "I hope they pardoned them [i.e., the Shaysites]," he told Abigail. "The spirit of resistance to government is so valuable on certain occasions, that I wish it to be always kept alive. . . . I like a little rebellion now and then. It is like a storm in the atmosphere." He had first proposed a similar formulation of the problem two months earlier in a letter to Ezra Stiles, the president of Yale. "If the happiness of the mass of the people can be secured at the expense of a little tempest now and then," he had written Stiles, "or even of a little blood, it will be a precious purchase." A month later he had written Madison in language almost identical to his message to Abigail. His boldest formulation came more months later, in November 1787, when he told William Stephens Smith that Shays's Rebellion was actually a symptom of America's political health: "What signify a few lives lost in a century or two?" he observed. "The tree of liberty must be refreshed from time to time with the blood of patriots and tyrants. It is its natural manure." Moreover, those alleged statesmen who wished to use Shays's Rebellion as an occasion to justify more coercive political institutions, he warned, "are setting up a kite to keep the hen yard in order."[71]

These were extremely radical statements, which, taken literally—or, for that matter, taken at all seriously—placed Jefferson far to the left of any responsible political leader of the revolutionary generation. For his remarks suggested that his deepest allegiances were not to the preservation of political stability but to its direct opposite. Given the radical and even anarchistic consequences of the ideas he seemed to be advocating in response to the Shays scare, one is tempted to put them down as hyperbolic occasions, or perhaps as momentary excesses prompted by his genuine aversion to the overreaction of those condemning the

Shays insurrection, an aversion rendered more plausible and comfortable by his distant and safe location in Paris.

But there is reason to believe that Jefferson meant what he said, indeed that his entire way of thinking about government was different from that of any other prominent American leader of the time. In January 1787, while Madison was studying the classic texts of Hume and Montesquieu in preparation for the Constitutional Convention later that spring, Jefferson wrote him to share his own thoughts on the appropriate political models for American society. While Madison was grappling with questions about political architecture—how to configure federal and state power; how to design institutions so as to balance interest groups without replicating the gridlock of the current government under the Articles of Confederation—Jefferson was thinking much more grandly, about the very ground on which any and all political structures must be constructed. While Madison was struggling with arrangements of authority in three branches of the government, Jefferson was identifying three kinds of society in which human beings might arrange themselves.

There was European society, with governments that ruled by force, usually monarchical in form, what Jefferson described as "a government of wolves over sheep." Then there was American and, to a slightly lesser extent, English society, with governments responsive to the populace as a whole, where "the mass of mankind enjoys a precious degree of liberty & happiness." Finally there was Indian society, which managed itself without any formal government at all by remaining small and assuring the internalization of common values among all members. If forced to choose, Jefferson preferred the Indian solution, while admitting that it was "inconsistent with any degree of population." He reiterated the point in a letter to Edward Carrington, a conservative Virginian planter and politician. "I am convinced," he explained, "that those societies (as the Indians) which live without government enjoy in their gen'l mass an infinitely greater degree of happiness than those who live under European governments."[72]

The Jeffersonian ideal, in short, was not a specific version of balanced republican government. It was a world in which individual citizens had internalized their social responsibilities so thoroughly that the political architecture Madison was designing was superfluous. Though prepared to acknowledge the need to make necessary compromises with his ideal for practical reasons—the size of the American population and the vastness of its territory obviously demanded some delegation of authority beyond the sovereign self—he did so grudgingly. And the elaborate reasoning about constitutional structure that so captivated political thinkers like Madison and the other delegates at the Constitutional Convention never animated the best energies of his mind, which drew its inspiration from a utopian vision of the liberated individual resisting all external coercion and regarding all forms of explicit government power as a necessary evil.

All this helps explain his initially hostile reaction to the news leaking out of Philadelphia about the shape of the new American Constitution in the summer of 1787. Madison had tried to prepare him for what was coming, suggesting that America needed an energetic federal government "with a negative *in all cases whatsoever* over the local legislatures." But Jefferson resisted the suggestion and questioned the decision to make wholesale changes in the current, albeit inadequate, national government: "The negative proposal . . . on all acts of the several [i.e., state] legislatures is now for the first time suggested to my mind," he told Madison. "Prima facie I do not like it. It fails in an essential character [by proposing] to mend a small hole by covering the whole garment." He expressed the same apprehension to Adams, claiming that "the good of the new constitution might have been couched in three or four articles to be added to the good, old, and venerable fabrick, which should have been preserved even as a religious relique." Edward Carrington also tried to prepare him for a fundamentally new kind of federal government, not just a minor revision of the Articles of Confederation. "The Ideas here suggested," Carrington wrote in June, "are far removed from those which prevailed when you was amongst us, and as they have arisen with the most able, from an actual view of events, it is probable you may not be prepared to expect them." Jefferson's location in Paris rather than Philadelphia proved a major advantage, by providing time to adjust to political ideas that ran counter to his own and that he would in all likelihood have opposed if present.[73]

He concealed his worries about what was brewing in Philadelphia from all his European correspondents, preferring to play his customary role as America's champion. "Our Federal convention is likely to sit till October," he wrote a French friend, "and we may be assured their propositions will be wise, as a more able assembly never sat in America. Happy for us, that when we find our constitutions defective and unsufficient to secure the happiness of our people, we can assemble with all the coolness of philosophers and set it to rights, while every other nation on earth must have recourse to arms. . . ." Meanwhile Madison apologized for his inability to provide a detailed account of the ongoing deliberations. "I am still under the mortification of being restrained from disclosing any part of their proceedings," he wrote in July. "As soon as I am at liberty I will endeavor to make amends for my silence and . . . give you pretty full gratification. I have taken lengthy notes of every thing that has yet passed. . . ."[74]

Madison was as good as his word. His letter of October 24, 1787, provided Jefferson with a lengthy report on the wide-ranging deliberations at the Constitutional Convention and a truly remarkable appraisal of the constitutional issues at stake. He described how the delegates had tried "to draw a line of demarkation which would give to the General Government every power requisite for general purposes, and leave to the States every power which might be most beneficially administered by them." This formulation blurred the relative powers of federal versus state authority, but in terms that clearly extended federal jurisdiction over domestic policy in ways that Jefferson staunchly opposed. Madison then went on to analyze the intricate and purposefully ambiguous layering of jurisdiction by the different branches of government and the different versions of representation. "Those who contend for a Simple Democracy, or a pure republic, actuated by a sense of the majority, and operating within narrow limits," he observed, "assume or suppose a case which is altogether fictitious." What Madison was terming "fictitious" was in fact the essence of Jefferson's thinking about government. Jefferson acknowledged as much in his response to Madison. "I own I am not a friend to a very energetic government," he confessed. "It is always oppressive. . . . After all, it is my principle that the will of the Majority should always prevail." Madison did not write back to explain that, at least as he saw it, the Constitution had been designed to subvert mere majority rule on the assumption that the chief threat to individual liberty in America was likely to come from that direction. Jefferson would have found such an argument unintelligible, since he found it impossible to regard popular majorities as dangerous or to think about the powers of government in positive ways. Madison's entire emphasis on social balance was at odds with Jefferson's commitment to personal liberation.[75]

Here was the first significant occasion—it would not be the last—when the special relationship between Jefferson and Madison assumed a human version of the checks and balances principle. Despite deep reservations about an energetic federal government, especially a federal government empowered to tax, Jefferson decided to follow the advice of his most loyal lieutenant and endorse ratification of the new Constitution. At first he declared himself neutral, telling Carrington that "there is a great mass of good in it . . . , but there is also to me a bitter pill or two," then directing him to confer with Madison for more specific information about his views. On all the specific provisions empowering the new national government to make laws for all the states, he decided to remain silent and let Madison speak for him. Over the course of the following months, as the ratification process went forward in the respective states, Jefferson worked out a responsibly critical posture: The new Constitution had his approval, even though he preferred specific limitations on the tenure of the president and an explicit bill or declaration of rights that defined those personal freedoms that no federal government could violate.[76]

Even Adams concurred on the latter point, as did many of the advocates of the Constitution in the state ratifying conventions. As for his apprehensions about excessive executive power, Jefferson wrote to Washington to assure the man who was virtually certain to be elected the first president that his worries were about the future, after Washington had left the office. They were also intensified by his European experience. "I was much an enemy to monarchy before I came to Europe," he apprised Washington, and was "ten thousand times more so now since I have seen what they [i.e., kings] are. . . . I can further say with safety there is not a crowned head in Europe whose talents or merits would entitle him to be elected a vestryman by the people of any parish in America." He had expressed his worries more directly to Adams, claiming that "the President seems a bad edition of the Polish king." But his preference for term limits—he favored one four-year term—did not place him outside the boundaries of respectable criticism.[77]

Nevertheless, word leaked back to America that Jefferson's support for the new Constitution was soft and perhaps even nonexistent. "Bye the Bye," wrote Francis Hopkinson from Philadelphia, "you have been often dish'd up to me as a strong Antifederalist, which is almost equivalent to what a Tory was in the Days of the War, for what reason I know not, but I don't believe it and have utterly denied the Insinuation." During the ratification debate in Virginia both Patrick Henry and George Mason, who led the opposition, claimed that mutual friends assured them that Jefferson also opposed the creation of a strong central government with powers over the states. Madison, however, rose to contradict the claim and, as he explained it to Jefferson, *"took the liberty to state some of your opinions on the favorable side."*[78]

Precisely what Jefferson himself would have said if he had been present in Virginia for the ratification debate is impossible to know. Madison, perhaps the most able parliamentary maneuverer in American politics, carried the Jeffersonian flag with him to victory in the Virginia convention. Jefferson's own remarks throughout the summer and fall of 1788 were inconsistent and contradictory. First he advocated support for the Constitution until nine states had ratified, then opposition so as to force amendments and acceptance of a bill of rights.

Then he backed away from that position, endorsing ratification but only on the condition that a bill of rights be added once the new government was in place. When Carrington sent him a copy of the recently published *Federalist Papers*, Jefferson sent his compliments to Madison, one of the main contributors, praising the work as "the best commentary on the principles of government which was ever written" and conceding that "it has rectified me in several points." In an earlier letter to Madison he had conceded that on the specific question of presidential term limits, "I readily therefore suppose my position wrong. . . ." But when asked by Hopkinson if he was a staunch Federalist, meaning supporter of the Constitution, he gave an equivocal answer that was rescued from its inherent ambivalence by the lyrical quality of its concluding line: "I am not a Federalist, because I never submitted the whole system of my opinions to the creed of any party of men whatever. . . . Such an addiction is the last degredation of a free and moral agent. If I could not go to heaven but with a party, I would not go there at all."79

In a very real sense, this statement, albeit unintentionally, captured the essence of Jefferson's ultimate position on the Constitution and indeed on all specific constitutional schemes. He found them excessively technical configurations of political power that did not speak directly to his own political creed, which transcended categories like "Federalist" and "Antifederalist" by inhabiting a more rarefied region where political parties, constitutional distinctions and even forms of government themselves were rendered irrelevant. His lifelong attitude toward the constitutional settlement of 1787–88 remained ambiguous and problematic. The trouble with most Europeans, he wrote to Hopkinson, was that they had been bred to prefer "a government which can be felt; a government of energy. God send that our country may never have a government, which it can feel." Madison and most Federalists believed that the new American Constitution was admirable for precisely the energetic qualities Jefferson denounced. As for Jefferson, his mind and heart longed for a world where government itself had disappeared. Given the terms of the constitutional debate that raged in

America in 1788, the one issue that best embodied his political convictions was the insistence on a bill of rights that transcended all the Madisonian complexities. That was pretty much what he chose to emphasize.

REVOLUTIONS AND GENERATIONS

AT ALMOST THE same time that the delegates to the Constitutional Convention were gathering in Philadelphia, the Assembly of Notables was convened by the French king, Louis XVI, in Versailles. The advantage of hindsight allows us to know that this gathering, rendered necessary by a financial crisis that threatened to bankrupt the French government, was actually the opening chapter in a bewilderingly complex and horridly bloody chain of events that tore French society to pieces and fundamentally altered the course of modern history. But neither Jefferson nor anyone else for that matter could be expected to recognize at the time that he was witnessing the start of the French Revolution, or that comfortably confident endorsements of "a little rebellion now and then" would take on such a very different meaning after the cataclysms of 1789.[80]

Jefferson's initial instinct was to see the Assembly of Notables as an inferior version of the Constitutional Convention, another illustration of his running argument about the inherent superiority of the American environment and the degraded condition of European politics. He kept up a standing joke with the Adams family in which the delegates at Philadelphia were described as demigods or modern-day Ciceros, while the French nobility gathered at Versailles were comic buffoons who delivered long soliloquies that bore only a tenuous relationship to the political issues at stake. (Lafayette, Jefferson's closest French friend and himself a delegate to the Assembly of Notables, joined in the banter by wondering if his colleagues should be called "not able.") By the summer of 1787 Jefferson could complain to Monroe that the latter's reports on the Constitutional Convention were brimming with excitement and vigorous arguments, while "I have nothing to give you in return but the history of the follies of nations in their dotage."[81]

His early characterizations of the king's behavior fitted into the same pattern of European corruption. "The king goes for nothing," Jefferson wrote Jay. "He hunts one half the day, is drunk the other, and signs whatever he is bid." His confidential and coded letters to Adams and Madison reiterated the image of a royal family drowning in wine and incapable of any form of political leadership, except serving as role models in the most advanced arts of sexual promiscuity. He was sufficiently confident that nothing significant would happen at Versailles—aristocratic bombast directed at a drunken monarch more resembled a political opera than an occasion for serious statecraft—that he went ahead with his plans to travel through southern France rather than remain in the capital.[82]

Although the motif of European degradation never completely disappeared from his thinking or his correspondence, by the summer of 1787 Jefferson had begun to recognize the seriousness of the political crisis France was facing. The frivolous tone of his earliest letters receded, his critical and condescending attitude toward Europe's hopelessly corrupt condition became a minor note and the major note became that of a respectful and cautiously optimistic witness to history in the making. His reports to Jay, who still retained overall responsibility for American foreign policy, emphasized the steady progress France was making: Representative assemblies had been created in the various provinces; the infamous corvées, requiring peasants to perform unpaid labor for feudal lords, had been abolished; some kind of parliamentary system of government seemed inevitable, albeit one in which the power of the king would probably remain greater than the English constitutional model. "All together," he wrote Jay, these were impressive reforms that "constitute a vast improvement in the condition of this nation."[83]

His shift from irreverent criticism to guarded optimism reflected his growing conviction that "the contagion of liberty" released onto the world by the American Revolution was now spreading to Europe and that France was the first European country to experience its liberating consequences. As one who had been present at the creation of this revolutionary movement in America, he felt almost providentially privileged to witness its arrival as a liberating army of ideas marching through France and, he hoped, eventually all Europe. If the detailed work of constitution making did not engage his fullest energies, the contemplation of more overarching political trends and truths did so naturally.

All this explains his extremely—and as subsequent events proved, excessively—optimistic appraisal of the ongoing political drama in revolutionary France. "So that I think it is probable that this country will within two or three years be in the enjoiment of a tolerably free constitution," he wrote Monroe in 1788, "and without its having cost them a drop of blood." When Adams expressed his concern that the different factions in the Estates-General would find compromise impossible, Jefferson assured him that "her [France's] internal affairs will be arranged without blood" because moderates in the new national legislature were in control. "In every event, I think the present disquiet will end well," he told Washington, explaining that the people of France "have been awaked by our revolution, they feel their strength, they are enlightened, their lights are spreading, and they will not retrograde." France looked to him like the America of Europe. It was struggling to create a new constitution; like America—echoes of Shays's Rebellion in the background—the threat of violence had been faced "but as yet not a life has been lost," and again like America, thoughtful leaders "are all employed in drawing plans of bills of rights."[84]

Later in his life, probably when he was reviewing his correspondence in preparation to write his autobiography in 1821, Jefferson was somewhat embarrassed at his unrelieved optimism in the late 1780s. For by then, of course, he knew that the Assembly of Notables would fail to reach agreement about a solution to the fiscal crisis, which would then lead to the calling of the Estates-General, which would fail to resolve the political crisis in a way acceptable to the nobility and bourgeoisie, which would then lead to mob action in Paris, bread riots throughout the countryside, mass executions, the Reign of Terror and eventually dictatorial rule by Napoleon. On at least one occasion toward the end of his life he doctored his correspondence, inserting a more cautionary statement designed to convince posterity that his affection for France had not blinded him to the possibility of unparalleled violence. "Should they attempt more than . . . the established habits of the people are ripe for," he later added to one letter from 1787, "they may lose all, and retard indefinitely the ultimate object of their aim." The undoctored correspondence, however, reveals no premonition of the looming convulsions and instead shows an abiding confidence that French political leaders would manage their way past trouble much as their counterparts in America were doing.[85]

So much history happened in prerevolutionary France during the last two years of Jefferson's ministry that it is not easy to summarize his shifting political positions, except perhaps to say that he presumed that France would emerge from the ferment as some kind of constitutional monarchy. Despite his earlier characterizations of the French king as a drunken sot, completely out of touch with the needs and frustrations of the French people, by the summer of 1788 he had come to regard Louis as an enlightened ruler who was anxious to play a crucial role in forging political alliances between the nobility and the members of the Third Estate. (In the end Louis XVI turned out to be like George III, fated to do precisely the wrong thing at just the right time, what Jefferson called "a machine for making revolutions.") But his fondest hopes for the recovery of political stability rested with the group of moderate and enlightened aristocrats, led by his good friend Lafayette, called the Patriots or the Patriot Party. Although he was prepared to acknowledge that the situations were fundamentally different, Jefferson seemed to regard the Patriots in France as counterparts to the Federalists in America; they were "sensible of the abusive government under which they lived, longed for occasions of reforming it" and were dedicated to "the establishment of a constitution which shall assure . . . a good degree of liberty." Lafayette was cast in the role of a French Madison, orchestrating the essential compromises among the different factions and thereby consolidating the energies of the revolution within a political framework that institutionalized the maximum gains that historical circumstances would allow.[86]

Jefferson was prepared to recognize that those circumstances were not ideal. The deeply rooted class divisions of French society were on display during the debates within the Estates-General that he attended in May and June 1789, as were the still-powerful legacies of feudalism, which had all but vanished in America but in Versailles took on the highly virulent and visible form of costumed lords and courtly processions. Given these entrenched impediments to a fully flowered revolution along American lines, Jefferson advised his friends in the Patriot Party to settle for the English constitutional model, supplemented by one important American addition—that is, he recommended the retention of the French monarchy, though with vastly reduced powers, the creation of a bicameral legislature with the upper chamber reserved for the clergy and nobility and—the American contribution—the insistence on a declaration of rights that protected basic liberties from violation by kings, lords or even elected legislators. Characteristically, he devoted most of his time and energy to drafting the Charter of Rights, which called for the abolition of all pecuniary privileges and exemptions enjoyed by the nobility, civilian rule over the military, equal treatment under the law and a modified version of freedom of the press. With France as with America, his fondest political topic was not the artful arrangement of government power but rather the cordoning off of a region where no government power could exist. He conveyed his draft to Lafayette in June 1789; it served as the basis for the Declaration of Rights that Lafayette presented to the National Assembly the following month.[87]

By that time Jefferson was confident that the danger of disintegration and violent revolution had been averted. "The great crisis being now over," he wrote to Jay, "I shall not have a matter interesting enough to trouble you with as often as I have lately." The Estates-General had not taken his advice and established a separate chamber for the clergy and nobility, but enough of the privileged classes had gone over to the Third Estate to make the newly established National Assembly a representative, if somewhat unwieldy, body. Nevertheless, as he explained to Tom Paine on July 11, 1789, the French Revolution was effectively over. "The National *assembly* (for that is the name they take) . . . are now in complete and undisputed possession of sovereignty. The executive and the aristocracy are now at their feet. The mass of the nation, the mass of the clergy, and the army are with them. They have prostrated the old government, and are now beginning to build one from the foundation."[88]

The following day Paris exploded in a series of riots and mob actions that have been memorialized in countless histories, novels and films on the French Revolution: the assault on the Customs House; the stoning and eventual massacre of the royal cavalry; the storming of the Bastille and subsequent beheading and dismemberment of its garrison. After five days of random violence and massive demonstrations, Jefferson described to Jay the scene as Louis XVI returned to the capital, with Lafayette at his side, to be greeted by "about 60,000 citizens of all forms and conditions armed with the muskets of the Bastille and . . . pistols, swords, pikes, pruning hooks, sythes, etc." and all shouting "vive la nation."[89]

If one were to conjure up a scene designed to weaken Jefferson's faith in the inherent benevolence of popular movements or to shake his apparent serenity toward popular rebellions, one could hardly do better. Therefore it is worth noting that, though shocked at first by the random and savage character of the mob violence, he never questioned his belief in the essential rightness of the cause or the ultimate triumph of its progressive principles. His letters to Jay and Madison described the carnage of July 1789 as an unfortunate but temporary aberration that in no way called into question the prospect for an enduring and peaceful political settlement. He seemed to regard the spasm of violence as the product of a misguided decision by the king or his ministers to increase the troop strength in the city rather than as ominous evidence of deep and irreconcilable class resentments. By early August, in fact, he was convinced that the storm (shades of

Shays's Rebellion) had passed and the future looked clear and bright: "Quiet is so well established here that I think there is nothing further to be apprehended. The harvest is so near that there is nothing to fear from the want of bread. The National assembly are wise, firm and moderate. They will establish the English constitution, purged of its numerous and capital defects."[90]

It was in this brave and buoyant mood that Jefferson sat down on September 6, 1789, to write what has subsequently proved to be one of the most famous letters in his vast correspondence. "The course of reflection in which we are immersed here on the elementary principles of society," he explained to Madison, "has presented the question to my mind." The question itself was not entirely new. It was "Whether one generation of men has a right to bind another," which Jefferson claimed had implications that had not been sufficiently appreciated in either Europe or America. His answer to the question had the kind of unequivocal ring that he normally reserved for documents like the Declaration of Independence. "I set out on this ground," he announced, "which I suppose to be self-evident, *that the earth belongs in usufruct to the living.*"

Exactly what Jefferson meant by this proposition has been the subject of endless debate among historians for some time. In the letter itself Jefferson seemed to be advocating some version of generational sovereignty. "We seem not to perceive," as he put it to Madison, "that, by the law of nature, one generation is to another as one independent nation is to another." He produced elaborate calculations based on Buffon's demographic tables to show that, on average, a generation lasted about nineteen years. It therefore followed from the principle—"the earth belongs always to the living generations"—that all personal and national debts, all laws, even all constitutions, should expire after that time.[91]

Madison, always the gentle critic of Jeffersonian ideas, complimented Jefferson on his "interesting reflections," then proceeded to demolish the idea of generational sovereignty, which was not really an idea at all, he suggested, but rather a dangerous fantasy. In the course of presenting his argument, Jefferson had asked Madison to imagine "a whole generation of men to be born on the same day, to attain mature age on the same day, and to die on the same day." Here, Madison observed not so diplomatically, was the chief clue that Jefferson was engaged in magic more than political philosophy. For there is not, and never can be, a generation in Jefferson's pure sense of the term. Generational cohorts simply do not come into the world as discrete units. There is instead a seamless web of arrivals and departures, along with an analogous web of obligatory connections between past and present generations. These connections are not only unavoidable but absolutely essential for the continuation of civilized society.[92]

Madison did not say it, but the whole tenor of his response implied that Jefferson's letter was an inadvertent repudiation of all the painstaking work that he and his Federalist colleagues had been doing for the past two years. For Jefferson's idea (or, if you will, fantasy) struck at the very stability and long-term legality that the new Constitution was designed to assure. The notion that all laws, contractual obligations and hard-won constitutional precedents would lapse every nineteen or twenty years was a recipe for anarchy. Like Jefferson's earlier remark about wanting to see "a little rebellion now and then," which it seemed to echo, the generational argument struck Madison as an utterly irresponsible and positively dangerous example of indulged speculation and just the kind of abstract reasoning that gave French political thinkers a reputation for building castles in the air.[93]

As usual, Jefferson listened to Madison's advice. He never put forward his generational argument as a serious legislative proposal, and he refrained from ever mentioning the matter to Madison again. But whatever practical problems the idea posed, whatever its inadequacies as a realistic rationale for legal reform, he clung to it tenaciously, introducing it in conversations and letters for the rest of his life. If, as Madison had suggested, the core of the idea was incompatible with the way the world actually worked, it was compatible with the way Jefferson's mind worked. Indeed, there is no single statement in the vast literature by and about Jefferson that provides as clear and deep a look into his thinking about the way the world ought to work. The notion that "the earth belongs to the living" is in fact a many-faceted product of his political imagination that brings together in one place his essential obsessions and core convictions.

It therefore behooves us to ask when and how Jefferson acquired the idea. One can detect the first inkling in an earlier letter to Madison, describing his impressions of the French countryside around Fontainebleau in 1785. His encounter with a peasant woman led him, he told Madison, "into a train of reflections on that unequal division of property which occasions the numberless instances of wretchedness which I had observed in this country and is to be observed all over Europe." These reflections then led him to the conclusion that "the earth is given as a common stock for man to labour and live on. If, for the encouragement of industry we allow it to be appropriated, we must take care that other employment be furnished to those excluded from the appropriation. If we do not the fundamental right to labour the earth returns to the unemployed." What seems to be driving Jefferson's thinking here is a fresh appreciation of the entrenched poverty afflicting Europe's peasant class and the discrepancy between that near-hopeless condition and "the fundamental right to labour the earth." What seems to be the culprit are the accumulated inequities and inherited inadequacies, the dead hand of the Europeans past—in a word, feudalism.[94]

The next installment of the idea appears in Jefferson's correspondence with Lafayette between January and July 1789. The correspondence itself is an elliptical and elusive source per se, but its major topic, the drafting of a Declaration of Rights, prompted both men to think about what Lafayette called "the right of succeeding generations" (*le droit des générations qui se succèdent*), a phrase included in the proposed Declaration of Rights that Lafayette submitted to the National Assembly in July. At one level the phrase was designed to assure subsequent constitutional reform, in the form of either amendments or conventions of the sort pioneered by the new American states. At a deeper level the thinking behind the language suggested the need to anticipate posterity's independent appraisal of its own best interests. After all, the current French political crisis had been prompted by fiscal problems that now required the present generation to assume the accumulated debts of its predecessors. Inherent in the French political situation, in other words, was a heightened sensitivity toward the burdens the past imposed on the present, especially in the form of debt but also in the form of legacies like clerical and aristocratic privileges. Jefferson and Lafayette seemed to be groping toward built-in constitutional mechanisms that would relieve future generations from the same burdens.[95]

The final sighting of the idea—that is before it took its enduring form in the letter to Madison—occurs in August and early September 1789. On August 26, responding to Lafayette's request, Jefferson hosted a working dinner for eight leading members of the Patriot Party, who gathered to debate a looming vote in the National Assembly over whether the king should have a veto over acts of the legislature. It was a far-ranging discussion, which Jefferson described as "truly worthy of being placed in parallel with the finest dialogue of antiquity, as handed to us by Xenophon, by Plato, and Cicero." While there is no direct evidence that the subject of generational sovereignty came up, the gathering conveniently symbolizes the informal and ultimately untraceable way in which new ideas were circulating in revolutionary Paris. And though neither Tom Paine nor the Marquis de Condorcet was present at the dinner, both men were members of the Patriot Party and had proposed their own versions of the generational argument. Condorcet, France's premier mathematician as well as an outspoken republican, advocated a version of the generational argument strikingly similar to Jefferson's, complete with demographic tables and the same calculations about the life span of a generation. What's more, Condorcet was friends with and a patient of Dr. Richard Gem, a physician who treated Jefferson for one of his recurrent migraine headaches during the first week of September. We know that Gem and Jefferson discussed the question of posterity's rights and that Gem handed Jefferson a written statement on the matter that asserted the principle "that one generation of men in civil society have no right to make acts to bind another, is a truth that cannot be contested."[96]

Rather than become entangled in an endless argument about intellectual originality and primacy, it seems more sensible to bypass such unanswerable questions and conclude that Jefferson's thinking about the present generation's obligations to the future developed in revolutionary France, that his formulation of the idea was probably influenced by the specific dilemmas faced by the French government at the time and that the notion of generational sovereignty was "in the air" within the French salon culture, in much the same way that the core ideas of the natural rights section of the Declaration of Independence were "in the air" in the summer of 1776. The question then becomes: Why did Jefferson pluck this particular idea out of the air in 1789 and give it the exalted status of a newly discovered self-evident truth?

Two different but overlapping answers suggest themselves. First, Jefferson's enhanced apprehensions about the destructive potential of inherited debt had both a public and a private dimension that converged in his mind about this time. The outstanding debt of the United States had undercut his best efforts as minister to France and blocked his diplomatic initiative to negotiate treaties with other European powers. And the volatile political situation in revolutionary France had been triggered by a fiscal crisis created by a massive national debt. Moreover, his personal finances—the cost of his accommodations, clothing, furniture, horses and carriage, what he called his "outfit"—had far outdistanced his allotted salary and forced him into embarrassing exchanges with his superiors back in Philadelphia about the gap between his living costs and his ministerial stipend.

But the debt he was running up in Paris was just the tip of the proverbial iceberg. For by the late 1780s he began to become aware that the debts he had inherited from his father-in-law's estate were compounding at a rate that he might never be able to repay. It first began to dawn on him that despite owning thousands of acres and about two hundred slaves, he owed his creditors such vast amounts that he might go to his grave a debtor. This realization was almost as much a burden as the debts themselves. "The torment of mind I endure till the moment shall arrive when I shall not owe a shilling on earth," he wrote his overseer at Monticello in 1787, "is such really as to render life of little value here." He was, in effect, both intellectually and psychologically primed to appreciate what debt does to nations and to individuals and therefore open to ideas designed to limit the damage.[97]

Moreover, the doctrine of generational sovereignty was yet another version of his utopian radicalism. Madison was surely correct to declare the entire scheme wildly impractical and utterly incapable of implementation. But that was beside the point. For the vision of each generation starting from scratch, liberated from the accumulated legacies of past debts, laws, institutionalized obligations and regulations, allowed Jefferson to conjure up his fondest dream, a world where the primal meaning of independence could flourish without any restrictions, where innocence had not yet been corrupted. This was the world of the prefeudal Saxon settlers, the world of the prepolitical Indian tribes, the world of the independent yeoman farmer on the edge of the frontier, the world after a rightful rebellion has cleared the air. It was a wholly voluntary world, where coercion was unknown and government unnecessary. Though transient—history would begin to make its inevitable inroads almost immediately—the idyllic harmonies sustained themselves for that one brief, shining moment. It was therefore the proper place to house the memories of the affair with Maria Cosway (though not Cosway herself) and to preserve the feminine values she symbolized at the peak of their remembered perfection. The belief that "the earth belongs to the living," in short, was another blow struck in behalf of Jefferson's most cherished dream: a society devoid of contaminating institutions and laws; an effort to routinize their removal so that the deadening hand of history was regularly slapped away in order to make room for a pristine encounter with what he believed to be the natural order.

COMING HOME

JEFFERSON HAD BEEN anticipating his return to America throughout the winter and spring of 1789. Even before Washington's election as president, which everyone considered a foregone conclusion, Jefferson's name had been bandied about as a prospective member of the new administration. In May Madison reported these rumors, adding that "the most prominent figures" (who presumably included Washington himself) were taking him aside to ask whether an appointment in the new government would be agreeable to the current American minister to France. "Being *unacquainted with your mind*," Madison wrote in coded language, "I have not *ventured on an answer*." Jefferson did not receive Madison's letter until August, but he responded crisply and immediately: "You ask me if I would accept my appointment on that side the water? You know the circumstances which led me from retirement, step by step from one nomination to the other, up to the present. My object is to return to the same retirement." The answer, in short, was no. He did want to return to Virginia to deposit Patsy and Polly back in the safer surroundings of their native land. And he wanted to put his personal affairs at Monticello in order. But after a few months at home he expected to return to his post in Paris—there is no reason to doubt his sincerity on this score—and then retire from public service.[98]

His last letters from France are intriguingly contradictory on the question of the ongoing French political crisis. On the one hand, he reiterated his optimism. "Tranquillity is pretty generally restored in this country," he explained, "and the National Assembly are going on well in forming their constitution. It will be difficult for them to form one which will appear the best possible to every mind but they will form a good one, in which liberty and property are placed on a surer footing than they are in England. I imagine they will be two or three months engaged in this business." He was prepared to recognize the existence within the National Assembly of a mischievous faction "with very dangerous views." But they should be easily overwhelmed because "the mass of the nation [is] so solidly united, that they seem to have abandoned all expectations of confusing the game."[99]

On the other hand, to a few correspondents he was more circumspect. "The crisis of this country is not yet over," he wrote to David Ramsay of South Carolina. "Should the want of bread begin a tumult, the consequences cannot be foreseen, because the leaven of other causes will rise with the fermentation." The mood of his letters to Jay was simultaneously upbeat and cautious. He expected the Patriot Party to dominate the National Assembly, thereby exerting a moderating effect on the extremists and leading France to stability as a constitutional monarchy. But there were some less attractive scenarios. If bread riots began in Paris, or the fiscal crisis worsened, or the king lost his nerve and attempted to flee Versailles, it would "be the signal of a St. Barthelemi [i.e., a massacre] against the aristocrats in Paris. . . ." With Jay at least, his official superior in charge of American foreign affairs, he was hedging his bets.[100]

The long trek back to Monticello began on September 28, 1789. Bad weather trapped him at Le Havre for two weeks, long enough to attract the attention of one fellow traveler, who described an attractive scene in which Jefferson waited out the weather with Patsy and Polly gathered around him, reading out loud to their father while he helped Polly pronounce difficult words. As they waited for the ship that would carry them to England and eventual passage to America, three different correspondents were writing him with important news: Maria Cosway bade him farewell, saying a bad cold prevented a final rendezvous in England; William Short reported from Paris that bread riots had broken out there and a mob of five thousand women was marching on Versailles; and George Washington wrote to offer him the post of America's first secretary of state.[101]

3

MONTICELLO: 1794–97

He built for himself at Monticello a château above contact with man. The rawness of political life was an incessant torture to him, and personal attacks made him keenly unhappy. . . . He shrank from whatever was rough or coarse, and his yearning for sympathy was almost feminine.

—HENRY ADAMS
History of the United States
During the Administrations of Thomas Jefferson
(1889–91)

From 1793 to 1797 I remained closely at home, saw none but those who came here, and at length became very sensible of the ill effect it had on my own mind. . . . I felt enough of the effect of withdrawing from the world then, to see that it led to an antisocial and misanthropic state of mind, which severely punishes him who gives in to it. And it will be a lesson I never shall forget as to myself.

—JEFFERSON TO MARIA JEFFERSON EPPES
MARCH 3, 1802

MONTICELLO WAS ALWAYS the preferred destination in Jefferson's imagination, but the American Revolution intervened, then the diplomatic mission in Paris, then the secretary of state responsibilities in the Washington administration. But by January 1794, at long last, he was finally convinced that his public career was over. "I hope to spend the remainder of my days," he declared, "in occupations infinitely more pleasing than those to which I have sacrificed 18 years of the prime of my life." In truth, at fifty-one years of age, he believed that the prime of his life was over and that he was considerably closer to the end than the beginning. For more than a year he had been pleading with Washington to release him from political duties so that he might live out his time as a farmer: "I am every day convinced that neither my talents, tone of mind, nor time of life fit me for public life."[1]

Incantations of virtuous retirement to rural solitude after a career of public service were familiar and even formulaic refrains within the leadership class of eighteenth-century America, none more so than within the Virginia dynasty. Everyone knew the classical models of latter-day seclusion represented by Cicero and Cincinnatus and the hymns to pastoral splendor in Virgil's *Georgics*. Declarations of principled withdrawal from the hurly-burly of political life to the natural rhythms of one's farm were so commonplace that John Adams, an aspiring Cicero himself, but also an inveterate skeptic about anyone else's pronouncements of rural virtue, had begun to doubt the entire Ciceronian syndrome. "It seems the Mode of becoming great is to retire," he wrote Abigail. "It is marvellous how political Plants grow in the shade." Adams was not referring specifically to Jefferson, but other Federalist critics were letting out the word in Philadelphia that the outgoing secretary of state was merely going home to lick his wounds, storing up his energies for the inevitable assault on the presidency, posturing as the retired farmer.[2]

But Jefferson was not posing. He confided to the ever-discreet Madison—it was an uncharacteristically candid confession—that he had once felt "the little spice of ambition, which I had in my younger days," but these internal urgings "had long since evaporated, and I set still less store by a posthumous than present fame." All he wanted in the time that remained to him, he told Angelica Church, was "to be liberated from the hated occupations of politics, and to remain in the bosom of my family, my farm, and my books." Until now Monticello had been a mirage that kept receding into the middle distance of his life. Now he was suddenly there himself. "I have my house to build, my fields to farm, and"—an intriguingly dutiful way to put it—"to watch for the happiness of those who labor for mine."

One of his black servants, this time Robert Hemings rather than Jupiter, was dutifully waiting at Fredericksburg with fresh horses on January 12, 1794, and the two rode together toward the foothills of the Blue Ridge and home. "The length of my tether is now fixed for life between Monticello and Richmond," Jefferson announced two weeks later. Ensconced on his mountaintop, he apprised Adams that the rural rhythms were already taking hold: "I put off answering my letters now, farmer-like, till a rainy day." He claimed to have become "thoroughly weened from newspapers and politics" and was pleased to "find my mind totally absorbed in my rural occupations."[3]

Perhaps the most palpable source of his resolution to retire was age. Having crossed over to the far side of the half century mark, he could not reasonably expect his good luck with health would continue that much longer. The biblical "three score and ten" left him only slightly more than a decade, and he had no way of knowing that, unlike his father and mother, he would defy the odds and make octogenarian. The first dents in his cast-iron constitution had in fact begun to appear in the form of soreness in his joints, which progressed to a severe case of rheumatism by the summer of 1794 and kept him on his back for two weeks. "I begin to feel the effects of age," he noted the following year, adding that this body was sending him signals "which give me to believe I shall not have much to encounter of the *tedium vitae*." The reddish blond hair was still full, though graying; the lean and somewhat long face still had the burnished glow of an outdoorsman, though it was now more weathered and creased at the edges of the eyes; the body was still taut and athletic in a slender way, still carried itself in that ramrod-straight posture, though the joints in his wrists and knees now tended to flare up in damp or cold weather. All in all, he still looked younger than his years, still could keep his seat on the largest and most spirited horses, still rose at dawn and worked sixteen-hour days without naps or rest periods, still projected in his regimen the vigorous image of a young country whose future lay before it. But his personal future—he now literally felt it in his bones—had a more limited duration. He wanted to spend the time that was left to him in his own private pursuits of happiness.[4]

All this would have been sufficient by itself to propel Jefferson out of public life, galloping with Robert Hemings down the road from Fredericksburg to Charlottesville and then up to his mountaintop. An essential part of him, as he himself acknowledged, never felt comfortable exercising political power or participating in the contentious debates that representative government seemed to require. Unlike Adams, who regarded an argument as the ideal form of a conversation, or Franklin, who had the capacity to float above the political infighting on the basis of seniority and wit, or Washington, who was already regarded as atop the American Olympus and therefore untouchable, Jefferson felt every criticism personally. Clashing opinions or arguments struck him as dissonant noise and therefore a crude refutation of the natural harmonies he believed in and heard inside himself. In a sense, his retirement to private life in 1794 was a long-delayed recognition that as a public figure he had always been miscast.

But no matter how sufficient these long-standing conditions might have been in theory, history had seen fit to double his dose of political anguish in practice by contriving to make the 1790s one of the most rancorous and disputatious decades in American history. From the time Jefferson assumed the duties of secretary of state in 1790 until he escaped Philadelphia in 1794, he was a central player in an ongoing political drama that proved to be more intense, almost to the point of paranoia, than any experience in his public life. He suffered psychic wounds during his time in the Washington administration that never completely healed. And he dispensed political invective of his own, or rather had surrogates do it in his behalf, that made him the chief symbol of opposition to the government in which he served. Whether the times changed him or merely marked him is an interesting question. But there is no question he emerged from the experience speaking a more distinctly partisan political language that was just beginning to be associated on a national level with his name. If we are to understand the heart and the head of the middle-aged man so eager to sequester himself at Monticello, we need to know a bit more about what had happened to him in the political world from which he was escaping.[5]

PASSIONS AND PARTIES

JEFFERSON'S TENURE as secretary of state coincided with the most uncharted era in American political history. Precisely because the new national government was new, every major decision set a precedent and every initiative in domestic or foreign policy threatened to establish a landmark principle. The distinguishing feature of the new Constitution was its purposeful ambiguity about the relationship between federal and state jurisdiction and about the overlapping authority of the respective branches of the federal government. The Constitution, in short, did not resolve the long-standing political disagreements that existed within the revolutionary generation so much as establish a fresh and more stable context within which they could be argued out.

As Jefferson and all the other major participants in that debate understood it, nothing less was at stake than the true meaning of the American Revolution. And since Jefferson had been serving in France throughout the latter half of the 1780s, when the first battles to define the positive powers of the federal government were waged, he entered the debates of the 1790s with his revolutionary values more intact than most of his colleagues, who had already concluded that securing the Revolution required compromises with political power at the national level that he was ideologically and psychologically unprepared to make.[6]

The most novel and wholly unforeseen development of the era was the emergence of political parties. Not that modern-day political parties, with their mechanisms for raising money, selecting candidates and waging election campaigns, were fully formed in the 1790s. (Full-scale political parties with all the institutional accouterments we associate with the term date from the 1830s and 1840s.) Nevertheless, what we might call the "makings" of political parties originated during Jefferson's time as secretary of state, and he had a crucial role in their creation. The trouble was that the term "party," and the very idea for which it stood, had yet to achieve any measure of respectability. A "party," as the term was commonly understood, was nothing more than a "faction," meaning an organized minority whose very purpose was to undercut the public will, usually by devious and corrupt means. To call someone a member of a political party was to accuse him of systematic selfishness and perhaps even outright treason. The modern notion of a legitimate organized opposition to the elected government did not exist. Indeed it would have struck most members of the revolutionary generation as a contradiction in terms.7

All this presented enormous intellectual and emotional problems for Jefferson, because along with Madison he established the rudiments of the Republican party between 1790 and 1794 and thereby created a discernible and organized alternative to the Federalists. To repeat, there were as yet no rules for what they were doing, no neutral vocabulary even for talking about it. In the eyes and minds of their Federalist critics, Jefferson and Madison were traitors, especially Jefferson, who actually served in the cabinet of the government he was opposing. This helps explain the vituperative and highly personal attacks on his character in the public press during those years; there was as yet no available language or mentality for a more detached interpretation of his behavior.

Sustaining this posture of organized but unofficial opposition required considerable confidence in one's political vision of what the American Revolution meant. It also required another quality that Jefferson had developed during his French phase, what might be called a cultivated tolerance for inconsistency that others might perceive as deception or hypocrisy. For as a titular party leader in an age when political parties were still anathema, Jefferson was forced to mislead and conceal on several occasions, and his success at doing so depended on his psychological agility, his canny manipulation of different voices and personae, on his capacity to play hide-and-seek within himself.

Finally, during the early 1790s the long-standing relationship between Jefferson and Madison reached a new level of collaboration, so much so that it is sometimes impossible to know where the thoughts of one end and the other begins. John Quincy Adams put it nicely when he observed that "the mutual influence of these two mighty minds upon each other is a phenomenon, like the invisible and mysterious movements of the magnet in the physical world, and in which the sagacity of the future historian may discover the solution of much of our national history not otherwise easily accountable." The habits of confidentiality and the experience at communicating in coded letters that the two men had established when Jefferson was in France served them well in the 1790s, when they teamed up to oppose the fiscal policies of Alexander Hamilton and began to develop the foundations for an opposition party. It is not quite fair to Madison's intelligence and leadership skills to regard him as the junior partner or as Jefferson's ever-willing surrogate in the political infighting that Jefferson found so offensive. In fact, during the early phases of the battle with Hamilton, from 1790 to 1792, Madison actually led the fight, especially against Hamilton's funding scheme and proposal for a national bank.[8]

But in general it seems fair to concur with those Federalists who considered Madison the "General" and Jefferson the "Generalissimo" of the emergent Republican opposition. Jefferson was the psychological superior and senior member of the team. He orchestrated the strategy and Madison implemented the tactics. Jefferson could afford to emphasize the broadest contours of a political problem because Madison was silently handling the messier specifics. (If God was in the details, so the story went, Madison was usually there to greet Him upon arrival.) The advantages of this arrangement were obvious: It placed an extremely talented spokesman at the point of attack while allowing Jefferson to remain behind the scenes and above the fray.

But there were also some less obvious disadvantages: It gave cre-

dence to the charge that Jefferson was a devious manipulator who
played cowardly games with the truth. While his defenders could and
did characterize his famous craving for personal privacy as a function
of shyness or discretion, claiming that "the boldness of his mind was
sheathed in a scabbard of politeness," even Dumas Malone, his most
admiring biographer, has been forced to acknowledge that during the
party wars of the 1790s Jefferson frequently crossed that dim line
between "courtesy and deception." More critical commentators date
his reputation as a mysterious and not-so-admirable version of the
American Sphinx from this phase of his career. "He did not always
speak exactly as he felt," wrote Charles Francis Adams, "either towards
his friends or his enemies. As a consequence, he has left hanging over a
part of his public life a vapor of duplicity . . . , the presence of which is
generally felt more than it is seen." Despite Madison's heroic efforts to
shield him from criticism, indeed in part because those efforts raised
questions about where Jefferson himself stood, most of the unfriendly
assessments of Jefferson's elusive personality originated in the superheated political climate of the 1790s. Here his character became controversial.[9]

So were his priorities and policies as secretary of state. In the wake
of Jefferson's retirement James Monroe sent him a consoling letter,
assuring his mentor that "notwithstanding the important and even tur-
bulent scenes you have passed through [you have] not only the approbation of your own heart, and of your countrymen generally, but the
silence and of course the constrained approbation of your enemies."
This seems a plausible if somewhat partisan appraisal.[10]

Jefferson helped launch American foreign policy in a direction that
served national purposes tolerably well throughout the next century.
He shared with the other major figures, especially Washington, Adams
and Hamilton, the fundamental recognition that the chief task facing
the young republic was internal and domestic, stabilizing the freshly
created political institutions and consolidating control over the North
American continent. This meant steering clear of European conflicts at
almost any cost and providing time and space for the emergent Ameri-

can national economy to develop its still-nascent potential. Despite bitter partisan fights over how to implement these foreign policy principles, not to mention the complete collapse of agreement over the relative threats posed by English or French challenges to American neutrality, the principles themselves remained a matter of consensus throughout the top reaches of the government. Jefferson was frequently accused, for good reason, of harboring pro-French sympathies that distorted his version of American neutrality. But the French minister, Pierre Adet, offered the most perceptive appraisal of Jefferson's deepest sympathies. "Mr. Jefferson likes us," wrote Adet, "because he detests England . . . , but he might change his opinion of us tomorrow, if tomorrow Great Britain should cease to inspire his fears. . . . Jefferson, I say, is American and, as such, he cannot be sincerely our friend. An American is the born enemy of all the European peoples." This shrewdly accurate assessment provides the fairest gloss on his overall goals as secretary of state, which were to negotiate American interests forcefully while avoiding any version of partisanship that might lead to war.[11]

That said, Adet's observation that Jefferson truly detested England was also demonstrably true. Indeed Jefferson's palpable hatred of all things English (except perhaps their gardens) colored his entire performance as secretary of state and on several occasions came perilously close to causing a breakdown in Anglo-American relations. In the Nootka Sound crisis of 1790, for example, when an incidental flare-up between England and Spain near present-day Vancouver threatened to provoke war throughout the entire trans-Mississippi West, Jefferson took an especially belligerent stand toward English designs on the region that risked war with England until the crisis fizzled away. In his negotiations with George Hammond, the British minister charged with resolving the long-standing differences over the terms of the Treaty of Paris, Jefferson was particularly wooden and unbending, almost constitutionally incapable of the kind of diplomatic demeanor that came so naturally to him in other contexts. And in 1793 his exhaustive report on American trade policy as a neutral nation recommended retaliatory tariffs against England that were economically suicidal and depended on a belief in American economic prowess vis-à-vis England that verged on sheer hallucination. The mere mention of England, it was clear, tapped some reservoir of hatred buried within the deeper folds of his personality that made diplomatic detachment almost impossible.[12]

The deepest sources of that hatred must remain a matter of speculation. It is worth recalling, for example, that he had launched his national career by drafting a bill of indictment against George III and added a wholesale condemnation of the English people; these were so vitriolic that his colleagues on the Continental Congress had seen fit to tone down the former and wholly delete the latter. (What others regarded as justifiable propaganda had always seemed to him the literal, indeed self-evident truth.) Had not George III confirmed that the loathing was mutual by ceremoniously turning his back on him and Adams before the entire English court? Before that Cornwallis's soldiers had burned his crops, carried off his livestock and slit the throats of those animals they could not take with them. During his Paris years he had also been exposed to the routinized arrogance of the English press, which seemed incapable of digesting the awkward fact that the American colonies had actually won their war for independence.

But English delusions were also symptomatic of what Jefferson saw as a palpable threat—namely, England's willingness to use its formidable economic and military power to thwart and perhaps even reverse the larger process set in motion by the American Revolution. Were not those English troops still stationed on America's western frontier an explicit statement of harmful intentions and England's prevailing hope that its former colonies might one day be reconquered? Was not English commercial policy, so implacably resistant to Jeffersonian pleas for free trade and so smugly confident of its hegemony in the world markets, evidence of a blatant English attempt to recolonize their former American empire? Finally, to top it off and make it deeply personal, did not he, along with a sizable portion of Virginia's planter class, still find himself deeply in debt to English and Scottish creditors, who were busy compounding the interest on those debts at rates that made personal independence increasingly problematic? It was a galling thought, but in fact was it not the case that he, Thomas Jefferson, who had done so much to make and shape the American Revolution, remained maddeningly subservient to British authority?[13]

Any effort to disentangle the personal from the public reasons for his Anglophobia, or perhaps his psychological from his ideological motives, would be a frustrating and ultimately futile task. Perhaps the best way to put it is that England was one subject on which his head and his heart saw no reason for debate. At the level of foreign policy, history eventually proved him wrong, as the Anglo-American alliance and the protection of the British fleet substantially assisted the maturation of the fledgling American nation throughout the nineteenth century. And his presumption that England was already on the downslope of history took a decisive blow in the unparalleled projection of English values during the Victorian era. But his instinctive sense that there was still unfinished business between England and America was shrewd; it was confirmed by the War of 1812. And his fear that England still contemplated the recovery of its lost American empire, while exaggerated, was a plausible apprehension that appears less credible to us now only because we have the advantage of knowing it did not happen.

A similar mixture of personal and public reasons shaped his affection for France and frequently gave his definition of American neutrality a decidedly French accent. What Jefferson called "fair neutrality" meant an American foreign policy that recognized the crucial role France had played as America's European ally during the American Revolution and the abiding obligations incurred in the Franco-American Treaty of 1778. He was successful in persuading Washington that American treaty obligations were made with the French nation, not with any particular government or individual, so that the execution of Louis XVI in 1793, then the bloody procession of shifting political factions that assumed power in revolutionary France, must not be used as an excuse to abandon the alliance. Though controversial at the time, and actively opposed by Hamilton and the so-called High Federalists, Jefferson's judgment appears sound in retrospect. But his posture toward the French minister, Edmond Genêt, was the mirror image of his attitude toward England's George Hammond, almost endlessly patient and infinitely forgiving, willing to tolerate Genêt's brazen meddling in American domestic politics and his apparent delusion that he was actually empowered to overrule the president of the United States. Even when Jefferson eventually decided to break with Genêt in August 1793, his motives were explicitly political and domestic. "I saw the necessity of quitting a wreck," he informed Madison, "which could not but sink all who would cling to it."[14]

Even Genêt's hopelessly arrogant behavior failed to destroy Jefferson's deep-rooted Gallic sympathies, which had their foundation in much more than his famous fondness for French cooking and Parisian architecture. These sympathies manifested themselves most tellingly in his almost casual endorsement of the horrific excesses then sweeping the French Revolution toward Jacobin rule and the Terror. "The tone of your letters had for some time given me pain," he apprised William Short, who had written from Paris about the murderous behavior of the mobs and the complete breakdown of social order. Jefferson then delivered a lecture on the human cost that sometimes must be paid when history is on the march: "The liberty of the whole earth was depending on the issue of the contest, and was ever such a prize won with so little blood? My own affections have been deeply wounded by some of the martyrs to this cause, but rather than it should have failed I would have seen half the earth desolated. Were there but an Adam and an Eve left in every country, and left free, it would be better than it is now."[15] Such an extreme version of what might be called revolutionary realism, which conjures up comparisons to the twentieth-century radicals in the Lenin or Mao mold, exposes a chilling side of Jefferson's character that seems so thoroughly incongruous with his temperament and so resolutely ideological. But his casual response to the atrocities of the French Revolution was in fact an integral part of a rather rarefied but deeply felt sense of where history was headed.

The main outlines of the picture he carried about in his mind's eye had been congealing ever since his Paris years. It envisioned the American Revolution as merely the opening shot in a global struggle that was eventually destined to sweep over the world. "This ball of liberty, I believe most piously," he informed one correspondent in a typical formulation, "is now so well in motion that it will roll around the globe." American independence from England was only the initial political manifestation of a much broader and more thoroughgoing process of liberation that would follow naturally, though obviously not without violent opposition, as the last vestiges of feudalism and monarchy were destroyed and swept into the dustbin of history. The book that best captured the essence of the Jeffersonian vision was Tom Paine's *The Rights of Man* (1791), which Jefferson had enthusiastically endorsed in its American edition and which created a sensation for its verbal flair in describing "the spirit of '76" and "the spirit of '89" as twin expressions of the same liberal impulse. From Jefferson's perspective, therefore, the rather striking differences between the American and French revolutions were insignificant incidentals—on this score Adams thought he was either blissfully ignorant or temporarily insane—when compared with their common purpose. Likewise, he believed that the random violence and careening course of the French Revolution were part of a lamentable but passing chapter in a larger story of triumphant global revolution. All specific decisions about American foreign policy needed to be informed by this overarching, almost cosmic pattern. In practice this meant, as it usually did for Jefferson, fitting the intricate complexities of foreign policy into a simple moral dichotomy. This one cast England in the role of counterrevolutionary villain and France in the role of revolutionary hero.[16]

Meanwhile his international vision had a discernible domestic analogue. After about a year of reasonably congenial political cooperation within Washington's cabinet, Jefferson began to articulate a view of American politics that was also moralistic in tone and populated with clearly delineated villains and heroes. The immediate cause of this change was Alexander Hamilton, or rather the combination of his offensive policies as secretary of the treasury and irritatingly imperial personality. Jefferson and Hamilton had quickly emerged as the dominant figures in Washington's cabinet. (John Adams, who might have been expected to carry equivalent weight, was shuttled to the side because of his vice presidential duties in the Senate, prompting him to observe that he occupied "the most insignificant office that ever the invention of man contrived or his imagination conceived," the first in a litany of colorful complaints by subsequent occupants of the post.) In what became known as "the dinner table bargain," Jefferson and Hamilton joined together in June 1790—Madison was present too and actually the chief negotiator—in order to forge a compromise that gave Hamilton sufficient votes in the Congress for passage of his proposal to have the federal government assume all outstanding state debts. This policy operated against the interests of Virginia, which had already retired the bulk of its debt, so Hamilton offered his support for a commitment to locate the national capital on the Potomac ten years hence. But the dinner table bargain proved to be the last bipartisan agreement between the two cabinet leaders. Jefferson was soon confessing that he had been "duped" by Hamilton and "made a tool for forwarding his schemes, not then sufficiently understood by me; and of all the errors of my political life, this has occasioned me the deepest regret." Throughout the remainder of their time in the government Jefferson and Hamilton were engaged in a bitter fight for the ear and mind of Washington and for what each man regarded as the very soul of the American republic.[17]

Although the deeper sources of the conflict were profoundly ideological, it also had a decidedly personal edge. Hamilton was the kind of man who might have been put on earth by God to refute all the Jeffersonian values. Dashing and direct in his demeanor, Hamilton possessed all the confidence of a military leader accustomed to command, just the kind of explicit exercise of authority Jefferson found so irritating. While perhaps rooted in Hamilton's military exploits as an officer on Washington's staff during the Revolutionary War (another heroic experience Jefferson could not claim), this palpable projection of authority called attention to its own brilliance in a style that was reminiscent of Patrick Henry's oratory, which Jefferson also mistrusted for its ostentation. Like Henry, Hamilton was a youthful prodigy of impoverished origins—John Adams later called him "a bastard brat of a Scotch pedlar"—whose visible craving for greatness violated the understated code of the true Virginia aristocrat. To make matters worse, Hamilton as an opponent was equally formidable on his feet and in print. Jefferson recalled his clashes with Hamilton in cabinet meetings as a form of martyrdom and warned Madison to draft all newspaper attacks against Hamilton personally, claiming that Hamilton was "a host within himself. . . ." Capable of mastering massive amounts of detail and tossing off sophisticated political essays against a tight deadline, Hamilton's mind projected relentless energy rather than Jeffersonian serenity. It also tended to begin with a palpable and practical problem—how to assault a British position, ratify a constitution or develop a national economy—then reason toward the overarching principles that provided the solution. Jefferson's mind moved along the same arc but in the opposite direction, from principled ideals to specific contexts or problems. This meant that Jefferson's disappointments occurred when reality failed to measure up to his expectations; Hamilton's occurred when his realistic proposals struck others as totally devoid of principle. Jefferson appeared to his enemies as an American version of Candide; Hamilton as an American Machiavelli.[18]

These mutual and highly personal animosities became matters of public record starting in 1792, when Hamilton and his followers, writing under several pseudonyms (i.e., Catullus and Scourge), attacked Jefferson in the press for his pro-French sympathies, his shifting position on the Constitution and the elusive core of his character: "Cautious and shy," wrote Hamilton, "wrapped up in impenetrable silence and mystery, he [Jefferson] reserves his *abhorrence* for the arcana of a certain snug sanctuary, where seated on his pivot chair, and involved in all the obscurity of political mystery and deception . . . he circulates his poison thro' the medium of the *National Gazette*." The final reference was to an anti-Hamilton newspaper edited by Philip Freneau, whom Jefferson had hired as a translator at the State Department in order to subsidize his editorial efforts against the government, all the while claiming that the arrangement violated no conflict of interest principles known to him. Meanwhile the Hamiltonians kept blazing away at the so-called Generalissimo of the opposition party, in the process providing the most scathing attack on Jefferson's career and character ever put before the public: "Had an inquisitive mind in those days sought for evidence of his Abilities as a Statesman, he would have been referred to the confusions in France, the offspring of certain political dogmas fostered by the American Minister, and to certain theoretical principles fit only for Utopia. As a Warrior, to his Exploits at *Monticelli;* as a Philosopher, to his discovery of the inferiority of Blacks to Whites, because they are more unsavory and secrete more by the kidnies; as a Mathematician, to his whirligig Chair."[19]

Apart from Freneau, Jefferson's chief defenders were all Virginians: the ever-loyal Madison and Monroe, plus the young congressman William Branch Giles, whom Jefferson encouraged to launch an official, though trumped-up, investigation of Hamilton's financial improprieties as secretary of the treasury. Jefferson himself never entered the public debate, always preferring to work through surrogates, and he was so skillful at covering his tracks that the extent of his involvement in the Giles investigation was not discovered for almost two hundred years.[20]

Beneath the purely personal animus between the two different-minded and temperamentally incompatible cabinet members, Jefferson and Hamilton had become convenient symbols for a more fundamental ideological division. By 1792 Jefferson was referring to the Federalist leadership as "monarchists," "tories," "anti-republicans" and the supporters of Hamilton's fiscal policies as "monocrats," "stock-jobbers" and "paper men." The story that was taking shape in Jefferson's mind assumed the contours of a plot to reverse the course of the American Revolution, with the chief characters on the other side cast as villainous conspirators covertly commanded by the diabolical secretary of the treasury, whom he described to Washington as "a man whose history, from the moment at which history can stoop to notice him, is a tissue of machinations against the liberty of the country which has . . . heaped its honors on his head." The hatred was palpable.[21]

Historians who have studied this volatile moment in Jefferson's career and in the political history of the early republic, searching for a way to render plausible what to the modern ear sounds obsessive and almost paranoid, have described it as a fresh application of the same Whig ideology he had brandished so successfully against the English ministry in the 1760s and 1770s. There is much to be said for this interpretation, which has the virtue of linking his earlier obsessions with English political corruption to his equally obsessive hatred of Hamilton's financial program and the Hamiltonian vision of a proactive national government, which Jefferson purportedly regarded as the latter-day apparition of a political dragon he thought he had slain in 1776. This way of understanding Jefferson's hyperbolic rhetoric in the 1790s—as a recurrence of the Country Party fears of the American Revolution—also has the virtue of undercutting criticism of his apparent extremism in the political crusade against Hamilton. For if one is going to question Jefferson's sanity in the 1790s, does that not then cast aspersions on his equivalently polemical assaults on George III during the most gloriously patriotic moment in American history?[22]

Jefferson was not—let us be clear and emphatic on this point—a mentally unstable person or a man with latent paranoid tendencies. The conspiratorial character of his political thinking in the 1790s, as all scholars of the Whig ideology have reminded us, was a common feature of the political literature of the time, and substantial traces of the same feverish mentality can be found in the private correspondence of the entire political leadership, including Adams, Madison and Hamilton. (Only Washington seems to have remained immune, but then he was immune to everything.) Unless one is prepared to make sweeping psychiatric charges against the vanguard members of the entire revolutionary generation, which is generally credited with being the most intellectually gifted group of political leaders in American history, then psychiatric appraisals of Jefferson himself should be recognized as both misleading and unfair. The leading scholar of the revolutionary era has also reminded us that conspiracy theories not only were prevalent ways of thinking and talking about political events by mainstream as well as marginal figures but also provided a secular way of explaining baffling social changes in terms that improved upon previous resorts to fate, providence or God's will.[23]

That said, Jefferson's simplistic and highly moralistic rendering of what the Federalists and especially the Hamiltonians were doing merits a moment of meditation, if for no other reason than the Country Party interpretation does not do full justice to the way Jefferson's mind actually worked. Perhaps the best way to put it is that because he began with a purer and more intensely idealistic conception of the levels of individual freedom possible in this world, especially after the final vestiges of kingly and clerical power had been blown away, Jefferson harbored a more acute sensitivity toward the explicit exercise of government power than any other member of the revolutionary generation. Because the primary colors of his political imagination were black and white, there were no shaded hues, no middle-range way stations where his apprehensions about the oppressive effects of political power could rest more comfortably once threats to his utopian goals materialized. Hamilton's plans for a proactive federal government empowered to shape markets and set both the financial and political agendas were certainly not monarchical in character—if anything, they were more a precocious precursor of twentieth-century New Deal values than an archaic attempt to resuscitate the arbitrary authority of medieval kings and courts—but in Jefferson's mind these distinctions made no appreciable difference. Energetic governmental power of any sort was intolerable because it originated outside the individual; it therefore violated his romantic ideal of personal autonomy. George III's edicts and Parliament's taxation policies, it is true, elicited the same fears back in the 1760s and 1770s. But Hamilton did not just conjure up bad memories of English oppression; he directly threatened the primal core of Jefferson's wistful world.[24]

In addition, Jefferson's emerging sense of himself as the leader of the Country Party assumed a distinctively Jeffersonian flavor that was different from the original English meaning of the term, for the rather obvious reason that "Country" meant different things for him than for a resident of Walpolian England. When he was asked to describe the social composition of the two parties, for example, his list of "anti-republicans" consisted of former loyalists and tories, American merchants trading with England, stock speculators and banking officials, federal employees and other office seekers and—an all-purpose psychological category—"nervous persons, whose languid fibres have more analogy with a passive than active state of things." The list of "republicans," on the other hand, was much shorter but included the vast majority of American voters. It was comprised of "the entire body of landholders throughout the United States" as well as "the body of labourers, not being landholders, whether in husbanding or the arts." Jefferson estimated that "the latter is to the aggregate of the former party probably as 500 to one."[25]

Here one gets an early whiff of the distinctively democratic odor with which Jefferson's name would eventually be associated. In the traditional Whig formulation the Country Party was an elite group of landowners who opposed the policies of the Court Party, and the two competing elites offered different prescriptions for what was in the best interest of the public. But Jefferson had come to see himself as the leader of a popular *majority* doing political battle against an elite *minority*. This was a new way of thinking about politics in the late eighteenth century. True, it drew upon traditional notions of conspiracy long associated with Whig ideology. The "anti-republican" supporters of Hamilton's policies, for example, though a mere minority, enjoyed "circumstances which give them an appearance of strength and numbers." Their chief advantage, Jefferson thought, was that "they all live in cities, together, and can act in a body readily and at all times," whereas his constituency was "dispersed over a great extent of country, [and] have little means of intercommunication with each other." (The chief disadvantage facing the Country Party, in other words, was that it lived in the country.) But the novel feature of Jefferson's formulation of American political life was that it was essentially a matter of numbers. He regarded himself as the spokesman for a latent majority of Americans who, if they could ever be mobilized, would assume their rightful place as true heirs to "the spirit of '76." And instead of talking about them as "the public," he began in the 1790s to speak in the more democratic idiom of "the people." These were prophetic tendencies.[26]

DREAMS AND DEBTS

VERY FEW LETTERS went out from Monticello during Jefferson's first year of retirement, and the ones that did conveyed the impression that the former secretary of state had successfully completed the long-awaited odyssey from the purgatory of politics to his own pastoral paradise. He wrote to Washington not as the president but as a fellow farmer, recalling that both men were familiar with a scheme to manufacture "an essence of dung, one pint of which could manure an acre," and that if any ingenious inventor could render it portable, Jefferson was now prepared to purchase a huge supply. To James Monroe, who was serving as the American minister in Paris, he apologized for the infrequency of his letters, blaming the long silence on "that sort of procrastination which so often takes place when no circumstance fixes a business to a particular time." When word reached him that his old Parisian infatuation, Maria Cosway, had left her husband, abandoned her young child and sequestered herself in an Italian convent, he wrote her in the old sentimental style of times past: "I regret the distance which separates us and will not permit myself to believe that we are no more to meet till you meet me where time and distance are nothing." But she was wrong to bury herself in a cloistered room where "the sun [is] ever excluded, the balmy breeze never felt. . . ." He had chosen the opposite direction for himself, spending his days out of doors like "a real farmer, measuring fields, following my ploughs, helping the haymakers, and never knowing a day which has not done something for futurity." He assured his friends that his serenity, like a field of planted flowers, had germinated and was now bursting out inside his soul. It was the lifelong Jeffersonian domestic ideal, now at midlife and in the proper rural context: to be "living like an Antedeluvian patriarch among my children and grandchildren, and tilling my soil."[27]

Certain features in this idyllic scene, especially the family dimension, apparently did come together for Jefferson at least momentarily in the mid-1790s. Patsy, now a full-grown woman whom Jefferson addressed as Martha, had married Thomas Mann Randolph, Jr., in 1790, soon after her return from France. When she was a young girl studying in Paris, Jefferson had worried out loud about the chances "that in marriage she will draw a blockhead," but Randolph put those worries to rest. A Virginia gentleman of the finest pedigree, Randolph had been educated at Edinburgh and in fact modeled himself after his new father-in-law. Tall, sinewy, like Jefferson, but with black hair and a dark complexion, he was a splendid horseman, one of the few Virginians who could outride Jefferson; as a young man he possessed the dashing charm and beguiling eccentricities associated with other male members of the Randolph clan, like saluting nonchalantly as his horse cleared a formidable fence. By 1795 he and Martha had already produced two grandchildren for Jefferson. Nine more were on the way. In addition to substantial holdings at Varina on the James River below Richmond, in 1792 Randolph purchased Edgehill, a fifteen-hundred-acre estate only two miles from Monticello, so he and Martha could be regular presences in Jefferson's domestic circle and full-fledged residents of Monticello throughout the summers.[28]

In June of 1796 a visiting French nobleman, the Duc de La Rochefoucauld-Liancourt, who was one of the aristocratic refugees from the current bloodbath in France, described Jefferson supervising his wheat harvest in the fields with Randolph alongside him, commenting that "from, the affection he [Jefferson] bears him," Randolph "seems to be his son rather than his son-in-law." La Rochefoucauld-Liancourt then went on to describe the other member of Jefferson's family unit at Monticello, the former Polly, now old enough to turn heads among all the eligible bachelors of Albemarle County and be referred to by her proper name: "Miss Maria constantly resides with her father; but as she is seventeen years old, and is remarkably handsome, she will, doubtless, soon find that there are duties which it is still sweeter to perform than those of a daughter." A year later Maria fulfilled this prediction by becoming engaged to John Wayles Eppes, whom Jefferson described as just the young man he would have chosen for his stunningly beautiful daughter "if I had had the whole earth free to have chosen a partner for her." Jefferson then explained to Martha how Maria's looming marriage provided the final ingredient for his long-standing plan of domestic harmony: "I now see our fireside formed in a group, no one member has a fibre in their composition which can ever produce any jarring or jealousies among us. No irregular passions, no dangerous bias, which may render problematic the future fortunes and happiness of our descendants. We are quieted as to their condition for at least one generation more."[29]

Like many of Jefferson's fondest and most heartfelt visions, this one proved too good to be true. Despite her father's wedding gift of eight hundred acres within sight of Monticello, designed to keep her close, Maria preferred to live on her husband's family lands at Eppington. And like her mother, she died prematurely during childbirth in 1804. Meanwhile Thomas Mann Randolph became afflicted with a mysterious nervous disorder soon after Jefferson took up residence as paterfamilias. Neither a tour through the cooler climate of New England nor several visits to the hot springs of Virginia produced the desired cure, leaving Jefferson himself to wonder what ailed his beloved son-in-law. Alcoholism became a problem in the ensuing years, and rumors began to circulate that young Randolph had inherited a streak of the eccentric behavior—enemies called it outright lunacy—that stalked the Randolph line. By 1802 he was confessing his feelings of inadequacy as a member of the Jefferson family, "like something extraneous, fallen in by accident and destroying the homogeneity," the self-declared "silly bird" who could never feel at ease among the swans.[30]

Indeed the only persevering portion of Jefferson's domestic dream was Martha, who devoted herself to her father and her children in the selfless fashion in which she had been reared, never talked about her husband's mounting emotional problems, in fact acknowledged in 1798 that her love for her husband had never really displaced "the first and best of nature," meaning her feelings for her father. Whether this rather extreme version of daughterly affection had something to do with Thomas Mann Randolph's slide into despair and eventual destitution is not clear. What is clear is that despite what must have been many idyllic moments soon after Jefferson's retirement, expectations of an abiding form of domestic bliss on his mountaintop were forced to adjust themselves to the emotional rivalries that had infiltrated his domestic circle.[31]

Jefferson's attitude toward whatever psychological conflicts were steadily eroding those dreams was self-conscious silence. When Maria once mentioned the dilemma posed by the persistent alcoholism of a distant relative, Jefferson advised her to avoid discussing the subject. "What is the use of rectifying him if the thing be unimportant," he asked rhetorically, "and if important, let it pass for the present. . . . It is wonderful how many persons are rendered unhappy by inattention to these little rules of prudence." Such acts of prudent obliviousness also had the decided advantage of sustaining the imaginary ideal. In the Jeffersonian family code, one not only kept secrets from outsiders; one kept secrets from oneself.[32]

Much like his domestic ideal, Jefferson's agrarian ideal was utterly sincere, an honest expression of how he wished to see himself but set so far from the messy and mundane realities of plantation life in postrevolutionary Virginia that collisions between interior preferences and exterior limitations were unavoidable, in the end tragically so. One of his most famous utterances, trailing only his classic statement on human rights in the Declaration of Independence as an eloquent contribution to American prose history, is the following passage from *Notes on Virginia:* "Those who labour in the earth are the chosen people of God, if ever he had a chosen people, whose breasts he has made his peculiar deposit of genuine virtue. It is the focus in which he keeps alive that sacred fire, which otherwise might escape from the face of the earth." As one modern-day scholar and farmer has observed, American agriculture has never quite recovered from this resounding compliment. Indeed the entire history of farming in nineteenth- and twentieth-century America can be written as a clash between the mythical status of the Jeffersonian tiller of the soil and the harsh realities of capricious weather and equally capricious markets. That long and often paradoxical story, it turns out, actually had its origins in the experience of Jefferson himself.[33]

Reality came at Jefferson in several overlapping waves, but the most elemental fact was that he was not an independent yeoman farmer but an indebted Virginia planter. By the time of his retirement as secretary of state he owed about forty-five hundred pounds to English creditors in Bristol and another two thousand pounds to a Glasgow firm. The bulk of this debt had been incurred in the 1770s, when he inherited the burdened estate of his father-in-law, John Wayles. But what he called his "thralldom of debt" had been further complicated by the wartime inflation that rendered his efforts at payment valueless, by the declining productivity of his lands during his long absences from Monticello from 1784 to 1794, as well as by his apparently constitutional inability to live within a budget or deny himself books, fine furnishings, expensive wines or other essentials of the good life. During the latter phase of his ministry in France he had become increasingly aware of the growing gap between his income and his expenses, indeed almost obsessively aware that the interest on his debts was compounding at a faster rate than his payments on the principal. When he left public office in 1794, while he had sounded the familiar Ciceronian note about his craving for bucolic simplicity, he apprised Washington, more practically, that he had retired in order to rescue himself from debt and his lands from "the ravages of overseers [which] has brought on them a degree of degredation far beyond what I had expected."[34]

His financial predicament was serious. Comparisons in modern-day terms are notoriously tricky to calculate, but can conservatively be estimated in the range of several hundred thousand dollars. But they were also fairly typical for the planter class of postrevolutionary Virginia. In

1790 residents of the Old Dominion owed £2.3 million to English and Scottish creditors, and the most prominent families of Virginia were also the most prominent names on the list of more than thirty thousand delinquent debtors kept by British merchants. Jefferson was profoundly aware of the massive indebtedness afflicting his friends and neighbors, once even explaining to a French admirer that the debts of Virginia's planters were "hereditary from father to son for so many generations, so that the planters were a species of property, annexed to certain mercantile houses in London." He said pretty much the same thing to his younger daughter: "The unprofitable condition of Virginia estates in general leaves it next to impossible for the holder of one to avoid ruin. And this condition will continue until some change takes place in the mode of working them. In the mean time, nothing can save us and our children from beggary but a determination to get a year beforehand, and restrain ourselves vigorously to the clear profits of the last. If a debt is once contracted by a farmer, it is never paid but by a sale [of the estate.]" Given his own indulged habits of consumption and the eventual fate of his beloved Monticello, this proved to be a highly ironic statement. But in the middle years of the 1790s he could neither foresee the future nor appreciate irony. What he could do, or at least try mightily to do, was make his lands more productive and pay off his debts. Farming, then, meant making money.[35]

His landed assets were impressive, but deceptively so. Jefferson owned nearly eleven thousand acres, about equally divided between estates surrounding Monticello in Albemarle County and western lands concentrated in Bedford County, about ninety miles away. He had sold off additional acreage lying along the James River to the southeast in Goochland and Cumberland counties, in part to pay off debts and in part to consolidate his holdings. Despite the sale, Jefferson remained one of the largest landowners in the state. One of the reasons he found it difficult to accept the full implications of his indebtedness was that he thought of wealth like an old-style Virginia aristocrat, in terms of land rather than money or more liquid forms of capital. For Jefferson, land was the best measure of a man's worth and, as he put it, "that of which I am the most tenacious." Despite the haunting presence of his English and Scottish creditors, he thought of himself as a landed and therefore a wealthy man.[36]

He expected the land to rescue him from those creditors once he took personal charge of managing its cultivation. His plan was clear. He would abandon tobacco as his chief cash crop in favor of wheat. In his *Notes on Virginia* he had described tobacco growing as "a culture productive of infinite wretchedness," in part because the noxious weed served no earthly purpose other than to feed a nasty habit, but also because the plant possessed an almost unique capacity to kill the land. Because his own lands were, as he put it, "as yet reclaimed from the barbarous state in which the slovenly business of tobacco making had left them," he would insist upon the adoption of a seven-step long-term plan of crop rotation designed to permit the soil to recover its former fertility. Throughout the spring and summer of 1794 Jefferson focused the bulk of his considerable energies on the details of his seven-step rotation plan, giving it all the concentrated attention he had previously given to American domestic politics or foreign policy.[37]

At least at the theoretical level, which was where Jefferson always did his most impressive thinking, his plan had much to recommend it. Wheat was becoming the crop of choice among Virginia's more progressive planters (Washington had helped lead the way here) because it did less damage to the soil and enjoyed several market advantages over tobacco, the chief ones being that people needed to eat more than they needed to smoke and that the ongoing war between England and France presented a golden opportunity to capture the European market for foodstuffs. The elaborateness of his seven-step rotation program meant that it would take a long time, at least seven years, before his fields were fully ready for extensive wheat cultivation, but that seemed a price worth paying to do the job right. The plan provides additional evidence that Jefferson saw himself as remaining at Monticello for the duration. He was planning for the long haul.

Of all the reasons why the plan failed—and after some initial success it did fail in just about every way possible—perhaps the main culprit was the bane of all farmers: bad weather and bad luck. Droughts and early frosts damaged Jefferson's wheat crop three years in succession. Heavy rains soaked his grain while it was being shipped by barge downriver. Later on the dreaded Hessian fly settled over his fields at regular intervals, consuming whatever had managed to survive the capricious elements. One cannot read through his *Farm Book*, where Jefferson recorded his seasonal encounters with the vagaries of the weather and the countless impediments to his best-laid plans, without concluding that however fortunate he was as a public figure, he was an extremely unlucky farmer.[38]

Beyond bad luck, however, there were two elemental reasons why Jefferson's plantations were not really capable of producing cash crops at a level sufficient to generate substantial profits. First, he simply did not have enough land under cultivation. When one conjures up the image of an eleven-thousand-acre plantation, it is difficult not to be influenced by the popular iconography of the huge agrarian factories of the antebellum South with their vast fields and gangs of slave laborers organized in quasi-military units. But Jefferson's lands, and indeed most of Virginia's plantations in the eighteenth century, did not look or function at all like that. Instead of one large tract stretching out to the horizon, Jefferson owned seven separate and disparate farms: Monticello, Shadwell, Tufton and Lego in Albemarle County; and Poplar Forest, Bear Creek and Tomahawk in Bedford. Moreover, only about a thousand acres of his total holdings were under cultivation. The rest was forest. In effect, Jefferson did not oversee a unified plantation in the familiar sense of the term so much as a series of modest-sized farms. Taken together, these scattered agrarian communities were capable of producing enough corn, oats, potatoes, rye, peas, barley and flax to support themselves and, in good years, to show a small profit. That in fact is what they managed to do year in and year out. But the acreage under cultivation was too small, and the organization of the enterprise too decentralized to permit much more.[39]

Second, the land Jefferson owned lacked the nutrients and the corresponding fertility necessary to produce a bumper cash crop. Even if

the weather and the fates had been kinder, they would have had a difficult time overcoming the geological realities. Jefferson liked to blame
the poor quality of his soil on the exhausting effects of tobacco and the
careless management of his lands by overseers during his absence in
France and Philadelphia. This was true enough, but it failed to
acknowledge the more elemental fact that his plantations were on the
eastern slope of a mountain range. Aesthetically and visually this location could claim few equals, commanding a spectacular view from
Monticello east toward the Tidewater. But though it looked down on
some of the richest soil in Virginia, the very height that made the view
so stunning also made the soil inferior for purposes of cultivation. (If
he had had access to twentieth-century fertilizers and farming techniques, things might have been different. Modern farmers in the area
earn their livings with livestock.) So while Jefferson preferred to believe
that his lands had been worn out—this meant that proper care by
means of a meticulous crop rotation system could reclaim their fertility—the less palatable truth was that the soil lacked the basic nutrients
essential for a flourishing plantation economy. The ground around
Monticello, for example, was clay-based and therefore excellent for
making bricks, but even as one admires the distinctive dark-red hues of
the mansion facade today, one is also looking at another underlying
reason why Jefferson was not destined to be a successful farmer.[40]

Although Jefferson never fully grasped the intractability of his economic predicament, he had a sharp sense of the need to generate
income, presumably to tide him over until his lands recovered their
productivity, so he decided early on to establish a nail-making business
on the grounds of Monticello. He described his reasoning in a letter to
a French correspondent in the spring of 1795: "In returning home after
an absence of ten years, I found my farms so much deranged that I saw
evidently . . . that it was necessary for me to find some other resource
in the meantime. . . . I concluded at length to begin a manufacture of
nails, which needs little or no capital, and I now employ a dozen little
boys from 10 to 16 years of age, overlooking all the details of their business myself and drawing from it profit on which I can get along till I

can put my farms into a course of yielding profit." He joked about his new occupation as manufacturer and factory foreman, claiming that "my new trade of nail-making is to me in this country what an additional title of nobility or the ensigns of a new order are in Europe," but he was deadly serious about supervising the operation personally and enforcing a rigid regimen for the teenage black slaves who constituted his labor force.

Every morning except Sunday he walked over to the nailery soon after dawn to weigh out the nail rod for each worker, then returned at dusk to weigh the nails each had made and calculate how much iron had been wasted by the most and least efficient workers. Isaac Jefferson recalled that his former master made it clear to all hands that the nailery was a personal priority and that special privileges would be accorded the best nailmakers. "[He] gave the boys in the nail factory a pound of meat a week. . . . Give them that wukked the best a suit of red or blue; encouraged them mightily." Jefferson even added the nailery to his familiar refrain in the pastoral mode. "I am so much immersed in farming and nail-making," he reported in the fall of 1794, "that politicks are entirely banished from my mind." He also immersed himself in the business side of nail making, demanding cheaper prices from his nail rod supplier in Philadelphia, noting increases in the price of iron, keeping track of retail sales of his product at local stores and worrying when "a deluge of British nails" flooded the local market "with a view as is said of putting down my work." (The fact that they were British nails meant that he took it personally.)[41]

From a financial perspective the nailery made perfect sense. In fact, in terms of his struggle to make his plantations profitable, the nailery was the one success story, earning almost a thousand dollars in a good year. But seen in the context of Jefferson's eloquent hymn to the bucolic beauties of the pastoral life, it was a massive incongruity. A historian with the ironic sensibility of, say, Henry Adams could have a field day contemplating the symbolic significance of a small factory, perched atop Monticello in the heart of Jefferson's agrarian utopia, perhaps concluding that it was America's original version of "the

machine in the garden." Or a novelist with the temperament of
Charles Dickens might have taken delight in comparing the regimen of
Jefferson's nailery with the sweatshops and dawn-to-dusk drudgery
of London's satanic mills. Jefferson himself, it should be noted, had no
comparable sense of irony or contradiction; he felt no need to apolo-
gize for bringing industry to Monticello. There is no evidence that it
ever occurred to him that his daily visits to the nail factory, with its
blazing forges and sweating black boys arranged along an assembly line
of hammers and anvils, offered a graphic preview of precisely the kind
of industrial world he devoutly wished America to avoid, or at least to
delay for as long as possible.[42]

At a more mundane level Jefferson's dedication to the meticulous
management of the nailery illustrates what compelled his fullest energies as master of Monticello. Both ex-slave Madison Hemings and former overseer Edmund Bacon, though recalling a later time in his life,
claimed that Jefferson showed "but little taste or care for agricultural
pursuits. . . . It was his mechanics he seemed mostly to direct, and in
their operations he took great interest." Though his first year of retirement in 1794–95 appears to have been an exception, his general rule
was to pass little time in his fields, preferring to leave their cultivation
to his overseers except at harvesttime. He spent no time at all behind a
plow and almost no time watching others perform the routine tasks of
farming. What most fascinated him and commanded his fullest attention were new projects that demanded mechanical or artisanal skill of
his laborers and that allowed him to design and superintend the entire
operation. The nailery was the first of such projects, but it was followed
by construction of a new threshing machine, plans for a flour mill and
an expensive canal in the Rivanna River.[43]

But the biggest project of all was Monticello itself. He had in fact
been contemplating a major overhaul of his mansion ever since his
return from France in 1789. From a financial point of view the idea of
renovating Monticello, unlike his plans for the nailery, made no sense
at all. But when it came to the elegance and comfort of his personal
living space, Jefferson's lifelong habit was to ignore cost altogether,

often going so far as to make expensive architectural changes in houses or hotels where he was only a temporary resident. His much grander plans for Monticello followed naturally from two idealistic impulses that seized his imagination with all the force of first principles: First, he needed more space, more than twice that of the original house, in order to accommodate his domestic dream of living out his life surrounded by his children and grandchildren; second, his revised version of Monticello needed to embody the neoclassical principles of the Palladian style that his European travels had allowed him to study firsthand. The conjunction of these two cravings had drastic implications, since the spatial expansion had to occur within severely constrained conceptions of symmetry and proportion dictated by the Palladian principles for beauty. The new structure could not just spread out like a series of boxcars, but neither could it rise vertically, since Palladian buildings must present at least the appearance of a one-story horizontal line, preferably capped by a dome. What this meant in effect was that the original house needed to be almost completely demolished and rebuilt from the cellar up.[44]

Brick-making started soon after his return home in 1794, but throughout that year and the next Jefferson focused most of his energies on his fields and the nailery. Some construction work must have begun right away, since Jefferson reported to George Wythe in October 1794 that he was "now living in a brick-kiln, for my house, in its present state is nothing more." But a year and a half later, in March 1796, he informed William Branch Giles that he had "just begun the demolition of my house," adding that Giles should "not let this discourage you from calling on us if you wander this way in the summer" and joking that he could stay in one of the unfinished, open-air rooms. An Irish traveler passing through in May of the same year described Monticello as "in an unfinished state, but if carried to the plan laid down, it will be one of the most elegant private habitations in the United States." Visits by two Frenchmen provide us with the only other direct testimony about the physical condition of life on the mountaintop at this time. The Duc de La Rochefoucauld-Liancourt tended to overlook the clutter and, like a good Jeffersonian, describe the promise: "His travels in Europe have supplied him with models; he has appropriated them to his design; and his new plan, which is already much advanced, will be accomplished before the end of next year...." (He was off by twelve or twenty-six years, depending on how one calculates completion.) Count François de Volney, another refugee from the French Revolution who wished to visit, received a welcoming note from Jefferson that included more candid advice about the view that would greet him: "[T]he noise, confusion and discomfort of the scene will require all your philosophy and patience."[45]

Throughout the vast bulk of Jefferson's sequestration, it seems clear, Monticello was a congested construction site replete with broken bricks, roofless rooms, lumber piles and, if some reports are to be believed, more than a hundred workmen digging, tearing and hammering away. The millions of twentieth-century visitors to the mansion are the real beneficiaries of Jefferson's irrational decision to redesign and rebuild Monticello in the 1790s, though they would be mistaken to think the house in which Jefferson lived looked the way it does now. It was in some state of repair or improvement throughout Jefferson's lifetime. More to our purposes, from 1794 to 1797 Monticello was part ruin, part shell and mostly still dream. Not only is it wrong to envision Jefferson's estates as an integrated agrarian enterprise along the lines of Tara in *Gone with the Wind,* not only is it misguided to imagine Jefferson walking behind a plow or spending much time supervising others walking behind a plow, but it is also misleading to think of him residing in a palatial home shaped by his distinctive tastes and filled with his favorite curiosities. Monticello was an excavation rather than a mansion at this stage. It was also his largest and most all-consuming project, the activity that soaked up his best energies and provided him with a sense of purpose. While his inspirational hymn to the virtuous farmer was unquestionably genuine, the truth was that farming bored him. Retirement to rural solitude did not mean tilling the soil, but digging it up to build something new and useful on it.

SLAVERY

ALMOST ALL THE WORK, whether in the fields, in the nailery or at
the construction site for Monticello itself was done by slaves. The total
slave population on Jefferson's several plantations was a fluctuating figure, oscillating above and below 200 and divided between Albemarle
and Bedford counties at the ratio of roughly three to two. Between
1784 and 1794, as Jefferson attempted to consolidate his landholdings
and reduce his debt, he had disposed of 161 slaves by sale or outright
gift. But natural increase had raised the slave population on all his
estates to 167 by 1796, and that number was to grow gradually over the
ensuing years. On his plantations in Albemarle County it would seem
safe to estimate that Jefferson was surrounded by about 100 slaves during his three-year retirement. It is, on the other hand, by no means safe
to estimate Jefferson's thoughts and feelings about what in effect constituted the overwhelming majority of residents at Monticello.[46]

Although Jefferson had made extended visits to Monticello during
his years as secretary of state, his duties in Paris and before then in
Philadelphia and Williamsburg meant that he was mostly an absentee
slaveowner for the better part of fifteen years. During that time his
views on the institution of slavery had fluctuated in much the same
way as the size of his own slave population, oscillating between outright condemnation of slavery as incompatible with republican values
and equally outright procrastination when pushed to offer practical
remedies to end it. Of course the gap between "what ought to be" and
"what the world allowed" constituted the central dilemma of Jefferson's overall cast of mind on almost all political topics. But the problem of slavery exposed the gap more dramatically than any other issue;
it also exposed his intellectual awkwardness in attempting to straddle
what was in fact a moral chasm between what he knew to be right and
what he could not do without. Even at the purely theoretical level,
then, his thinking about slavery as a matter of public policy was deeply

paradoxical and tinctured with personal considerations. The return to Monticello in 1794 and his apparently permanent encampment among "those who labor for my happiness" put an even sharper edge on the paradox by making the theoretical problem into a palpable, day-by-day set of personal interactions.⁴⁷

If Jefferson had a discernible public position on slavery in the mid-1790s, it was that the subject should be allowed to retire gracefully from the field of political warfare, much as he was doing by retiring to Monticello. This represented a decided shift from his position as a younger man, when he had assumed a leadership role in pushing slavery onto the agenda in the Virginia Assembly and the federal Congress. His most famous formulations, it is true, were rhetorical: blaming the slave trade and the establishment of slavery itself on George III in the Declaration of Independence; denouncing slavery as a morally bankrupt institution that was doomed to extinction in *Notes on Virginia*. His most practical proposals, all of which came in the early 1780s, envisioned a program of gradual abolition that featured an end to the slave trade, the prohibition of slavery in all the western territories and the establishment of a fixed date, he suggested 1800, after which all newly born children of slaves would be emancipated. To repeat, up through this stage of his political career, he was a member of the vanguard that insisted on the incompatibility of slavery with the principles on which the American republic was founded. Throughout this early phase of his life it would have been unfair to accuse him of hypocrisy for owning slaves or to berate him for failing to provide moral leadership on America's most sensitive political subject. It would in fact have been much fairer to applaud his efforts, most of them admittedly futile, to inaugurate antislavery reform and to wonder admiringly how this product of Virginia's planter class had managed to develop such liberal convictions.

Dating the origins of a long silence is an inherently imprecise business, but it would seem that Jefferson's posture toward slavery began to shift in the mid- to late 1780s during his ministry to France. This is ironic, since during this same time he was telling his French audience misleadingly optimistic stories about the imminent demise of slavery in his native Virginia and playing the Parisian version of the American antislavery champion. But he was simultaneously beginning to back away from any leadership role in the American debate over slavery. "I have long since given up the expectation of any early provision for the extinguishment of slavery among us," he wrote in 1805, going on to reiterate his belief that slavery was an anomaly in republican America; but his abiding posture was that the current configuration of political forces blocked any meaningful reform at present, so that all one could realistically do was wait for the future to prepare public opinion for the inevitable. This more passive and fatalistic position, which he maintained for the remainder of his life, was the product of several different lines of thought that converged in his mind after 1785. It was in fact a more intellectually and psychologically complex view than it appears at first, and since it was the view he carried in his head to Monticello in 1794, its origins merit a moment of our attention.[48]

First, as we have seen, Jefferson's withdrawal from the antislavery vanguard followed directly upon publication of *Notes on Virginia*. The ringing denunciations of slavery presented there, which Jefferson had never intended for an American audience, made him a controversial figure, especially within the slave-owning class of Virginia, and the prospective leader of the still quite small group of progressive southern planters advocating some form of gradual emancipation. It was a prominent public role that ran against the grain of all his instincts for privacy. His deep-seated aversion to controversy actually caused him to exaggerate the expected personal criticism that *Notes*, or so he feared, would generate. But whether his apprehensions were mostly justified or mostly imagined was beside the point. He was simply not equipped temperamentally to stay at the cutting edge of the antislavery movement after he got a dose of the sharp feelings it aroused.

Second, the more pessimistic implications of the argument he had made in *Notes* began to settle in and cause him to realize, for the first time, that he had no workable answer to the unavoidable question: what happens once the slaves are freed? This was the kind of practical question that Jefferson had demonstrated great ingenuity in avoiding on a host of other major political issues. Indeed, one of the most seductive features of his political thinking in general was its beguiling faith that the future could take care of itself. Slavery, however, proved to be the exception to this larger pattern of calculated obliviousness. For one brief moment, in 1789, he seemed to entertain a bold, if somewhat bizarre, scheme whereby emancipated slaves would be "intermingled" with imported German peasants on fifty-acre farms where both groups could learn proper work habits. But even this short-lived proposal served only to expose the inherent intractability of the postemancipation world as Jefferson tried to imagine it. His fundamental conviction, one that he never questioned, was that white and black Americans could not live together in harmony. He had already explained why in *Notes:* "Deep rooted prejudices entertained by the whites; ten thousand recollections, by the blacks, of the injuries they have sustained; new provocations; the real distinctions that nature has made; and many other circumstances, will divide us into parties, and produce convulsions which will probably never end but in the extermination of one or the other race." Here was the single instance, with the most singularly significant consequences, when Jefferson was incapable of believing that "the dead hand of the past" could not be swept aside by the liberating forces unleashed by the American Revolution. Blacks and whites were inherently different, and though he was careful to advance the view "as a suspicion only," people of African descent were sufficiently inferior to whites in mental aptitude that any emancipation policy permitting racial interaction was a criminal injustice to the freed slaves as well as a biological travesty against "the real distinctions that nature has made." The unavoidable conclusion, then, was that slavery was morally wrong, but racial segregation was morally right. And until a practical solution to the problem of what to do with the freed slaves could be found, it made no sense to press for emancipation.[49]

3   Third, during the latter phase of his French experience Jefferson became more intensely aware how much his own financial well-being

depended upon the monetary value and labor of his slaves. As the depth of his own indebtedness began to sink in, there were three ways to raise large amounts of capital to appease his creditors: He could sell off land, as he did somewhat reluctantly by disposing of holdings in Cumberland and Goochland counties; he could sell slaves outright; and he could rent or lease the labor of his slaves to neighboring planters. He expressed considerable guilt about pursuing the last two options, suggesting it was a betrayal of his paternal obligations to the black members of his extended "family." He gave specific instructions that particular slaves who had been with him for some time not be sold or hired out unless they wished it. But much as he disliked selling his slaves or temporarily transferring control over them to others, he recognized that such a course constituted "my only salvation." In short, once he grasped the full measure of his personal economic predicament, the larger question of emancipation appeared in a new and decidedly less favorable light. It was now a matter on which he could not afford to be open-minded; nor, as it turned out, were the exigencies of this debt-induced predicament to change over his lifetime, except to grow worse.[50]

The net result of all these influences was a somewhat tortured position on slavery that combined unequivocal condemnation of the institution in the abstract with blatant procrastination whenever specific emancipation schemes were suggested. The Duc de La Rochefoucauld-Liancourt captured the essential features and general flavor of Jefferson's slavery stance during his visit to Monticello in June 1796: "The generous and enlightened Mr. Jefferson cannot but demonstrate a desire to see these negroes emancipated. But he sees so many difficulties in their emancipation, even postponed, he adds so many conditions to render it practicable, that it is thus reduced to the impossible. He keeps, for example, the opinion he advanced in his notes, that the negroes of Virginia can only be emancipated all at once, and by exporting to a distance the whole black race. He bases his opinion on the certain danger, if there were nothing else, of seeing blood mixed without means of preventing it.[51]

If his position on slavery as a young man merits a salute for its forthright and progressive character, his position as a mature man invites skepticism for its self-serving paralysis and questionable integrity. But latter-day moral judgments are notoriously easy to render from the comfortable perch that hindsight always provides. And such judgments ought not become a substitute for recovering Jefferson's own understanding, no matter how flawed, of what he was doing when he resumed his role as master of Monticello. He saw himself, even more than his slaves, as the victim of history's stubborn refusal to proceed along the path that all enlightened observers regarded as inevitable. In that sense he and his African-American charges were trapped together in a lingering moment, a historical backwater in which nature's laws would be sorely tested as both sides waited together for the larger story of human liberation to proceed. In this overly extended transitional moment, his primary obligation was to serve as a steward for those temporarily entrusted to his care and to think of his slaves, as in fact he listed them in his *Farm Book,* as members of "my family," to be cared for as foster children until more permanent and geographically distant accommodations could be found.[52]

Although the self-serving character of this paternalistic posture might have an offensive odor and fraudulent look to us, it had decided advantages for Jefferson's slaves as well as for Jefferson himself. The major reason why his many returns to Monticello were always greeted by the black population on the mountain as cause for celebration was that it meant the temporary end of control by overseers and the resumption of Jefferson's more benevolent and generous authority. His residence meant fewer whippings, more dependable food and clothing distributions and the assurance of a more fair-minded arbiter of work schedules. No reliable evidence exists to document any instance in which Jefferson personally flogged a slave or dispensed any physical punishment himself. On rare occasions, and as a last resort, he ordered overseers to use the lash, but his general policy was to sell off troublemakers, effectively banishing them from his extended family as recalcitrant children. He was extremely reluctant to sell slaves against their will. When forced by his creditors to sell eleven slaves in 1792, he ordered that they all be selected from his more remote Bedford plantations and that the sale itself be carried out in a distant location, acknowledging that he "did not like to have my name annexed in the public papers to the sale of property." On the other hand, he tried to respect the wishes of those slaves who asked to be sold, usually to be united with their families. In 1792, for example, he approved the sale of Mary Hemings to Thomas Bell, a local merchant, studiously avoiding mention of the fact that Bell, a white man, was the father of Mary's two youngest children and the sale "according to her desire" would allow them to live together as common-law husband and wife.⁵³

Jefferson's own highly developed network of interior defenses also helped sustain his paternalistic self-image by blocking out incongruous evidence (like the Hemings-Bell relationship) or consigning it to some oblivious region of his mind that was cut off from communication with the conscious world, a kind of internal banishment of recalcitrant ideas. Just as he could look squarely at the most atrocious acts of mob violence in revolutionary Paris and see only a momentary excess of human liberty, or could put Philip Freneau on his payroll as a partisan in the party wars without acknowledging a conflict of interest, or not even admit that he and Madison were orchestrating the political tactics of an opposition party, Jefferson possessed the psychological dexterity to overrule awkward perceptions, including the day-by-day realities of slave life. He was the kind of man who would have been able to take an oath—and if the technology for a lie detector test had been available, to have passed it—certifying that his slaves were more content and better off as members of his extended family than under any other imaginable circumstance. And like a general ensconced at headquarters, he conveyed a clear signal to his overseers in the fields that unpleasant incidents should not filter their way back up the mountain.

Partly by geographic accident, partly by his own design, the organization of slave labor at Jefferson's plantations reinforced this shielding mentality in several crucial ways. Recall, first of all, that his cultivated lands were widely distributed, half of them at Bedford, several days' ride away. Until he built his second house at Poplar Forest during his final retirement, Jefferson seldom visited those remote estates. Recall too that, except for the temporary enthusiasm of 1794–95, he seldom ventured into his fields at Monticello or Shadwell except at harvest-time, leaving daily management of routine farming tasks to overseers. While he kept elaborate records of his entire slave population in his *Farm Book*, including the names and ages of all hands, his direct expo-sure to field laborers was limited. His cryptic notation on the division of slave labor is also revealing in this regard: "Children till 10 years of age to serve as nurses. From 10 to 16 the boys make nails, the girls spin. At 16 go into the ground or learn trades." The ominous phrase "go into the ground" accurately conveyed Jefferson's personal contact with that considerable majority of adult slaves who worked his fields. Except as names in his record books, they practically disappeared.[54]

When Jefferson did encounter them, it was usually in the context of work on one of his several construction projects or as apprentices in the nailery. Most of his face-to-face contact with laboring slaves occurred in nonagrarian settings—the nailery, the sawmill, the con-struction site around the mansion—where he supervised them as work-ers doing skilled and semiskilled jobs. Even the nailery, with its overtones of assembly-line monotony and Dickensian drudgery, allowed him to think about the work of the slave boys as an apprentice experience providing them with a marketable trade. In explanation of Jefferson's compulsive tendency to launch so many mechanical and construction projects at Monticello, it is possible that they not only served as outlets for his personal energies but also allowed him to design a more palatable context for interacting with his slaves as hired employees rather than as chattel.

Finally, all the slaves working in the household, and most of those living along Mulberry Row on the mountaintop, were members of two families that had been with Jefferson since the earliest days of his mar-riage to Martha. They enjoyed a privileged status within the slave hier-archy at Monticello, were given larger food and clothing rations, considerably greater latitude of movement and even the discretion to choose jobs or reject them on occasion. Great George and his wife, Ursula, referred to as King George (a joke on George III) and Queen Ursula, were slaves in name only and effectively exercised control over management of the household. (When Jefferson asked Thomas Mann Randolph to tell Little George, their son, to perform a particular task, Randolph claimed that "George I am sure would not stoop to my authority. . . .") The other and larger slave family were all Hemingses, headed by the matriarch, Betty Hemings, whom Jefferson had inherited from his father-in-law, John Wayles, along with ten of her twelve children in 1773. It was an open secret within the slave community at Monticello that the privileged status enjoyed by the Hemings family derived from its mixed blood. Several of Betty's children, perhaps as many as six, had most probably been fathered by John Wayles. In the literal, not just figurative sense of the term, they were part of Jefferson's extended family. All the slaves he eventually freed were Hemingses, including Robert and James in 1794 and 1796 respectively. If what struck the other slaves at Monticello was the quasi-independent character of the Hemings clan with its blood claim on Jefferson's paternal instincts, what most visitors tended to notice was their color. La Rochefoucauld-Liancourt left this account in 1796: "In Virginia mongrel negroes are found in greater number than in Carolina and Georgia; and I have even seen, especially at Mr. Jefferson's, slaves, who, neither in point of colour or features, showed the least trace of their original descent; but their mothers being slaves, they retain, of consequence, the same condition."[55]

Since the members of the Hemings family were the front-and-center slaves at Monticello, most guests and visitors to the mountaintop experienced the Jeffersonian version of slavery primarily as a less black and less oppressive phenomenon than it actually was. As overseer Edmund Bacon recalled, "there were no Negro and other outhouses around the mansion, as you generally see on [other] plantations," so the physical arrangement of appearances also disguised the full meaning of the slave experience. In short, Jefferson had so designed his slave community that his most frequent interactions occurred with African-

Americans who were not treated like full-fledged slaves and who did not even look like full-blooded Africans because, in fact, they were not. In terms of daily encounters and routinized interactions, his sense of himself as less a slave master than a paternalistic employer and guardian received constant reinforcement.[56]

By the same token, if slavery was a doomed institution whose only practical justification was to preserve the separation of the races until the day of deliverance arrived at some unspecified time in the future, Jefferson was surrounded by dramatic evidence that it was failing miserably at that task. Miscegenation at Monticello was obviously a flourishing enterprise, much more so than his wheat fields. Several of Betty Hemings's grandchildren looked almost completely white, graphic testimony that whatever had begun with John Wayles had certainly not stopped back then. Jefferson's stated aversion to racial mixture had somehow to negotiate its visible examples all around him. In a sense what he saw only confirmed his deepest fears about an amalgamation of the races, though his code of silence dictated that no mention of the matter be permitted in public. Despite his remarkable powers of avoidance, this is one topic we can be sure he brooded about, even if he never talked about it for the record. The eloquence of his silence provides the best evidence of what Monticello was like as a real place rather than an imagined ideal. If literary allusions afford the best mode of description, we need to dispense with Virgil's pastoral odes and begin to contemplate William Faulkner's fiction.

MADISONIAN MINUET

JAMES MADISON probably knew Jefferson as well as or better than anyone else alive, and he recognized from the very start of the sequestration at Monticello that two Jeffersonian truths needed to coexist peacefully for at least the foreseeable future: First, his political mentor and partner regarded his retirement from public life as final; his recovery of some measure of serenity therefore depended on sustaining the illusion that he was done with politics forever. Second, as time passed and his political wounds healed, Jefferson would find it difficult to remain on the sidelines, especially if the cause that had compelled their collaboration appeared at risk. So as he set out for the fall session of Congress in October 1794, the alleged "General" wrote to the putative "Generalissimo" that he would "always receive your commands with pleasure, and shall continue to drop you a line as occasions turn up."[57]

It was essentially a resumption of the old relationship of the Paris years, with Madison sending regular reports from the political cockpit in Philadelphia and Jefferson receiving them in a distant location that afforded him the tranquility to listen and respond in the meditative mode he preferred. For the first year Jefferson's indifference to political news was nearly total. Madison's detailed reports on the prospects for Republican candidates in various state elections produced only yawning silence from Monticello, along with the reminder that he did not really follow such matters anymore and had stopped subscribing to newspapers so as not to be bothered with the petty details. When Madison passed along diplomatic correspondence with queries about the proper course for American foreign policy, Jefferson expressed no interest: "Make any answer you please for me. If it had been on the rotation of my crops, I would have answered myself, lengthily perhaps, but certainly *con gusto.*" Or when Attorney General Edmund Randolph wrote asking if he might be willing to head up the American negotiating effort with Spain, Jefferson slammed the door defiantly: "No circumstances, my dear Sir, will ever more tempt me to engage in anything public. I thought myself perfectly fixed in this determination when I left Philadelphia, but every day and hour since has added to its inflexibility." No matter what his friends in Philadelphia were secretly thinking, much less his enemies not so secretly saying, he was done with politics forever.[58]

The first tiny cracks in this adamant position began to appear in the winter of 1794–95. During the previous summer a popular insurgency in four counties of western Pennsylvania had prompted Washington to call out the militia. The rebels were protesting collection of an excise tax on whiskey that Hamilton had advocated in order to pay for the federal assumption of state debts in 1791. Western farmers considered the tax unfair because it fell disproportionately on their most exportable product—whiskey was the most convenient way to market their grain—and a self-proclaimed army of seven thousand whiskey rebels had marched through Pittsburgh in a massive display of frontier protest. An even more massive display of federal military power, nearly thirteen thousand troops, had put down the rebellion quickly and with a minimum of violence. Jefferson tended to view the entire affair as a shameful repetition of the Shays's Rebellion fiasco, in which an essentially healthy and rather harmless expression of popular discontent by ordinary American farmers had prompted a military response by the government vastly more repressive than the situation required. Nevertheless, he refrained from making any comment throughout the fall of 1794, despite overtures from Madison to condemn what he regarded as the government's overreaction.[59]

What drew him into the debate was a speech Washington delivered to Congress in the aftermath of the Whiskey Rebellion, denouncing "certain self-created societies" as subversive organizations that fomented discontent and defied the authority of the legitimate government. Washington's attack on the so-called Democratic-Republican societies prompted Madison to sound an alarm designed to pierce the rural serenity surrounding his friend at Monticello. Washington's speech was, Madison said, an "attack on the most sacred principle of our Constitution and Republicanism" and was artfully orchestrated, undoubtedly by Hamilton, to link the Republican critics of the Federalist government with whiskey and rebellion. Madison smelled a conspiracy of just the sort Jefferson had often warned against, the covert "monarchists" in the executive branch of the government scheming to subvert the liberties of "the people." It was imperative that Jefferson rouse himself from his lair and join the fight: "If the people of America are so far degenerated as not to see . . . that the Citadel of their liberties is menaced by the precedent before their eyes, they require abler advocates than they now have, to save them from the consequences."[60]

Jefferson in effect budged, but he did not move. Madison's assessment of what was afoot was obviously correct. "The denunciation of the democratic societies," Jefferson agreed, "is one of the extraordinary acts of boldness of which we have seen so many from the faction of Monocrats." Washington was just as obviously a prop for Hamilton's political ambitions; the president's speech reminded him of "shreds of stuff from Aesop's fables and Tom Thumb," clear evidence the president himself did not write it. But then came a sudden and, at least as far as Madison was concerned, an unexpected reversal:

> Hold on then, my dear friend. . . . I do not see in the minds of those with whom I converse a greater affliction than the fear of your retirement; but this must not be, unless to a more splendid and efficacious post. There I should rejoice to see you. . . . But double delicacies have kept me silent. I ought perhaps to say, while I would not give up my own retirement for the empire of the Universe, how can I justify wishing one, whose happiness I have as much at heart as yours, to take the front of the battle which is fighting for my security.

This was an elegantly indirect way of refusing the invitation to end his own retirement, along with a clear invitation to Madison to assume complete command of the Republican cause and prepare himself for a run at the presidency. Though aroused by the news from Philadelphia, he wanted Madison to know that, like it or not, the torch had been passed to him.[61]

Although Jefferson meant what he said, the debate over the Democratic-Republican societies stirred up the old juices. His letters during the first half of 1795 contained periodic bursts of political invective in the midst of longer and more languid conversations about his wheat crop and the weather. He wrote William Branch Giles that the use of federal troops "to retain the liberty of our citizens meeting together" had signaled a decisive shift toward tyranny "a full century earlier than I expected." Even Washington, who had been spared direct criticism on the questionable supposition that Hamilton was manipulating his words and decisions, now came in for attack: Washington had provided the Hamiltonians with "the sanction of a name which has done too much good not to be sufficient to cover harm also." But these political outbursts, to repeat, usually occurred within the context of more temperate and philosophical musings in the bucolic mode and firm resolutions of pastoral contentment. Letters to Madison probably best reflected the mixed state of Jefferson's mind at this time; requests for copies of his previous correspondence as secretary of state with Edmond Genêt coming right before requests for the most recent pamphlet on crop rotation, news on the elections to the House of Representatives from Virginia districts followed by a lengthy exegesis on the marvelous curative power of vetch as a fallow crop in his old tobacco fields. The happily retired farmer-philosopher was doing battle with the reluctant but ready leader of the Republican party at some subconscious level of Jefferson's personality. But he preferred to keep the conflict below the surface, invisible even to himself, all the better to sustain what remained the dominant impression: that he was still immune to political temptation.[62]

If one were looking to find a precise moment when Jefferson's political interests began to win the interior struggle, a good choice would be the day after Christmas 1795. On that date he mailed eight dollars to Benjamin Franklin Bache for a year's subscription to Bache's *Aurora*, a leading Republican newspaper. While not yet ready to enter the public debate, he had moved to the point of acknowledging that he wished to follow it.[63]

But of course Jefferson's evolution toward a resumption of his public career was a process more than a moment. The pace of his commentary on politics quickened in his letters in late 1795 and early 1796, which was also the time when the demolition efforts at Monticello went forward at full speed, suggesting that he was fully capable of juggling several versions of his future life without any sense of contradiction. Hamilton was in the news at this time: He had announced his decision to resign from the cabinet; a congressional investigation of accounting irregularities in his office was proceeding apace. Anything involving a prospective exposure of Hamilton caught Jefferson's attention—he utterly loathed the man—and the investigation seemed to sanction Jefferson's own, albeit surreptitious, efforts to catch Hamilton cooking the books three years earlier: "I do not at all wonder at the condition in which the finances of the U.S. are found," he wrote Madison. "Hamilton's object from the beginning was to throw them into forms which would be utterly undecypherable. I even said he did not understand their condition himself."[64]

Coming as they did from a man whose own meticulous accounting of his personal finances never seemed capable of producing a realistic rendering of the proverbial bottom line, Jefferson's critical remarks on Hamilton's financial confusion are richly ironic. They also call attention to yet another possible influence on Jefferson's thinking about a return to the public arena, this time at a depth that not only eluded his conscious scrutiny but also puts a strain on our own limited knowledge about the irrational sources of human motivation in general.

For Jefferson's congenital suspicion of Hamilton's cavalier way with budgets merely hinted at his much deeper suspicion that Hamilton's real intention was to increase the national debt in order to justify expanding federal power over the economy, including the power to tax, manipulate credit rates and establish all the accouterments of a modern nation-state along English lines. (On this score he was not entirely wrong.) Debt, then, was the key device that made the whole Hamiltonian scheme possible. So if Jefferson were to reenter the political arena, one of his highest priorities would be the reduction and elimination of the public debt. But his obsession with public debt rested cheek by jowl with his own cavalier way with his personal debt. Just how this intriguing disjunction between personal habit and public policy actually operated inside Jefferson's character is difficult to capture confidently, though paradox is obviously at work. At the personal level Jefferson's intricate record-keeping probably bolstered his false confidence that his own debt problem was under control. (It clearly was not, and the decision to rebuild Monticello helped assure that it never would be.) The looming decision to end his retirement and reenter politics could be seen, then, as a flight from the apparently intractable problem of his personal indebtedness; he would solve publicly what he could not solve privately. Whatever the interactive pattern might have been, it seems fair to say that the problem of debt haunted him at both levels, that his hatred of Hamilton was fueled by personal demons he did not fully understand himself and that the process of thinking about returning to public life involved a complex blend of emotional and ideological considerations.[65]

The decisive event in that process was much more explicit and readily identifiable—namely, the passage of the Jay Treaty, which was simultaneously a landmark in the shaping of American foreign policy, a decisive influence on the constitutional question of executive power in foreign affairs and the occasion for Jefferson's resumption of leadership in the Republican party. If Jefferson was already leaning toward returning to the political wars in Philadelphia, claiming all the while that his retirement was forever and meaning every word, the battle over the Jay Treaty pulled him all the way over and ended all pretenses of remaining a Ciceronian presence in American politics. The passage of the Jay Treaty was a great victory for the Federalists, but it was Jefferson who understood, more than anyone else, that it was a victory from which his enemies would never fully recover. It turned out to be the launching site of his eventually successful campaign for the presidency.[66]

The story had its origins in the early months of 1795. Madison sent reports to Monticello that the terms of the treaty that John Jay had negotiated with England were still secret but that Federalists with inside information "do not assume an air of triumph," from which "it is inferred that the bargain is much less in our favor than ought be expected. . . ." It would be wrong to prejudge, he cautioned, "but I suspect that Jay has been betrayed by his anxiety to couple us with England, and to avoid returning with his finger in his mouth." At this early stage of the story Jefferson refused to rise to the bait. His letters back to Madison did not mention the ominous implications of the Jay Treaty at all, preferring instead to discuss a somewhat bizarre proposal to transfer the University of Geneva to Virginia, request delivery of a letter to a prospective fresco painter for Monticello's new walls and wax eloquent on vetch as the ideal rotation crop.[67]

Madison's fears about the terms of the treaty seemed more than justified, as knowledge of its contents leaked out from the special session of the Senate called to vote on it in the summer of 1795; it then spread, as Madison put it, "with an electric velocity to every part of the Union." The initial public reaction was almost wholly negative. John Jay later claimed the entire eastern seaboard of the United States was illuminated each evening by the fires from burning effigies of his likeness. Popular opinion rallied around the Republican charge that Jay had betrayed American honor as well as American interests in return for a few scraps of English patronage. In New York Alexander Hamilton was struck in the head by a rock and forced to withdraw while attempting to address a rally against the treaty, and the local militia proposed a mock toast to Jay and Federalist Senator Rufus King: "May the cage constructed to coop up the American eagle prove a trap for none but Jays and Kingbirds."[68]

Jefferson's initial response combined outrage with exhortation. He began giving orders again. Madison must take on Hamilton, who was already heating up the public presses with editorials in behalf of the treaty. "Hamilton is really a collossus to the antirepublican party. Without numbers, he is a host within himself. They have got themselves in a defile, where they might be finished, but too much security on the Republican part, will give time to his talents. . . . We have had only midling performances to oppose him. In truth, when he comes forward, there is nobody but yourself who can meet him." Monticello soon began to function as headquarters for the Republican campaign against the treaty. Madison paid an extended visit to the mountaintop in October 1795 in order to plan strategy for opposing the treaty in the

Virginia legislature, a kind of dress rehearsal for the projected debate in the federal Congress later that year. He left with Jefferson the only copy of his "Notes on the Debates at the Constitutional Convention," a clear signal that Jefferson needed to bone up on the constitutional questions at issue, which would form the centerpiece of the Republican position in the congressional debate over ratification. What has come to be called "the great collaboration" was now back in operation and functioning in its familiar fashion. A steady stream of correspondence began to flow from Monticello throughout the fall, rallying Republican support around the position that the Jay Treaty was "really nothing more than a treaty of alliance between England and the Anglomen of this country against the legislature and people of the United States."[69]

Indeed, if the gods had seen fit to conjure up a single statement about American foreign policy that was designed to inflame all of Jefferson's deepest fears and most abiding hatreds, they could not have done better than the Jay Treaty. It accepted the fact of English commercial and naval supremacy and thereby endorsed a pro-English version of American neutrality, just the opposite of Jefferson's pro-French version of "fair neutrality." It repudiated Jefferson's efforts as secretary of state to place duties on English imports while accepting England's right to retain tariffs on American imports. Finally it committed the United States to compensate British creditors on outstanding prerevolutionary debts, most of which were owed by Virginia's planters. Its sole positive feature from the Jeffersonian perspective was the agreement to abide by the promise made in 1783 to evacuate British troops from their posts on the western frontier, but even that concession merely reflected a willingness to implement what the Treaty of Paris had long ago required. What's more, the chief supporters of the treaty were the merchants and bankers of America's port cities. And, a clinching condemnation, its major advocate was Alexander Hamilton. In effect, as Jefferson saw it, the Jay Treaty was a repudiation of the Declaration of Independence, the Franco-American alliance, the revolutionary movement sweeping through Europe and all the political principles on which he had staked his public career as an American statesman.

Subsequent generations of historians, with all the advantages of hindsight, have not seen the same picture that Jefferson saw. The more balanced consensus of posterity is that the Jay Treaty was a realistic bargain that avoided a war with England at a time when the United States was ill prepared to fight one. It effectively postponed the Anglo-American conflict that Jefferson felt in his bones to be inevitable until 1812, when America was economically stronger and politically more stable. In the even longer view it linked American security and economic development to the British fleet, which provided a protective shield of incalculable value throughout the nineteenth century. It bet, in effect, on England rather than France as the hegemonic European power of the future. It therefore repudiated the Jeffersonian presumption that England was an inherently counterrevolutionary force on the downward slope of history.[70]

None of these historical insights of course was available to Jefferson, who was caught up in an ongoing controversy that put his most cherished political convictions at risk and made all the promises of pastoral seclusion he had made to himself seem like quaint vestiges of a bygone era. Madison had already tried to warn him of what destiny was arranging for him: "You ought to be preparing yourself to hear truths, which no inflexibility will be able to withstand." Loosely translated, this meant that Jefferson, not Madison, was the consensus choice of the Republican party to succeed Washington in the presidency. Now that the Jay Treaty had given the Republicans a popular issue on which to discredit the Federalists, and now that Washington's retirement after two terms was a virtual certainty, Jefferson's reentry into the political arena had massive implications. Writing in coded language to Monroe in France, Madison explained that "the *republicans* knowing that *Jefferson alone* can be *started with hope of success mean to push him.*" By the early spring of 1796, whether he knew it or not, he had become the standard-bearer for the Republican party.[71]

This did not mean that Jefferson formally declared his candidacy for the presidency; no self-respecting statesman of the day did that. It meant that he merely neglected to make a public statement declaring his withdrawal. But since Jefferson did not permit the perception of his candidacy to gain access to his conscious mind, even though it was being bandied about throughout the Republican network and in several newspapers, he really had no reason to declare his withdrawal. Madison understood the elaborate system of internal valves that Jefferson could turn off and on so deftly. He therefore understood—it was a critical dimension of their remarkable collaboration—that Jefferson's willingness to reenter the political arena depended upon sustaining the fiction that it would never happen. Although Madison spent the entire summer and early fall of 1796 at Montpelier only a few miles from Jefferson, he chose not to visit his mentor at Monticello for fear of being drawn into conversations that upset Jefferson's denial mechanisms. "I have not seen Jefferson," he wrote Monroe in coded language, "and have *thought it best* to present *him no opportunity of protesting* to his *friend against* being *embarked on this contest.*"⁷²

This psychological minuet enjoyed the advantage of allowing Jefferson to dance back into public life without quite knowing it was happening. On the downside, since he did not yet acknowledge to himself that his remarks were anything but those of a private citizen, he did not feel accountable to anyone but himself or internalize any need to be guarded in his correspondence. His most damaging statement came in a letter to his Italian friend Philip Mazzei, in April 1796, that effectively ended his cordial relationship with Washington when it was picked up in the American press the following year: "It would give you a fever were I to name to you the apostates who have gone over to these heresies, men who were Samsons in the field and Solomons in the council, but who have had their head shaved by the harlot England. . . . We have only to awake and snap the Lilliputian cords which they have been entangling us during the first sleep which succeeded our labors.⁷³ If, as everyone at the time assumed, Samson was George Washington and the reference to shaved heads was a comment on his support for the Jay Treaty, Jefferson's letter was both grossly unfair and extremely impolitic. Characteristically, he claimed that the version printed in American newspapers was a distortion of his meaning produced by a bad translation from the Italian papers, where it originally appeared. But the simple truth was that his sentiments had not been garbled in translation, nor were they a temporary aberration, as some latter-day biographers have claimed. This was how he genuinely saw his political opponents at the time, as apostates and heretics and traitors to the cause of American independence. The moral dichotomies were clear and pure. The colors were black and white. There was no room in his mental universe for the notion that honest and principled men could disagree on a landmark issue like the Jay Treaty and make mutually compelling claims to the truth.

He also made some loose comments on the constitutional issues posed in the debate on the Jay Treaty that he would almost certainly have avoided if his guard had been up. Madison had lent him his personal copy of "Notes on the Debates at the Constitutional Convention" in the fall of 1795 because it was clear by then that the Republican strategy to block passage of the Jay Treaty depended upon throwing the question into the House of Representatives, where the Republicans enjoyed a majority; this required a good deal of constitutional ingenuity because the power to make treaties rested with the president and the Senate. (Indeed, a review of Madison's "Notes on the Debates" revealed that Madison himself had been one of the staunchest opponents of infringements on executive power over foreign policy at the Constitutional Convention.) Jefferson's bold and bald solution to this dilemma was to declare that "the true theory of our constitution" allowed the elected representatives in the House an equal share of power over treaties with the president and the Senate. Because he regarded the House of Representatives as the most democratic branch of the government with the closest ties to popular opinion, "the representatives are as free as the President and the Senate were to consider whether the national interest requires or forbids their giving the forms and force of law to the articles over which they have a power." Indeed, Jefferson claimed that to deny the House a role was to transfer control from the American people to "any other Indian, Algerine or other chief." He even went so far as to tell Monroe that he had no problem in shifting the main responsibility for approving all the treaties to the House and "in annihilating the whole treaty making power [of the executive branch], except as to making peace."[74]

These were radical prescriptions that, if taken seriously, would have thrown American foreign policy into the cauldron of domestic politics on every controversial occasion. They contrast with Madison's more narrow and careful constitutional argument, which became the official Republican position, that the House could block passage of the Jay Treaty because certain provisions required funding for their implementation and the House was the proper branch to decide all money bills. Madison's more careful argument made no frontal assault on executive power but still achieved the desired goal of allowing the Republican majority in the House to hold the Jay Treaty hostage. Jefferson's more extreme position reflected his more cavalier attitude toward constitutional questions in general. Unlike Madison, who had a deep appreciation for the Constitution as an artful arrangement of juxtaposed principles and powers with abiding influence over future generations, Jefferson tended to view it as a merely convenient agreement about political institutions that ought not to bind future generations or prevent the seminal source of all political power—popular opinion—from dictating government policy. His casual remarks in the spring of 1796 during the height of the debate over the Jay Treaty were uncharacteristic only in the sense that Jefferson customarily left constitutional questions in Madison's capable hands. But precisely because he did not feel the obligation to filter his opinions through Madison, his statements more accurately reflected his greater willingness to bend constitutional arguments to serve what he saw as a higher purpose, which in this case was defeat of the counterrevolutionary alliance with England. Upsetting delicate constitutional balances or setting dangerous precedents did not trouble him in such moments.[75]

Madison served as the floor manager for the Republicans during the debate in the House of Representatives—it was the first instance when they met in caucus as an opposition party—and the humiliation fell on him when the Republican majority melted away. John Adams observed that "Mr. Madison looks worried to death. Pale, withered, haggard." When the final vote came in late April 1796, Madison attributed the narrow Federalist victory to an urban conspiracy led by "the Banks, the British Merchts., the insurance Comps." In truth, the swing votes had come from western representatives, whose constituents had decided to support the treaty because the removal of British troops from the frontier promised to open up the Mississippi Valley for settlement. Madison apprised Jefferson that "the exertions and influence of Aristocracy, Anglicism, and mercantilism" had combined to "overwhelm the Republican cause, [and] has left it in a very crippled condition. . . ." The disaster was so total and so unexpected that, as Madison explained his dismay to Jefferson, "my consolation . . . is in the effect they have in riveting my future purposes." He was played out and ready for retirement.[76]

Jefferson, who had the advantage of viewing the devastation from Monticello, had a fundamentally different and more politically astute appraisal. The primary reason for the Federalist victory, he told Monroe in France, was the gigantic prestige of Washington, "the one man who outweighs them all in influence over the people" and whose support for the Jay Treaty proved in the end too much to overcome. Jefferson's conclusion was shrewdly prophetic:

> The Anglomen have in the end got their treaty through, and so far have triumphed over the cause of republicanism. Yet it has been to them a dear bought victory . . . and there is no doubt they would be glad to be replaced on the ground they possessed the instant before Jay's nomination extraordinary. They see that nothing can support them but the Colossus of the President's merits with the people, and the moment he retires, that his successor, if a Monocrat, will be overborne by the republican sense. . . . In the meantime, patience.[77]

Jefferson was usually even more disposed than Madison to regard any Federalist success as the result of corruption and conspiracy. After all, if the vast majority of the citizenry allegedly opposed a particular policy, and it nevertheless kept winning victories, the only logical explanation must be conspiratorial. What Jefferson saw clearly in the wake of the Jay Treaty debate, and Madison was simply too closely involved to notice, was that the resolution of the questions raised by the treaty had been reached by a new kind of politics in which both sides acknowledged that success depended upon an appeal to popular opinion. Washington's nearly unassailable popularity had given the Federalists a decided edge in this particular contest. But once the game had been defined in these terms—that is, once republicanism became more democratic in character—the Federalists were doomed.[78]

LUCKY LOSERS

IN SEPTEMBER 1796 Fisher Ames, the oracular champion of the Federalist cause, observed that Washington's Farewell Address was "a signal, like dropping a hat, for the party races to start." In fact the Republicans had been organizing for several months. Jefferson's candidacy had been a foregone conclusion for almost a year; as early as May 1796 Madison had apprised Monroe that the presidential election was likely to pit *"Jefferson the object on one side* [and] *Adams apparently on the other."* Neither man was expected to campaign. The emergence of an early form of democratic politics had not yet reached that stage of development. It was still considered unbecoming for a serious statesman to prostitute his integrity by a direct appeal to voters.[79]

This lingering aristocratic code fitted Jefferson's mood perfectly, for it allowed him to remain sequestered at Monticello throughout the summer, publicly oblivious of the campaign that Madison was waging in his behalf and even privately capable of sustaining the pretense that he would live out his life in retirement. Madison was the complicitous partner in this psychological game, never corresponding with Jefferson about the looming election until it was over. Even then, when he finally wrote Jefferson in December 1796, his political report studiously avoided mention of Jefferson's candidacy. "It is not improbable that Pinckney will step in between the two who have been treated as the principals in this question," he observed, a reference to efforts by Hamilton to run a third candidate, Thomas Pinckney of South Carolina, who might displace Adams as the Federalist choice for president. "This Jockeyship is accounted for by the enmity of Adams to Banks and funding systems," Madison went on, "and by an apprehension that he is too headstrong to be a fit puppet for the intriguers behind the skreen." Adams, in other words, was not a loyal Hamiltonian—the truth was that Adams disliked Hamilton almost as much as Jefferson did, and after learning about this Pinckney scheme, he loathed him even more—so the next occupant of the presidency was going to be either Jefferson or a man the Republicans could tolerate.[80]

Jefferson's first acknowledgement of his own candidacy came in response to Madison's letter. While not attempting to affect complete surprise, Jefferson maintained the posture that Madison had always remained his preferred choice: "The first wish of my heart was that you should have been proposed for the administration of government. On your declining it I wish any body rather than myself. And there is nothing I so anxiously hope as that my name may come out second or third. These would be indifferent to me; as the last would leave me at home the whole year, and the other [the vice presidency] the other two thirds of it." Jefferson then informed Madison to put out the word that if the election ended in a tie, he wished it known that Adams should be declared the winner. "He has always been my senior from the commencement of our public life," Jefferson observed with becoming modesty, a circumstance "that ought to give him preference," adding as a final thought that he had "no confidence in myself for the undertaking."[81]

Over the ensuing weeks, as the results of the electoral vote in the fourteen states became clear, Jefferson sustained a public posture of personal reluctance and political deference to Adams. Even before the votes had been counted, he wrote to his old colleague from Philadelphia and Paris days, regretting "the various little incidents [that] have happened or been contrived to separate us" and disavowing any competitive urges. "I have no ambition to govern men," he confided. "It is a painful and thankless task." He was obviously paying close attention to press reports on the voting, since he was one of the first to predict that Adams would win by three electoral votes (71–68), which turned out to be the exact result. But he wished to squelch all rumors that he had any objection to serving under Adams: "I was his junior in life, was his junior in Congress, his junior in the diplomatic line, his junior lately in our civil government." Besides, Adams was "perhaps the only sure barrier against Hamilton's getting in." The office of the vice presidency was a "tranquil and unoffending station" that would effectively allow Jefferson to remain in semiretirement. He expected to spend "philosophical evenings in the winter, and rural days in the summer."[82]

Beneath such expressions of reluctance and deference, which accurately reflected a genuine feeling at one layer of his personality, there existed another, much more realistic assessment of the political situation. While reiterating his political innocence, claiming that "I never in my life exchanged a word with any person on the subject, till I found my name brought forward generally, in competition with that of Mr. Adams," he also offered a shrewd analysis of what was in store for the winner. "The second office of this government is honorable and easy," he explained; "the first is but a splendid misery." The chief problem was the long shadow of George Washington. In an uncharacteristically mixed metaphor, he offered Madison this uncanny insight: "The President is fortunate to get off just as the bubble is bursting, leaving others to hold the bag. Yet, as his departure will mark the moment when the difficulties begin to work, you will see, that they will be ascribed to the new administration, and that he will have his usual good fortune of reaping credit from the good acts of others, and leaving to them that of his errors." In short, whoever followed Washington was virtually assured of failure, and "no man will bring out of that office the reputation which carries him into it." The Republicans had been lucky to lose.[83]

Neither Madison, who was too busy trying to diagnose the likely course of an Adams presidency, nor Adams himself, whose combination of vanity and obsession with public duty never permitted such political detachment, was capable of seeing things so clearly. To his credit, Jefferson's first reaction was to share this political appraisal with his long-standing friend from Quincy. He assumed the Ciceronian posture of the retired farmer; he was living, as he put it to Adams, in a secluded canton where "I learn little of what is passing; pamphlets, I never see, papers but a few; and the fewer the happier." Though disingenuous, it was a posture Adams understood for what it was and in keeping with the somewhat contrived civility that both men had assumed toward each other in recent years. After congratulating Adams on his victory and assuring him that he "never one single moment expected a different issue," Jefferson tried to warn him of the storm into which he was riding. First, there was "the subtlety of your arch-friend of New York"—Hamilton's duplicity was a sure source of complete consensus—who "will be disappointed as to you" and "contrive behind the scenes" to manipulate his protégés in the cabinet. More generally, both the foreign and domestic affairs of the nation were victims of partisan squabbling: "Since the day on which you signed the treaty of Paris our horizon was never so overcast." He concluded with a reference to earlier and better days, "when we were working for our independence," and a vague promise to renew the old partnership.[84]

Instead of posting the letter directly to Adams, Jefferson decided to run it past Madison first, just to assure its propriety. Madison counseled against sending the letter, offering six reasons why its sentiments might be misconstrued. The last and most politically significant reason was telling: "Considering the probability that Mr. A's course of administration may force an opposition to it from the Republican quarter, and the general uncertainty of the posture which our affairs may take, there may be real embarrassments from giving written possession to him, of the degree of compliment and confidence which your personal delicacy and friendship have suggested." In other words, Jefferson's well-known affection for Adams was admirable, but it must not be allowed to become an impediment to the Republican cause. If Jefferson were correct about the political earthquakes about to shake the Adams presidency, best to keep one's distance.[85]

This was excellent political advice that Jefferson immediately recognized as such, but it came at a price. For the bond Jefferson felt toward Adams was palpable. "Mr. A. and myself were cordial friends from the beginning of the revolution," he explained to Madison, and although they had parted company on several issues in the early 1790s, these differences had "not made me less sensible of the rectitude of his heart. And I wished him to know this. . . ." What's more, Adams was no hard-line Federalist of the Hamiltonian stripe. He had in fact opposed Hamilton's banking and funding schemes and offered only lukewarm support for the Jay Treaty. Furthermore, Jefferson knew that Adams mistrusted the English as much as he did. (The problem was that he mistrusted the French even more.) In short, Adams did not fit the Federalist stereotype that both Jefferson and Madison carried around in their heads. Indeed Adams's first instinct as president-elect was to ask if Madison would be willing to head the American diplomatic delegation to France and if Jefferson would consider serving in the cabinet rather than waste his talents in the Senate. It was a clear bipartisan gesture designed to offer the Republicans a significant role in the new administration.[86]

Jefferson's decision to distance himself from Adams, then, was both personally poignant and politically fateful. At the political level one can only speculate about the prospects of a bipartisan government headed by the Adams-Jefferson tandem, which would have enjoyed at least a fighting chance of inhabiting Washington's massive legacy. But such speculation is idle, not just because of Jefferson's decision but also because the Federalists whom Adams unwisely chose to retain in his cabinet were just as opposed to a vigorous Jeffersonian presence in the new administration as was Madison; they threatened to resign en masse if it occurred.

At the personal level Jefferson was effectively forced to choose between his long-standing loyalty to a friend and his responsibility to the Republican agenda. He was psychologically incapable of seeing himself as a party leader, but that in fact was what he once again had become. In his own mind he was taken off the hook in March 1797, when, after a cordial dinner at Washington's house in Philadelphia, he and Adams walked home together along Market Street and Adams apprised him that his Federalist associates had vetoed the bipartisan initiative as preposterous. As Jefferson remembered it later, the two old allies took different directions, "his being down Market Street, mine off along Fifth, and we took leave; and he never after that said one word to me on the subject or ever consulted me as to any measure of the government." Adams too, when forced to choose, had opted for party over friendship.[87]

Neither man, it should be noted, saw his decision in quite those terms. Adams regarded himself as the American version of "the patriot king," the virtuous chief magistrate who would oppose all factions on behalf of the public interest, even if it meant repudiating his own Federalist colleagues, as it eventually did. Jefferson, on the other hand, saw himself as head of the government-in-exile, again placed in the anomalous position of serving officially in the administration he opposed. At his swearing-in ceremony he joked about his rusty recall of parliamentary procedure, a clear signal that his time in Philadelphia would be spent in the harmless business of monitoring debates in the Senate. Three weeks later, on March 20, he was already back at Monticello, waiting for the inevitable catastrophes to befall the Federalists and, all in good time, deliver the full promise of the American Revolution into its rightful hands.[88]

4

Washington, D.C., 1801–04

We are all republicans—we are all federalists.
—THOMAS JEFFERSON
INAUGURAL ADDRESS, MARCH 4, 1801

I shall take no other revenge, than, by a steady pursuit of economy and peace, and by the steady establishment of republican principles, in substance and in form, to sink federalism into an abyss from which there shall be no resurrection of it.
—JEFFERSON TO LEVI LINCOLN
OCTOBER 25, 1802

LEGEND HAS IT that he rode to his inauguration as president in splendid isolation and with becoming modesty. According to the apocryphal account, which was based on the fraudulent report of an English tourist, at just before noon on March 4, 1801, Jefferson proceeded down a dusty Pennsylvania Avenue in a scene that subsequent image makers ought to have entitled "Mr. Jefferson Comes to Washington": "His dress was of plain cloth, and he rode on horseback to the Capitol without a single guard or even servant in his train, dismounted without assistance, and hitched the bridle of his horse to the palisades." He then entered the Senate chamber, so the story goes, and gave his Inaugural Address in an unassuming style and in a voice that one witness, Margaret Bayard Smith, described as "almost femininely soft." Indeed his delivery was so subdued that very few members of the audience could hear what he said. Then, after taking the oath of office, he left quickly and without fanfare and rode back alone to his lodgings at Conrad and McCunn's boardinghouse. There he placed himself at the far end of the table away from the fireplace—his customary location—and looked to all the world like just another ordinary citizen of the American republic breaking bread with his equals.[1]

The democratic themes of individualism and equality come marching, or perhaps riding, right at us in this legendary rendering. And since Jefferson's ascendance to the presidency is so closely associated with the emergence of a more democratic American society in the early years of the nineteenth century, it seems perfectly plausible to fit him into the trappings of democratic mythology. Jefferson himself inadvertently contributed to this interpretation when, several years after the event, he referred to his election as "the revolution of 1800," then went on to explain that it was "as real a revolution in the principles of our government as that of 1776 was in its form."[2] But what Jefferson actually meant by these words, and what most of his contemporaries thought his election meant at the time, do not rest very comfortably within the mythical imperatives of a democratic culture. Perhaps the best way to dramatize the difference between the democratic legend and the more historically correct reality is to begin with a detached description of what we know about the actual events of March 4, 1801.

There is no horse in the picture. It was only a short distance from his rooms at Conrad and McCunn's to Capitol Hill, only a few hundred yards, so he walked. But he was not walking alone. Ahead of him marched a detachment of militia officers from neighboring Alexandria with drawn swords, followed by a delegation of marshals from the District of Columbia. Behind him was a small parade of dignitaries led by a cadre of Republican congressmen and two members of the outgoing cabinet, whose presence was intended to illustrate continuity with the Adams presidency. Adams himself was conspicuously absent, having taken the four o'clock stage out of town that morning.

There was nearly unanimous recognition among witnesses that the relative simplicity of this "little parade" was intended to make a political statement. Most commentators emphasized the relative lack of pomp and pageantry and contrasted Jefferson's modest entourage with the coach and sixes used by Washington and Adams at their respective inaugurations. But the operative word was "republican" rather than "democratic." No one at the time was disposed to describe Jefferson's election as the coming of the common man. The only observers willing to characterize him as a "democrat" were a few diehard Federalists; and they used the term as an epithet (i.e., "dangerous democrat"). Jefferson himself had seldom used the word "democracy" in his public statements or private letters prior to 1800, and he did not start doing so once elected. In a letter to Maria a few weeks before the inauguration, he adopted his most familiar formulation of the Jeffersonian sense of what was happening: "I feel a sincere wish, indeed, to see our Government brought back to its republican principles, to see that kind of government firmly fixed to which my whole life has been devoted." He saw himself as the instrument for a recovery of "pure republicanism," by which he meant the political principles forged in the crucible of the American Revolution, principles that had then been corrupted by the Federalists (i.e., "Anglomen," "monarchists") since 1776.[3]

In both his own mind and the minds of his supporters, then, Jefferson's elevation to the presidency did not symbolize the ascendance of the ordinary so much as the restoration of revolutionary austerity. The studied simplicity of his clothing and the unassuming demeanor of his "little parade" as it marched up Capitol Hill was seen as a backward-looking statement about "the spirit of '76." In Jefferson's mind great historical leaps forward were almost always the product of a purging, which freed societies from the accumulated debris of the past and thereby allowed the previously obstructed natural forces to flow forward into the future. Simplicity and austerity, not equality or individualism, were the messages of his inaugural march. It was a minimalist statement about a purging of excess and a recovery of essence.

REPUBLICAN CITY

IF THIS WAS what "pure republicanism" meant to Jefferson and his contemporaries, their intended message enjoyed a perfect natural habitat in the new national capital. For Washington, D.C., in 1801 was the ideal location in which to launch a crusade against excesses. It would have been impossible to imagine courtiers scheming in corridors or conspirators plotting behind locked palace doors, since there were no courts, no palaces, in truth very few buildings at all. Congressmen who tried to caucus in the corridors of the unfinished Capitol had to compete with the frequent sound of rifle fire from hunters shooting quail and wild turkeys within a hundred yards of Capitol Hill. Washington was the perfect republican city in the awkward sense that it was not really a city at all. The stumps still protruded in several spots up and down Pennsylvania Avenue (perhaps another reason why Jefferson was not conveyed to his inauguration in a coach), and several travelers who stopped to inquire where the new capital of America was located were informed that they were standing squarely in its center. It was doubly appropriate that the first president to take up residence was on record as believing that cities were sores on the body political, since Washington struck most observers as more bucolic than urban, an open wound bleeding into the Potomac River.[4]

Jefferson had long regretted "the dinner table bargain" that led to the southern location of the national capital on the banks of the Potomac; he called it the most misguided decision of his entire public career. But he was referring to Hamilton's crafty diplomacy in seducing him to accept federal assumption of the state debts, not the unlikely placement of the capital in the Chesapeake marshland. Washington himself had made the key decisions about the swampy site and ungainly size of the place. He had selected a natural depression with saucerlike sides that efficiently captured and trapped heat and humidity while serving as an ideal breeding ground for mosquitoes. The surrounding hills were just high enough to impede the movement of air and just low enough to preclude the presence of vistas. Washington had also fused together both urban plans proposed to him, thereby expanding the borders of the city. As a result, instead of beginning with a concentrated population center and spreading out, the city that bore his name began as an expansive but almost empty space that only gradually filled in. European and American tourists were invariably confused upon entering the American capital because the city managers had published elaborate maps and prints showing the layout of the envisioned streets and buildings without explaining that it would take decades for reality to catch up with the vision. Washington's last words on the project, eerily accurate as usual when it came to essential matters, predicted that the vacant spaces would allow the national capital to grow into greatness "in about a century."[5]

That made Washington a model Jeffersonian city in yet another sense—namely, it was a bold, some would say preposterous, promise about the nation's latent potential, as if a young man just starting out in life were to draw up a plan for his dream house and then wait confidently for the future to fulfill his expectations. Foreign visitors routinely recorded their disapproval of the presumptuous neoclassical style of the President's House and the Capitol—the only public buildings standing in 1801—which were plopped down in the midst of a marshy field. "The streets are filled with mud in winter, and with dust in summer," ran one comic account, "and instead of splendid edifices you can see nothing but cornfields, and plains, dry canals and dirty marshes, where frogs make love in a most sonorous and exquisite strain, and bellow forth their attachments as if they were determined to make no secret of it." Renaming Goose Creek the Tiber served as a source of many jokes about the ridiculousness of an American Rome. A young Irish poet, Thomas Moore, captured the caustic mood in verse, even taking a swipe at Jefferson himself in the process:

> This fam'd metropolis, where fancy sees
> Squares in morasses, obelisks in trees.

Which second sighted seers e'en now adorn
With shrines unbuilt and heroes yet unborn.

Though now but woods and J——they see,
Where streets should run and sages ought to be.[6]

Whatever deficiencies such doggerel displayed as poetry, it correctly called attention to the obvious disjunction between the physical reality of Washington as a motley collection of villages and the rather presumptuous claim, which over the long stretch of time miraculously turned out to be nearly true, that this pseudometropolis was the epicenter of a political earthquake destined to topple all the monarchs and despots on the planet. But at the time this remarkable paradox looked more like a simple contradiction. The unfinished state of the Capitol made the point graphically. What Jefferson saw as he completed his "little parade" was a construction site. The center of the Capitol was missing altogether, and the columns designed to support the front facade were lying flat on the lawn. The north wing, where the House of Representatives met, was still a shell with an unfinished roof; congressmen referred to it as "the oven." Jefferson had chosen to be sworn in as president in the Senate chamber primarily because it was the only public building available.[7]

Of course urban and architectural symbolism can carry us only so far in recovering the original sense of Jefferson's inauguration. Once inside the Senate chamber we enter an interior region in several senses of that term. All the seats on the Senate floor were filled, and the gallery was crowded to capacity. Reporters estimated the audience at about a thousand people. If we can be sure that they had not come to hear about the arrival of Jeffersonian Democracy but rather about the restoration of "pure republicanism," it was by no means clear what that meant. Some sense of the drama and tension lying beneath the surface of the scene greeted Jefferson as he approached the small stage at the bottom of the well of the Senate floor. Waiting to meet him were Vice President Aaron

Burr, who had been sworn in earlier that morning, and Chief Justice John Marshall, who was present to administer the oath to Jefferson.

Any gathering that included Burr possessed the potential to look like a conspiracy. He was, by the lights of his contemporaries, the most mysterious and mercurial member of the revolutionary generation. John Adams believed that Burr was the only man capable of edging out Hamilton in the race to become an American Napoleon. He was dashing and brilliant in the Hamiltonian style, and his singular advantage over Hamilton, and indeed all competitors, was a total disregard for any moral or political principle that obstructed his path to power. "As to Burr," wrote Hamilton in December 1800, "his private character is not defended by his most partial friends," adding that "Mr. Burr [is] the most unfit man in the United States for the office of President." Hamilton seemed to sense in Burr a more virulent version of his own throbbing political ambition, just as Burr seemed to sense in Hamilton the only American statesman with the audacity to challenge his own pretensions. The very similarity of their respective temperaments defined their rivalry in life-and-death terms. If only in retrospect, it seemed eminently predictable that the two antagonists would face off with pistols on the plains of Weehawken three years later and that Burr, unburdened by any quaint code of honor, would coolly send a bullet into Hamilton's spinal column.[8]

Why was such an un-Jeffersonian character standing there in the Senate chamber, greeting Jefferson as his second-in-command? The short answer is that Burr was primarily responsible for Jefferson's election. In the presidential campaign of 1800 Jefferson had once again been matched against Adams. Although Republican candidates for Congress and state office won sweeping victories, Adams ran ahead of the other Federalist candidates at the top of the ticket. In all states except New York, Adams actually matched or exceeded his electoral votes in the 1796 contest, which he had won by a narrow margin. But New York had gone decisively for Jefferson, providing his slim margin of victory. And the man who had delivered the electors of New York to Jefferson's camp was the irrepressible Aaron Burr, whose price for this important contribution was a place on the ballot alongside Jefferson.[9]

An all-important epilogue to this political story occurred during the weeks following Jefferson's victory. It then became distressingly clear that because of a quirk in the electoral system that prevented electors from distinguishing between votes for president and vice president (subsequently corrected by the Twelfth Amendment), Jefferson and Burr had received the identical number of electoral votes. This threw the election into the House of Representatives, where the Federalists were able to block the majority necessary for Jefferson's selection for six days and thirty-six ballots. Even though everyone acknowledged that the American electorate had intended to choose Jefferson as its president, Burr had done nothing to indicate his willingness to defer. (Altruistic acts of deference were alien to Burr's style.) So the man greeting Jefferson as he entered the Senate chamber was an infamous political schemer who only a few weeks earlier had passively given himself to a Federalist conspiracy designed to cheat Jefferson of the very office he was coming to claim.[10]

Then there was John Marshall. By all rights Marshall should have been a Jeffersonian disciple. A fellow Virginian, even a distant cousin via the ubiquitous Randolph clan, Marshall was a contemporary of Madison and Monroe who had somehow wiggled through the net that usually gathered Virginia's talented young men into Jefferson's political family. By the time of the Jay Treaty he had become one of the most prominent of the Federalists; Jefferson wrote him off as a man of "lax lounging manners . . . and a profound hypocrisy," Jefferson's way of designating Marshall a traitor to Virginia's version of republicanism. Marshall's talents attracted Adams's attention by 1797, and he was appointed a member of the all-important American delegation to France, then secretary of state, and finally, during Adams's last weeks as the lame-duck president, chief justice of the United States.[11]

To say that Jefferson and Marshall hated each other would be going too far in 1801; hatred came later with greater exposure. In a curious way Marshall presented difficulties that were a mirror image of those represented by Burr, for Marshall always managed to cloak his personal feelings toward Jefferson behind an elaborately constructed screen of impartial-sounding arguments that invariably ended up leaving him no choice but to align himself on the other side. Just as Hamilton's dislike of Burr was rooted in the recognition of their overlapping ambitions and their common affinity for a flamboyant brand of decisiveness, so Jefferson's mistrust of Marshall was exacerbated by their mutual preference for a more subtle and indirect style that probably had its origins in the Virginia code of politeness. If Hamilton came at you with a saber, Marshall preferred the stiletto.

On the other hand, Marshall's massive probity was powered by a mind that worked in ways fundamentally different from Jefferson's, which tended to filter and fit experience through primal categories of right and wrong. Marshall worked in more shaded hues and colors in the middle of the spectrum and, much like Madison, was more intellectually agile in a lawyerlike way in making distinctions that broke down the Jeffersonian dichotomies into smaller components. He was a genius at what Jefferson later called "twistifications"—that is, intricate arguments that seemed to be headed in the proper Jeffersonian direction but then somehow doubled back and landed decisively on the other side. Much like Hamilton's dexterity with account books and complex fiscal figures, Marshall's reasoning usually appeared to Jefferson like the diabolical maneuvers of an evil wizard. He was also extremely adroit at doing the greatest damage to one's cause by apparently attempting to defend it. In the weeks before the inauguration, for example, he had admitted to having "insufferable objections" to Jefferson's election and to believing that Jefferson's political prejudices made him "totally . . . unfit for the chief magistracy of a nation which cannot indulge these prejudices without sustaining deep and permanent injury." But despite these reservations, he wished it known that some Federalist critics of the president-elect were unfair. If the Jeffersonians were divided between "speculative theorists and absolute terrorists," Jefferson himself did not strike him as a member of the latter category.[12]

At a more political but less personal level, the man waiting to administer the oath of office to Jefferson in the crowded Senate chamber was especially offensive because he stood as the ultimate embodiment of "the midnight judges." That phrase did not originate with Jefferson, though he quickly adopted it as a way of referring to the judicial appointments that Adams had made, allegedly during his last hours in office. The phrase itself was somewhat misleading, since it conjured up an image of Adams spending his last night in the presidential mansion furiously signing appointment letters beneath the midnight oil in a last-ditch spasm of political vindictiveness before catching the early-morning stage out of town. In fact Adams had made the vast majority of his judicial appointments, including that of Marshall as chief justice, several weeks earlier, soon after the passage of the Judiciary Act in February 1801. What was true, however, was that all of them, including Marshall's, had occurred after the results of the presidential election of 1800 were known, so in that sense they constituted a partisan action designed to force Federalist judges on the incoming Republican president. Adams could claim, as he did, that he was simply doing what Washington had done during his last weeks in office; but that precedent was rather weak because Jefferson's election represented a fundamental repudiation of the incumbent Federalist administration, whereas Adams had represented a continuation.[3]

To make matters worse, Marshall's appointment had no term. It was a lifetime seat that could be vacated only if Marshall committed "treasonable acts" or was found guilty of "high crimes and misdemeanors." This made him a kind of unmovable Trojan horse placed squarely in the middle of the Jefferson presidency, the official commander of a Federalist judiciary apparently impervious to executive influence or popular opinion. Nor was Marshall unaware of his truly singular position and his nearly open-ended opportunity—he saw it as a duty—to make trouble. On inauguration day, just before he walked over to the Capitol, he wrote a reassuring letter to a Federalist colleague. "Of the importance of the judiciary at all times, but more especially the present I am fully impressed," he explained, "and I shall endeavor in the new office to which I am called not to disappoint my friends." Jefferson of course did not know about this letter, but he knew enough to suspect perpetual mischief from Marshall's protected corner. The preceding day, anticipating that Marshall might show up late for the ceremony as a way of spoiling the serenity of the proceedings, Jefferson sent him a terse note reminding him to be present at twelve o'clock sharp. Marshall wrote back to reassure the president-elect that he was always punctual.[14]

Whatever mutual dislike and distrust the awkward trio of Burr, Marshall and Jefferson harbored toward one another, it could be dismissed as a merely private or personal drama. At the larger public level the tension present in the Senate chamber derived from two overlapping apprehensions: First, the ascendancy of Jefferson and the Republicans to power was unprecedented in the sense that the Federalists had controlled the federal government since its inception in 1789; second, Jefferson's dominant political message throughout the 1790s had been almost entirely negative, in the sense that he had led the opposition to Federalist versions of federal power and objected to the creation of an energetic national government on the ground that it violated the original intentions of the American Revolution. Taken together, these two conditions raised serious questions about the very survival of a federal government the incoming president had threatened to dismantle.[15]

The answer to the first set of questions seemed clear and reassuring and was essentially inherent in the very inaugural ceremony itself. Margaret Bayard Smith, the wife of the editor of the pro-Jefferson *National Intelligencer* and a member of the audience, put it most succinctly: "The changes of administration, which in every government and in every age have most generally been epochs of confusion, villainy and bloodshed, in this happy country take place without any species of distraction, or disorder." More elemental than the ostentatious simplicity and republican symbolism of the inaugural parade was the fundamental fact that it had occurred at all. The peaceful transfer of political power from one regime to another, a problem that had haunted European governments of all sizes, shapes and forms from time immemorial—and indeed continues to bedevil some of the most powerful nations of the modern world—had happened in a remarkably matter-of-fact fashion. The defeated Federalists were bitter, to be sure, but they had deferred to the will of the electorate. During the protracted debate and balloting in the House of Representatives in February, Thomas McKean, the Republican governor of Pennsylvania, had threatened to call out twenty thousand militia if the Federalists tried to cheat Jefferson of his victory. Another Pennsylvanian, Hugh Henry Brackenridge, had advised Jefferson to seize power and convene the government without waiting for the House of Representatives to resolve the impasse with Burr. Several Virginians had recommended calling for a new constitutional convention to restructure the federal government in anticipation of Federalist skulduggery. But all such alarmists had gone unheeded, and their sense of foreboding had proved exaggerated. Although it was not what Jefferson meant by the phrase "the revolution of 1800," the most revolutionary feature of his elevation to the presidency was its routine character. To put it differently, the most significant events were those that did not happen.[16]

The answer to the second set of questions—about Jefferson's political agenda as president—was much more problematic. No one knew for sure what he meant by "pure republicanism," except perhaps that it entailed reducing the size and scope of the federal government. "Mr. Jefferson is well calculated to pull down any political edifice," wrote one Virginia Federalist, "and those will not be disappointed who have feared he would employ himself . . . in taking to pieces the national building . . ."; he warned that "even the foundation will be razed in less than four years." The reference to "the foundation" hinted at the chief Federalist fear, which was that Jefferson intended to disavow the constitutional settlement of 1788. He had, after all, been elected as the leader of a political party whose central premise had been hostility to any exercise of power by the federal government in domestic affairs. What Jefferson referred to admiringly as "the antient Whig principles" were entirely oppositional in character, having developed in England as the dissenting tradition against the accumulated power of king and court, then in America as the ideological basis for opposition to both royal and parliamentary power over the colonies. Clearly Jefferson and his Republican supporters regarded the Federalist policies of the 1790s, especially the Hamilton fiscal program, as a betrayal of "pure republicanism." But given the inherently oppositional logic of Jeffersonian thought, it was not just plausible, it seemed almost obligatory, that he also reject as excessive the powers vested in the national government under the Constitution. This meant turning the clock back past the 1790s and into the 1780s, when the powers of the national government under the Articles of Confederation were extremely weak. Indeed, considering Jefferson's deep-seated aversion to political coercion of any sort and his long-standing commitment to a dissenting tradition that regarded all government power as inherently arbitrary and corruptive in character, it was difficult to know where he drew the line that separated the legitimate exercise of political authority from the oppressive and abusive infringement of personal freedom. How could he take an oath to preserve, protect and defend the Constitution of the United States, the Federalists asked, if his primary goal as president was to dismantle the federal institutions created by that very document?[17]

The answer he seemed to leak out to his Republican supporters in the months preceding his inauguration was that his intention was not to dismantle the federal government but to shrink it. "The true theory of our Constitution," he told Gideon Granger, is that "the states are independent as to everything within themselves, and united as to everything respecting foreign nations." This sounded very much like the position he had taken in the 1780s, when the Constitution was being drafted and before Madison had persuaded him to support its ratification. It was also consistent with his view in 1798, when he and Madison had worked together to draft the Kentucky and Virginia Resolutions in order to block implementation of the Alien and Sedition Acts, the one significant act of his vice presidency. There Jefferson had gone considerably further than Madison in recognizing the right of a state to nullify a federal law within its own borders, even describing federal intrusion in state matters as interference by a foreign government. In October 1801 he had also let it be known that he supported a proposal being circulated in Virginia by John Taylor and Edmund Pendleton that called for a one-term presidency with reduced executive power, shorter terms for senators, federal judges removable by a vote of Congress and constitutional limits on the borrowing power of the federal government. Whether one characterized these hints as "shrinking" or "dismantling," they lent credibility to the Federalist rumors that Jefferson meant to destroy the current foundation of the central government and thereby allow the United States to become, like Europe, a series of separate nation-states in the manner of France, Italy and Austria.[18]

If there was a consensus within both Republican and Federalist circles that Jefferson's election meant a radical reduction in the powers of the federal government, the only question being how much and the only political disagreement being that the Republicans were overjoyed and the Federalists were terrified, the one dissenting voice belonged to none other than Alexander Hamilton. Acknowledging that "it is too late for me to become his apologist" and that he "did not really have any disposition to do it" anyway, Hamilton went on to offer a back-handed defense of Jefferson's political principles: "I admit that his politics are tinctured with fanaticism, that he is too much in earnest in his democracy, that he has been a mischievous enemy to the principal measures of the past administration, that he is crafty and persevering in his objects, that he is not scrupulous about the means of success, nor very mindful of truth, and that he is a contemptible hypocrite." But despite all these personal weaknesses, indeed in part because of them, Hamilton predicted that Jefferson "is as likely as any man I know to temporize . . . ; and the probable result of such a temper is the preservation of systems, though originally opposed, which being once established, could not be overturned without danger to the person who did it." Like everyone else, Hamilton conceded, he was only guessing, but he did not believe that Jefferson had the disposition to sustain the kind of pressure required to dismantle the federal government. "To my mind," Hamilton concluded, "a true estimate of Mr. J's character warrants the expectation of a temporizing rather than a violent system."[19]

These, then, were the personal or private vibrations as well as the larger political speculations present in the Senate chamber when Jefferson turned to the audience and began to read his Inaugural Address. One feature of the legendary account is absolutely correct—his voice was so soft and inaudible that few listeners beyond the first row could hear what he said—but he had worked on his address with the same diligence he had once given to the Declaration of Independence. And this time the words were all his, unedited by intrusive committees or meddling delegates. What's more, he had finished making his revisions in time to have the final draft available for the printers and the *National Intelligencer* on the day of its delivery, so it is possible that some members of the audience had advance copies that allowed them to follow his speech despite the poor projection of his voice. What they heard, or perhaps read, turned out to be one of the two or three most significant inaugural addresses in American history and, apart from the hallowed Declaration, the most artful and eloquent public document that Jefferson ever crafted.[20]

FIRST INAUGURAL

LIKE ANY SEMINAL statement in American history, though unlike the vast majority of inaugural addresses by other American presidents, Jefferson's speech of March 4, 1801, can be read with profit on several levels. At the highest and most rarefied level, a place where Jefferson's stylistic skills felt most comfortable and functioned with near-poetic felicity, his speech contained several passages that echo across the ages with memorable phrasings. As an eloquent statement of the becoming modesty joined with panoramic wisdom that we look for in a new president, for example, none has said it better:

> I have learned to expect that it will rarely fall to the lot of imperfect man to retire from this station with the reputation and the favor which bring him into it. . . . I shall often go wrong through defect of judgment. When right I shall often be thought wrong

by those whose positions will not command a view of the whole ground. I ask for your indulgence for my own errors, which will never be intentional; and your support against the errors of others, who may condemn what they would not if seen in all its parts.[21]

Or if one were searching for a classic rendering of the principle of free speech, no American statesman had ever put it so succinctly: "If there be any among us who would wish to dissolve this union or to change its republican form, let them stand undisturbed as monuments of the safety with which error of opinion may be tolerated where reason is left free to combat it." Or to take a final illustration out of several equally eloquent entries, there is this concise formulation of America's domestic and foreign policy goals: "Equal and exact justice to all men, of whatever state or persuasion, religious or political; peace, commerce, and honest friendship, with all nations—entangling alliances with none." It was Jefferson, not Washington, who coined the term "entangling alliances."[22]

But the most oft-quoted words, which can also reach across time as a lyrical expression of transcendent truth, are in fact fully comprehensible only when seen within the context of American politics in 1801. Apart from the natural rights section of the Declaration of Independence, this is probably the most famous political statement that Jefferson ever made: "But every difference of opinion is not a difference of principle. We have called by different names brethren of the same principle. We are all republicans—we are all federalists." This was also the passage that virtually all the reporters and interested observers fastened upon at the time because it seemed to represent Jefferson's clear, indeed grand, statement of conciliation and moderation. It signaled that the bitter party battles of the 1790s would not continue in the Jefferson presidency, that the incoming Republicans would not seek revenge for past Federalist atrocities like the Alien and Sedition Acts and, most significant, that Jefferson's understanding of "pure republicanism" did not mean a radical break with Federalist policies or a dramatic repudiation of the governmental framework established in the Constitution. Hamilton spoke for the relieved Federalists who viewed the address as "a candid retraction of past misapprehensions, and a pledge to the community that the new President will not lend himself to dangerous innovations, but in essential points will tread in the steps of his predecessors."[23]

But Jefferson did not really mean what Hamilton and all the other commentators thought they heard him say. Part of the problem was actually a matter of translation. In the version of his address printed in the *National Intelligencer* and then released to the newspapers throughout the country, the key passage read: "We are all Republicans—we are all Federalists." By capitalizing the operative terms, the printed version had Jefferson making a gracious statement about the overlapping goals of the two political parties. But in the handwritten version of the speech that Jefferson delivered, the key words were not capitalized. Jefferson was therefore referring not to the common ground shared by the two parties but to the common belief, shared by all American citizens, that a republican form of government and a federal bond among the states were most preferable. Since one would have been hard pressed to discover a handful of American citizens who disagreed with this observation, his statement was more a political platitude than an ideological concession. The impression that Jefferson had publicly retracted his previous statements about the party conflict as a moral struggle between the forces of light and the forces of darkness was, as it turned out, badly mistaken.

There were several suggestive passages that provided clues to Jefferson's truly visionary version of "pure republicanism," but most commentators were too transfixed by the apparent message of moderation to notice. John Marshall, who was presumably close enough to the podium to hear the speech as delivered, went straight back to his home and recorded his impression: "I have administered the oath to the President. . . . It [the Inaugural Address] is in direct terms giving the lie to the violent party declamation which had elected him; but it is strongly characteristic of his political theory." Marshall was right, though he did not specify what he meant by "political theory." But this was hardly the chief justice's fault. A crucial component of Jefferson's genius was his ability to project his vision of American politics at a level of generalization that defied specificity and in a language that seemed to occupy an altitude where one felt obliged to look up and admire without being absolutely certain about the details.[24]

One such passage in the Inaugural Address occurred when Jefferson was enumerating the natural advantages enjoyed by American citizens, who were "separated by nature and a wide ocean from the exterminating havoc of one quarter of the globe" and had the good fortune to possess "a chosen country, with room enough for our descendants to the hundredth and thousandth generation." Then he concluded the list of assets with what he called "one thing more": "a wise and frugal government, which shall restrain men from injuring one another, which shall leave them free to regulate their pursuits of industry and improvement, and shall not take from the mouth of labor the bread it has earned. This is the sum of good government, and this is necessary to close the circle of our felicities." This was Jefferson's clearest statement of his minimalist theory of government. While Federalists were listening nervously for clarifications of his position on executive authority, the role of the judiciary and the proper jurisdiction of federal versus state law, Jefferson framed his answer at a level where all such distinctions dissolved. The very notion of government itself was the core problem. In that sense he remained true to the Whig tradition, which stigmatized all forms of political power as inherently corrupt, as well as to his own ideal of personal autonomy, which regarded any explicit exercise of authority that was not consensual or voluntary as inherently invasive. Though an old and venerable political tradition and a long-standing Jeffersonian conviction, this perspective assumed a novel shape in the Inaugural Address because it meant that Jefferson was declaring that his primary responsibility as president was to render ineffectual and invisible the very government he was elected to lead. On the face of it, this seemed to put him in a strange and anomalous position, much like naming Luther to head the Catholic Church.[25]

The obvious question that followed logically from this disavowal of a positive role for government was not lost on Jefferson himself. He raised it midway through his speech and made at least a glancing attempt at an answer:

> I know, indeed, that some honest men fear that a republican government cannot be strong; that this government is not strong enough. But would the honest patriot, in the full tide of successful experiment, abandon a government which has so far kept us free and firm, on the theoretic and visionary fear that this government, the world's best hope, may possibly want energy to preserve itself? I trust not. I believe this, on the contrary, the strongest government on earth. I believe it is the only one where every man, at the call of the laws, would fly to the standard of the law, and would meet invasions of the public order as his own personal concern.[26]

This is both the richest and most elusive passage in Jefferson's Inaugural Address. It acknowledged, at least implicitly, that his election had prompted widespread apprehension about the dismemberment of the federal government and the resulting dissolution of the national union. But then Jefferson inverted the argument, claiming that his critics had been seized by a "theoretic and visionary fear." This in fact was precisely the accusation being leveled against *him*—namely, that he was a naive visionary who lacked a realistic understanding of how much national stability depended upon an energetic federal government that he (not his Federalist critics, as he seemed to say) had pledged to dismantle. Jefferson had somehow transformed himself into the defender of a national government as "the world's best hope"—a phrase Abraham Lincoln was to pick up and improve upon as "last, best hope" in his own First Inaugural—and consigned his critics to the role of skeptics who lacked his republican faith.

But the truly creative transformation, again more implied than asserted, was Jefferson's suggestion that the true, indeed only source of energy in a republic was not the government per se but the voluntary popular opinion on which it rested. The traditional presumption, which was a bedrock conviction among all Federalists, was that an active federal government was necessary to embody authority and focus national policy. In the absence of such governmental leadership, it was assumed that the American republic would spin off into a series of factions and interest groups and eventually into separate regional units. Without a strong central government, in short, one could not have a coherent American nation. In Jefferson's formulation, however, which must have seemed counterintuitive to the Federalists, the release of national energy increased as the power of government decreased. Whereas the Federalist way of thinking about government concerned itself with sustaining discipline, stability and balance, the Jeffersonian mentality bypassed such traditional concerns and celebrated the ideal of liberation. Lurking in his language about what makes a republican government strong was a belief in the inherent coherence of an American society that did not require the mechanisms of the state to maintain national stability.

In the weeks following the delivery and distribution of his Inaugural Address, Jefferson made a point of writing to surviving signers of the Declaration of Independence, as well as other colleagues from the Continental Congress who had also been "present at the creation," to share his celebratory sense that the version of "pure republicanism" he had professed in his speech was a recovery of what they all had intended back in 1776. Whatever new and ideologically experimental ideas were lurking within the rhetorical recesses of the Inaugural Address, Jefferson was absolutely certain that his message represented a restoration of the vision shared by the original revolutionaries as "the antient and sacred truths" on which American independence had been based. He explained to Benjamin Rush, the old revolutionary gadfly in Philadelphia, that "these sentiments have been long and radically mine," and Rush concurred that Jefferson's address gave poetic expression to the values they all had thought they were fighting for in the glory days. Something magical and spiritual had happened at the founding moment, a kind of primal encounter with political purity that all the original participants experienced as a collective epiphany. Jefferson's first instinct was to share with his fellow survivors and sharers of that experience—outsiders and the younger generation could not understand—that the true "spirit of '76" was back. The sinners had at least been cast out of the temple, and the saints were once again in control.[27]

His emphasis on austerity and simplicity, both in the inaugural ceremony itself and in his prescriptions for a stripped-down federal government, represented his core conviction about the recovered meaning of what the American Revolution had been about and what his own election to the presidency had reestablished. Much like his fondness for "a little rebellion now and then" or for "sweeping away" the accumulated debris of history every generation, Jefferson regarded his ascendance to power as a mandate to purge the American government of all the excess institutional baggage it had acquired since its pristine birth a quarter century earlier. While his Federalist critics and even some of his moderate Republican supporters worried out loud how far Jeffersonian reform would go (did it include eliminating the national bank? the federal judiciary? the navy?), Jefferson's own mind simply did not work at that level of specificity. His thinking about his presidential agenda, like his lyrical language in the Inaugural Address, hovered above such particulars. As he explained to John Dickinson, another of the revolutionary "band of brothers," the American government was like a ship that had passed through some very rough seas: "We shall put her back on her republican tack, and she will show by the beauty of her motion the skill of her builders." Once the nation was put on its proper course, in short, forces as natural as the wind and tide would take over and carry America toward its destiny. God was not in the details for Jefferson; he was in the sky and stars. If one could just align the ship of state with them again, all those minor squabbles about executive power or federal jurisdiction would become irrelevant and sink from sight. Those who kept raising nettlesome questions about such items were inadvertently confessing that they lacked the pure republican faith.[28]

THE TEXTUAL PRESIDENCY

WHEREVER ONE might wish to locate God's abiding presence, its political manifestation was very much on Jefferson's side at the start of his presidency. As it turned out, Adams had been the perfect predecessor. His irascible and all too human executive style had contrasted unfavorably with the Olympian presence of the godlike Washington, thereby making Adams unpopular and lowering expectations for his own successor. What's more, the most unpopular and unilateral act of the Adams presidency, to send an American delegation to Paris with instructions to negotiate an end to the "quasi war" with France, had proved to be a brilliant success. The terms of the new peace treaty arrived too late to help Adams in the presidential election of 1800 but in time to end the "quasi war" before Jefferson took office. And not only was America at peace with the European powers, but France and England had agreed to what was in effect an armistice in their seemingly perpetual struggle for the domination of Europe. Jefferson inherited the most stable and peaceful international scene since the United States had declared its independence.[29]

On the home front, providence proved just as kind. The much-despised Alien and Sedition Acts, which had allowed the Federalists to prosecute their most outspoken Republican opponents for treason, had in fact backfired, helping mobilize popular support for Republican candidates in the congressional elections of 1800. In the new Congress coming to Washington with Jefferson, the Republicans enjoyed a two-to-one majority in the House and a smaller but decided majority in the Senate. What's more, the legislation that had created the Alien and Sedition Acts was due to lapse in the early months of Jefferson's presidency, so he needed to do nothing on that score but wait. Add to this happy set of circumstances the resumption of a flourishing West Indian trade now that peace with France was restored, an overall expansion of American commerce with a now-peaceful Europe and an agrarian economy that was humming along at unprecedented levels of productivity, and Jefferson's vision of a minimalist federal government—pursuing what he described as "a noiseless course . . . , unattractive of notice"—began to look like a sensible act of hands-off statesmanship. With history dealing out cards like this, who would not want to stand pat?[30]

As it turned out, even the most invisible and unobtrusive federal government required executive leadership, if for no other reason than to implement the principle of republican austerity. Here again Jefferson was the beneficiary of the Adams administration, but this time as a graphic example of how not to do it. "My wish is to collect in a mass around the administration all the abilities and the respectability to which the offices exercised here can give employ," Jefferson explained, adding that he was determined to "give none of them to secondary characters." Adams, not certain about how much discretion he possessed as incoming president, had felt obliged to retain Washington's cabinet as his own. It proved to be the most disastrous decision of his presidency and the chief source of his political frustrations, since he inherited the "secondary characters" Jefferson was referring to, as well as a cabinet more loyal to Hamilton and to memories of Washington than to Adams himself. (Jefferson later recalled that Adams became so frustrated by the recalcitrance of his own cabinet that he ended up convening it in order to scream obscenities at its advice while stomping around the cabinet meeting room and "dashing and trampling his wig on the floor.") The cabinet choices Jefferson made were governed by two criteria: proven ability and complete loyalty to the Jeffersonian version of republicanism. On this score he was extremely shrewd as well as blessed. His cabinet proved to be one of the ablest and the most stable collection of executive advisers in the history of the American presidency.[31]

The two most prominent and invaluable members were James

Madison and Albert Gallatin. Madison had long been a foregone conclusion as secretary of state. He was Jefferson's lifetime lieutenant and protégé, a fellow member of the Virginia dynasty, a battle-tested veteran of the party wars of the 1790s and the shrewdest student of the Jefferson psyche ever placed on earth. Gallatin was a Swiss-born émigré to America who had settled in Pennsylvania and quickly risen in the Republican ranks on the basis of his deft way with both words and numbers. He was short, balding and hawk-nosed, but his unimpressive appearance and lingering Genevan accent belied intellectual powers second to none among the rising generation of Republican leaders. Gallatin was only forty, and he was the one man in America capable of going toe-to-toe with Hamilton in debate over fiscal policy and comfortably holding his own. Since Jefferson's considerable experience in foreign policy meant that—no offense to Madison's extraordinary competence—he could and often would serve as his own secretary of state, Gallatin as secretary of the treasury was the most invaluable and strategically positioned member of the cabinet.[32]

The other members, if not "secondary characters," were lesser figures. Levi Lincoln, the attorney general, was a respected lawyer from Massachusetts. Along with Henry Dearborn, secretary of war, who was from the Maine district of Massachusetts, Lincoln was that singular phenomenon, a New England Jeffersonian whose Republican credentials had proved themselves by surviving in the homeland of Federalism. "Both are men of 1776," observed Gallatin, "and decided Republicans." The same could be said of Gideon Granger, who as postmaster general was not officially a member of the cabinet but had important responsibilities dispensing patronage. Granger was that rarest of species, a Republican from Connecticut, where rumor had it that a Yale degree was a prerequisite for success in politics or the pulpit, and a vow of eternal hostility to the infidel from Monticello was a mandatory part of the Yale commencement ceremony. The eventual choice as secretary of the navy, after much unsuccessful lobbying of other candidates, was Robert Smith, a prominent Baltimore lawyer. Jefferson joked that he "shall have to advertise for a Secretary of Navy," because of the widespread presumption, which proved correct, that the main mission of the job was to scuttle much of the infant American fleet in order to implement the Jeffersonian goal of republican austerity.[33]

Most students of the Jefferson presidency explain his leadership style in terms of the positive lessons he had learned from Washington and the negative ones learned from Adams. It is true that Jefferson himself referred to these obvious and opposing models as his guides, with the Adams model (i.e., sulking patriarch) less personally appealing and politically effective than Washington's model (i.e., military commander-in-chief surrounded by staff officers). In one sense Jefferson's organization of the executive branch represented an adaptation of the Washington scheme. All business had to go through the appropriate department heads first. On every working day each department head sent Jefferson a written summary of all decisions or issues in his area. Jefferson responded in writing, if possible on the same day, and also made himself available for individual conferences before his daily horseback ride at one o'clock. Unlike Washington, Jefferson preferred not to schedule regular meetings of the full cabinet, convening the entire group only when difficult decisions or a looming crisis required it. This arrangement made the president, as Jefferson put it, "the hub of a wheel" with the business of the nation done at the rim, conveyed through the departmental spokes but all supervised at the center. It was a system that maximized control while simultaneously creating necessary distance from details.[34]

Washington's example certainly loomed large for Jefferson, but it is more correct to understand his executive style as a projection of his own experience and personality. After all, the symbolic significance of Jefferson's inauguration was intended as a republican repudiation of courtly pomp and monarchial affectations, which were all a piece of the Washington model. And the military framework that Washington carried over from his experience as commander of the Continental Army was too explicitly authoritarian to fit with Jefferson's temperament, which preferred a more indirect expression of authority and attempted to create a consensual context within which all decisions had at least the appearance of being voluntary. He had in effect been practicing this more indirect leadership style in different ways throughout his mature life. It was the diplomatic style of the elegantly elusive American in Paris. It was the political style of the invisible but effective party leader who honestly claimed to despise political parties. It was the paternalistic style of the plantation master who had designed Monticello so as to make slavery almost invisible. It was the domestic style of the benevolent patriarch surrounded by an extended family bonded together in seemingly perfect harmony by unalloyed affection. It was, finally, the republican style of the president-elect, declaring that his chief duty was to render the federal government over which he was to assume control unobtrusive and politically impotent. The common ingredient in all these contexts was Jefferson's urge to cloak his exercise of power from others and from himself.

His own characterization of cabinet meetings, for example, emphasized the harmonious atmosphere; it borrowed from the sentimental language he customarily used to describe family gatherings. "There never arose, during the whole time," he recalled in 1811, "an instance of an unpleasant thought or word between the members. We sometimes met under differences of opinion, but scarcely ever failed . . . to produce an unanimous result." The consensual character of Jefferson's cabinet meetings was real enough, in great part deriving from the fact that Jefferson had selected men who shared his views. But he also orchestrated events to prevent conflict. One reason he kept full meetings of the cabinet to a minimum was to avoid argumentative debates. "The method of separate consultations," he explained, "prevents disagreeable collisions." When a heated exchange occurred in one meeting, he asked Madison to maneuver behind the scenes and let his colleagues know that such unbecoming conduct would not be tolerated in the future: "Will you be so good as to endeavor, in an unsuspected way, to observe to the other gentlemen the advantages of sometimes resorting to separate consultation? To Mr. Gallatin may be remarked the incipient indisposition which we noted in two of our brethren on a late consultation; and to the others may be suggested the other important considerations in its favor." Full-throated debate within the cabinet struck him as uncivil. He wanted his department heads to work out their disagreements in private so as not to contaminate cabinet meetings with a contentious spirit. If the democratic ethos welcomed a wide-open, deuces-wild brand of political jostling, Jefferson's version of republican serenity was incompatible with it.[35]

He seemed to want the operation of the federal government to be noiseless, invisible and completely collegial. Soon after he formed his cabinet he instituted the practice of scheduling three dinner parties each week at the presidential mansion in order to bring together members of Congress and their wives with representatives of the executive branch and foreign diplomats stationed in Washington. Some of the most vivid physical descriptions of President Jefferson come from personal reminiscences of guests at these intimate (twelve to twenty people) social occasions. Edward Thornton, the British chargé, was struck by Jefferson's almost theatrical effort "to inculcate upon the people his attachment to a republican simplicity of manners and his unwillingness to admit the smallest distinction, that may separate him from the mass of his fellow citizens." Margaret Bayard Smith read his spare and unassuming social style as a mark of true humility. Louisa Catherine Adams, wife of John Quincy, saw it as an aristocrat's clumsy effort to affect ordinariness. The most talked-about incident occurred in 1803, when the newly arrived British minister, Anthony Merry, raised a huge fuss about the awkward evening he and his wife spent at a presidential dinner. In his famous *History* Henry Adams made the episode into a delectably malicious set piece in which the courtly expectations and insufferable affectations of Mrs. Merry run hilariously into the Jeffersonian "pêle mêle" rules of etiquette, which struck her as a barbaric free-for-all for seating.[36]

But the contrasting descriptions of Jefferson's social demeanor were merely another measure of how richly enigmatic Jefferson's self-conscious republican style appeared to observers with different political agenda. The truly significant fact about the dinners was their underlying purpose. They imposed a huge social obligation on Jefferson, especially during the months when Congress was in session. He continued them throughout his presidency because they enhanced the prospects for creating personal bonds and emotional attachments that might help override political disagreements. If people sat down to dinner together and were obliged to observe the customary civilities, they were less likely to be at one another's throats on the floor of Congress the next day. But the laudable intentions behind the presidential dinners were greatly diluted by the very motives that inspired them. Early on Jefferson established the rule, which must have struck some congressmen as bizarre, that explicitly political conversations were prohibited at the table. And after attempting to mix Federalist and Republican guests for a short while, he abandoned the experiment in order to avoid the threat of volatile exchanges or politically edged jokes about his French wine. Thereafter invitations were sent out strictly according to party affiliations. Even more than the cabinet meetings, the much-desired harmony of the dinner parties was highly orchestrated.[37]

The dinners served another purpose that needs noticing, especially because our modern-day assumptions about instant access to the images and sounds of our elected officials impedes a faithful recovery of the way it was back then. To put it simply, the dinners represented the primary occasion for seeing President Jefferson. (This was the chief reason why so many of the visual descriptions of Jefferson that survive came from dinner guests.) Apart from his daily horseback rides through the woods and on the bridle paths of semirural Washington, Jefferson made no public appearances whatsoever. This constituted a break with precedent, since both Washington and Adams had delivered periodic public addresses before crowds and had appeared before Congress at least once a year to deliver their annual messages. Jefferson discontinued the practice of presenting his Annual Message as a speech, claiming that a written version was more efficient. It also eliminated the spectacle of the presidential entourage parading up Capitol Hill in conspicuous imitation of European royalty, then placing the members of Congress in the position of subjects passively listening to his proclamation. Jefferson believed that a republican president should be inconspicuous. He wanted to institutionalize a self-consciously nonimperial presidency. As far as we know, the only two public speeches he delivered throughout his eight years in office were his two inaugural addresses.[38]

The chief business of the executive branch under Jefferson was done almost entirely in writing. Indeed, if we wish to conjure up a historically correct picture of Jefferson as president, he would not be riding or walking toward Capitol Hill for his inauguration but would be seated at his writing table about ten hours a day. He usually rose before daybreak, around five o'clock, worked at his desk alone until nine, when cabinet officers and congressmen were permitted to visit. He went riding in the early afternoon, returning in time for dinner at three-thirty. He was back at his desk between six and seven o'clock and in bed by ten. As he explained to a friend, he was "in the habit, from considerations of health, of never going out in the evening." Apart from the months of August and September, when the heat and humidity of Washington drove him back to his mountaintop at Monticello, he was desk-bound. In his first year as president he received 1,881 letters, not including internal correspondence from his cabinet, and sent out 677 letters of his own. This reclusive regimen made him practically invisible to the public. He even seemed determined to obliterate any traces of his written record as president, insisting that all his public correspondence be filed under one of the other executive departments "so that I shall never add a single paper to those constituting the records of the President's office."[39]

It was all of a piece. A minimalist federal government required a minimalist presidency. Political power, to fit the republican model, needed to be exercised unobtrusively, needed neither to feel nor to look like power at all. Jefferson's notoriously inadequate oratorical skills were conveniently rendered irrelevant or perhaps made into a virtuous liability. The real work of the job played right into that remarkable hand, which could craft words more deftly than any public figure of his time, and into Jefferson's preference for splendid isolation, where improvisational skills were unnecessary, control over ideas was nearly total and making public policy was essentially a textual problem.

Indeed one might most aptly describe Jefferson's self-consciously unimperial executive style as the textual presidency. The art of making decisions was synonymous with the art of drafting and revising texts. Policy debates within the cabinet took the form of editorial exchanges about word choice and syntax. When Jefferson prepared his first Annual Message to Congress, for example, all the department heads were asked to submit memoranda suggesting items for inclusion. He composed a draft based on their written advice and then submitted that draft for their comments. He asked Madison to pay special attention to language: "Will you give this enclosed a revisal, not only as to matter, but diction. Where strictness of grammar does not weaken expression, it should be attended to in complaisance to the purists of New England. But where by small grammatical negligences the energy of an idea is condensed, or a word stands for a sentence, I hold grammatical rigor in contempt."

Gallatin tended to make more editorial suggestions than any other cabinet member, often writing out revisions more than twice as lengthy as the original Jeffersonian draft and infusing his remarks with a critical edge that would have been unacceptably argumentative in a full cabinet meeting but became palatable when offered in the privacy of written prose. "As to style," he wrote in 1802, "I am a bad judge, but I do not like, in the first paragraph, the idea of limiting the quantum of thankfulness due to the supreme being; and there is also, it seems, too much said of the Indians in the enumeration of our blessings in the next sentence."[40]

This extraordinary reliance on the written word had some ironic consequences. On the one hand, it allowed Jefferson to remain one of the most secluded and publicly invisible presidents in American history. On the other hand, it produced a paper trail that has made the decision-making process of his presidency more accessible and visible to historians than any other—that is, until the installation of electronic recordings under John Kennedy and the sensational revelations produced by the White House tapes of Richard Nixon. And because Jefferson's annual messages were polished documents designed to be read for content—and because his mastery of language was unmatched by any subsequent American president save Lincoln—they present a remarkably cogent and peerlessly concise statement of what, in fact and not just in theory, he thought "pure republicanism" meant.

DEBTS, FEDERALISTS, INDIANS

Above all, it meant eliminating the national debt. During the nerve-racking days when the electoral vote tie between Jefferson and Burr was thrown into the House of Representatives, several Federalists had tried to elicit a promise from Jefferson that he would honor the obligation to retire the federal debt, implying that the Jeffersonian version of republicanism was incompatible with fiscal responsibility. Little did they know how unnecessary such worries were. As Jefferson later explained to Gallatin, "I consider the fortunes of our republic as depending, in an eminent degree, on the extinguishment of the public debt . . . ," adding that failure to discharge the debt would send America careening down "the English career of debt, corruption and rottenness, closing with revolution." Redeeming the national debt, for Jefferson, was truly a matter of national redemption, a matter "vital to the destinies of our government. . . ." He informed Gallatin that it was the highest priority of his presidency and that it was unlikely that America would "ever see another President and Secretary of Treasury making all other objects subordinate to this."[41]

He was not exaggerating. In 1801 the national debt stood at $112 million, most of which had accrued as a result of Hamilton's program to assume the state debts. (Jefferson always regarded this decision as a political version of America's original sin, for which he was forever doing penance because of his own complicity.) Following Jefferson's instructions, Gallatin came up with a plan to retire the debt within sixteen years at the rate of $7 million a year. Since the annual income of the federal government, mostly from customs duties and the sale of public lands, was about $9 million, this left only slightly more than $2 million to fund the annual expenses of the entire government. But that was precisely what Jefferson proposed to do.[42]

In an ironic sense, both Jefferson and Hamilton regarded the national debt as the cornerstone of national policy. For Hamilton it was a national blessing because it created the need for taxes, banks and federal fiscal policies that amplified the powers of the national government. For Jefferson it was a national curse; it conjured up all the demonic images associated with European monarchies, especially the layered levels of consolidated corruption represented by the political juggernaut that was the English government. It was also, however, a blessing in disguise, because it defined and disciplined the core mission of his administration. The central impulse of Whig ideology, as we have noted earlier, was oppositional; it required a "clear and present danger" to focus its energies. The debt gave Jefferson his essential enemy. Gallatin's program to retire the debt required reductions in the size of the number of federal employees, shrinking the army and significant cuts in the navy. The debt, in this sense, was a godsend because it became the budgetary tool for enforcing austerity and reducing the size of the government. It defined, in an eminently practical way, how a president used executive power to limit governmental power.

It is difficult for us in present-day America to appreciate, for that matter to understand at all, Jefferson's obsession with a national debt that looks so comparatively small. The number of federal employees in Washington in 1801 totaled 130, and the national debt of $17 million is considerably less than the hourly interest payments that accrue on the current national debt of several trillion dollars. Moreover, the accumulated wisdom of economists and economic historians has taught us to realize that we ought not to think about the national debt in the same straightforward way we regard personal and family debt, as an unalloyed burden to be eliminated with as much deliberate speed as possible. Hindsight also suggests that even for those disposed to reject the

Hamiltonian vision of an integrated and expansive commercial republic, the national debt Jefferson inherited should have been viewed as a
wholly plausible investment in America's future development, a prudent loan, if you will, more than covered by the collateral of prospective economic growth. In all these present-minded ways Jefferson's
fixation on the national debt looks simplistic and silly.[43]

In a certain sense it was, even in its own time. The single-minded
passion he brought to the subject was extreme. Several of his more
moderate Republican colleagues and a good many Federalists thought
his debt-driven fiscal policy was excessively austere. Adams sequestered
in Quincy and licking his political wounds while preparing to settle
scores in his autobiography, worried most about the dismantling of the
navy, which might one day prove shortsighted. (The War of 1812 proved
him right.) But Jefferson's attitude toward the debt must be compre-
hended on its own Jeffersonian terms. This means recognizing the
deep pools of ideological and psychological conviction from which it
drew its nonnegotiable character.[44]

Public debt was the unmistakable engine of government corruption
according to "the antient Whig principles." It set off all the trip wires
and blew all the fuses of the Jeffersonian ideological circuitry, which
then exploded in a flashing vision of Anglomen, monarchists and
scheming bankers conspiring among the ruins of the American republic. This, it is true, was a conspiratorial mentality; it was misguided in
its pathological association of debt with corruption and with its virulent version of Anglophobia. But it had been hallowed as a central article of the republican faith during the American Revolution, and
Jefferson embraced it with all the heartfelt intensity of a true believer.

Psychologically, debt set off another kind of chain reaction inside
Jefferson. Not only had he watched a disarming number of Virginia's
planter class spend and borrow themselves into bankruptcy, but he
knew personally what it felt like to remain one short step ahead of his
creditors, even to experience the sickening sense that they would eventually hunt him down too. In his personal life, of course, we know that
the looming specter of crushing debt had no discernible effect on his

indulgent habits of consumption. (The wine bill alone for his first term as president approached ten thousand dollars, and the expensive and apparently eternal renovations of Monticello continued apace throughout his presidency.) Perhaps the soundest way to put it is that just as an extended exposure to slavery seemed to give Jefferson a particularly intense appreciation of individual freedom, so his private habits of indulgence gave him a peculiarly powerful appreciation of government austerity. In both cases his public fervor grew directly out of his experience of private failure.[45]

In Jefferson's personal life as an indebted planter the elaborate plans for financial recovery never quite worked; the numbers never added up. As president, however, the flow of history (as well as the managerial competence of Gallatin) was on his side. The exponential growth in American exports increased federal revenues even faster than Gallatin had predicted, allowing for an even more rapid retirement of the debt. The chief opposition to the austerity budget came from Federalists in the Senate, who warned that cuts in the military put American security at risk. But the Republican majority easily overrode the dissenting Federalists, and the extended European peace made Jefferson's gamble on a reduced navy look prescient. In his first Annual Message to Congress in December of 1801 Jefferson felt sufficiently confident to recommend the abolition of all internal taxes. He made the classic republican analysis: "Sound principles will not justify our taxing the industry of our fellow citizens to accumulate treasure for wars to happen we know not when, and which might not perhaps happen but from the temptations offered by that treasure." Armies and navies did not deter wars; they usually caused them. Meanwhile the elimination of internal taxes further reduced the public visibility of the federal government in the most sensitive area of popular opinion, tax collection. By the end of his first term Jefferson was able to ask the rhetorical question: "What farmer, what mechanic, what laborer ever sees a tax-gatherer of the United States?"[46]

All the while the budget constraints imposed by the commitment to debt reduction served as a purring engine steadily eating away at what Jefferson devoutly regarded as a bloated federal bureaucracy. "We are hunting out and abolishing multitudes of useless offices," he reported enthusiastically to his son-in-law, "striking off jobs, lopping them down silently. . . ." He apprised William Short, still based in Paris, that he and Madison were giving serious consideration to letting all foreign treaties lapse and closing down American embassies in Europe. (This idea was eventually abandoned.) Gallatin was able to persuade him that the national bank and the customs collectors should be spared; they actually facilitated debt reduction; in modern parlance, they were "cost-effective." Jefferson reluctantly agreed. "It mortifies me to be strengthening principles which I deem radically vicious," he complained, but Gallatin was probably right "that we can never completely get rid of his [Hamilton's] financial system." Nevertheless, the abiding commitment must be to simplify financial records, hack away at the entrenched layers of accountants, civil servants and—the core Republican agenda—"bring things back to that simple and intelligible system on which they should have been organized at first."[47]

Leading the battle of the budget came to him naturally and drew from deep personal resources that all flowed together in the same direction. But the comparatively mundane task of distributing patronage bedeviled him from the start of his presidency. He wrote more letters and expressed more contradictory opinions on this subject than any other. His most colorful statement—that Federalist incumbents in government jobs prevented the creation of vacancies, that "those by death are few; by resignation none"—was made when he was in the mood for "a sweep," meaning a wholescale removal of Federalists to make room for loyal Republicans. On other occasions he adopted a more conciliatory line, claiming he would leave Federalists in most government jobs and replace them only as vacancies arose; at times he sounded an even more benevolent note, suggesting that rank-and-file Federalists should be appointed and only the most diehard Federalist leaders, "whom I abandon as incurables," should be excluded. "If we can hit on the true line of conduct," he wrote to Horatio Gates, "which may conciliate the honest part of those who were called federalists, and do justice to those who have so long been excluded from it, I shall hope to be able to obliterate, or rather unite the names of federalists and republicans." This sounded like the most generous reading of the "We are all republicans—we are all federalists" line in his Inaugural Address. For several months he oscillated back and forth among these different positions.⁴⁸

Jefferson's patronage dilemma grew out of the unprecedented political situation created by his election. He was the first leader of an opposition party elected to the presidency and the first recognized party leader to face the "loaves and fishes" problem with all the middle- and lower-level federal offices still occupied by the outgoing administration. In subsequent years it became common practice and a matter of mutual understanding that victory in a presidential election meant a wholesale changing of the guard along party lines. Nothing terribly principled or massively moral was at stake. Patronage was a simple by-product of political power. But the victorious Republican party had come to power believing in its own virtue and claiming to represent a restoration of principles that dispensed with politics as usual. As Henry Adams put it, "Such a state of things could never occur again, for only a new country could be inexperienced in politics." It was awkward for Jefferson to start behaving like a party leader after a decade of denying that the Republicans were a political party at all.⁴⁹

The practical resolution of this dilemma is less significant per se than for what it revealed about Jefferson's inherently moralistic mentality. Throughout the 1790s he had described the Federalists as an evil faction of cryptomonarchists and closet-tories who had commandeered the original purpose of the American Revolution and carried the government to the brink of irreversible corruption. This highly charged diagnosis had never been factually accurate. Very few of the Federalists were outright monarchists. Indeed, if one were searching for such creatures, the top candidate would have been Burr, who was a Republican and Jefferson's vice president to boot. The underlying issues separating Federalists and Republicans were not really moral so much as constitutional and strategic: The Federalists preferred a more consolidated federal government in which more power was allocated to the executive and judicial branches and America's primary European ally and role model was England. The Republicans wanted a smaller and weaker federal government in which the House of Representatives was the dominant force; they looked to France as our chief European friend. While these were hardly incidental differences—they had their origins in fundamentally juxtaposed ideas about the proper allocation of political power in a republican government—they did not really translate into the kind of moral imperatives that Jefferson's mind required to mobilize its political energies. Yet for Jefferson to mean what so many readers of his Inaugural Address thought he meant—that the differences between Federalists and Republicans were eminently negotiable—would have required him to acknowledge that his moral crusade of the 1790s had been misguided.

By the summer of 1801 Jefferson had reached his conclusion: There were Federalists and there were federalists. The former were unredeemable monarchists, "incurable monocrats" and "the desperadoes of the quondam faction." He claimed to "wish nothing but their eternal hatred," and if that were to cease, "I should become suspicious to myself." The latter were misguided followers, who preferred a somewhat stronger executive but in their heart of hearts were really republicans and therefore "entitled to the confidence of their fellow citizens." The beauty of this simplistic distinction was that it allowed Jefferson to retain his moral categories, indeed to focus his hatred even more intently on the surviving pockets of recalcitrant Federalist influence, especially in New England, while simultaneously adopting a conciliatory posture elsewhere and encouraging mass defections to the Republican party. In Connecticut, for example, he claimed that most citizens remained mesmerized by the vilest version of the Federalist persuasion: "Their steady habits exclude the advances of information and they seem exactly where they were when they separated from the Saints of Oliver Cromwell." They were, he believed, willing to "follow the bark of liberty only by the help of a tow-rope." Connecticut therefore demanded a "general sweep" of Federalists from office. Appointing a Federalist there was "like appointing an atheist to the priest-hood." Massachusetts was only slightly better, though Jefferson held out the hope that "as the Indian says, they are clearing the dust out of their eyes there also," so that eventually "the republican portion will at length arise, and the sediment of monarchism will be left as lees at the bottom." Until then, however, "a clean sweep" was necessary in Massa-chusetts too.[50]

Jefferson's moral distinctions were lost on most Federalists, who regarded the mass removals in New England as a betrayal of his inau-gural promise. "The truth is," noted the editors of the *New York Evening Post,* "it has become ridiculous in Mr. Jefferson and his supporters to pretend that, in the present system of hunting the Federalists like wild beasts, they are governed by any principle or principles which will bear avowal or can be for a moment supported under any pretence whatso-ever." The real truth was that pretense was very important to the Republicans; they did not want to think of themselves as typical politi-cians who traded their principles for raw power upon entering office. As for Jefferson himself, the messy matter of patronage exposed how his mind was capable of moving on parallel tracks, one side fiercely vindictive and merciless, the other accommodating and charitable. It all depended on where one landed in the inherently moral world that was Jefferson country.[51]

The patronage episode also revealed how alien Jefferson was to the pluralistic ethos so central to modern-day political liberalism, which accords respect to fundamentally different values and defines integrity as a civil, if spirited, dialogue among opposing ideas. His was the more traditional and universalistic conviction: There was one truth, not many. He could be endlessly patient and pragmatic about minor dif-ferences, but once it was clear your views lay on the other side of the line, it was war to the death. What saved the bulk of the Federalists, it turned out, was not generosity of spirit so much as the fervent hope that they were really latent Republicans primed for conversion.

It was a characteristically Jeffersonian outlook, and it contributed to his paradoxical reputation as an extremely cool and serenely civil man of considerable grace who periodically unleashed sudden torrents of anger and hostility at his enemies. At the private level it gave his otherwise smooth and soft demeanor a dangerous edge, especially for those who mistook his reticent style for indifference and blundered into one of the deeply felt subjects. At the semipublic level, such as cabinet meetings or one-on-one sessions in the presidential office, it enhanced his authority by suggesting a subterranean region forever concealed from view and inhabited by fearful forces that, if inadvertently unlocked, would take no prisoners. At the public level the New England Federalists triggered the moral explosions, much as George III and then the Hamiltonians had done in previous years. But the most dramatic display of this Jeffersonian syndrome during his presidency, which also had the greatest consequence on domestic policy and subsequent American history, occurred in his treatment of Native Americans.

Jefferson's attitude toward the Indian population of the United States has always seemed as profoundly paradoxical as his attitude toward slavery. On the one hand, he devoted an entire chapter in his *Notes on Virginia* to a celebration of the indigenous culture of America's original inhabitants, recalling the impressive oratorical skills of tribal chiefs, recommending the serious study of the different Indian languages and dialects, even going so far as to contrast Indians favorably with blacks in terms of their mental and physical aptitude and their capacity for assimilation into white American society. As president he greeted visiting Indian delegations with becoming graciousness and visible respect. On several occasions he went out of his way to describe the Indian people of North America as a noble race who were the innocent victims of history: "Endowed with the faculties and rights of men, breathing an ardent love of liberty and independence," as he so eloquently put it, "and occupying a country which left them no desire but to be undisturbed . . . they have been overwhelmed by the current, or driven before it." One senses in so many of Jefferson's observations on Indians an authentic admiration mingled with a truly poignant sense of tragedy about their fate as a people.[52]

On the other hand, it was during Jefferson's presidency that the basic decisions were made that required the deportation of massive segments of the Indian population to land west of the Mississippi. In the language of the leading scholar on the subject, "the seeds of extinction" for Native American culture were sown under Jefferson. The essence of Jefferson's thinking about Indian removal was expressed in a letter to the territorial governor of Ohio in 1803:

> In this way our settlements will gradually circumscribe and approach the Indians and they will in time either incorporate with us as citizens of the United States or remove beyond the Mississippi. The former is certainly the termination of their history most happy for themselves, but, in the whole course of this, it is essential to cultivate their love. As to their fear, we presume that our strength and their weakness is now so visible that they must see we have only to shut our hand to crush them, and that all our liberalities to them proceed from motives of pure humanity only.[53]

This is a striking statement in several senses: its casual sense of assurance about what history intended; its eerie mixture of charity and cruelty; its presumptive and paternalistic tone. In Jefferson's mind the Indians occupied the same problematic space as the Federalists. They were a doomed species. Their dooming had not been his doing, but he had no compunctions or doubts about serving as the instrument of their destruction. And just as the rank-and-file Federalists should recognize that their political survival depended on embracing the central tenets of republicanism (as defined by the Republican party), so the Indians should recognize that their cultural survival depended upon abandoning their nomadic hunting societies—these required too much land—and adopting an agricultural way of life, eventually the English language, and gradually assimilating into white American society. In short, Indian culture could survive by ceasing to be Indian, just as the Federalists could survive by ceasing to be Federalists.[54]

Those Indians who resisted assimilation, again like the recalcitrant Federalist leaders in Connecticut and Massachusetts, deserved nothing less than extermination or banishment. Like the Federalist ideologues in New England, Indian leaders who clung tenaciously to tribal mores and insisted on inculcating "a sanctimonious reverence for the custom of their ancestors" must be shown no mercy. Jefferson believed that banishment to the currently unoccupied lands west of the Mississippi was only a temporary solution since the white migration would eventually overflow these lands too and pose the same questions at a later date. But he was not burdened by any doubts about what constituted the right answer. When James Monroe, in his capacity as Virginia's governor, wrote him to raise the possibility of creating a western reserve for emancipated slaves, Jefferson opposed the idea on grounds that boded ill for Indians as well as blacks: "[I]t is impossible not to look forward to distant times, when our rapid multiplication will . . . cover the whole northern, if not the southern continent, with a people speaking the same language, governed in similar forms, and by similar laws; nor can we contemplate with satisfaction either blot or mixture on that surface." Just as he found it impossible to imagine a pluralistic American politics in which competing convictions about the meaning of the American Revolution coexisted, he had no place in his imagination for an American society of diverse cultures in which Native Americans lived alongside whites while retaining their own Indian values.[55]

WESTERN MAGIC

THERE WAS ALSO a sharp line running through Jefferson's constitutional thinking between foreign and domestic policy. Actually, to speak of "constitutional thinking" is a bit misleading since Jefferson's mind preferred broader moral categories that hovered over the more conventional constitutional distinctions. In his own Jeffersonian way, however, he believed that the House of Representatives had primary responsibility for domestic policy and the executive had equivalent responsibility over foreign affairs, though he seemed to have embraced a somewhat fuzzy caveat during the debate over the Jay Treaty that gave the House veto power over foreign treaties. At any rate, it would be fair to say that Jefferson did not think that the office of president should be as inconspicuous or invisible to foreign nations as it should to American citizens.[56]

Only two months after his inauguration the Barbary pirates on the North African coast put this theory to the test when the pasha of Tripoli declared war on the United States. (The pasha was incensed upon learning that the tribute he was receiving from the Americans was less than that which was being paid to Algiers.) This was an old story to Jefferson, who had argued unsuccessfully with Adams in their Paris years that paying bribes to these seafaring terrorists of the Muslim world was dishonorable. Now, as president, he was in a position to implement his long-standing preference for military action. "I am an enemy to all these doceurs, tributes and humiliations," he explained to Madison, and "I know that nothing will stop the eternal increase from these pirates but the presence of an armed force. . . ." Fortunately, and with an irony that only Adams could have fully appreciated, the buildup of the American navy that Adams had insisted on during his presidency, despite the opposition of Jefferson and the Republicans, meant that a fleet of frigates was available for Jefferson to dispatch to the Mediterranean. With the consent of his cabinet—only Gallatin, whose job was to worry about the budget, objected on cost grounds— Jefferson ordered a naval squadron to patrol the North African coast.[57]

Throughout his first term, then, and well into his second, the United States was engaged in a small-scale naval war in the Mediterranean that never achieved the decisive conclusion that Jefferson wanted. He revived his old scheme of creating an international task force comprised of European and American warships to police the region—perhaps a forerunner of the United Nations peacekeeping force—but it never materialized. At least at the symbolic level, however, the ongoing conflict with the Barbary pirates became America's first "splendid little war" by generating patriotic rallies throughout the country. These reached a crescendo in 1804, when Stephen Decatur, an American naval officer, brazenly sailed into the Bay of Tripoli to rescue American prisoners of war on board the captured *Philadelphia* and then proceeded to revenge his brother's death by killing his Muslim murderers in hand-to-hand combat. (No less an authority than Lord Nelson of the British Admiralty called it "the most bold and daring act of the age.") Decatur's exploits were memorialized in verse and dramatic productions as the North African version of Bunker Hill; he became America's first nineteenth-century military hero.[58]

The Jefferson administration benefited from this nationalistic surge, though Jefferson was careful to remind all concerned that the naval operation in the Mediterranean was a mere sideshow and would not deter his plans to dry-dock a hefty portion of the American fleet. In the grand scheme of things the centerpiece of his foreign policy remained the avoidance of war at almost any cost. Retiring the debt and sustaining republican austerity had to take precedence. In that sense the campaign against the Barbary pirates was perfect: It was a safe and limited projection of American power abroad, it displayed Jefferson's resolve as president, it produced convenient heroes to celebrate and it cost very little. It was, if you will, the ideal miniature war for Jefferson's minimalist presidency.[59]

There was nothing miniature about the American West, nothing less than grandiose about Jefferson's vision of its future role in American history and nothing but extraordinary presidential leadership, matched with even more extraordinary good fortune, that produced the Louisiana Purchase. When word reached Washington in 1803 (on July 4 no less) that France had agreed to the sale of the Louisiana Territory for fifteen million dollars, the American republic doubled in size overnight. Even compared with the legendary purchase of Manhattan from the Indians for a pittance, the acquisition of half a continent for about three cents an acre was a bigger steal. It was unquestionably the greatest achievement of the Jefferson presidency and, with room left for scholarly quibbling about Abraham Lincoln in 1861, Franklin Roosevelt in the 1930s and Harry Truman in 1945, one of the most consequential executive actions in all of American history.[60]

It was fashionable for many years to tell the story of the transaction primarily as a meditation on the influence of dumb luck. "Napoleon threw the province, so to speak, at Livingston, Monroe, Madison and Jefferson," wrote one historian, "and they share between [sic] them—equally—whatever credit there was in catching it and holding it—that is all." This interpretation represented a continuation of Federalist explanations at the time. "[T]he acquisition has been solely owing to a fortuitous concurrence of unforeseen and unexpected circumstances," said an editor in the *New York Evening Post,* "and not to any wise or vigorous measures on the part of the American government." The fairer judgment would seem to be that Jefferson was both more fortunate and more prescient than anyone realized at the time. And his nearly mystical sense of the American West made him more flexible in the implementation of his political principles than at any other time in his public life. To seize an empire, it turned out, required an imperial president.[61]

Although he himself had never been west of the Shenandoah Valley, Jefferson's proprietary attitude toward the Mississippi Valley and beyond was long-standing. In the 1780s, when rumors spread that John Jay was negotiating the surrender of American navigation rights on the Mississippi to Spain, both Jefferson and Madison expressed outrage. They consistently described the Mississippi as the major artery of the American body politic, "the Hudson, the Delaware, the Potomac, and all the navigable rivers of the Atlantic, formed into one stream." While secretary of state, most pointedly during the Nootka Sound crisis of 1790, Jefferson had been prepared to risk war in order to prevent either England or France from displacing Spain as the European presence in the trans-Mississippi West. From that time forward Jefferson regarded Spanish ownership of the vast western region of North America as essentially a temporary occupation that conveniently bided time for the inevitable American sweep across the continent. Of all the European powers, Spain, the chronically weak "sick man of Europe," was, as Rufus King put it, "the most proper to possess a great empire with insignificance." When rumors reached Washington in 1802 that Spain had ceded its rights in North America, including the all-important control over the Mississippi, to Napoleon and France, Jefferson immediately recognized the French presence as a fundamental shift in the strategic situation; it both threatened American security and blocked westward American expansion. Without quite shouldering Madison to the sidelines, Jefferson assumed personal control over the diplomatic initiative to remove this unacceptable intrusion of a major European power onto the American continent.[62]

His instructions to Robert Livingston, the newly appointed American ambassador to France, minced no words. He apologized for temporarily displacing the secretary of state but explained that he "cannot forbear recurring to it personally, so deep is the impression it makes in my mind." The sale of the Louisiana region to France was a major disaster that "completely reverses all the political relations of the United States and will form a new epoch in our political course." It constituted, he believed, the greatest challenge to American independence and national integrity since the American Revolution: "There is on the globe one single spot, the possessor of which is our natural and habitual enemy," he explained to Livingston. That epicenter of American national interest was New Orleans. Despite past friendship with France and despite his own personal affinity for the Franco-American alliance, the moment France occupied New Orleans the two nations must become mortal enemies. "From that moment," he concluded ominously, "we must marry ourselves to the British fleet and nation." Given his deep and lifelong hatred of England, Jefferson was effectively describing French control of the Mississippi as the equivalent of an international earthquake that moved all the geological templates into a new pattern.[63]

Though eminently capable, Livingston possessed the singular disadvantage of not being a Virginian. Jefferson wanted someone on the ground in Paris whom he could trust implicitly. So he in effect ordered James Monroe, a Jefferson protégé currently serving as governor of Virginia, to become a special envoy to France. "[T]he circumstances are such as to render it impossible to decline," Jefferson observed dramatically, because "on the event of this mission, depends the future destinies of this republic." Monroe's instructions authorized the purchase of New Orleans and as much of the Mississippi Valley as possible—the geographic boundaries of the French acquisition from Spain were fuzzy—for up to ten million dollars. Even the paramount domestic goal of debt reduction was subordinated to recovering control over America's interior.[64]

During the winter and spring of 1803, while the outcome of the Monroe mission remained up in the air, Jefferson's management of the prospective crisis was deft and shrewd. He saw to it that du Pont de Nemours, an old French friend, was provided information about America's deadly serious intentions that could be leaked in the proper corridors at Versailles. When the Spanish official still governing New Orleans abruptly closed the port to American commerce, Jefferson came under considerable pressure to launch a unilateral military expedition to seize both the city and the Floridas, thereby abandoning diplomacy in favor of war with both Spain and France. Hamilton, writing as Pericles, endorsed the military solution, arguing that "in an emergency like the present, energy is wisdom." Despite an authorization from Congress empowering the president to raise eighty thousand volunteers for a military campaign, Jefferson remained calm. Even if the ongoing negotiations in Paris failed, he explained—and of course they did not—outright war was both unwise and unnecessary. Time and demography were on the American side, justifying a patient policy "till we have planted such a population on the Mississippi as will be able to do their own business, without the necessity of marching men from the shores of the Atlantic 1500 or 2000 miles thither. . . ."[65]

Jefferson was also extremely fortunate, in some ways ironically so. Napoleon's decision to sell not just New Orleans but also the entire

Mississippi Valley and modern-day American Midwest was prompted by the resumption of the Anglo-French war in 1802. Ambassador Livingston had earlier complained that negotiating with France was impossible: "There is no people, no Legislature, no counsellors. One man is everything. He seldom asks advice, and never hears it unasked." This, of course, was the essence of the Napoleonic all-or-nothing style. But once Napoleon decided to cut his losses in America in return for money that would subsidize his European army, the same style worked to Jefferson's advantage; Napoleon sold all his North American possessions for practically nothing. The early Federalist attempts to undercut Jefferson's coup in acquiring the Louisiana Territory emphasized the impulsive character of Napoleon's decision, which had nothing to do with Jefferson's diplomatic maneuverings and everything to do with the shifting European context and the unpredictable Napoleonic character.[66]

The deeper truth was that Louisiana was a providential gift from the insurgent slaves and the malaria-carrying mosquitoes of Santo Domingo (now the Dominican Republic and Haiti). The immediate cause of Napoleon's decision to abandon his dreams of a French empire in America was the disastrous failure of a twenty-five-thousand-man expeditionary force headed by Charles Leclerc, Napoleon's brother-in-law, that had been dispatched to Santo Domingo to suppress the slave insurrection there under the charismatic leadership of a black man named Toussaint L'Ouverture. Believing that a show of American support against the revolutionary government of Toussaint might win Napoleon's favor, Jefferson had informed the French government that "nothing would be easier than to furnish your army and fleet with everything, and to reduce Toussaint to starvation." As it happened, Leclerc's troops were decimated in the savage fighting against the slave insurrectionaries before American aid could arrive, and the mosquitoes killed off the rest. The virtual extinction of the French expeditionary force, which had been scheduled to proceed to New Orleans after dispatching the blacks of Santo Domingo, was the immediate cause of Napoleon's decision to cut his losses in the Western

Hemisphere. In that sense, Jefferson was not only extraordinarily lucky but also beholden to historical forces that he had actually opposed.[67]

If, then, one ever wished to construct a monument in New Orleans memorializing the Louisiana Purchase, Jefferson would have to be a central figure, but he would also need to be flanked by busts of Toussaint and his fellow black insurrectionaries, plus perhaps a tribute to the deadly mosquito. And the most appropriately eloquent quotation would come from Talleyrand, that ubiquitous and famously unscrupulous French foreign minister. "I can give you no direction," he said to Livingston, "you have made a noble bargain for yourselves, and I suppose you will make the most of it." Talleyrand was referring to the imprecise and therefore controversial borders of French Louisiana, but his statement accurately described Jefferson's presidential style in the immediate aftermath of the sale. He violated his most cherished political principles several times over in order to guarantee the most expansive version of the "noble bargain," and he temporarily made himself into just the kind of monarchical chief magistrate he had warned against. "It is incumbent on those who accept great charges," he explained afterward, "to risk themselves on great occasions," adding that "to lose our country by a scrupulous adherence to written laws, would be to lose the law itself. . . ."[68]

With regard to the borders question, Jefferson had acted preemptively, even before knowing whether Napoleon would sell all or part of Louisiana. He commissioned his private secretary, Meriwether Lewis, to organize an expedition comprised of "ten or twelve chosen men" to explore the trans-Mississippi region and discover the most direct water route, if any existed, to the Pacific. Since France and Spain still owned the huge tract Lewis would be exploring, Jefferson obtained authorization from Congress on the pretense that this was a scientific venture or "a literary pursuit" and that it would go no farther west than the Mississippi basin. This official explanation "satisfied curiosity," he informed Lewis, "and masks sufficiently the real destination." News of the Louisiana Purchase arrived just as what history has come to know as the Lewis and Clark Expedition departed Washington, so from the very start they knew themselves to be a covert reconnaissance team exploring the western borders, and beyond, of America's newest possession.[69]

Once Lewis was launched into the vast and unmapped interior of the trans-Mississippi West, Jefferson turned his attention to the Gulf Coast. Back at Monticello during the late summer of 1803 he studied old maps and determined to his own satisfaction that the southeastern border of French Louisiana was the Perdido River, near present-day Pensacola. Subsequent scrutiny of the maps also satisfied him that the southwestern border was the Rio Grande. This meant that the United States had acquired all the land west of modern Florida along the Gulf Coast through present-day Texas. France had no objections to this somewhat expansive interpretation of the treaty. As Talleyrand had indicated, France was washing its hands of the entire American business, and no one in France knew the location of the Perdido or Rio Grande from the Hudson or Potomac anyway.[70]

Spain, however, took a somewhat less charitable view of the American claims, insisting that neither the Gulf Coast (called West Florida) nor any land southwest of New Orleans was included in the purchase. Jefferson instructed Monroe to leave Paris for Madrid and there make a modest effort to buy West Florida from Spain. "We scarcely expect any liberal or just settlement with Spain," Jefferson observed, but it made little difference since "whatever may be the views of Spain, there will be no difficulty . . . in getting thro' with our purposes." In short, Spain being Spain, it should be regarded as a mere holding company for the United States, "and if, as soon as she is at war, we push them strongly with one hand, holding out a price in the other, we shall certainly obtain the Floridas, and all in good time." Though it required another fifteen years, plus the military adventurism of Andrew Jackson, that is exactly what happened.[71]

Finally, and most famously, there were the constitutional questions raised by the acquisition of so vast a tract, whatever the borders.

Although Madison and Gallatin tried to persuade him otherwise, Jefferson remained convinced that the enlargement of the Union required an amendment to the Constitution: "The constitution has made no provision for our holding foreign territory . . ." he acknowledged. "The Executive in seizing the fugitive occurrence, have done an act beyond the Constitution." As Jefferson explained to Senator John Breckinridge of Kentucky, he had been placed in the awkward position of a guardian who, presented with an unprecedented investment opportunity, had decided to act without obtaining the consent of his clients, saying in effect, "I thought it my duty to risk myself for you." But he was now under moral obligation to request a constitutional amendment from the Congress at the same time he forwarded the treaty for ratification.[72]

By the time the special session of Congress convened in October 1803, however, Jefferson had changed his mind. Reports from Paris indicated that the ever-impulsive Napoleon was having second thoughts; at the same time the Spanish were threatening to challenge the entire treaty on the ground that no one really knew the proper boundaries of Louisiana. Fearing that any delay might put the purchase at risk, Jefferson concluded that "the less that is said about my constitutional difficulty, the better; and that it will be desirable for Congress to do what is necessary *in silence*." If the choice was between sustaining his strict interpretation of executive authority or losing half a continent, he chose the more pragmatic course, all the while expressing the hope that "the good sense of our country will correct the evil of [broad] construction when it shall produce ill effects."[73]

The constitutional embarrassments became worse over the succeeding months. The huge Republican majority in Congress ratified the Louisiana Purchase, as one senator put it, "in less time than required for the most trivial Indian contract," then passed enabling legislation that delegated to the president nearly autocratic power over decisions about a provisional government in the Louisiana Territory. John Quincy Adams, one of the few senators to oppose the legislation, observed that Jefferson would possess "an assumption of implied power greater . . . than all the assumptions of implied powers in the years of the Washington and Adams administrations put together." The old enemy of George III now wielded more arbitrary power over the residents of Louisiana than any British king had wielded over the American colonists.[74]

Moreover, Jefferson chose to use that executive power to propose a blatantly nonrepublican territorial government. His outline for a proposed constitution was accompanied by a cover letter to Senator Breckinridge, swearing him to secrecy. "You must never let any person know that I have put pen to paper," he warned, "and should destroy the original" immediately after making a copy. "I am this particular," Jefferson explained, "because you know with what bloody teeth and fangs the federalists will attack any sentiment or principle known to come from me, and what blackguardisms and personalities they make it the occasion of vomiting forth."[75]

The chief reason for Jefferson's apprehension was that the provisional government of the territory he proposed consisted of a governor appointed by the president and a nonelected council or senate, which Jefferson called the "Assembly of Notables." This was precisely the kind of constitutional arrangement one might have expected from John Adams, who was more comfortable with aristocratic entrustments of authority, preferred ornate titles and might have argued that the predominantly French residents of Louisiana would appreciate a familiar political framework reminiscent of the *ancien régime*. But this was also precisely the kind of government Jefferson had condemned the Federalists for preferring, since it deprived the residents of any elective rights and, as Madison privately admitted, "will leave the people of that District for a while without the organization of power dictated by the Republican theory."[76]

During the debate over Jefferson's proposal in the Senate, John Quincy Adams, undoubtedly enjoying the irony and fully aware the Republicans would vote whatever Jefferson wanted, attempted to add a provision protecting the rights of the Louisiana residents against being taxed without their consent. The following year a delegation of three agents from the territory came to Washington to present a remonstrance, protesting the violation of their rights and their de facto status as colonists. "Do the political axioms on the Atlantic become problems," they asked rhetorically, "when transplanted to the shores of the Mississippi?" Jefferson avoided any contact with the delegation or conversation about their remonstrance. In his private correspondence he explained that "our new fellow citizens [in Louisiana] are as yet incapable of self-government as children, yet some cannot bring themselves to suspend [republican] principles for a single moment." The suspension was only temporary, he promised, until he could be assured that the political temperature had sufficiently lowered to avoid the risk of insurrection.[77]

From the long-term historical perspective, and with all the advantages of hindsight, Jefferson's controversial decisions about the Louisiana Territory can be—most of them indeed should be—defended as wise. The decision to bypass the constitutional issue was unquestionably correct, for the practical reason that the debate over a constitutional amendment would have raised a constellation of nettlesome questions—about slavery and the slave trade, Indian lands, Spanish land claims and a host of other jurisdictional issues—that might have put the entire purchase at risk. The hard-boiled and dismissive attitude toward Spanish arguments about borders, especially in West Florida, followed naturally from a realistic assessment of Spanish impotence and American demographic destiny. Even the decision to install an essentially arbitrary and despotic provisional government over the Louisiana Territory to carry it through the early years of assimilation cannot be condemned outright, since both the sheer size of the region and the ethnic diversity of the Creole population posed governance problems that justified a firmer hand at the start.[78]

The issue, then, is not whether Jefferson's policies toward Louisiana were right or wrong but rather how he managed to implement decisions that defied in so many ways his long-standing commitment to limitations on executive power and the near-sacred character of repub-

lican principles. Two of the more conventional answers to this question do not ring true: First, Jefferson was not simply seized by power-
hungry impulses once he assumed the presidency, since in a broad
range of other policy areas he exhibited considerable discipline over
the executive branch and habitual deference to the Congress; second,
he did not suddenly discover a pragmatic streak in his political philosophy, since on issues like the debt and, later on, the embargo he clung
tenaciously to Jeffersonian principles despite massive evidence that
they were at odds with reality. The pragmatic interpretation fails to
explain why he was capable of putting his belief in "pure republicanism" aside in this instance and not in others.

The answer would seem to be the special, indeed almost mystical
place the West had in his thinking. When history presented him with
an unexpected and unprecedented opportunity to eliminate forever
the presence on America's western border of any major European
power (Spain did not count here), it triggered his most visionary energies, which then overrode his traditional republican injunctions. For
Jefferson more than any other major figure in the revolutionary generation, the West was America's future. Securing a huge swatch of it for
posterity meant prolonging for several generations the systemic release
of national energy that accompanied the explosive movement of settle-
ments across the unsettled spaces. (The Indians, like Spain, did not
count in this calculus.) What Frederick Jackson Turner later called a
safety valve was for Jefferson more like a self-renewing engine that
drove the American republic forward. The West was the place where
his agrarian idyll could be regularly rediscovered, thereby postponing
into the indefinite future the crowded conditions and political conges-
tions of European society. Jefferson liked to think of the West in much
the same way that some modern optimists think of technology, as
almost endlessly renewable and boundlessly prolific. It was the secret
weapon that made the American experiment in republicanism
immune to the national aging process, at least for the remainder of the
century. It was America's fountain of youth.[79]

As a result, any issue involving the fate of the American West possessed the potential to trump his other political convictions. Jefferson's visionary sense of what the West meant for America also made him virtually immune to the doubts, prevalent among Federalists and even shared by some of his Republican colleagues, about the country's capacity to assimilate the vast Louisiana Territory. After all, when such a massive area had come under British control after the French and Indian War in 1763, it had led directly to political problems that eventually resulted in the American Revolution and the dissolution of the British Empire in America. While easterners, especially New England Federalists, worried that their influence would erode as more western states entered the Union, the predominant fear was fragmentation, that the expanded version of the United States would split up into several regional units in the European mode. Jefferson's reaction to such fear was almost cavalierly dismissive: "Whether we remain in one confederacy, or form into Atlantic and Mississippi confederacies, I believe not very important to the happiness of either part. Those of the western confederacy will be as much our children and descendants as those of the eastern, and I feel myself as much identified with that country, in future time, as with this."[80]

This was a remarkable statement since it conveyed an almost ostentatious nonchalance toward the preservation of national union, the dominant political issue of the next half century. Jefferson did not worry about the integration of the West into the United States because he thought about the process more dynamically and as part of a larger transformation. From his perspective, the United States was not just integrating the West into the Union; the West was actually integrating the older United States into a newer and ever-changing version of America. In spirit, if not in fact, Jefferson was a westerner, captivated by the apparently endless horizons and the exciting unknowns that Meriwether Lewis might bring back to nourish the present with news of the future. It also helped that the vast majority of westerners were likely to prove staunch Republicans.

SCANDALS

IF THE WEST was that future place where the creative juices of the expanding American republic flowed most freely, then New England was the past, where, as Jefferson saw it, Federalism stewed in its own poisonous juices while adjusting to its abiding irrelevancy. Unfortunately for Jefferson, whose impressive intellectual range did not extend to an appreciation of the compressed energies of New England Puritanism, his declaration of war to the death against the "incurables" of Federalism alienated some of the most formidable figures among the best-educated population in the country. Jefferson was an excellent hater and a skillful polemicist, but he more than met his match in the Federalist press and pulpit, where the expiring condition of Federalism as a viable political movement only intensified the desperation of its defenders. Later in life, after Jefferson and Adams had reconciled and resumed their correspondence, they kept up a running joke about which one could assemble the larger volume of vindictive criticism directed at him during his presidency. This was one area of playful competition where Jefferson was the indisputable winner. The assaults on his character were unparalleled in the history of the early republic.[81]

That does not mean they were unprecedented. During the presidential campaign of 1800 Adams had been subjected to several attempts at character assassination, the chief blow coming from Hamilton, who published a lengthy indictment of the president's explosive personality. The gist of the charge was that Adams was mentally deranged and fully capable of destroying the infant American republic during one of his spasms of lunacy. Even the godlike Washington had become a target of abuse during his second term, when he was accused of senility as well as pro-Hamilton favoritism that derived from the groundless but sensational allegation that Hamilton was secretly his illegitimate son. Hamilton himself was charged with a variety of indiscretions, the most scandalous being that his sexual affair with a married woman exposed him to blackmail by the woman's husband, who demanded political favors for his silence. Ever the master of audacity, Hamilton took out newspaper space to announce that the charges of infidelity were sadly true but that, despite this personal failure, his public virtue as a government official had never been compromised. The line of demarcation that he attempted to draw between his private life and his public integrity was precisely the line that newspaper editors and political pundits refused to recognize. By the time Jefferson ascended to the presidency, then, the private lives of public figures were clearly regarded as fair game by the press, and Jefferson, who had been active behind the scenes in paying off hired character assassins in the party wars of the 1790s, knew perfectly well that he could expect the same treatment. "They say we lied them out of power," he observed in reference to the Federalists, "and openly avow they will do the same by us."[82]

The Federalist barrage started right away, though the earliest shots tended to be aimed to wound rather than kill, poking fun at such targets as the distinctive Jeffersonian literary style, with its fondness for exalted phrasings and frequent alliterations. "Man is, by nature, a mighty megalonyx," wrote one Federalist in mock imitation of the Declaration of Independence, "produced purposely, in a philosophical view, to prowl, pillage, propagate, and putrify." The publication of five new editions of *Notes on Virginia* in 1801, presumably an effort by publishers to cash in on Jefferson's new visibility as president, offered Federalist editors a broad range of easy targets. For some reason they tended to fasten upon Jefferson's claim that huge, hairy prehistoric beasts called mammoths still lived on in the unexplored American West, one of those pre-Darwinian ideas Jefferson found attractive because it supported his anti-Buffon contention that the American environment produced large animals. Federalist wits ridiculed his "mammoth theory" over and over again, and the motif became a centerpiece of opposition sarcasm toward Jefferson's pretensions as a scientist. In the same quasi-playful mode, Jefferson's defenders countered the mammoth onslaught by presenting him with a "mammoth cheese" weighing 1,235 pounds, reputedly from the milk of nine hundred cows, "not one of them a federalist."[83]

The truly serious assaults on his character first came on the religious front. In his *Notes on Virginia* Jefferson had presented an argument for religious freedom that concluded with a clever comment on his own open-mindedness: "But it does me no injury for my neighbor to say there are twenty gods or no gods. It neither picks my pocket nor breaks my leg." The Federalist clergy of New England seized on this remark as conclusive evidence that Jefferson was some combination of pagan, infidel, atheist and heretic. Editorials throughout New England played on the theme that the most Christian country in the world was now headed by a man who denied the central tenets of Christianity. While Jefferson does not appear to have been personally hurt by the charge, he recognized the political damage it was doing to his party; so he composed a brief essay on the merits of Jesus as a role model, which was actually based on a similar essay by Joseph Priestley, the English deist, that compared Jesus and Socrates as splendid embodiments of humanistic values. Jefferson saw to it that his essay was leaked to Republican friends in order to counter what he called "the anti-Christian system imputed to me by those who know nothing of my opinions." Yes, he explained to Benjamin Rush, he did reject "the corruptions of Christianity," but not "the genuine precepts of Jesus himself."[84]

Such distinctions were wasted of course on his Federalist critics, who were looking for ammunition rather than truth. Jefferson provided them with more than they could have hoped for when, only two weeks after his inauguration, he offered passage on a government ship to Tom Paine, who was attempting to return to America from France after barely escaping the guillotine. Jefferson's letter to Paine was picked up by the American press from the Paris papers, where Paine himself had probably planted it to publicize the honor of Jefferson's testimonial. "I am in hopes," Jefferson wrote to Paine, "you will find us returned generally to sentiments worthy of former times. In these it will be your glory to have steadily laboured and with as much effect as any man living. That you may long live to continue your useful labours and reap reward in the thankfulness of nations is my sincere prayer. Accept assurance of my high esteem and effectionate attachment."[85]

From Jefferson's perspective Tom Paine was an authentic American hero, a charter member of "the band of brothers" that had made the American Revolution happen and had then carried "the spirit of '76" to France, where it had produced more collateral damage than either man had anticipated, true enough, but where the future would surely recover the original ethos. Unfortunately for Jefferson, Paine's reputation in America had not aged well. When he landed in Baltimore, the local newspaper caught the mood by observing sarcastically that "our pious President thought it expedient to dispatch a frigate for the accommodation of this loathsome reptile." Paine's chief offense was not that he was a practicing alcoholic with the social graces of a derelict, though that was true, but rather that he had written *The Age of Reason,* which was as full-throated an attack on Christianity as *Common Sense* had been on monarchy. By publicly associating with Paine, Jefferson exposed himself to the full-broadside blasts of the Federalist press as an "arch infidel," "a defiler of Christian virtue" and "a companion of the most vile, corrupt, obnoxious sinner of the century." All Americans who took Christianity seriously now had to make a choice, said one editor, between "renouncing their savior, or their president. . . ." The attacks were relentless and unequaled in the early history of the young nation for their polemical intensity. As Henry Adams put it, if Jefferson had decided to congratulate Napoleon for his despotic seizure of power in France, "he could not have excited in the minds of the New England Calvinists so deep a sense of disgust by seeming to identify himself with Paine." It was, in a real sense, one of Jefferson's finer moments, since he was fully aware of Paine's notoriety but stuck by him to the end, even inviting him to live and dine at the presidential mansion for several weeks. Federalist editors had a field day describing "the two Toms" walking arm in arm, allegedly comparing notes on the ideal way to promote atheism or their past successes in despoiling Christian virgins.[86]

"The *circle* of our President's *felicities* is greatly enlarged," observed the editor of the Federalist *Port Folio,* "by the indulgence of Sally the sable, and the auspicious arrival of Tom Paine the pious." The reference to "Sally the sable" was a casual insertion of the most sensational accusation made against Jefferson, a charge of sexual (and in its own day racial) impropriety. Virtually every Federalist newspaper in the country picked up the story, which first appeared in the *Richmond Recorder* in September 1802. "It is well known," the story began, "that the man, *whom it delighteth the people to honor,* keeps, and for many years past has kept, as his concubine, one of his own slaves. Her name is SALLY. . . . The name of her eldest son is TOM. His features are said to bear a striking, although sable resemblance to those of the President himself." For several months the Federalist press printed editorials disclaiming knowledge as to whether the allegations were true, but then proceeding to provide readers with colorful variations on the provocative gossip, some even set to verse:

> *Of all the damsels on the green*
> *On mountain or in valley*
> *A lass so luscious ne'er was seen*
> *As Monticellan Sally.*

Editorials referred to "Dusky Sally," "Black Sal," the "African Venus" and the "mahogoney colored charmer." The Boston press was especially interested in how the fifty-nine-year-old president managed to make love with a much younger (Sally was thirty-one or thirty-two) woman. The answer was her African features:

> *Thick pouting lips! how sweet their grace!*
> *When passion fires to kiss them!*
> *Wide spreading over half the face,*
> *Impossible to miss them.*

And so on.[87]

It was a publicist's dream at the time because it gave the Federalists, who were growing more desperate with each Republican victory in the ongoing state elections, the kind of small but sharp-edged piece of scandal that cut across all party or policy disagreements and straight into the core question of Jefferson's character. It has been a publicist's dream ever since, because the charges could not until recently be conclusively proved or disproved and because advocates on each side of the debate possessed just enough evidence at their disposal to block a comfortable verdict for the opposition. (See "A Note on the Sally Hemings Scandal" at the end, for a concise summary of the evidence.) John Adams had one of the shrewdest reactions to the charges when they first surfaced. Adams was still in his anti-Jefferson phase, so his response was not conditioned by their former friendship. As a victim of similarly venomous vendettas Adams claimed to empathize with Jefferson. On the other hand, the allegations were "a natural and almost inevitable consequence of a foul contagion in the human character, Negro Slavery." Jefferson was not only contaminated by that contagion, but also not above suspicion because "there was not a planter in Virginia," Adams observed, "who could not reckon among his slaves a number of his children." The charge of sexual impropriety therefore placed "a blot on his Character" that was not completely implausible. It possessed a certain moral truth because it raised to relief the inherently immoral condition in which all slaveowners, Jefferson included, lived their lives.[88]

What Adams did not say for the record, but almost surely thought, was that there was an analogous sense of poetic justice about the allegations, because they originated with a former Republican scandalmonger named James Callender, whose previous career had been spent vilifying Jefferson's opponents, Adams among them, in much the same truth-be-damned fashion and with Jefferson's support and approval. Callender had been the reporter to break the story of Hamilton's shady escapades in 1797 and the following year had slandered Adams as "the corrupt and despotic monarch of Braintree" in a pamphlet entitled *The Prospect Before Us*. Jefferson had endorsed and helped pay for *Prospect*, but Callender, whose only consistency was a perverse flair for treachery, turned against him when Jefferson refused to reward his labors with the postmaster's job in Richmond. According to one Federalist account, probably apocryphal, Callender lingered outside the presidential mansion for several days hoping for a personal interview. When he spotted Jefferson at an upstairs window, he shouted out his threat: "Sir, you know that by lying I made you President, and I'll be d————d if I do not unmake you by telling the truth." Jefferson denounced Callender as "a lying renegade from Republicanism," then had Monroe, still governor of Virginia at the time, release statements denying that Jefferson had ever befriended or salaried Callender or had anything to do with his earlier diatribes against Adams. But Callender had saved his copies of Jefferson's incriminating letters and immediately distributed them to the Federalist press. "I thank you for the proof-sheets you enclosed me," Jefferson had written to Callender in reference to *Prospect;* "such papers cannot fail to produce the best effect."[89]

The duplicity that was exposed in his dealings with Callender was wholly in character for Jefferson. It was the Freneau deception and the Mazzei mischief all over again, with Jefferson denying to himself and then to the world his complicity in behind-the-scenes political skullduggery, then being genuinely surprised when the truth came out. Now, with the publication of his ill-considered correspondence with Callender, he was caught in a lie, which was bad enough, but the lie also enhanced the credibility of Callender's other charges about more titillating behind-the-scenes escapades with Sally Hemings.

There was one additional reason that Callender's charges disturbed Jefferson's quite remarkable powers of deception and denial. Namely, they were essentially true. While we cannot know with any degree of certainty what the emotional character of Jefferson's sexual relationship with Sally Hemings may have been, we can be reasonably sure that it was long-standing, most probably dating from his last two years in Paris. It was also most probably consensual, at least to the extent that any inherently unequal relationship between master and slave can permit mutual consent. It clearly satisfied basic biological needs that

Jefferson was unable or unwilling to deny himself, since the liaison continued for several years after the Callender exposé.

Mostly, however, it was covert, secret in several senses of the term. Not a trace of evidence about the relationship ever found its way into Jefferson's vast personal correspondence. (So adept at covering his tracks was Jefferson that it required nearly two centuries and the most advanced genetic detective work of modern science to establish the case for his paternity of Sally's children.) Moreover, within the interior world of Monticello, which Jefferson always described in his most heartfelt fashion as an idyllic haven of domestic serenity, there must have been a veritable labyrinth of sealed-off physical and psychological spaces.

Martha Jefferson Randolph, his eldest daughter, lived with her growing brood of children at Monticello throughout the duration of Jefferson's relationship with Sally Hemings. How she could have avoided knowing the truth strains even our most sophisticated under-standing of the human capacity for denial. But Martha went to her grave insisting the Callender accusations were untrue, defending her father's reputation, somehow convincing herself in the process of per-suading others. And then there was Jefferson himself, dutifully record-ing the names of Sally's children in his *Farm Book* as slaves, treating them as such while they grew up, as if there were no connection between them and him, indeed as if the man who fathered them and the man who owned them were different people.

At the public level the consequences of the Callender accusations did not linger so poignantly, while the scar on Jefferson's reputation never went away, and the New England Federalists did their best to keep the accusations alive in the public press, even going so far as to put the matter of Jefferson's character on the official agenda of the Massachusetts legislature, the political damage to his presidency proved less serious than the lingering stigma that attached itself to his image with posterity. The damage control teams in the Republican press helped the cause, Jefferson's posture of total silence on the matter prevented any prolonged debate from feeding on itself and, most sig-nificant, the steady string of Republican successes—the debt was being retired, taxes were being eliminated, the economy was humming along nicely, half a continent was peacefully acquired—simply crowded out the bad news. At the height of the Sally stories, John Quincy Adams suggested that the Federalists were forced to resort to such scandal-mongering because their political program had been "completely and irrevocably, abandoned and rejected by the popular voice." Whatever alarm Jefferson's supporters felt, he observed, would prove short-lived. "What they take for breakers," Adams noted, "are mere clouds of unsubstantiated vapour."[90] This became Jefferson's public position as well. The frantic behavior of the Federalist press was symptomatic of its utter desperation, he insisted, as its cause slid beneath the surface of American politics forever. The Federalists were simply clutching at dirt as they went under.

But the experience took its toll on Jefferson's view of the American press. His eloquent statement in the Inaugural Address—"let them stand undisturbed as monuments of the safety which error of opinion may be tolerated where reason is left free to combat it"—implied that complete freedom of the press was both inviolable and self-correcting. Now he was not so sure. "Our newspapers, for the most part, present only the charicatures of disaffected minds," he concluded in 1803, and what he called "the abuses of the freedom of the press" had generated a scatological political culture "never before known or borne by any civilized nation." Jefferson actually had a point, since his presidency coincided with an exponential increase in the sheer number of American newspapers, as well as the abiding sense—left over from the 1790s—that there were no official or unofficial rules of conduct governing what would or should be printed.[91]

Jefferson wanted the press to be free, but he had also presumed that a free press would maintain some measure of respect for the truth. The free-for-all mentality and ricochet style of the multiplying newspapers allowed him to persuade himself that the very principle of freedom of the press was being destroyed by its own excesses. "This is a dangerous state of things," he explained to Thomas McKean of Pennsylvania, "and the press ought to be restored to its credibility if possible." He did not have anything so heavy-handed as the Sedition Act in mind. Instead he suggested that Republican governors in selected states target the most offensive Federalist editors for libel: "And I have therefore long thought," he apprised McKean, "that a few prosecutions of the most prominent offenders would have a wholesome effect in restoring the integrity of the presses. Not a general prosecution, for that would look like persecution [i.e., the Federalist approach with the Sedition Act], but a selected one." Governors McKean in Pennsylvania and De Witt Clinton in New York took the suggestion as a command to release their lawyers on the most recalcitrant Federalist editors. As Jefferson saw it, he was not violating a principle so much as rescuing it from its own abusive and self-destructive tendencies. But it was clearly at least a half step backward from his earlier incantations to unbridled freedom of speech.[92]

GIBRALTAR

THE SAME LINE in his mind that separated salvageable Federalists from "incurables," good Indians from bad, also separated responsible journalists from loathsome liars. Until that line was crossed, he could be the essence of tolerant amiability. On the other side of the line, however, there could be no mercy, since the moral issues at stake were not susceptible to negotiation or compromise. Within this powerful moralistic scheme, one group was permanently planted on the far side of the Jeffersonian divide and in fact served as the most visible symbol of the institutionalized evil that still managed to defy the "pure republicanism" Jefferson wished to restore. These were the judges of the federal courts, especially the so-called midnight judges Adams had appointed during his lame-duck phase. Soon after Jefferson named Levi Lincoln as his attorney general, he told him that "the removal of the excrescences from the judiciary is the universal demand." William Branch Giles, his Virginian protégé who was elected to the Senate in the Republican avalanche of 1800, reminded Jefferson that "the revolution is incomplete, so long as that strong fortress is in possession of the enemy." Since the Jeffersonian mentality actually required discernible enemies in order to unlock its dynamic energies, one could argue that Adams had done him a backhanded favor by his judicial legacy. But if the federal judiciary was a convenient target that mobilized all the Jeffersonian firepower, it was also, as the editor of the *National Intelligencer* put it, "the Gibraltar" of Federalism, sitting squarely and impregnably in the midst of Republican waters. Jefferson spent much of his first term circling this Federalist fortress, sending his most devoted soldiers, like Giles, against it, but never breaching its formidable defenses.[93]

It is important to distinguish between Jefferson's animosity toward the midnight judges as political appointments and his more general hostility toward the federal judiciary as an institution. In 1804, as part of an unsuccessful effort to resume friendly relations with John and Abigail Adams, he explained to her that "the one act of Mr. Adams' life" that had genuinely upset him and struck him "as personally unkind" was the appointment of Federalists to the federal courts. "They were among my most ardent political enemies," he complained, "and from whom no faithful cooperation could ever be expected. . . . It seemed but common justice to leave a successor free to act by instruments of his own Choice." The most offensive appointment, of course, was John Marshall's selection as chief justice, which was especially loathsome for several reasons: first, because it was a lifetime appointment, second, because it placed a Federalist atop the entire national judiciary system and third, because Marshall himself was, in his own different way, more formidable an adversary than Hamilton. Marshall was that rarest of creatures, a Federalist with a Jeffersonian style. He was the one man whom Jefferson did not believe he could outduel in behind-the-scenes political fighting: "When conversing with Marshall," he confessed, "I never admit anything. So sure as you admit any position to be good, no matter how remote from the conclusion he seeks to establish, you are gone. So great is his sophistry you must never give him an affirmative answer or you will be forced to grant his conclusion. Why if he were to ask me if it were daylight or not, I'd reply, 'Sir, I don't know, I can't tell.' "[94]

Beyond the personal hatred and the understandable bitterness at being saddled with the Adams appointments lay Jefferson's more tortured sense of hostility toward the entire federal judicial system per se. Part of the problem with recovering his mentality in this area is that it does not fit neatly into the logical and legal categories that constitutional scholars, who have done the best work on the general subject, have tended to bring with them. Questions about federal versus state jurisdiction, for example, or the highly controversial question about judicial review did not engage his full attention except as specific episodes in a larger political drama about the true meaning of the American Revolution. And the simple truth was that the original American revolutionaries had not envisioned a national judiciary at all. At times Jefferson seemed to believe that to be true to the original "spirit of '76" all federal courts should be abolished completely and the judicial decisions left to the states. But such thoughts did not emerge out of specific legal arguments so much as a grander sense of "sweeping away" the institutional residue that had built up since the Revolution.

Similarly, Jefferson did not have a consistent or cogently constructed position on the ultimate questions of constitutional sovereignty. In his more radical moments he seemed to believe that all fundamental constitutional questions should be settled by a popular referendum, since the doctrine of popular sovereignty empowered only the people at large to render such judgments. This was obviously burdensome, if not completely impractical, but it drew inspiration from the same visionary impulse that welcomed a "sweeping away" of all laws every generation. In his first Annual Message to Congress he proposed a more moderate idea that each branch of the federal government was sovereign and therefore empowered to interpret the Constitution for itself. Gallatin and Madison, recognizing the confusion inherent in such a position, persuaded him to delete the paragraph.[95]

To be fair, Jefferson was hardly alone in grappling unsuccessfully with the proper role of the federal judiciary, especially the Supreme Court. The judicial institutions were still congealing as integral parts of the national government. Nor had there been any clear consensus at

the Constitutional Convention about the role of the Supreme Court
as the ultimate arbiter of the Constitution's meaning. Hamilton had
made the clearest case on behalf of the principle of judicial review in
Federalist 78, but it was part of the genius of the constitutional settlement of 1788 to leave such controversial questions blurry and unresolved. In that sense Jefferson's confusion accurately mirrored the
crisscrossing currents of constitutional opinion prevalent at the time.[96]

But Jefferson's mind preferred to operate at a higher altitude, where
the details and technicalities disappeared from sight and the larger
moral patterns assumed a clear shape. From that perspective, he saw
the federal judiciary and its capstone in the Supreme Court as a source
of unmitigated danger. If the West for Jefferson was the dynamic
engine of expansion and national liberation that continually vitalized
the American republic with its energy, the federal judiciary was the
engine of centralization and consolidation that sucked the energies of
the new nation into a stifling sinkhole. The fact that all the crucial
offices were filled with Federalists was obviously bad enough, but the
federal judiciary itself embodied counterrevolutionary tendencies fundamentally at odds with the deepest impulses of "pure republicanism"
as Jefferson understood it. Jefferson's views were distinctive and radical
on this score. Both Adams and Madison recognized the need for a
judicial counterpoise to majority rule. The fact that federal judges
served for life and were least accountable to popular opinion was, as
they saw it, an important asset, for such requirements helped balance
the democratic excesses of the more directly elected branches of government. Jefferson, however, saw no need for such balancing mechanisms. For him, the American Revolution was about release, not
restraint. In addition to being a Federalist Gibraltar occupied by his
most devoted enemies, then, the national judiciary was a permanent
brake placed on the wheels of the ongoing American Revolution.[97]

The battle over the judiciary took the form of three distinct skir-
mishes. The first, in the winter of 1802, occurred in the Congress, where
the Republicans used their majority to repeal the Judiciary Act of 1801.
Jefferson had launched the attack in his first Annual Message. "The

judiciary system . . . and especially that portion of it recently erected," he declared, "will of course present itself to the contemplation of Congress." He was referring specifically to the Judiciary Act of 1801, which was offensive to Republicans for several reasons: It was a partisan measure passed by the lame-duck Congress in February, when the Federalists were scrambling to shore up their control over the court system before Jefferson took office; it established a separate circuit court with sixteen new judges, essentially creating a new layer of federal jurisdiction between the Supreme Court and the district courts; and most of the midnight judges appointed by Adams filled these new circuit court posts. Although Jefferson was active in mobilizing the Republican forces behind the scenes, he made a point of maintaining a distance from the congressional debates, which were heated, and attempted to present his opposition to the circuit courts in the most innocuous terms, claiming that there were simply not enough cases to justify the new layer of federal judges. Rather than raise the controversial constitutional or ideological issues about the entire judicial system, he preferred to cast the issues in terms of republican austerity. Given the Republican dominance in the Congress, victory was a foregone conclusion. Gallatin had already prepared the budget estimates for 1802 on the presumption that the circuit court judges would be eliminated.[98]

The second skirmish occurred in 1803 in the unfriendly arena of the Supreme Court, where Marshall's influence and intellectual agility worked its customary magic to produce an embarrassing defeat for Jefferson. The matter at issue was unquestionably trivial: the appointment of William Marbury to a low-level post as justice of the peace in the District of Columbia. The subsequent historical significance of Marshall's decision was just as unquestionably massive; it became the landmark precedent for the principle of judicial review and for the Supreme Court's sovereign right to interpret the meaning of the Constitution. But in the historical context of the time Marshall's celebrated opinion in *Marbury* v. *Madison* occupied an inherently middle ground, neither trivial nor dramatically principled. It provided the occasion for Marshall to lecture Jefferson for failing to uphold the law by refusing to appoint Marbury. The message was clear to all the interested parties of the day: The Republican assault on the federal judiciary may have been successful at eliminating the circuit courts, but the Supreme Court was off-limits. The Federalist fortress on Gibraltar could fire back.[99]

The legal genius of Marshall's opinion, what Jefferson described as "sophistry" and later as Marshall's "twistifications," derived from the chief justice's rearrangement of the questions presented to the Court, which allowed him to rule against Marbury's petition only after lecturing the president and ruling on the constitutionality of an act of Congress, the Judiciary Act of 1789. If he had taken up the questions in the order in which they were presented, there would have been no need to address the broader issues. The political genius of Marshall's opinion was double-barreled: He enhanced the power of the Supreme Court by denying its jurisdiction, and he patronized the president while deciding the case in his favor. It was vintage Marshall at his most maddeningly covert. It also revealed that Marshall, much like Jefferson, preferred to avoid a direct confrontation on the abiding role of the federal judiciary, since he had masked his assertion of judicial review under the veil of impotence and had ruled that Jefferson, though in violation of the law, did not need to appoint Marbury after all. Having sallied forth from his fortress, Marshall had returned quietly to the safety of Gibraltar.

The third skirmish came at the end of Jefferson's first term, when the Republicans in Congress, at the president's instigation, unsuccessfully attempted to impeach Justice Samuel Chase. Next to Marshall, Chase was the most formidable Federalist presence on the Supreme Court, a white-maned giant who preferred to play the role of Jehovah with all Jeffersonians who had the misfortune to land in his courtroom. He had attracted sharp criticism for his strenuous support of the Sedition Act, most especially (and ironically for Jefferson himself) because of his intemperate conduct in dispatching James Callender to a Richmond jail during Callender's anti-Federalist phase. If Marshall was the master of stealth and guerrilla tactics, Chase preferred to lead cavalry assaults. In May 1803, after reading about Chase's inflammatory charge to a Baltimore jury, Jefferson wrote to a Republican leader in the House: "Might this seditious and official attack on the principles of our Constitution . . . go unpunished? And to whom so pointedly as yourself will the public look for the necessary measures. I ask these questions for your consideration. For myself, it is better that I should not interfere." This was the equivalent of a command to his Republican lieutenants in Congress to launch impeachment proceedings against Chase.[100]

But impeachment, as Jefferson readily acknowledged, was a clumsy instrument, requiring as it did evidence of "treason, bribery, or high crimes and misdemeanors." Though the Republicans attempted to wrap themselves in the trappings of legality, the trial in the Senate had a distinctly partisan flavor that struck several observers as a Republican version of the Sedition Act. Jefferson followed the proceedings closely; he kept a running tabulation of the votes on each count for conviction but maintained official silence. Chase was eventually acquitted on all the charges. His Federalist defenders enjoyed the advantage of the narrow requirements imposed by the Constitution for removing judges; they could plausibly describe Chase as a political target and victim; and they particularly relished the opportunity to remind Jefferson that the principle of an independent judiciary had been a rallying cry in 1776 as well as one of the sacred truths that Jefferson had once accused George III of violating.[101]

Over the subsequent course of American history several presidents also attempted to take on the Supreme Court, and all came away with a similar sense of frustration as Jefferson. But these latter-day challenges to the judicial branch all occurred after the Supreme Court had achieved quasi-sacred status as the one American political institution that was presumed to receive its instructions directly from God rather than from the electorate. Jefferson's campaign against the judiciary predated the public enshrinement of federal courts, most especially the Supreme Court, as the designated Olympian element in the government. Indeed Jefferson's campaign was driven by the conviction that, as he put it, "independence of the will of the nation is a solecism, at least in a republican government. . . ." What appears almost sacrilegious to us was then still in the process of carving out its place in American political theology.[102]

For Jefferson the religious wellspring that inspired his vision of the sacred remained the "pure republicanism" of the American Revolution. The federal judiciary had no prominent place in that vision, indeed no place at all, and Jefferson went to his grave believing that Marshall and his colleagues on the Supreme Court were an evil conclave, a gang of "sappers and miners" sabotaging the republican experiment from within. But if his ideological convictions were clear and unwavering, his reluctance to declare unlimited war on the federal judiciary stands out as the defining feature of the conflict. Perhaps at some level he recognized that a national government required some kind of national system of laws, that those moderate Republicans who regarded the Constitution and the constitutional settlement of 1787–88 as the sacred corollary to the revolutionary magic of 1776 had at least half a point. If so, he never acknowledged this concession publicly or privately. (It might have been one of those silent occasions when Madison's invisible influence proved decisive.) Or perhaps Hamilton was right after all: that Jefferson's aversion to conflict dictated a policy of caution for purely personal reasons, in spite of his moral certainty that the federal judiciary was a blot on the face of "pure republicanism." Or perhaps his own belief in the inherent limitations that republicanism imposed on the executive branch—the unimperial presidency—made more decisive action impossible for him. One cannot be sure of the right answer here, or even be sure that Jefferson himself knew what it was, if it existed at all. For it was in this context, after all, that Henry Adams composed his most arresting portrait of Jefferson's elusive character: "Almost every other American statesman might be described in a parenthesis," Adams observed. "A few broad strokes of the brush would paint the portraits of all the early Presidents with this exception . . . , but Jefferson could be painted only touch by touch, with a fine pencil, and the perfection of the likeness depended upon the shifting and uncertain flicker of its semi-transcendent shadows."[103]

LISTS AND LOSSES

At some point during the year before his elevation to the presidency Jefferson wrote an uncharacteristically personal note to himself under the title "Memorandum of Services." "I have sometimes asked myself whether my country is the better for my having lived at all," he mused to himself. "I have been the instrument of doing the following things; but they would have been done by others; some of them, perhaps, a little better." He then went on to list a curious version of his public accomplishments, placing the dredging of the Rivanna River alongside the drafting of the Declaration of Independence, importing olive plants from France beside the efforts to end the slave trade. An updated version of the list composed at the end of his first term as president would surely have added appreciably to his achievements. The two presidential accomplishments that gave him the most satisfaction were the Louisiana Purchase and the retirement of a substantial portion of the national debt. Although pockets of Federalism held out in parts of New England, as a viable national party the Federalists were finished. Except for the ongoing naval action against the Barbary pirates, a limited affair, America was at peace with the world. And that symbol of government's unwelcome reach into private lives, the tax collector, had been banished, along with the circuit court judges, much of the army and navy, a boatload of civil servants and several tribes of recalcitrant Indians. He had no way of knowing it, of course, but Jefferson's first term was to go down as one of the two or three most uniformly successful in American presidential history in achieving its stated objectives.[104]

In more personal terms, the Federalist attacks on his character had taken an emotional toll. But he claimed that it was precisely "the unfounded calumnies of the federal party" that persuaded him to run for a second term. He had always presumed, he explained to Elbridge Gerry, that he would retire after four years, but the lingering presence of Federalist propaganda in the press, though like letters from the dead, needed to be silenced completely. "They force my continuance," he claimed. "If I can keep the vessel of state as steadily on her course another four years, my earthly purposes will be accomplished, and I shall be free to enjoy"–then the familiar refrain–"my family, my farm, and my books." His reelection, if he chose to run, was a foregone conclusion.[105]

But something had gone out of him even as he decided to prolong his presidency. The burdens of the office undoubtedly accumulated with time. The Federalist assaults on his personal honor also inflicted wounds that never completely healed. His physical constitution, though still remarkably robust for a sixty-one-year-old man, was now bedeviled by recurrent bouts of diarrhea that periodically sapped him of energy. The most devastating blow, however, came in April 1804, when Maria died from complications in childbirth, much as her mother had done. "Others may lose of their abundance," he wrote to John Page, his lifelong soul mate, "but I of my want, have lost even the half of all I had." His prospects, he believed, "now hang on the slender thread of a single life." This was Martha, the only one left to populate the family circle from the original Jefferson dream, which he now described as "fearfully blighted." He was never really the same after Maria's death, less exuberant and more fatalistic, and history was already preparing a series of unpleasant surprises on the international scene that were destined to make his second term as president a headlong fall from grace.[106]

5

Monticello, 1816–26

I like the dreams of the future better than the history of the past.
—JEFFERSON TO JOHN ADAMS
AUGUST 1, 1816

I regret that I am now to die in the belief that the useless sacrifice of themselves by the generation of 1776 . . . is to be thrown away by the unwise and unworthy passions of their sons, and that my only consolation is to be, that I live not to weep over it.
—JEFFERSON TO JOHN HOLMES
APRIL 22, 1820

VISITORS DURING his last decade could catch a glimpse of the ex-president astride his favorite horse in the early afternoon of most days, when he rode Eagle for two or three hours through the fields and woods around Monticello. Time had taken its inevitable toll on his aging body in all the little ways that accumulate in the joints and arteries of formerly athletic young men past their prime. But the nagging disabilities that made rising from a chair or walking through his garden more difficult somehow disappeared once he was on horseback. (In 1809, when he was sixty-five, he had taken his final ride home from Washington to permanent retirement without assistance and had pressed on for the final eight hours through a driving snowstorm.) As Eagle aged along with him and became Old Eagle, the members of the family worried that these solitary rides each afternoon placed both man and mount at some risk. But Jefferson brushed aside such cautionary concerns, explaining that, while an old man on his own legs, he was still a young man in the saddle. Even after he broke his arm in a fall off the back steps of Monticello in 1822, he insisted on his daily ride. He had Old Eagle brought up to the terrace so that he could be mounted from the height of the porch, eased himself into the saddle with his good arm while the horse leaned patiently against the terrace wall, then assumed the bolt-straight posture of a born rider and trotted off like a natural aristocrat keeping his appointment with destiny.[1]

We know more about his physical appearance and daily regimen during his last decade than at any other period of his life. He was, after all, a prominent member of America's founding generation, obviously destined to take his place in the history books, so visitors felt a special urge to record their impressions of the Sage of Monticello for posterity. The inexorable ravages of the aging process also forced Jefferson himself to chronicle the physical and medical realities as they encroached upon his earlier indifference to such matters. He remained to the end congenitally suspicious of all doctors, claiming that whenever he saw three physicians together, "he looked up to see if there was not a turkey-buzzard in the neighborhood." But he also recognized, as he reported to Adams, that "our machines have been now running for 70 or 80 years, and we must expect that worn as they are; here a pivot, there a wheel, now a pinion, next a spring, will be giving way."[2]

The old argument over the color of his hair—was it red or blond?—was now displaced by the common description of family and friends that it was completely gray. He also cut it shorter, eliminating the tied queue in the back, in part because it was easier to care for, in part because the longer style was beginning to seem old-fashioned. When walking outside or riding, he tended to wear a large, round, broad-brimmed hat to shield his face from the sun. Despite this protection, his facial skin was blotchy and usually peeling from exposure; the capillaries just beneath the surface were easily ruptured, giving his face irregular coloration; biologically as well as psychologically, he was thin-skinned. Recurrent diarrhea and intestinal disorders sapped his energy—this was the ailment that eventually killed him—so he needed a cane much of the time he was on his feet, and his loyal black servant, Burwell, the successor to Jupiter and James Hemings, accompanied him at all times except during his afternoon ride. His posture remained remarkably erect despite the cane, though several visitors noted that his head and neck now inclined forward, as if he were always leaning into the wind.[3]

When guests joined him for a tour of the grounds, they tended to be surprised at his passionate and animated way of talking and the rapidity of his speech, which tended to come in bursts of varying length and was accompanied by an emphatic shrugging of his shoulders and gesturing with his long arms and large hands. An itinerant bookseller, clearly expecting a more sedate and stoic demeanor, described him as "less a philosopher than a partizan." Jefferson's preferred mode of dress also caught some visitors off guard because of its informality. He tended to wear a brightly colored (usually red) vest underneath a gray waistcoat and loosely fitting pantaloons or corduroy pants that were usually tucked into his riding boots. He dressed, in other words, less like a former statesman or aspiring national icon than a working Virginia planter. Despite the cane and the blotchy skin and the disjunction between his nonchalant demeanor and the godlike expectations, almost all observers commented on his relatively youthful appearance. At eighty he looked sixty.[4]

His diet and daily regimen continued to follow the old patterns. He ate very little red meat, preferring vegetables, poultry and shellfish, though regular fish did not agree with his digestive system. He drank coffee and tea at breakfast, malt liquor and cider at dinner. While he avoided all hard liquors, he enjoyed three or four glasses of wine each day. He rose with the sun regardless of the season, usually getting five to eight hours of sleep, the length contingent upon the retirement hour, which itself depended on the quality of conversation when there were guests in the house or his interest in the book he was reading that evening. He bathed his feet in cold water every morning, devoted the early part of each day to his correspondence and his garden, rode each afternoon, then made himself sociable with family and guests at dinner until dark. His hearing remained good except, as he put it, "when several voices cut across each other," which meant that he could not always follow conversations over dinner. His eyesight was excellent at a distance, but he relied on glasses for reading, especially at night.[5]

Certain poignant scenes, like verbal tableaux, have been passed down in the reminiscences of his grandchildren. Like the description of his daily excursion aboard Old Eagle, they conjure up some of the most attractive and nearly idyllic moments, when his retirement years managed to capture the pastoral and domestic serenity he had been pursuing throughout his life. There is the scene in his garden just after breakfast, working beside Wormley, his gardener, who is tending the spade and hoe while Jefferson aligns the rows of flowers and vegetables with a measuring line or clips off excess buds and leaves with his pruning knife. Or there is the scene on the terrace after dinner, as Jefferson organizes footraces for his grandchildren around the house, dropping a white handkerchief for the start, then seeing to it that the younger and slower children receive pieces of fruit just like the winners.[6]

There were two minor but naggingly persistent intrusions into the domestic serenities on the mountaintop, and both were direct consequences of Jefferson's stature as one of the last survivors of 1776. First, the steady flow of guests, tourists and self-proclaimed Jeffersonians made Monticello into a virtual hotel for at least eight months of the year. "I need not tell you what open doors he lives," one visitor reported in 1815, "as you well know his mountain is made a sort of Mecca." Members of Congress, foreign dignitaries, Indian agents, retired army and naval officers, Protestant missionaries, itinerant booksellers, aspiring Virginia politicians—all felt the obligation to make the pilgrimage to Monticello. Once there, a distressingly large number chose to regard Jefferson's generic offer of hospitality as a personal invitation to stay for several days. Martha's daughter, Ellen, recalled that her mother sometimes had to feed and entertain fifty overnight guests. Total strangers who were simply passing through seemed to believe that Monticello was a national shrine where they could declare sanctuary. They often peered through the windows when the family was seated at dinner, walked right into the front hallway, chipped off pieces of brick or wood as souvenirs, even joined the invited guests over tea or wine and struck up conversations with the patriarch himself, who was sometimes not sure whether he was addressing a guest or an interloper. By 1816, as this persistent stream of visitors became a virtual flood, Jefferson retreated three or four times a year to his estate in Bedford County about ninety miles from Monticello. He supervised the finishing touches on what became his Poplar Forest home away from home, a smaller but even more architecturally distinctive dwelling than Monticello (Poplar Forest was shaped as a perfect octagon) and used it as his personal refuge whenever Monticello became overoccupied.[7]

Second, his correspondence became a massive and time-consuming burden. Jefferson received more than 1,000 letters each year of his retirement. In 1820 he made a point of keeping an accurate record and counted 1,267 separate letters, most from people he did not know, many requesting long answers to historical questions. He spent three or four hours each morning trying to respond, then often returned to the writing desk before retiring at night. "Is this life?" he asked Adams, answering his own question by describing himself as "a mill-horse, who sees no end to his circle but in death." Adams commiserated with what Jefferson had called his "epistolary corvée," noting mischievously that he did not have Jefferson's problem because he had been prescient enough to make himself unpopular. Moreover, as Adams explained, he simply neglected to answer the letters from cranks and well-intentioned strangers, so that he could devote his remaining energies to correspondents who counted, the chief one being Jefferson himself.[8]

But Adams's sense of humor was lost on Jefferson, who somehow felt a relentless obligation to respond personally to everyone. Madison advised him to prepare a formulaic letter, "a standard response that the family can send out expressing thanks," but he could not comply.

Especially after arthritis in his wrist and fingers worsened with age, he complained that "the unceasing drudgery of writing keeps me in unceasing pain and peevishness." Only a few months before his death he lamented that his rescue from the writing table rested "on the hitherto illusive hope that the discretion of those who have no claims upon me, will at length advert to the circumstances of my age and ill health, and feel the duty of sparing both." But it was not meant to be. Neither the presumptuous pilgrims to Monticello nor the countless correspondents throughout the country could be made to respect his privacy and leave him alone. As a living legend he had become public property.[9]

He claimed that there was one shadowy acquaintance whom he was fully prepared to receive at Monticello at any time. The prospect of death did not unnerve him so much as the fear of what he called "a doting old age." For more than twenty years he had been telling friends that his physical health was so good that he sometimes worried about living too long. The ultimate fear was senility, what Adams referred to as "dying at the top." Almost as worrisome was a gradual physical degeneration that would deprive him of any semblance of autonomy and personal sovereignty. (One reason the daily ride on Old Eagle was so important to him was that it symbolized the survival of his independent spirit.) Finally there was the uniquely Jeffersonian sense that one should not linger beyond the allotted time of one's generation, that one had almost a moral obligation to clear the ground for the next generation by placing oneself underneath it. "Mine is the next turn," he wrote to his old love Maria Cosway in 1820, "and I shall meet it with good will; and after one's friends are all gone before them, and our faculties leaving us, too, one by one, why wish to linger in mere vegetation, as a solitary trunk in a desolate field, from which all its former companions have disappeared." This feeling of having outlived his time intensified with age. In the year before his death he claimed that looking back over his own life was "like looking over a field of battle. All, all dead! and ourselves left alone midst a new generation whom we know not, and who know not us."[10]

Another memorable scene made the point with almost visual clarity. In 1824 Lafayette paid a final visit to America and naturally scheduled a rendezvous with the Sage of Monticello. An escort of 120 mounted men and a crowd of 200 onlookers accompanied Lafayette up the mountain to witness the reunion of the former comrades. Madison described the general as "in fine health and spirits but so much increased in bulk and changed in aspect that I should not have known him." (Lafayette had spent several years in a Swiss dungeon, confined by the radicals for siding with the moderate faction in the French Revolution, then ballooned upon his release.) Meanwhile Lafayette described Jefferson as "feeble and much aged," though "in full possession of all the vigor of his mind and heart." As the two aging patriarchs tottered toward each other and embraced before the crowd, witnesses claimed they saw two ghosts from a bygone era materializing one final time for the benefit of the present generation. Given the urge to make Jefferson into a historical icon, it seemed almost awkward to realize that he was still alive.[11]

Or there was the highly symbolic but scary scene the following year, in 1825, when Jefferson consented to sit for a "life mask" that would allow posterity to possess a reliable likeness of the American hero, an iconographic rendering of the living icon based on a special technique designed to subordinate artistic interpretation to the actual shape and contours of his face. The American sculptor John Henri Browere poured successive coats of a mysterious plasterlike substance over Jefferson's head, but the liquid dried and hardened more rapidly than anticipated, causing Jefferson considerable discomfort and forcing Browere, as Jefferson put it, to "use freely the mallet and chisel to break it into pieces" with a series of heavy blows that "would have been sensible almost to a loggerhead. . . ." The experience convinced Jefferson to "bid adieu for ever to busts and even portraits." In addition to illustrating the dominant perception of Jefferson as a living relic of America's glorious past, the Browere incident inadvertently signaled the subsequent problems that would afflict anyone intent upon establishing a close fit between Jefferson's image and the man he really was.

Even Browere's plaster cast was based on the reassembled fragments of the fractured "life mask." Like the man himself, even his face seemed to resist realistic renderings.[12]

But the faithful recovery of revealing moments—riding Old Eagle, greeting Lafayette, enduring the preservative techniques of Browere—provides us with only glimpses of the real person who was Jefferson in his most patriarchal phase. Such scenes also telescope, and therefore distort in their well-intentioned way, Jefferson's own final stage of evolution during a ten-year period when, despite the nagging intrusions of visitors and the equally nagging afflictions of age, he enjoyed the opportunity to meditate more freely and fully about his legacy than any other time in his life. One last scene, though only another momentary glimpse, offers what is probably the best angle from which to catch the main drift of Jefferson's mentality throughout his final decade by providing a thematic clue to the abiding concerns that were on his mind and in his heart.

It was the last morning of his life, which, as if orchestrated by providence, happened to be July 4, 1826, the fiftieth anniversary to the day of the publication of the Declaration of Independence. He had fallen into coma the preceding evening and awoken to ask the physician and family gathered around the bedside, "Is it the Fourth?" It was obvious to all, including himself, that this was his final illness, and for several days visitors and family had been paying their respects, noting the persistence of his independent spirit; he insisted on sleeping at night with only the trusted Burwell in the room and on flicking away the flies during the day himself. The prayer of the family that he would make it to the Fourth was answered, though he was unconscious for most of the final hours. He stirred briefly, mumbling something that the doctor and family could not understand, until Burwell, the only one to comprehend what his master was asking, stepped forward to adjust the pillows. His last request, in effect, was answered by a slave, just as first memory, at least as legend has it, was of being carried on a pillow as a young child by a slave. His last sounds were semiconscious ramblings, apparently based on his dreams. He was back in the 1770s, giving instructions about the Committees of Safety and the need to stand firm against British tyranny. He went to his maker shortly after noon on July 4, reliving the tumultuous early years of the American Revolution. This was both poignant and symptomatic. For the meaning of the American Revolution—his personal role in it and his abiding sense of what it meant for posterity—was also his central obsession throughout the final decade of his retirement.[13]

WORDS AND MUSIC

ALTHOUGH AN OBSESSION, by definition, does not need any urging, in Jefferson's case a good deal of looking back occurred at the urging, one might even say at the frantic insistence of John Adams. The resumption of correspondence between the two patriarchs seems, in retrospect, almost inevitable. "You and I ought not to die," as Adams so eloquently put it, "before We have explained ourselves to each other." But for many years what now appears inevitable and almost elegiac looked utterly impossible. Jefferson's narrow victory in the presidential election of 1800 had sent Adams into retirement at Quincy, where he spent nearly twelve years groveling and grimacing and twitching away in barely suppressed resentment, then firing away in his best Adams style, sending a salvo of words toward all his political enemies, Jefferson among them. "Mr. Jefferson has reason to reflect upon himself," Adams observed grudgingly upon Jefferson's retirement from the presidency. "How he will get rid of his remorse in his retirement, I know not. He must know that he leaves the government infinitely worse than he found it, and that from his own error or ignorance. I wish his telescopes and mathematical instruments, however, may secure his felicity." Adams had a way of exposing his deep-seated anger toward Jefferson in the same breath that he tried to deny its existence. "I have no resentments against him," he explained to Benjamin Rush, "though he has honoured and salaried almost every villain he could find who had been an enemy to me."[14]

This last reference was to the Republican propaganda campaign against Adams during his presidency, chiefly the libelous accusations of James Callender in *The Prospect Before Us,* which Jefferson had in fact subsidized and approved. It described Adams as a vain (true), dangerously unbalanced (exaggerated distortion of the truth) and covertly monarchical (mostly untrue) instrument of Federalist corruption (completely untrue). Jefferson had made a concerted effort to reopen the lines of communication with the Sage of Quincy in 1804, trying the indirect route through Abigail. But he made the double mistake of mentioning his own anger at Adams for the appointment of the midnight judges and then claiming complete ignorance of the whole Callender business. Abigail responded like a lioness protecting her pride. Jefferson had once been a trusted friend, she explained, and some residue of affection "still resides in the Bosom, even after esteem has taken its flight." But she no longer respected or trusted a man so capable of either hypocrisy or self-deception, and she acknowledged a personal sense of poetic justice when "the serpent you cherished and warmed [i.e., Callender], bit the hand that nourished him," a reference to the Sally Hemings accusations. "Faithful are the wounds of a Friend," she observed caustically, then declared any subsequent correspondence unnecessary. (Adams himself did not see any of these letters until a few months later, when Abigail showed them to him, and he jotted in the margins: "I have no remarks to make upon it at this time and place.") No more words were exchanged between Quincy and Monticello for another eight years.[15]

If Adams spent much of that time licking his political wounds, Jefferson was having a whole new series of political wounds inflicted on him. Adams's harsh appraisal of Jefferson's latter years as president was only a more intense version of the generally negative verdict. Everything that had flowed together so serenely during his first term seemed to collapse in disastrous heaps of misfortune in his second. The root cause of the later failures, it turns out, was located in the same place as the earlier successes—namely, the European conflict between England and France. The temporary peace between these two perpetual combatants had permitted American commerce to flourish between 1800 and 1803; this in turn had allowed Jefferson, with Gallatin's able assistance, to perform the political magic of retiring the debt while also cutting taxes. Even as the Anglo-French war had resumed in 1803, Jefferson and his administration were the immediate beneficiaries when Napoleon decided to cut his losses in North America by selling the Louisiana Territory for a mere pittance. But the resumption of full-scale war on the Continent in 1803, then the imposition of naval blockades in the Atlantic and Caribbean, threw the American economic engine into reverse. And since Jefferson's dedication to fiscal austerity had required the dry docking or destruction of America's infant navy, there was really very little strategic room in which Jefferson could maneuver as American commercial vessels were scooped up by English or French frigates on the high seas.[16]

Jefferson's answer to these multiple challenges was the Embargo Act of 1807, which essentially closed American ports to all foreign trade. The idea for the embargo originated with Madison, who had convinced himself that closing down American exports and domestic markets would eventually force England and France to alter their policies. This was always an illusion, but it blended nicely with Jefferson's more moralistic vision, which was simply to sever all connections with the corrupt, belligerent nations of Europe. The result was an unadulterated calamity that virtually wrecked the American economy, had no discernible effect on either the policies or economies of England or France and required the federal government to exercise coercive powers to enforce the embargo, thereby contradicting the Jeffersonian principle of limited government. To make matters worse, just as the international crisis was intensifying, Jefferson had to deal with a domestic crisis with equivalently catastrophic potential when Aaron Burr, his former vice president, was caught conspiring to launch a fabulously ambitious scheme—even today Burr's bizarre goals are murky—to detach a substantial chunk of the American Southwest and set up an independent nation-state with himself as the benevolent despot. Burr's capture and eventual trial produced only more trouble for Jefferson, who was so eager to see Burr convicted of treason that he was willing to violate basic constitutional principles to get his way, but once again found that way blocked by that high priest of Federalist defiance, the irrepressible John Marshall, who found Burr not guilty.[17]

All in all, then, Jefferson's second term had proved just as disastrous as his first term had been glorious. He announced his decision to observe Washington's precedent and retire after two terms in December 1807, just as the Embargo Act was approved by the Congress. From that time forward, for more than a year, he surrendered all essential decisions to Madison and Gallatin, thereby creating a sense of drift in American policy at the very moment that the unpopular and cumbersome embargo required executive leadership. There was loose talk, even in Republican circles, of Pontius Pilate washing his hands of unpleasant responsibilities. Among the Federalists there were gleefully mischievous comparisons to his infamous flight from British soldiers during his final days as governor in revolutionary Virginia. He was clearly played out as president. "Never did a prisoner, released from his chains," he observed the day before Madison's inauguration, "feel such relief as I shall on shaking off the shackles of power."[18]

It was a rather awkward and somewhat hollow end to more than forty years of almost uninterrupted public service. As he himself had predicted in his First Inaugural Address, no man was likely to leave the office of president with the same high reputation that he had when he entered it. With all the advantages of hindsight it is now easy to see that the failures of his second term had root causes in the Napoleonic Wars that were beyond his or, for that matter, anyone's control. His earlier presidential luck had simply run out. Nevertheless, the somber character of the end cast a pall over his entire presidency; it helps explain why he did not choose to list this phase of his public career on his tombstone. Up in Quincy, Adams, writing to Benjamin Rush the day after Jefferson's term ended, claimed to know all about disappointing conclusions. But at least his own end as president, Adams noted, had the clear and crisp character of an electoral defeat. Anyone attempting to deliver a benediction on Jefferson's presidency would be hard pressed to know what to say. "Jefferson expired and Madison came to life last night at twelve o'clock," Adams joked to Rush. "Will you be so good to take a Nap and dream for my instruction and Edification a character of Jefferson and his administration?" The safe thing to say of course was that "only posterity could judge."[19]

Both Adams and Jefferson had their sights set on posterity's judgment, so perhaps the first thing to keep in mind when we consider the eloquent correspondence of their twilight years is that they were self-consciously writing to us as well as to each other. Adams had been under persistent prodding from Rush to break the silence between Quincy and Monticello for several years, Rush claiming that he kept having dreams of the two patriarchs recovering the affinity of their early years, when they constituted, in Rush's memorable phrase, "the North and South Poles of the American Revolution." Initially Adams told Rush that such dreams struck him as nightmares; Jefferson was a mysterious "shadow man" whose character was "like the great rivers, whose bottoms we cannot see and make no noise."[20]

But gradually the ice melted at Quincy. He harbored "no Resentment or Animosity against the Gentleman" and would certainly respond "if I should receive a letter from him . . . ," meaning that Jefferson would have to write first. Then Adams became downright playful about the matter, declaring that he would rename his Quincy estate "Montezillo," a miniature version of Jefferson's grand home, wondering out loud to Rush what had caused the separation with Jefferson in the first place and concluding "that the only Flit between Jefferson and me concerned hairstyles." He preferred it straight and Jefferson preferred it curled. Or was it the other way around? Adams was clearly edging his way toward a rapprochement.[21]

Eventually, on January 1, 1812, he made the decisive move with a short and cordial note, protesting all the while that there was nothing momentous or historic about the reconciliation. "Jefferson was always a Boy to me," he joked; "I am bold to say that I was his Preceptor on Politicks and taught him every thing that has been good and solid in his whole Political Conduct." How could one hold a grudge against one's own disciple? The differences between them, Adams implied, were the product of exaggerated distortions put out by their mutual enemies, especially Hamilton. The friendship could be recovered easily because it had never really been lost. "It was only as if one sailor had met a brother sailor, after twenty-five years' absence," Adams quipped, "and had accosted him, how fare you, Jack?" All these playful half-truths and benign rationalizations helped Adams avoid facing the fact that he was extending his hand over what had become a huge personal and political chasm.[22]

Over the course of the next fourteen years they exchanged 158 letters and created what many historians have come to regard as the greatest correspondence between prominent statesmen in all of American history. What comes through to most modern readers of the letters is the elegiac tone and the seductive serenity of two American versions of the philosopher-king, meditating out loud to each other about all the timeless topics, sometimes dueling for the prize in eloquence like two precocious schoolboys. "My temperament is sanguine," Jefferson writes in 1816. "I steer my bark with Hope in the head, leaving Fear astern." Adams responds in kind: "I admire your Navigation and should like to sail with you, either in your Bark or in my own, along side of yours; Hope with her gay Ensigns displayed at the Prow; fear with her Hobgoblins behind the Stern." Then there is their mutual posturing in the Ciceronian mode. "But whither is senile garrulity leading me?" Jefferson asks rhetorically: "Into politics, of which I have taken final leave. . . . I have given up newspapers in exchange for Tacitus and Thucydides, for Newton and Euclid; and I find myself much happier." Adams answers with a display of his own literary firepower: "I have read Thucydides and Tacitus, so often, and at such distant periods of my Life, that elegant, profound and enchanting is their Style, I am weary of them"; he jokes that "My Senectutal Loquacity has more than retaliated your 'Senile Garrulity' " and then finishes with a flourish that is almost Jeffersonian in its alliterative style: "Whatever a peevish Patriarch might say, I have never seen the day in which I could say I had no Pleasure; or that I have had more Pain than Pleasure."[23]

They wrote each other with similar gusto and self-conscious flair about a host of safe subjects: the aging process; the beauties and the corruptions of Christianity; the bizarre and sometimes loony characters who inflicted themselves on busy presidents (Adams claiming that whenever self-styled prophets requested an interview during his presidency, he required that they perform miracles beforehand, thereby avoiding all such wasteful encounters); the books worth rereading; the impressive development of an indigenous American language. Jefferson was particularly outspoken about the need to allow new words like "belittle" and "neologism" into usage. "Dictionaries are but the depositories of words already legitimated by usage," he observed, and everyday conversation "is the workshop in which new ones are elaborated." Adams agreed wholeheartedly, arguing that they should join forces again to oppose British tyranny, this time repudiating England's despotic control over words. "We are no more bound by Johnson's Dictionary," Adams observed, "than by the . . . Cannon Law of England."

Adams acknowledged that words were Jefferson's special province. (It was one of the reasons, he liked to tell friends, that he had asked the young Jefferson to draft the Declaration of Independence.) "We shall all be asterisked very soon," Adams noted in 1821, adding, "Sic transit Gloriola (is there such a Latin Word?) mundi." Jefferson concurred about the dwindling size of the survivors from 1776, then confirmed that Cicero himself had used the word "Gloriola," which meant "little bit of glory," an appropriately modest description of what he and Adams and their revolutionary compatriots were due. Adams countered with the prediction that Jefferson, "as you are the youngest and the most energetic in mind and body," would be the final survivor. Like the last person in the household to retire at night, it was therefore Jefferson's responsibility to close up the fireplace "and rake the ashes over the coals. . . ."[24]

The emotional climax of the correspondence as a classical dialogue between reunited patriarchs came in 1823. During the early years of his retirement Adams had written several letters in which he had condemned Jefferson for his duplicity and criticized his policies as president. When several of these letters were published in the newspapers in 1823 without his permission, Adams was embarrassed and worried that they would undermine the newly recovered friendship. But Jefferson rose to the occasion with great style: "Be assured, my dear Sir," he wrote, "that I am incapable of receiving the slightest impression from the effort now made to plant thorns on the pillow of age, worth, and wisdom, and to sow tares between friends who have been such for nearly half a century. Beseeching you then not to suffer your mind to be disquieted by this wicked attempt to poison its peace, and praying you to throw it by. . . ." Adams was overjoyed, insisting that Jefferson's letter be read aloud to his family at the breakfast table. It was "the best letter that ever was written . . . , just such a letter as I expected, only it was infinitely better expressed." He closed with another typically Adams salvo against "the peevish and fretful effusions of politicians . . . [who] are not worth remembering, much less of laying to heart. . . . I salute your fire-side with cordial esteem and affection," then signed off as "J. A. In the 89 year of his age still too fat to last much longer.[25]

And so, even though both men were posturing for posterity, there is considerable truth in the classical portrait of Adams and Jefferson as reunited sages, speaking to each other and then across the ages to us, in their unique role as American originals. (At least one would be hard pressed, and at the same point reduced to sardonic laughter, to find an equivalent level of literacy and intellectual sophistication among all the retired presidents of American history.) Another picture, however, contains additional pieces of the truth that are especially important for an understanding of Jefferson's mentality in his final years. In this picture Jefferson is standing tall and straight with arms folded across his chest, as was his custom, and Adams is briskly pacing back and forth in front of him, talking in his mile-a-minute style, periodically stopping to grab Jefferson by the lapels to make his controversial and animated points. There really was a good deal of unfinished business between the two patriarchs, especially if Adams was determined to take seriously, as he obviously was, his conviction that they ought not to die before explaining themselves to each other. Adams was perhaps the one man in the world capable of challenging, often in a defiantly aggressive fashion, Jefferson's most cherished convictions about what the American Revolution had truly meant.

Jefferson liked to distinguish between his genuine affection for Adams as a wise and courageous man of unimpeachable character, one of the original "band of brothers" who made the American Revolution happen, and his disagreement with the Adams brand of political thinking. As he put it to Rush, he had always defended Adams's character "with the single exception as to political opinions." But given Adams's seamless integration of politics and personality, this was a bit like saying that one always listened loyally to the pope except when he spoke on matters of faith and morals. In addition, Adams enjoyed a certain psychological superiority over Jefferson on the bases of age and of having preceded Jefferson in each of their mutual missions: in the Continental Congress in the 1770s, Europe in the 1780s, vice president in the 1790s, and then the presidency. Although Adams was joking when he described Jefferson as his youthful disciple, there was at least a kernel of truth to the joke. For all these reasons, Jefferson tended to defer to Adams in much the same manner that his own protégés—Madison, Monroe, Gallatin—deferred to him. Moreover, while the other Federalist leaders, chiefly Hamilton and Marshall, were unadulterated enemies who stood clearly on the far side of the moral line in Jefferson's mind that separated the forces of light and the forces of darkness, Adams seemed to straddle that line, in fact to deny that such a line even existed. He simply did not fit neatly into any of the Jeffersonian categories. To top it all off, Adams had a maddeningly effusive style of writing that accurately mirrored his famously unbuckled brand of conversation, in which one idea ricocheted off another at such unpredictable angles and high velocities that the notion of a prudent and diplomatic exchange that avoided the unsafe subjects was inherently impossible.[26]

Perhaps the most graphic point of contention, which also exposed how much both men had invested in shaping the story of the Revolution to enhance their own respective reputations, involved their memories of the Declaration of Independence. When the document was first published and sent out to the world in 1776, only the delegates to the Continental Congress had known that Jefferson was the principal author. Not until the middle of the 1780s, when Jefferson was in Paris, was there any public recognition of a linkage between the words of the Declaration and any one person. Over the ensuing years, however, as the Fourth of July became the established occasion to celebrate the nation's birthday, Jefferson's association with the language of the Declaration became firmly established, and his reputation ascended alongside the hallowed text. Madison's last official act as president, in the spring of 1817, was to select four paintings by John Trumbull for the Capitol Rotunda, which was being restored after being burned by jthe British during the War of 1812. The first selection was Trumbull's depiction of Jefferson handing over his draft of the Declaration to the president of the Continental Congress, with Adams and the other members of the drafting committee in the background.[27]

One can sense the throbbing Adams ego just beneath the surface of all his complaints about the symbolism of this scene. In 1819, for example, a document surfaced in Mecklenburg County, North Carolina, purporting to date from March 1775, more than a year before the Declaration was written, and containing language that was eerily similar to the sacred text itself. The implication was clear: If authentic, the Mecklenburg Resolves cast a shadow over Jefferson's claim to originality. Adams rather mischievously asked Jefferson whether he knew anything about this surprising discovery. Jefferson responded immediately, suggesting that the Mecklenburg Resolves were almost certainly a forgery, and in any event he had never seen them before. Although Adams wrote back to Jefferson to say he took him at his word, he told other friends just the opposite. "I could as soon believe that the dozen flowers of the Hydrangia now before my Eyes were the work of chance," he gossiped, "as that the Mecklenburg Resolutions and Mr. Jefferson's declaration were not derived the one from the other."[28]

In general, however, Adams tended not to question the authenticity of Jefferson's authorship so much as the significance of the drafting process or even the Declaration itself. In the Adams version of the story, first presented in his autobiography and then subsequently conveyed in letters to anyone who asked, the drafting committee had appointed him chair of the two-person subcommittee composed of Jefferson and himself. Then he had delegated the actual drafting chore to Jefferson. When this version got back to Jefferson, he immediately recognized that Adams was attempting to steal a share of the credit and agency for the magic words (pushing himself forward in the Trumbull portrait, if you will), and he quickly issued a polite but firm rejoinder: "Mr. Adams' memory has led him into unquestionable error. At the age of 88, and 47 years after the transactions of Independence, this is not wonderful. Nor should I, at the age of 80, on the small advantage of that difference only, venture to oppose my memory to his, were it not supported by written notes, taken by myself at the moment and on the spot." Jefferson's notes, which he transcribed into his own autobiography, showed that he and Adams had indeed consulted before the drafting process began, but that the consultation had then been "misremembered into the actings of a sub-committee." There was no partnership, even of an administrative sort, at the moment of creation. Jefferson went out of his way to disavow any pretense of philosophical originality in the Declaration. As Madison so succinctly put it, Jefferson's goal "was to assert not to discover truths, and to make them the basis of the Revolutionary Act." But in so doing, Jefferson insisted, he acted alone.[29]

Historical jockeying of this sort might seem petty in retrospect, but it graphically illustrated how both men fully recognized the symbolic significance the Declaration had achieved, even in their lifetimes, and therefore how much their places in the American pantheon depended upon their association with its creation. That very fact rankled Adams more than anything else. "Was there ever a Coup de Theatre, that had so great an effect as Jefferson's Penmanship of the Declaration of Independence?" he asked Rush. He was candid enough to tell Jefferson that the significance of the Declaration was vastly overrated; it was "like children's play at marbles or push pin. . . . Dress and ornament rather than Body, Soul and substance." No one at the Continental Congress, he claimed, regarded the language of the Declaration as anything more than eloquent propaganda. It was merely "a theatrical side show" that subsequent generations had made into the main event. As a result, "Jefferson ran away with the stage effect . . . and all the glory of it."[30]

What, then, was the true story of the American Revolution? Both men agreed that it would probably go to the grave with them and never find its way into the history books. Adams liked to note the proliferation of falsified accounts already contaminating the record and the self-serving memoirs that, as he and Jefferson could testify, were fictitious versions of what was really said in the corridors and at private meetings where the real decisions were made. Jefferson concurred that only the "external facts" would ever get into the written histories and that "the life and soul of history must forever be unknown." In the Adams version of the true story, however, the culminating moment was not July 4, 1776, and the decisive document was not the Declaration of Independence. The war itself was already raging by that time. Most of the delegates to the Continental Congress regarded the Declaration as a ceremonial confirmation of what had already occurred; its chief practical value, apart from publicizing a foregone conclusion in lyrical terms, was to enhance the prospects of a wartime alliance with France, and all the revolutionary leaders understood the French alliance to be the urgent issue at the time. Jefferson's Declaration was like the thunder in an electrical storm; it made much noise, but the lightning had flashed earlier and already done the real work.[31]

For Adams the culminating moment had occurred on May 15, 1776, when the Continental Congress passed a resolution—not so coincidentally, he had proposed it—calling for new constitutions in each of the states. This was the decisive act, as Adams saw it, for three reasons: First, it was the decision that required the creation of separate and independent American governments; second, the resolution stipulated that each state call a convention to draft its constitution, thereby endorsing the doctrine of popular sovereignty, the hallowed idea that "the People were the Source of all Authority and [the] Original of all Power"; third, and most tellingly for the Adams version, it meant that the American Revolution was a responsible and positive commitment to new forms of political discipline, not just an irresponsible and negative assertion of separation from England based on a seductive promise of unlimited liberation. According to Adams, Jefferson was one of the few, perhaps the only participant in the debates, to take the language of the natural rights section of the Declaration seriously as a clean and thoroughgoing break with the accumulated political wisdom of the past. On the other hand, according to Jefferson, if Adams was right, the American Revolution was not really a revolution at all.[32]

This seminal disagreement exposed the underlying tension throughout the Adams-Jefferson correspondence. It never came completely to the surface for a full and free exchange of views because neither man wished to place their latter-day reconciliation at risk. The diplomatic imperatives of the dialogue in effect made it impossible for the American patriarchs to fulfill the Adams promise and explain themselves to each other before they died. Indeed, if Jefferson had had his way, the sensitive subjects would have been avoided altogether, in part because he despised conflict just as much as Adams relished it and in part because his affection for Adams was more important to him than any clarification of their political differences. As a result, their correspondence is like those high-level diplomatic statements that policy specialists study for pregnant silences and shaded meanings. The central dynamic of the dialogue tended to follow an episodic pattern: Jefferson would inadvertently raise one of the volatile issues and touch off a round of Adams's verbal airbursts, which momentarily illuminated their ideological differences; then the exchange would settle back to its idyllic mode.

One such episode in fact was occasioned by the very term "ideology." This was one of those new words that both men believed should be allowed to fight their way into the lexicon. Jefferson first used it in 1816, in reference to the writings of Destutt de Tracy, a French philosophe who had popularized the term in France. "What does it mean?" asked Adams. "I was delighted with it, upon the Common Principle of delight in every Thing We cannot understand. Does it mean Idiotism? The Science of Non compos Menticism? The Science of Lunacy?" The Adams list of preposterous and humorous definitions went on for several lines, along with the mock suggestion that since this was obviously one of those French words that Jefferson now wished to smuggle into the American language, it should be obliged to pay an import duty. But beneath the comic veneer Adams wanted to smuggle into his own dialogue with Jefferson a deadly serious point— namely, that Jefferson's style of political thinking was "much indebted to the invention of the word IDEOLOGY" because Jefferson harbored a set of attractive ideals, like the belief in human perfection or social equality, that he mistakenly believed could be implemented in this world merely because they existed in his head. This was the French way of thinking about politics, an a priori and implicitly utopian habit of mind that, as Adams recalled it, he and Jefferson had encountered in prerevolutionary Paris in the conversations of Lafayette, Turgot and Condorcet. It was an intellectual tradition that Adams described as "the school of folly" for its systematic confusion of what one could imagine with what was practical and possible. He was essentially accusing Jefferson of embracing attractive dreams, then condemning all critics of his naiveté as enemies of the goals themselves when in fact they were only criticizing their illusory character. It was the classic criticism of an idealist by a realist.[33]

Another illuminating airburst occurred in 1816, when Jefferson, while attempting to make the apparently harmless point that one ought not to wallow in grief, asked the rhetorical question "What is the use of grief on the [human] economy, and of what good is it the cause . . . ?" Adams proceeded to explode in a series of tirades on "the uses of grief," a subject on which he claimed to be one of America's leading experts. Grief, as he saw it, was a crucial human emotion that "sharpens the Understanding and Softens the heart." Grief was to human achievement as the thorn was to the roses. Had Jefferson never noticed that the portraits or statues of all the great men of history showed their faces filled with furrows of grief? Jefferson tried to send up the white flag: "To the question indeed on the Utility of Grief, no answer remains to be given. You have exhausted the subject." But Adams was just getting started. Besides the various "uses of grief" there were many more "abuses of grief," including—Jefferson could certainly appreciate this one—the misuse of Washington's reputation by Hamilton to gain support for his banking schemes. Grief, it turned out, was a many-sided and many-splendored emotion.[34]

Jefferson tried to counter the Adams onslaught with the clever argument that, since there seemed to be an equal number of uses and abuses of grief, then perhaps they canceled each other out and therefore rendered the entire subject superfluous. Adams could not have disagreed more. The study of human emotions was the statesman's highest duty, Adams claimed: "Our Passions . . . possess so much metaphysical Subtilty and so much overpowering Eloquence, that they insinuate themselves into the Understanding and the Conscience and convert both to their Party. . . ." Jefferson's unshakable faith in the eventual triumph of human reason over prejudice and superstition was, Adams conceded, an admirable hope. But as far as he was concerned, and as the whole sweep of history showed, "it would seem that human Reason and human Conscience, though I believe there are such things, are not a Match, for human Passions, human Imaginations and human Enthusiasm." It was the classic debate between a rationalist and an empiricist.[35]

Finally there was the most sustained and direct exchange over political principles in the entire correspondence. Jefferson accidentally started it with a familiar and, he must have thought, wholly unexceptional statement of the Jeffersonian vision of political parties:

The same political parties which now agitate the U.S. have existed thro' all time. Whether the power of the people, or that of the *aristoi* should prevail, were questions which kept the states of Greece and Rome in eternal convulsions; as they now schismatize every people whose minds and mouths are not shut up by

the gag of a despot. . . . To me it appears that there have been . . .
party differences from the first establishment of governments, to
the present day . . . every one takes his side in favor of the many,
or the few.[36]

As he quickly realized, Jefferson had wandered into the most dangerous political territory of all. For the Jeffersonian formulation rendered
all political history into a moral clash between benevolent popular
majorities and despotic elites, which in turn cast Adams and the Federalists in the unsavory role of the corrupt guardians of the privileged
few, systematically defying the will of the American majority. Obviously this was not a rhetorical posture that Adams would find comfortable or acceptable.

Even the ever-combative Sage of Quincy sensed this was heavily
mined ground that demanded caution. His first instinct was to search
for a safe haven. "Precisely," he wrote back to Jefferson; the distinction between the few and the many was "as old as Aristotle," one reason why he had claimed that politics, unlike the other sciences, was
"little better understood; little better practiced now than 3 or 4 thousand Years ago." And if Jefferson meant that the American Revolution
had committed the new nation to the Lockean principle of popular
sovereignty—that is, the doctrine that all political power derived from
the people—then they were in perfect agreement. But, and here
Adams began to touch the explosive charges buried beneath their
friendship, the simple dichotomy between benign majorities and
malevolent elites worked better as rhetoric than as a description of
political reality. Danger could come from several directions, from the
many as well as the few. "The fundamental Article of my political
Creed," Adams announced defiantly, "is, that Despotism, or unlimited Sovereignty, or absolute Power is the same in a Majority of a popular Assembly, an Aristocratical Counsel, an oligarchical Junto and a
single Emperor."[37]

The full implications of this exchange were too threatening to the
friendship for either man to pursue them to their logical conclusion in

the correspondence. Adams moved the dialogue to a collateral issue, the character of aristocracies, which he recalled that Jefferson had urged him to write about when they were together in Paris, claiming that he had been "writing on the Subject ever since," the only problem being that "I have been so unfortunate as never to make myself understood." The core of the Adams position was that elites had always been and always would be a permanent fixture in society. Why? Because "Inequalities of Mind and Body are so established by God Almighty in his constitution of Human Nature that no Art or policy can ever plain them down to a level." Adams went on a long and colorful tirade against the illusion of social equality, concluding that he had "never read Reasoning more absurd, Sophisty more gross, in proof of the Athanasian Creed, or Transubstantiation, than the subtle labors . . . to demonstrate the Natural Equality of Mankind." Now it was Adams who was trespassing on Jefferson's most cherished ground, essentially calling the Jeffersonian ideal of human equality a seductive delusion that mischievously confused a fond hope (i.e., "ideology") with the messier and less attractive social realities. In effect, he was accusing Jefferson of telling Americans what they wanted to hear, leaving Adams with the more difficult task of telling them what they needed to know.[38]

Jefferson recognized that the correspondence had drifted into one of those volatile subjects on which he and Adams could never agree. "We are both too old to change opinions," he acknowledged, "which are the result of a long life of inquiry and reflection." Nevertheless, he attempted to rescue the exchange from an embarrassing impasse by making what he hoped would be two face-saving distinctions. First, he suggested that Adams's view of aristocratic power was appropriate for Europe, where feudal privileges, family titles and more limited economic opportunities created conditions that sustained class distinctions. In America, on the other hand, the elimination of primogeniture and entail and the existence of an unspoiled continent meant that "everyone may have land to labor for himself as he chuses," so enduring elites were highly unlikely here. Second, Jefferson distinguished between the natural aristocracy, based on virtue and talent, and the pseudoaristocracy, "founded on wealth and birth, without either virtue or talents." Adams's strictures against aristocracy, he suggested, were really warnings against the pseudoaristocracy, which Jefferson agreed was "a mischievous ingredient in government, and provision should be made to prevent its ascendancy." Given the favorable laws and the abundant land of America, it was reasonable to expect that "rank, and birth, and tinsel-aristocracy will finally shrink into insignificance. . . ."[39]

Adams would have none of it. "Your distinction between natural and artificial aristocracy," he insisted, "does not appear to me well founded." One might be able to separate wealth and talent in theory or imagine idealistic worlds where they were not mutually dependent ("ideology" again), but in the real world they were inextricably connected in ways that defied Jefferson's theoretical dissections. Adams was also critical of Jefferson's vision of a classless American society. "No Romance could be more amusing," he chided, since the wide-open American environment would only ensure more massive inequalities and more unequal accumulations of property unless government stepped in to redistribute the wealth. Unless one believed that human nature had somehow changed in the migration from Europe to America, the disproportionate power of "the few" would bedevil political life in the American nation too. The Jeffersonian ideal of social equality, in short, was an illusion, and by maintaining the pretense that it was a reality, one only enhanced the likelihood of making matters worse. Here was another classic confrontation, indeed the most explicit political argument in the correspondence, though it defies a simple label. (Liberal versus conservative will not quite do.) Perhaps one can call it the clash between a romantic optimist and an enlightened pessimist.[40]

When Rush had referred to Adams and Jefferson as "the North and South Poles of the American Revolution," he was probably intending to make a purely geographic point. But the dialogue between the New

Englander and the Virginian revealed that Rush's metaphor had much more sweeping implications. Beneath the idyllic and somewhat contrived veneer as American sages, the two aging revolutionaries created a dialogue between two distinctive and different understandings of just what the American Revolution meant as a political movement. For most of his adult life Jefferson had regarded "the spirit of '76" and the doctrines of "pure republicanism" as unequivocally clear expressions of a clean break with the past and with all traditional forms of political organization that imposed unnecessary limitations on personal freedom. He had therefore concluded that the Federalists were traitors, who had betrayed these allegedly self-evident principles in favor of a coercive federal government that restored the very institutional mechanisms the Revolution was intended to remove. Now, here was Adams, whose credentials as a maker and shaper of the American Revolution could not be denied, insisting that this version of the story was not what he remembered, indeed suggesting that Jefferson's understanding was highly idiosyncratic in its emphasis on a radical break with the past and its antigovernment ethos.

At the symbolic and psychological level Jefferson's fourteen-year dialogue with Adams is important because Jefferson found it impossible to dismiss his irascible old colleague. Despite his aversion to conflict, he allowed Adams to draw him into an extended argument that created a literary monument to their beloved Revolution as a complex event with multiple meanings. They were the proverbial opposites that attracted. Or if the American Revolution had become a national hymn, they were its words and its music. The ironies abound, since the self-made son of a New England farmer and shoemaker was insisting that neither individual freedom nor social equality was ever a goal of the revolutionary generation, while the Virginia aristocrat with an inherited plantation of lands and slaves was insisting that both were. At the same time that Jefferson was beginning to develop his idea of the University of Virginia as a capstone to his career and a monument to his legacy, he was inadvertently, and at times against his own instincts, creating with Adams what turned out to be the ultimate literary monument to the American Revolution as an ongoing argument between idealistic and realistic impulses.

In his last letter to Adams, written just before he slid into his final illness, Jefferson asked if his grandson and namesake, Thomas Jefferson Randolph (or "Jeffy"), might pay a visit to the Sage of Quincy during his visit to Boston. "Like other young people," Jefferson explained, "he wishes to be able, in the winter nights of old age, to recount to those around him what he has heard and learnt of the Heroic age . . . and which of the Argonauts particularly he was in time to have seen." Like mythical gods frozen into classical postures, Jefferson and Adams had become living statues to the rising generation. What their correspondence preserved for posterity was the dynamic and contentious character of the Revolution they had mutually fought and wrought.[41]

RETROSPECTIVES

IF THEIR CORRESPONDENCE was a bit like a posed picture, periodically rescued from a still-life version of the American Revolution by Adams's inability to sit still or hold his tongue, it is worth noting that both men had been posing for many years. Like all the leading members of the revolutionary generation, Adams and Jefferson had early on developed a keen sense of themselves as Founding Fathers with a prominent place in the history books. (Adams, after all, had begun to make copies of all his letters in 1776, and Jefferson had been preserving most of his correspondence since 1782.) Alfred North Whitehead once observed that there were only two instances in recorded history when the political leadership of an emerging empire performed as well as one could realistically expect: The first was Rome under Caesar Augustus, and the second was the United States in the revolutionary era. While historians have offered several explanations for this remarkable explosion of leadership at the very start of the American republic—and it truly was remarkable—the self-conscious sense that the future was watching elevated the standards and expectations for all concerned. At least in a small way, we are complicitous in their achievement because we were the ultimate audience for their performances.[42]

While Jefferson had never been oblivious to the matter of posterity's judgment, in about 1816 his interest in what history would say about him intensified. The obvious reason for this discernible shift was age. Whatever revisions or additions he might wish to make for the historical record could not wait much longer because his time was running out. The correspondence with Adams, by forcing him into a dialogue with a lovable antagonist, probably also prompted his retrospective tendencies. In 1816, moreover, he was drawn into the debate about William Wirt's highly successful biography of Patrick Henry. Wirt had consulted Jefferson about the sources of Henry's histrionic style. "You have given them quite as much lustre as themselves would have asked," Jefferson apprised Wirt, thereby expressing in diplomatic fashion his long-standing opinion that Henry was vastly overrated. Jefferson suggested only one revision, a passage in which Wirt described Henry actually reading a book. "The study and learning ascribed to him, in this passage," Jefferson so delicately observed, would be inconsistent with "the excellent and just picture of his indolence through the rest of the work." In partial compensation for the obvious fact that he despised Henry, Jefferson allowed himself to be quoted in the published book to the effect that Henry deserved credit for fomenting opposition to British policies in the 1760s, saying that "Mr. Henry certainly gave the first impulse to the ball of revolution."[43]

This apparently harmless remark produced a loud howl from several New Englanders, including the ever-ready Adams, who interpreted the celebration of Henry's early efforts in behalf of American independence as a sly plot to make Virginia rather than Massachusetts the real cockpit of the Revolution. Jefferson expressed his surprise at the vehemence of the New England retaliation. He was the last man to champion Henry as a significant figure, and the whole argument about who was first was silly, like asking "who discovered gravity." But the debate dragged on—Adams was inspired to put forward James Otis of Massachusetts as Henry's predecessor in the contest for primacy as "the first American revolutionary"—until Jefferson issued a concession. He had "never meant to intercept the just fame of Massachusetts, for the promptitude and persevereance of her early resistance." He was even willing to cede her the title as "the cradle of independence," though he felt obliged to add that with regard to principles of the Revolution, "some of us believe that she had deflected from them in her course," even as "we retain full confidence in her ultimate return to them."[44]

Jefferson preferred to avoid such trivial arguments about specific events or personalities, except when the contested topic was the Declaration of Independence; there he was ready to defend his own version against all encroachments, sensing that it was the historical equivalent of the motherlode. His major concern was the larger outline of the story that would get passed down to posterity about the meaning of the American Revolution. Madison's retirement from the presidency in 1817 raised expectations that his old partner in the political wars would devote his energies to writing a Jeffersonian version of American history. He urged Madison to "apply your retirement to the best use possible, to a work which we have both wished to see well done. . . ." He promised to place all his personal letters and notes "entirely at your command." As in the party battles of the 1790s, Jefferson wanted Madison to take the point; it was essential to his own stature, as well as a temperamental imperative, that Jefferson himself remain behind the scenes and above the fray. But this time Madison pleaded declining health and sheer fatigue and turned down the invitation.[45]

As Jefferson saw it, this left the field almost entirely in the hands of the enemy. Hamilton's son, it was well known, was already writing a biography of his father, which would, Jefferson warned, surely promote "the rancor of the fiercest federalism." Then there was that treasure trove of un-Jeffersonian wisdom stockpiled at Quincy. "Mr. Adams' papers," Jefferson noted ominously, "and his biography, will descend of course to his son [John Quincy Adams], whose pen . . . is pointed, and his prejudices not in our favor." All the old moral dichotomies took command of Jefferson's imagination again: the Whigs versus the Tories; the Republicans versus the Federalists; "pure republicanism" versus corrupted impostors. Having won all the major battles during their lifetimes, Jefferson feared that he and his political disciples were about to lose the decisive war for posterity after they were dead.[46]

In fact the chief traitor had already struck and littered the historical record with lies that, again as Jefferson saw it, falsified the true story of the American Revolution beyond recognition. The culprit was none other than Jefferson's chief tormentor, the ever-resourceful John Marshall, who had somehow found time while serving as chief justice to publish between 1804 and 1807 a five-volume biography of George Washington. Adams, who might have been expected to find Marshall's Federalist interpretation to his liking, instead described the mammoth work as "a Mausoleum, 100 feet square at the base and 200 feet high," and predicted that it would prove "as durable as the Washington benevolent Societies"; in other words, it would sink from its own weight and ponderous prose. But Jefferson was just as certain that Marshall's biography, which was based on Washington's actual correspondence and benefited from Marshall's reputation for thoroughness and probity, would establish itself as the closest thing to an official history of the era. Marshall's narrative followed a story line that Jefferson considered an artful lie. The most offensive fifth volume offered this summary statement:

> [T]he continent was divided into two great political parties, the one of which contemplated America as a nation, and laboured incessantly to invest the federal head with powers competent to its preservation of the union. The other attached itself to the state authorities, viewed all the powers of congress with jealousy, and assented reluctantly to measures which would enable the head to act, in any respect, independently of the members. Men of enlarged and liberal minds . . . arranged themselves generally in the first party.

Marshall was arguing a constitutional interpretation that depicted the
political coalitions of the 1790s as products of the conflicting perceptions of the constitutional settlement of 1787–88. For Jefferson, on the
other hand, the core differences were more ideological than constitutional, the seminal decades were the 1770s, when the true faith was
declared, and the 1790s, when it was betrayed. As he put it, the real difference was not federal versus state authority, but "different degrees of
inclination to monarchy or republicanism."[47]

Given Madison's understandable reluctance to devote his retirement years to the task of countering Marshall's history, Jefferson was
thrown back upon his own devices. In 1818 he decided to edit and have
bound together for posthumous publication three volumes of private
letters, notes and memoranda from his years as secretary of state,
thereby creating an archival trail designed to lure subsequent historians
away from the false path blazed by Marshall. The modern editors of
Jefferson's papers suggest that we call these documents "Jeffersoniana"
instead of the term used by earlier editors, the "Anas," which is Latin
for a collection of anecdotes, table talk and gossip. Whatever we call
them, Jefferson's edited notes, made, as he recalled in 1818, on "loose
scraps of paper, taken out of my pocket in the moment and . . . therefore ragged, rubbed, and scribbled as they were," were intended to
have the look and sound of the *real* history; these were the secret stories and covert conversations that occurred in corridors and behind
closed doors, where the *real* decisions were made, the *real* arguments
were hammered out, the *real* power was exercised. Jefferson's clear purpose was to suggest that Marshall's account of the Washington administration was only the official version; it never got beneath the polite
surface to the messier truths. Jefferson was planting in the record his
own handmade explosive device, designed to go off after he was dead
and expose the Marshall history as a Federalist fable. His "Anas" or
"Jeffersoniana" might be construed, then, as our early American version of such twentieth-century revelations as *The Pentagon Papers*.[48]

Jefferson's story, which he wanted posterity to know as his final testament of the true history of revolutionary America, took the form of a

melodramatic plot populated by schemers, conspirators and corrupt connivers, all driven by a dedication to intrigue. He cast himself in the role of the American innocent, recently returned from his long absence in France, who discovers upon his arrival in New York City in 1790 that the republican principles he has been cherishing so faithfully have in fact been abandoned by a majority of the officials in the Washington administration. At almost all the dinner parties he attended soon after his arrival, the conversation turned toward the subject of monarchy, how its restoration offered the only hope for political stability and how Washington needed to be persuaded to accept the royal mantle. When Jefferson tried to make the case for a kingless version of republican government along the lines intended in 1776, he claimed he could "scarcely find . . . a single co-advocate . . . unless some old member of Congress happened to be present." The old "band of brothers" had been replaced by a gang of closet royalists. Hamilton was the archmonarchist, indeed "not only a monarchist, but for a monarchy bottomed on corruption." Even Adams, the old warhorse of '76, had been "taken up by the monarchical federalists," who played on his notorious vanity and political ambition to make him a "stalking horse" for the Hamiltonians. The evidence for all this consisted of multiple anecdotes, hearsay reports of private conversations and reliable gossip about what one cabinet member claimed to have heard Hamilton or his cronies whispering to each other over port and cigars.[49]

It was crucial for Jefferson's conspiratorial version of history to claim that Washington himself was oblivious to the plot. This was not easy to do, since Washington was the unquestioned leader of the Federalists and the alleged candidate for coronation by all the other members of the cabinet. Jefferson's solution was to suggest that Washington was unaware of much that was going on around him. His image of Washington had never been all reverence and flattery. "His mind was great and powerful," Jefferson observed, "without being of the very first order"; his conversational talents "were not above mediocrity," and in many public situations, "when called for a sudden opinion, he was unready, short, and embarrassed." He was, in effect, more a man of action than deep understanding; that made him susceptible to clever and crafty intriguers like Hamilton. Jefferson also devoted a substantial portion of his secret history to providing an account of his many private meetings with Washington, in all of which the latter showed himself to be in complete agreement with Jefferson about the need to establish "pure republicanism." Even those infamous presidential levees, where Washington supposedly held court like an American king, were misleading. Washington's private secretary had told the attorney general, who had told Madison, who then told Jefferson, that Washington despised the royal trappings of these occasions. No matter what Marshall's official and officious biography said, Washington's deepest sentiments agreed completely with Jefferson's. It was a rather extraordinary revelation and a stunning piece of revisionist history, but the elemental truth about America's most elemental hero was that he subscribed wholeheartedly to the Republican rather than Federalist persuasion.[50]

Although this attempt to capture Washington from the Federalists, indeed to make Washington a Jeffersonian, was—to put it most politely—a highly problematic version of American political history, Jefferson was absolutely correct to recognize that, in the history wars as in the political wars of the 1790s, whoever had Washington on their side possessed a decisive advantage. Unfortunately for Jefferson's purposes, the early editor of his papers never published the documents he had edited in 1818 in the format he had intended. As a political bombshell designed to detonate after he was gone, the "Anas" or "Jeffersoniana" proved to be a dud. Historians have not been sure how to categorize it, what to say about it, even what to call it. The best of the most recent scholarly appraisals sees it as a graphic example of the way "political gossip" shaped the ideological alignments in the early republic, also as another illustration of how the unprecedented and still-fragile character of political institutions in the 1790s generated a conspiratorial mentality on all sides, indeed a level of mutual suspicion and intrigue that looks utterly paranoid to us, at least until we recog-

nize how uncertain and unstable the political world of postrevolutionary America looked to them.[51]

For our purposes, however, Jefferson's retrospective on the old party
battles for the soul of the American Revolution reveals more about
how his mind worked than about the battles themselves. Even in his
old age, when one might have expected nostalgia and the misty accumulations of sentiment between then and now to have produced a certain mellowing tendency, he remained a dedicated political warrior.
Even with Adams urging him in his irresistibly unbridled way to give
up the simple moral categories of "us" versus "them," he clung to those
categories more tenaciously than ever. The primal colors of his political imagination remained black and white. The story of the American
Revolution that he saw in his head remained, as it had been in 1776, a
moralistic melodrama. Whatever final adjustments or accommodations he might be tempted to make as concessions to history's bedeviling complexity would have to occur within that nonnegotiable moral
framework.

There were, in fact, several such adjustments, all the product of the
increasingly retrospective character of his writing in the last decade. In
1821 he spent six months working on his autobiography, carrying the
story from his birth up to 1790, where the secret history he had compiled from his notes would presumably take over the narrative. (He
chose not to write anything at all about his presidency.) The autobiography was devoted to retelling two familiar stories in the way he
wanted them remembered. The first was about the drafting and subsequent debate in the Continental Congress over the Declaration of
Independence. He not only wanted to clarify for all time his authorship of the seminal document but also to reproduce his original draft,
before it was edited by the Congress. In effect, he delivered in his autobiography the defense of his original language that his congenital shyness had prevented him from delivering on the floor of the Congress at
the time. He also made a point of insisting, against the testimony and
memory of everyone else, that all the delegates actually signed the

Declaration on July 4. It was obviously important to him to certify the historical accuracy of the date subsequently celebrated as the nation's birthday.[52]

The second story was about the coming of the French Revolution. Here his chief purpose was to counter the charge, which his Federalist critics had made into a familiar refrain, that he had contributed to the radical utopianism of those French philosophes who led France into a bloodbath, or at least had drifted toward disaster with them in the dreamy days before the guillotine. His version of the crucial months emphasized the responsible character of the moderate French aristocrats led by Lafayette. The French Revolution would have been a bloodless and wholly peaceful transition, Jefferson argued, but for the cowardice and indecision of Louis Capet. And the king's failure to side with the future rather than the past was, he claimed, largely the result of his wife's influence over him. "I have ever believed," Jefferson wrote, "that had there been no queen, there would have been no revolution." The entire tragedy was due not to long-standing historical forces that proved unmanageable but to the ill-timed meddling of one woman.[53]

Beyond the boundaries of his autobiography, mostly in his extensive and increasingly burdensome correspondence, he attempted to make three significant modifications in the way he wished to be remembered. The first represented a revision of his much-quoted tribute to the agrarian life initially published in his *Notes on Virginia*. He wanted it known, and gave permission to be quoted on the matter in the newspapers, that the world had changed dramatically since he wrote *Notes*, when he had urged Americans to till the land and shun any and all forms of manufacturing. "We must now place the manufacturer by the side of the agriculturist," he acknowledged, endorsing a commitment to small-scale domestic manufacturing or home industry. Anyone who opposed this modest shift in America's economy was out of touch with reality and "must be for reducing us either to dependence on that foreign nation [England], or to be clothed in skins, and to live like wild beasts in dens and caverns."[54]

On the other hand–he did not want to be misunderstood on this point–America should remain a predominantly agricultural economy and society. Domestic manufacturing was permissible, but large factories should be resisted. Most important, the English model of a thoroughly commercial and industrial society in which the economy was dominated by merchants, bankers and industrialists should be avoided at all costs. "We may exclude them from our territory," he warned, "as we do persons afflicted with disease," going so far as to recommend that if one region of the United States should ever become thoroughly commercialized, the remaining agrarian region should secede in order to remain immune to the attendant corruptions. He conceded that his insistence on an agrarian character "may be the dreams of an old man, or that the occasions of realizing them may have passed away without return." But the goal of all statesmen dedicated to the values he cherished most should be to preserve as much of the agrarian character of America as possible. If that turned out to mean merely delaying the inevitable, so be it.[55]

A second significant clarification concerned his religious convictions. The Federalist press and New England clergy had been particularly vicious on this score during his presidency, citing his friendship with Tom Paine and his historic stand against any connection between church and state as evidence that he was probably an atheist and certainly not a Christian. In 1816 he announced the completion of what he called "a wee-book," which was really an outline for a book entitled *The Morals and Life of Jesus of Nazareth*. The culmination of a similar project begun in 1802, when the attacks on his religious beliefs had begun in earnest, Jefferson intended his sketch of Jesus as moral exemplar to be "a document in proof that *I am a real Christian,* that is to say, a disciple of the doctrines of Jesus. . . ." What he really meant was that he admired the moral values embodied in the life of Jesus but preferred to separate "what is really his from the rubbish in which it is buried" much in the way "as the diamond from the dunghill." Primitive Christianity, in his view, was similar to the original meaning of the American Revolution: a profoundly simple faith subsequently corrupted by its institutionalization. In the case of the Christian denominations, "the metaphysical abstractions of Athanasius, and the maniacal ravings of Calvin, tinctured plentifully with the foggy dreams of Plato, have so loaded it with absurdities and incomprehensibilities" that it was almost impossible to recover "its native simplicity and purity." He was particularly harsh on Yale, Harvard and Andover as "seminaries of despotism." If he had been completely scrupulous, he would have described himself as a deist who admired the ethical teachings of Jesus as a man rather than as the son of God. (In modern-day parlance, he was a secular humanist.) But by insisting on his status as a quasi-Christian, or at least placing on the record his personal acceptance of the term, he blunted one of the most pointed challenges to his prominent place in the mainstream of American history.[56]

Finally, Jefferson's twilight retrospecting allowed him to see his own political achievement from a more long-range perspective and therefore to talk about it in a new idiom. The act of preparing his secret history of the 1790s, for instance, required him to revisit and then reiterate his sense of the Revolution as a liberation movement to free America not just from English tyranny but from all forms of political oppression. This movement was halted and almost overturned by the Federalists in the 1790s, then was rescued and revived by the Republicans in 1800. In a sense, he had always carried this story line around in his head, but in old age he saw it even more clearly, clearly enough in fact to give its climax a name. In 1819, for the first time, he used the phrase "the revolution of 1800" to describe his own election, claiming that it was "as real a revolution in the principles of our government as that of 1776 was in its form." The act of providing a fresh descriptive label for his ascendance to the presidency did not really alter his long-standing belief in its significance, but it did make the event more memorable and give his version of history a more accessible handle. Subsequent generations of historians did not fail to grab it, thereby implicitly endorsing the Jeffersonian interpretation of the entire revolutionary era.[57]

Coining a new phrase is not the same thing, of course, as discovering a new idea. Starting in 1816, however, there is a clear trail of evidence in Jefferson's correspondence to indicate that he was thinking about what he called "the principles of 1776" in new ways. Again, the correspondence with Adams may have prompted this development, since Adams had remarked in a much-quoted aside that the term "republicanism" was one of those weasel words that different people understood to mean different things. Jefferson's most familiar formulation tended to follow his binary system of political thought, juxtaposing "republican" and "monarchy," but then leaving the matter at that, not specifying what "republican" meant beyond the elimination of royal prerogatives and divine right presumptions of power. Indeed one of the most alluring features of Jefferson's formulation was its eloquent silence on the whole question of what a republican government actually entailed. (Adams had written four fat volumes on this very subject, and Madison had given the matter equivalent analytical attention in *The Federalist Papers*.) Perhaps the most beguiling facet of Jefferson's habit of mind was its implicit assumption that one need not worry or even talk about such complex questions, that the destruction of monarchy and feudal trappings led naturally to a new political order. The best name for that new order had always been "republican."

By 1816 he began to find this language inadequate. "In truth, the abuses of monarchy had so filled all the space of political contemplation," he remarked, "that we imagined everything republican which was not monarchy." But subsequent events demonstrated that "we had not yet penetrated to the mother principle, that 'governments are republican only in proportion as they embody the will of the people, and execute it.' " He made the same point in a slightly different way to John Taylor, his fellow Virginian and even more fervent agrarian enthusiast: "The further the departure from direct and constant control by the citizens, the less has the government the ingredient of republicanism." In answer to the Adams claim that "republicanism may mean anything or everything," Jefferson apprised Taylor that the true doctrine was that "governments are more or less republican as they have more or less of the element of popular election and control in their composition." Whatever evils might flow from what he called "the duperies of the people" were infinitely less threatening or injurious "than those from the egoism of their agents." Without fully realizing it at the time, he and his fellow revolutionaries in 1776 had launched a political movement whose full implications were only now seeping into conscious articulation. Here, for the first time, Jefferson embraced the idea that would eventually and then everlastingly be associated with his name. What he had always called "pure republicanism" was really "democracy," and what he had actually done in "the revolution of 1800" was to restore the democratic impulse of the American Revolution after its betrayal by the Federalists.[58]

In a sense, pretty much as Jefferson claimed, the democratic implications of the American Revolution had been there all along, but once he began to feel more comfortable with the term, describing all Americans, for instance, as "constitutionally and conscientiously democrats," the very usage of the term forced a fuller explication of its portentous significance and cast a new light over his old attitudes toward government. The voluntary consent of the individual citizen, it was now clear, was the elemental principle and political power source. Jefferson's level of mistrust toward the different branches of the federal government had followed naturally from this principle: The federal courts were the furthest removed from popular consent, and he hated them the most; the Senate came next, followed closely by the president, then the House of Representatives; the state legislatures were then closer to the popular will; county representatives were closer still, and town or what he called ward officials stood face-to-face with the elemental source itself, the semisacred "will of the people."[59]

Jefferson's idealization of local government as the epitome of the democratic experience was probably connected to a statewide educational scheme he was devising for Virginia about this time (more on this shortly) that divided each county into ten to twelve wards, where he wanted state-supported primary schools established. The intimate, face-to-face character of government at the ward level helped Jefferson visualize the democratic essence. Almost every other political thinker of note in America, especially and exhaustively Adams and Madison, had begun with the presumption that the intimacy of local politics could not be replicated at the national level, which therefore required different and more complex political principles and institutional mechanisms to work effectively, indeed to work at all. But Jefferson did not think about politics in this conventional fashion. For him democracy was to politics as agrarianism was to the economy or health was to the human body. It could never be completely perfect, but the more of it, the better. His discovery of the wards as the primal democratic unit or the "pure and elementary republics" led him to what we might call a theory of democratic contagion: Combine the wards and they will congeal to form a democratic state; then, as the states interact to form a nation, they "will make of the whole a true democracy."[60]

In general, the depictions of democracy he provided in his correspondence after 1816 tended to operate at imaginary extremes. On the one hand, there was the individual voter in the town or ward, registering his personal preference. On the other, there was an impersonal and faceless aggregate called the people. When pressed to sharpen the focus on "the people," he developed an explanation based on who was *not* in the picture. Infants and children were obviously excluded, as were women, who "could not mix promiscuously in the public meetings with men." Slaves were also absent, on the principle that those "who have no will could be permitted to exercise none in the popular assembly." The picture of "the people" that he saw in his head, then, included "qualified citizens only." On the question of whether citizenship required the ownership of property he remained silent until near the very end. In 1824, however, in response to a request about the revision of the Virginia constitution, he came out in favor of the elimination of the property requirement for voting, saying it disenfranchised men who otherwise were expected to serve in the militia. His final verdict on the social composition of "the people," then, was that it included all the adult white males of the population.[61]

When not pressed, however, Jefferson preferred to keep the focus fuzzy. Specific questions about who should vote missed the larger point, which was that, thanks to the American Revolution, consent had replaced coercion as the operative principle of government, and political power, if it aspired to become legitimate authority, needed to pass muster with a majority of the citizenry. Efforts to clarify the somewhat misty and mystical notion of "the people" or "the will of the people" never made much headway with him, perhaps suggesting that he understood that if democracy were to become a political religion, it needed to preserve a sense of mystery at the core. He even opposed efforts to organize discrete interest groups to represent segments of the popular will to the federal government, what we would now call lobbyists. He regarded such associations as "dangerous machines," which should be "frowned down" as mere "clubbists of Washington" that were "unnecessary, presumptuous, and of dangerous example." The sprawling and inchoate character of popular opinion, it seems, was one of its chief blessings, not to be tampered with, orchestrated or analyzed. Even the term "democracy" itself, though he used it more frequently in those latter years, never achieved a secure and prominent place in his political vocabulary, retaining, as it did for him, some of the old eighteenth-century connotations of mob rule or anarchy, which he obviously opposed, or conveying to the younger generation, especially westerners, the rightful ascendance of ordinary citizens to public office, which he also found unacceptable. It was the vital idea beneath all the distinctions and definitions that mattered most to him, and the realization that, at least in retrospect, he had helped bring it to life.[62]

CONSOLIDATION AND DIFFUSION

ONE AREA OF latter-day revisionism merits special attention, both because of its dramatic and long-term historical implications and because of the passionate intensity Jefferson brought to its reconsideration. This of course was slavery, a subject on which Jefferson had been an outspoken opponent early in his career, but only a tentative and elusive commentator later on. He regarded it as absolutely imperative for the historical record, as well as for his own place in the American pantheon, that his moral revulsion against slavery be made clear to posterity, along with his sincere conviction that it was incompatible with the principles on which the republic was founded. He therefore saw to it that one of his most unequivocal condemnations of slavery was prominently placed in his autobiography: "Nothing is more certainly written in the book of fate than that these people are to be free. Indeed I tremble for my country when I reflect that God is just, that his justice cannot sleep forever, that considering numbers, nature and natural means only, a revolution of the wheel of fortune, an exchange of situation, is among possible events. . . . The Almighty has no attribute which can take sides with us in such a contest."[63] The ringing clarity of this pronouncement was designed to leave no doubt about his final thoughts on America's great anomaly. When Abraham Lincoln eventually made the decision to emancipate the slaves, he harked back to Jefferson as his moral beacon, even appropriating some of the language from Jefferson's autobiographical pronouncement in his own Second Inaugural Address.

Moral pronouncements aside, Jefferson had also left a long and clear record of procrastination and denial on the slavery issue. Despite prodding from several northern friends, whose consciences were admittedly not cluttered with the practical and financial impediments he faced as a slaveowner, and from a few southern friends, who wanted him to assume moral leadership for the cause of gradual abolition in Virginia, Jefferson had steadfastly refused to speak out. "I have most carefully avoided every possible act or manifestation on that subject," he wrote to a Quaker petitioner in what had become his standard response. "Should an occasion ever occur in which I can interpose with decisive effect," he explained, "I shall certainly know and do my duty." In the meantime any public statement "would only be disarming myself of influence to be taking small means." The propitious moment for decisive action, however, kept receding into the middle distance so that by 1817, upon receiving another plan for gradual emancipation from a northern admirer, he endorsed it in the most general terms ("The subordinate details might be easily arranged"), then declared his disappointment that the rising generation of American statesmen, "in which I once had sanguine hopes," had not been able to work out these details themselves. He was no longer convinced that the end of slavery was near. Certainly he would never live to see it: "I leave it, therefore, to time." Silence had become his official policy.[64]

What broke the silence and thrust his reputation squarely into the middle of the national spotlight, and in a way he would have preferred to avoid at almost any cost, was the debate over slavery in the Missouri Territory. It began in 1819 when a congressman from New York, James Tallmadge, Jr., proposed an amendment to the bill admitting Missouri into the Union that was designed to prohibit slavery in the new state. In his correspondence with Adams, Jefferson's initial reaction to what was being called the Missouri Question was calm and assured. He expressed the hope that the issue would pass "like waves in a storm pass under the ship." But as the national debate over the Missouri Question mounted, Jefferson lost his sense of confidence and his political balance. He began to describe the crisis as "the most portentous one which ever yet threatened our Union" and the greatest threat to the survival of the American republic "since the gloomiest days of the [Revolutionary] war." An old colleague from presidential days who visited Monticello in 1820 described him as obsessed with the Missouri Question, gesturing dramatically as he walked the grounds, warning of imminent civil war, which would lead to racial war and then to "a war of extermination toward the African in our land."[65]

His most graphic statement, which became an enduring part of the historical record because of its memorable metaphors, came in a letter to John Holmes, a congressman from Massachusetts. Jefferson explained that until recently he had been content to avoid newspapers and to regard himself as "a passenger in our bark to the shore from which I am not distant." But the Missouri Question had roused him "like a fire bell in the night, awakened and filled me with terror." He went on to claim that no man on earth wanted an end to slavery more than he did, that banishing slavery from all America "would not cost me a second thought, if, in that way a general emancipation and *expatriation* could be affected. . . ." But no workable plan for compensating owners and relocating the freed slaves had yet been devised. So, "as it is, we have the wolf by the ears, and we can neither hold him, nor safely let him go." It was an intolerable and insoluble dilemma: "Justice is in one scale and self-preservation in the other." He concluded the letter to Holmes with the most pessimistic and fatalistic remark about America he ever made: "I regret that I am now to die in the belief, that the useless sacrifice of themselves by the generation of 1776 . . . is to be thrown away by the unwise and unworthy passions of their sons, and that my only consolation is to be, that I live not to weep over it."[66]

What was behind, or perhaps beneath, this sudden torrent of outrage and despair? After all, the Missouri Question was hardly unprecedented; it merely raised in a new location the question of slavery in the western territories, which Jefferson had encountered in the 1780s and answered with a clear and resounding negative; it had been lurking in the political shadows ever since his single most brilliant stroke of presidential leadership, the Louisiana Purchase, had placed the entire Mississippi Valley within the national domain. What's more, the idea of prohibiting the extension of slavery into the western territories could more readily be seen as a fulfillment rather than a repudiation of the American Revolution, indeed as a fulfillment of Jefferson's own early vision of an expansive republic populated by independent farmers unburdened by the one legacy that defied the principles of 1776. Adams in fact interpreted the Missouri Question in precisely those terms, apprising several of his friends that the extension of slavery violated his sense of what the founders had intended; the present crisis, he thought, represented a welcome opportunity to take a moral stand against "an evil of Colossal magnitude" before it grew so large and intractable that it put the survival of the American republic at risk.[67]

He did not write Jefferson in this vein; it was another one of those sensitive subjects that put the fragile friendship at risk. When told that several of Jefferson's southern disciples were arguing that the core issue was constitutional—that the federal government lacked the authority to legislate in this area—Adams insisted that the core issue was obviously moral, not constitutional, and he relished the chance to remind his southern friends that Jefferson had established the constitutional precedent in 1803. "That the purchase of Louisiana was unconstitutional or extra Constitutional I never had a doubt—but I think the Southern gentlemen who thought it Constitutional then ought not to think it unconstitutional in Congress to restrain the extension of slavery in that territory now."[68]

Jefferson had in fact worried out loud about the constitutional precedent he was setting with the acquisition of Louisiana in 1803. In that sense his worries proved to be warranted. The entire congressional debate of 1819–20 over the Missouri Question turned on the question of federal versus state sovereignty, essentially a constitutional conflict in which Jefferson's long-standing opposition to federal power was clear and unequivocal, the Louisiana Purchase being the one exception that was now coming back to haunt him. But just as the constitutional character of the congressional debate served only to mask the deeper moral and ideological issues at stake, Jefferson's own sense of regret at his complicity in providing the constitutional precedent for the Tallmadge amendment merely scratched the surface of his despair. For him, as for Adams, the deeper issues were moral and historical, the original intent of the revolutionary generation they so poignantly symbolized. And for him, as for the members of Congress, the unmentionable subject was slavery. In the many letters on the Missouri Question he wrote in 1819–20, as in the congressional debate at the same time, the word "slavery" seldom appears, but like the proverbial ghost at the banquet, it dominated the underlying dialogue within the Congress and within Jefferson's own mind. It forced him to declare himself on the question of his own original and final intentions about the unmentionable subject in terms that he knew would not look attractive to posterity.

One remark prompted by the Missouri crisis that Adams *did* think he could safely send to Monticello provides a window into the deeper regions of Jefferson's despair. "Slavery in this Country I have seen hanging over it like a black cloud for half a century," Adams wrote: "I might probably say I had seen Armies of Negroes marching and counter-marching in the air, shining in Armour. I have been so terrified with this Phenomenon that I constantly said in former times to the Southern Gentlemen, I cannot comprehend this object. I must leave it to you. I will vote for forceing no measure against your judgments." Here Adams was making explicit the unspoken understanding that, so he claimed, had shaped the behavior of the revolutionary generation toward the potentially volatile politics of the slavery issue—namely, that northerners would delegate the touchy matter of its resolution to southerners, who obviously had so much more at stake. This was perhaps the most dramatic and hidden meaning of Benjamin Rush's description of Adams and Jefferson as "the North and South Poles of the American Revolution." From this perspective, what most rankled Jefferson about the debate over the Missouri Question was that it was occurring at all. For the debate represented a violation of the sectional understanding and the vow of silence that Adams, the quintessential New England patriot, had faithfully observed. In that sense the real revolutionary legacy on the slavery question was not a belief in emancipation but rather a common commitment to delay and a common trust that northerners would not interfere with southern leadership in effecting a gradual policy of emancipation. This was why Jefferson so deeply resented northern leadership on the Missouri Question, claiming that "they [the northerners] are wasting Jeremiads on the miseries of slavery, as if we were advocates for it." The sectional alliance that the Adams-Jefferson friendship so eloquently symbolized was being repudiated by the rising generation of northern politicians.[69]

Although the civility of their correspondence did not allow it, Adams might have reminded Jefferson that their unspoken understanding was contingent upon some discernible measure of progress toward ending slavery. In fact the Missouri debate did prompt several fresh initiatives in Virginia, one sponsored by Jefferson's son-in-law, Thomas Mann Randolph, Jr., for a gradual emancipation scheme, coupled with hypothetical plans to deport the freed slaves to either Africa or Santo Domingo. The Missouri crisis seemed to stimulate Jefferson himself to take a more active role in lending his support to these initiatives and to think more specifically about what he had earlier dismissed as mere details. In 1824 he compiled the fullest analysis of the demographic and economic facts he ever attempted and calculated that it would take nine hundred million dollars to free and then deport the 1.5 million slaves in the United States over a twenty-five-year period. The daunting character of the costs, he acknowledged, made it "impossible to look at this question a second time." Moreover, to make matters worse, the 1.5 million slaves would have doubled in number during the time the plans were being implemented, and many of the freed slaves, when offered passage to Africa or the West Indies, would surely say, " '[W]e will not go.' "[70]

In effect, the more one thought about the subject, the more one realized that no useful purpose could be served by thinking about it. Only a gradual policy of emancipation was feasible, but the mounting size of the slave population made any gradual policy unfeasible because the population would increase at a faster rate than it could be removed. No one, certainly not Jefferson, wanted to say it out loud or face it squarely, but whatever opportunity might have once existed to end slavery gradually and peacefully had itself ended, especially if one presumed, as Jefferson did, that the freed blacks could not be allowed to remain in the United States. If there had been an unofficial and unspoken understanding that slavery was a problem that southerners should be allowed to resolve without northern interference, by 1820 it had become abundantly clear that procrastination and avoidance, which were Jefferson's cardinal convictions on the subject, had rendered any southern-sponsored solution extremely unlikely. Jefferson's wistful remarks on the intractability of it all left open only a tiny crack of hope. "The march of events has not been able to render its completion practicable within the limits of time alloted to me," he admitted, "and I leave its accomplishment to the work of another generation."

Or, in the same vein: "On the subject of emancipation I have ceased to think because [it is] not to be the work of my day." In terms of his legacy, and within the context of the silent sectional agreement shared by the leadership of the revolutionary generation, now passing away, this constituted a confession of failure. The enlightened southern branch of the revolutionary generation, which Jefferson unequivocally headed, had not kept its promise. The Missouri crisis made that unpalatable fact more obvious than ever before and made it more diffi-cult, even for Jefferson, to avoid its unattractive implications.[71]

At yet another level the debate over Missouri transformed the huge midwestern region that Jefferson had acquired in 1803 from a source of release and relief to a source of ongoing contention. The West, as Jef-ferson had always envisioned it, was a place where festering social and political problems went to find answers. But the Missouri Question seemed to reverse the Jeffersonian process; it made the West a new the-ater of conflict, creating hostilities that then flowed back to Washing-ton and exacerbated the old political and sectional tensions. If the West had once seemed like America's fountain of youth, Missouri now poisoned it with the single most lethal subject the American republic could devise.

The position that Jefferson eventually adopted on the Missouri Question depended to a considerable extent on his refusal to abandon a quasi-mystical faith in the curative powers of the West. In effect, he argued that the vast lands of the trans-Mississippi region would dilute and then dissolve the toxic properties of the slavery issue and eventu-ally slavery itself. He called his answer "diffusion," the belief that allowing slavery to spread into the western territories would lead to its gradual extinction. As he put it, "diffusion over a greater surface would make them [slaves] individually happier, and proportionally facilitate the accomplishment of their emancipation, by dividing the burden on a greater number of coadjutors." In a letter to Henry Dearborn, his for-mer secretary of war, Jefferson hinted that he was extending the line of argument that Madison had first made in *Federalist 10*. "I still believe

that the Western extension of our confederacy will ensure its duration," he explained, "by overruling local factions, which might shake a
smaller association." He seemed to be suggesting, albeit in an imprecise way that requires inspired guesswork on our part to complete his
thoughts, that by enlarging the geographic area in which slavery
existed, one might multiply the factions for and against its continuance, thereby averting a clear sectional division between North and
South that might lead to civil war. If this was what he meant by "diffusion" and by "dividing the burden on a greater number of coadjutors,"
it was a plan designed to enlist the support of westerners and provide
the isolated slaveholders of the South with new partners in a policy of
gradual emancipation. The political dimensions of his thinking are
fuzzy. The picture he saw in his imagination is much clearer: Slavery
would migrate to the West and simply disappear in the vastness of
empty space.[72]

When Adams heard that his old friend, along with Madison and
Monroe, advocated allowing slavery to spread as a way to ameliorate
its effects and eventually kill it, he expressed astonishment, firing off
letters to his son John Quincy and daughter-in-law Louisa Catherine
Adams declaring that the Virginia dynasty had lost its collective mind.
As Adams saw it, slavery was a cancer; claiming that its spread throughout the body politic would somehow lessen its lethality was bizarre. He
also insisted that this new doctrine of diffusion contradicted the original intentions of the revolutionary generation, or at least that segment
of the leadership, which surely included Jefferson, dedicated to the
gradual abolition of slavery. All had then agreed that ending slavery
depended on confining it to the South. The emergence of cotton as a
lucrative cash crop and the concomitant spread of slavery into the new
states of the Deep South had exposed the weakness of this strategy, but
no one until now had ever claimed that this expansion of slavery was
helpful to the cause of abolition. Precisely the opposite, the spread of
slavery rendered the prospects for emancipation ever more distant.
While Jefferson believed that northern insistence on banishing slavery

from the western territories violated the sectional understanding within the founding generation, Adams accused Jefferson of repudiating the long-shared presumption that ending slavery meant isolating it in the South.[73]

In this debate over the true meaning of the American Revolution, which never became explicit because once again, it was too volatile a subject for the two patriarchs to share, Adams had the greater portion of historical evidence on his side. Indeed the ultimate source of Jefferson's extreme frustration with the Missouri Question, as well as the source of his frantic and farfetched efforts to answer it without surrendering his antislavery credentials, was that he was trapped within the contradictions created by his own posture of procrastination and denial. Missouri made the long-standing paradox of slavery that he had been living so deftly into an undeniable contradiction. He had all along been living a lie.

This was not a tolerable realization, just as it was not tolerable to recognize that northern politicians had seized the high moral ground, which was normally Jefferson country, from which they were now casting a long shadow over his legacy. Given the intolerable character of this situation, Jefferson reached down once again to the primal categories of his political imagination, which were, as always, moral and binary. The more he thought about the debate over Missouri, the more he convinced himself that the real agenda had little to do with slavery at all. That was merely a pretext, a master stroke of manipulation by the same sinister forces that had been trying to undermine the American republic from its very inception. They were called tories in the 1770s, monarchists or monocrats in the 1790s, diehard Federalists during his presidency, but they were all really agents of the same corrupt cause. "The Missouri Question is a mere party trick," he explained to Charles Pinckney. "The leaders of federalism, defeated in their schemes of obtaining power, have changed their tack and thrown out another barrel to the whale." Although it had been defeated time and time again, this surviving remnant of Federalist corruption was up to its old tricks, "taking advantage of the virtuous feelings of the people" in order to recover political power, using the antislavery message as a new instrument to consolidate its control.[74]

"Consolidation" was the new term that Jefferson embraced—other Virginians were using it too—to label the covert goals of these alleged conspirators. In one sense consolidationists were simply the old monarchists in slightly different guise. Or they were a reconfiguration of the courtiers and political henchmen around George III in the revolutionary era. At bottom they all were dedicated to the same purpose: accruing political power for themselves in tight bundles of coercion far removed from any popular restraints or public responsibilities, using slavery in the same way the Hamiltonians had formerly used debt to justify their plot. However flawed this bogeyman explanation was as an accurate description of the political forces that had mobilized around the Missouri Question, it was Jefferson's time-tested response to all complex political conflicts—namely, transform the swirling forces into a two-sided contest between good and evil. Simplification and exaggeration had always served him well in the past: George III had not really intended to enslave the American colonists, but rather to tighten imperial control over far-flung colonies; neither Hamilton nor Adams was really a monarchist, but rather advocates of a stronger executive and more energetic federal government. Moreover, his new label for the enemy—consolidationists—was actually a more accurate description of what had always distressed him about the primal concentration of political evil he saw in his mind's eye: It was organized and clustered together so as to maximize its coercive influence over popular opinion. Diffusion, on the other hand, accurately conveyed the core feature of all truly legitimate political power as he conceived it in his imagination: It was unorganized; it achieved its goals in a silent, slow and seeping fashion that never resorted to willful coercion; it was natural, almost unconscious.

As Jefferson saw it, then, the crisis of 1820 was yet another version of the ongoing struggle that he had waged and won in 1776 and again in 1800. "The same parties exist now which existed before," he wrote to

Lafayette in 1822, only now the enemy has realized "that monarchism is a hopeless wish in this country, and are rallying anew to the next best point, a consolidated government." The next day he wrote in the same vein to Gallatin, expanding his definition of the consolidation conspiracy to include the proposals for federal control over roads and canals—that is, all "internal improvements." While serving in Jefferson's cabinet, Gallatin had in fact authored the first study of a national system of roads and canals, and most Republicans had long since accepted the principle of federal responsibility for an interstate network of transportation to bind together the geographic regions and connect the coastal states to the interior. Now, however, Jefferson apprised Gallatin that internal improvements were yet another dimension of the consolidationists' plot. "Although this is not yet avowed (as that of monarchism, you know, never was) it exists decidedly," he assured Gallatin, "and is the true key to the debates in Congress. . . ."[75]

What Gallatin actually thought about Jefferson's conspiracy theory has not been preserved in the historical record. But the more expansive and inclusive version of Jefferson's demonic vision, which now went beyond the matter of slavery in Missouri to include the entire national program for internal improvements, made it difficult to understand his moral crusade against consolidation as he himself understood it—that is, as another chapter in the ongoing story of the American Revolution. The ancestral voices he heard and the ghosts of Federalism he saw now had the decided look of a massive delusion. Even worse, the embarrassing truth was that he was allowing the enormous prestige associated with his name to be captured by the most reactionary segment of southern political culture, with its attendant defense of slavery and its doctrine of states' rights.[76]

His language became more hysterical and apocalyptic. The decision to limit the expansion of slavery was a mere pretext for ruling slavery illegal throughout the United States, "in which case all the whites south of the Potomac and Ohio must evacuate their States, and most fortunate those who can do it first." It was precisely the same kind of scheme Parliament had tried in the 1760s, whereby the right to tax the

colonists was a mere opening wedge to establish tyranny in full fashion. He and his colleagues of the revolutionary generation had seen
through this trickery, but their successors "having nothing in them of
the feelings or principles of '76" were now completely duped into sup-
porting "a single and splendid government of an aristocracy, founded
on banking institutions, and moneyed corporations . . . riding and ruling over the plundered ploughman and beggared yeomanry." It was
the old Whig rhetoric, but now harnessed to the most provincial interests of Virginia politics. Though he expressed the fervent hope that he
would not live to see it, "there can be no hesitation," he concluded, if
faced with a choice between "the dissolution of our Union . . . or submission to a government without limitation of powers." Secession was
preferable to consolidation. It was a sad and pathetic spectacle, all the
more so because it seemed to ring all the familiar chords of 1776 and
1800, but he was in fact linking his legacy to the destruction of the
republic he had helped create.[77]

REBEL REACTIONARY

THERE WERE extenuating circumstances, which Jefferson's most
ardent admirers, both in his own time and ever after, have been at pains
to point out. One way to explain his descent into a nearly pathological
mentality is to see it more as a consequence of the panic of 1819 than
the Missouri crisis, two events occurring at the same time. The panic
depressed prices and land values throughout Virginia. Jefferson's financial problems and long-standing debts had forced him to sell his huge
(nearly seven thousand volumes) library in 1815 for the relatively meager
price of $23,950. And the economic depression that began in 1819 was
probably sufficient to ruin whatever slim prospects he ever had to pay
off his creditors. But the crowning blow came when he co-signed a
note of $20,000 for Wilson Cary Nicholas, a wealthy old friend and rel-
ative by marriage. The panic destroyed the value of Nicholas's extensive landholdings, forcing him to default on his loan and leaving

Jefferson with annual interest payments of $1,200. Jefferson immediately recognized this misfortune as what he called his *"coup de grace."* He was rescued from total despair only by the inimitable Jeffersonian style. "A call on me to the amount of any endorsements for you," he wrote Nicholas, "would indeed close my course by a catastrophe I had never calculated." His financial situation was undeniably hopeless after 1819. All his political statements after that date, so the argument goes, must be regarded as the ramblings of a depressed old man paralyzed by the realization that his bankruptcy would deprive his heirs of Monticello. His major domestic legacy was going to be debt. His political pronouncements of these last years, again so the argument goes, were colored by the pervasive sense of gloom that his financial misfortunes generated.[78]

He was also the victim of his own self-imposed isolation. "I read no newspaper now but Ritchie's," he wrote Nathaniel Macon in 1819, and "I feel much greater interest in knowing what has passed two or three thousand years ago, than what is now passing." Thomas Ritchie was editor of the *Richmond Enquirer,* a vehicle for militant states' rights polemics, and Macon was another staunch old Republican who regarded the Missouri crisis as a plot to end slavery in the South. Apart from Adams, almost all of Jefferson's regular correspondents were fellow Virginians like Macon, William Branch Giles and John Taylor, the latter the most verbose defender of agrarian values and states' rights in the entire country. Outside the Old Dominion, Jefferson's chief source of information on constitutional questions was William Johnson, a Supreme Court judge from South Carolina whose main claim to fame was his sporadic and usually inadequate efforts to oppose Chief Justice Marshall's ringing endorsements of federal authority over the states. All in all, then, Jefferson's sources of political information were highly partisan and narrowly provincial. Small wonder that his own views became distorted by similar prejudices.[79]

Finally, there is the much-quoted defense by Madison. Jefferson had asked his old disciple "to take care of me when dead," a poignant request that the ever-loyal Madison did not fail to fulfill in the 1830s, when southern secessionists tried to claim Jefferson as their own. No one could challenge Madison's claim that he knew Jefferson better than any man alive, and he expressed his clear conviction that "the charges against Mr. Jefferson," meaning the claims on his patrimony by secessionists and resolute states' righters, "can be duly refuted." Madison observed that "allowances also ought to be made for a habit in Mr. Jefferson as in others of great genius of expressing in strong and round terms, impressions of the moment." A few latter-day utterances, lifted out of context, ought not to be allowed to align Jefferson's long legacy with the most reactionary elements in the South. Coming as it did from Jefferson's closest confidant, who was also a Virginian with impeccable credentials as a defender of southern interests, Madison's insistence that Jefferson not be taken literally as a supporter of secession was both plausible and compelling.[80]

Each of these efforts at extenuation and helpful explication is true enough, especially Madison's warning that Jefferson's most disarmingly extreme statements not be seized upon in isolation as fair samples of his final thoughts. But it is also true that efforts to dismiss his latter-day political pronouncements as aberrations will not do. Whatever impact his financial predicament had on his emotional stability, he found ways to shield himself from the full implication of his indebtedness until only a few months before his death, using the same denial mechanisms that had served him so well throughout his life. And the narrowly partisan character of his correspondents was not just some accident of fate; Jefferson chose to focus his exchanges on politics with spokesmen for a "Virginia-writ-large" version of America because they tended to share his sense of impending doom for an agrarian society and a way of life that was inextricably bound up with slavery. Even Madison's persuasive defense—that Jefferson had an inherently rhetorical way with ideas that ought not always be taken literally—must be challenged, since the rhetorical power of Jefferson's political utterances was a central feature of their appeal and the singularly most significant key to the endurance of his legacy. In sum, Jefferson's final thoughts on the meaning of the American Revolution and what that meaning meant for the government of the emergent American nation *were* extreme, but not in the sense of being aberrant or wildly misrepresentative; they were intensifications and purifications of what he had been saying all along.

Perhaps alone among Jefferson's contemporaries, Madison understood all this. (Adams kept trying to understand, but his classical assumptions about the need to discipline and balance political power prevented him from grasping the seminal source of Jefferson's message.) Madison's defense of Jefferson was in fact more than a bit disingenuous, since his own personal correspondence and conversations with his mentor during the last five years of Jefferson's life gave him unique access to the final expression of Jeffersonian political wisdom, which was eminently vulnerable to capture by the southern secessionists. But Madison also understood better than anyone else that Jefferson was more a political visionary than a political thinker. In that ultimate sense his message defied capture by any single faction or interest group, including the ascendant southern secessionists; indeed it defied all traditional assumptions about what was possible in politics.

Madison tended to share Jefferson's foreboding fears of consolidation. Like Jefferson, he was trapped by the unattractive implications of the slavery question; he also opposed the restrictions on slavery imposed by the Missouri Compromise and sought relief in the illusion of diffusion, as well as the equally illusory belief that gradual emancipation was somehow still feasible. Moreover, one of his last acts as president was to veto the bill for internal improvements on the ground that it granted the federal government unconstitutional powers. In all these crucial ways he and Jefferson agreed, making it possible for Madison to commiserate in good conscience with his aging mentor and his tortured thoughts after 1820.[81]

One area, however, where Madison preferred to maintain a discreet silence was Jefferson's familiar refrain about what had been intended at the Constitutional Convention. "Can it be believed," Jefferson asked rhetorically, "that under the jealousies prevailing against the General Government, at the adoption of the Constitution, the States meant to surrender the authority of preserving order, of enforcing moral duties and restraining vice, within their own territory?" Jefferson's long-standing formula was straightforward: "I believe the States can best govern our home concerns and the General Government our foreign ones." Or, as he put it in his most graphic formulation, "the federal is, in truth, our foreign government. . . ." Madison preferred to answer such assertions with elliptical statements. "The Gordion Knot of the Constitution," he observed, "seems to lie in the problem of collision between the federal and State powers. . . ." While Madison himself wanted to blur both the sovereignty question and the extent of his disagreement with Jefferson, his wife, Dolley, in a note appended to her husband's papers soon after his death, spoke more candidly: "Thomas Jefferson was not in America pending the framing of the Constitution, whose information in all that occurred in the Convention, and of the motives and intents of the framers, was derived from Mr. Madison, whose opinions guided him in the construction of that instrument, was looked up to many as its father and almost unanimously as its only true repositor." When it came to constitutional questions, in short, Jefferson often did not know what he was talking about.[82]

The disagreement came to a head, as it logically and legally was almost obliged to do, over Jefferson's colorful denunciations of the Supreme Court. The ultimate symbol of consolidation for Jefferson was the Marshall Court, sitting atop the federal government like a Federalist sanctuary, with Marshall dispensing his judicial verdicts like some malignant Buddha. "The great object of my fear is the federal judiciary," Jefferson wrote in 1821. "That body, like gravity, ever acting, with noiseless foot, and unalarming advance, gaining ground step by step, and holding what it gains, is engulphing insidiously the special governments into the jaws of that which feeds them." His most frequent image was of the Supreme Court as "the subtle corps of sappers and miners constantly working under ground to undermine the foundations of our confederated republic." Most frustrating of all was Marshall himself, who seemed to possess magical powers of influence over his fellow justices. "An opinion is huddled up in conclave," Jefferson

noted in disgust, "delivered as if unanimous, and with the silent acqui-
escence of lazy or timid associates, by a crafty chief judge, who sophis-
ticates the law to his mind, by the turn of his own reasoning." At the
very least, Jefferson urged, Marshall's quiet despotism should be challenged by requiring all Supreme Court justices to submit separate "seriatim opinions," so that dissent within the Court could be exposed and
the illusion of godlike unanimity—Marshall's preferred effect—could be
destroyed.[83]

Madison tended to agree with Jefferson about Marshall's formidable influence and the need for seriatim opinions by all the justices on
the court. As long as the chief justice remained in place, one could
expect no limits on the encroachments of the federal government
when it came either to the slavery question in the western territories or
to the presumption of federal control over internal improvements. But
Jefferson went much further, denying altogether the power of the
Supreme Court to decide on questions of constitutionality. "The ultimate arbiter," he insisted, "is the people of the Union, assembled by
their deputies in convention, at the call of Congress, or of two thirds of
the States." In other words, Jefferson denied the principle of judicial
review and argued that the provisions made for amending the Constitution were the only proper procedures for deciding all questions of
constitutionality.[84]

Madison, ever the diplomat with his lifelong colleague and friend,
tried to avoid an open break by first suggesting that Jefferson's preferred modus operandi was rather cumbersome, then concurring that
Marshall's decisions were indeed enough to test one's patience. Then,
however, came the devastating clincher: "But the abuse of a trust does
not disprove its existence." Madison accepted, and had all along
accepted, the principle of judicial review. If there was the spirit of '76,
which Jefferson could plausibly claim to know firsthand, there was also
the spirit of '87, which Madison could claim with equivalent plausibil-
ity to know with comparable intimacy. The clear intention of the
framers of the Constitution, Madison told his friend, was to make the
Supreme Court the ultimate arbiter of federal versus state jurisdiction,

the final judge, as Madison put it, of any "trial of strength between the Posse headed by the Marshal and the Posse headed by the Sheriff."[85]

It was a rather astounding fact that the two Virginians had worked together so closely, so harmoniously for so many years and this elemental difference of opinion had never surfaced before. Despite Madison's gentle and, as always, deferential tone toward his old friend, Jefferson could not have missed the point, for it came up again little more than a year later in another context. Jefferson had prepared a draft proposal entitled "The Solemn Declaration and Protest of the Commonwealth of Virginia" in which he attempted to carve out a position that would permit his home state to oppose federal legislation for internal improvements. He identified control over its domestic affairs as one of "the rights retained by the states, rights which never have been yielded, and which this state will never voluntarily yield. . . ." Then, after disavowing any desire to threaten the Union or risk any "immediate rupture," declaring "such a rupture as among the greatest calamities which could befall them," he threatened precisely the action that he had disavowed: Destroying the Union would produce a calamity, to be sure, "but not the greatest" calamity; there was "yet one greater, submission to a government of unlimited powers." He sent the draft proposal to Madison with a note, saying that he "would not hazard so important a measure against your opinion, nor even without its support."[86]

Madison wrote back within the week. "You asked an early answer," he observed, "and I have hurried one, at the risk of crudeness in some of its views of the subject." The essence of the lengthy answer was that Jefferson's proposed draft was "an anomaly without any operative character." Congress had passed the act funding internal improvements by a decisive majority. The only ground on which the act could be overturned was for the Supreme Court to find it unconstitutional, a course that was unlikely in the extreme given Marshall's predilections and, irony of ironies, a course that Jefferson considered illegal anyway. Whatever one thought about internal improvements as a stalking-horse for the evils of consolidation, Virginia had to obey the law. To suggest otherwise was to raise the specter that states need not abide by laws they found objectionable. This was a recipe for civil war and eventual anarchy, precisely the danger the Constitution was designed to avoid and, Madison urged ever so discreetly, hardly the course Jefferson wished associated with his name. Jefferson almost always listened when Madison offered constitutional advice. "I have read the last with entire approbation and adoption of its views," he reported back to Madison, and "have therefore suppressed my paper. . . ." A few years later, when Madison was defending Jefferson's legacy against the claims of extreme states' righters during the Nullification Crisis, Jefferson's decision to withdraw his proposal made Madison's task much easier, and the benign duplicity of his defense more justifiable.[87]

Nevertheless, this last exchange and eventual collaboration with Madison are extremely revealing, and for reasons that extend far beyond the matter of Jefferson's vulnerability to, or rescue from, emergent southern secessionists. Adams had been telling Jefferson for several years that the Jeffersonian version of what the American Revolution actually meant was both idiosyncratic and irresponsible. Now Madison was telling him that he had failed to grasp the central achievement of the constitutional settlement of 1787–88, which was to grant the federal government sufficient sovereignty to assure a national system of laws that all states and all individuals were obliged to obey. Both Adams and Madison, in their different ways, were informing Jefferson that the outstanding accomplishment of the revolutionary generation had been the realistic recognition of the need for limits as well as liberation, that the American republic had endured because its creators made sensible compromises with political power, that the genius of the American Revolution resided in its capacity to harness, indeed to consolidate, the energies released by the movement for independence.

But Jefferson, it turned out, had not seen it that way at all. He regarded himself as the untamed essence of the original revolutionary impulse, uncontaminated by any implicit understandings of 1776 (here he parted with Adams) or any explicit compromises with political power in 1787–88 (here he parted with Madison). Indeed what his two old friends regarded as realistic limitations designed to assure the stability of the republican experiment, he believed betrayals of the true meaning of the American Revolution, which was not to harness individual energies but to release them. Even such intimate collaborators as Adams and Madison might consider his vision alluringly irresponsible, the kind of dangerously romantic aversion to established authority that one needed to get over. But Jefferson's statements during his last years of life, far from being aberrant ramblings, represented a consistent rededication to his visionary principles. All compromises with political power were pacts with the devil. All efforts at political consolidation were treasonable acts.

In that sense, at least, Madison was right to insist that his old mentor would have disavowed any claims on his legacy by southern states' righters. His abiding legacy was a profound suspicion of governmental power of any sort and a political rhetoric that depicted any relationship between the people and their government as problematic and contingent. The only unkind observation about Madison that Jefferson ever made, at least the only one that found its way into the historical record, came on his deathbed, in the final hours when he was passing in and out of consciousness: "But ah!" he blurted out. "He could never in his life stand up against strenuous opposition." While not fully fair to his most loyal friend, the remark captured Jefferson's derogatory sense of all political accommodation as a betrayal of principle. He remained a rebel to the very end.[88]

EDUCATIONAL DREAMS

THE HAPPIEST MOMENTS in those increasingly unhappy last years were unquestionably private occasions: the hours in his garden; the afternoons on horseback; the early-evening romps with his grandchildren on the back lawns of Monticello. The one bright spot amid the deepening sense of gloom about public affairs was provided by the project taking shape a few miles away in Charlottesville, barely visible on a clear day from his mountaintop, which Jefferson called his "academic village." Now known, of course, as the University of Virginia and recognized at the bicentennial celebrations of 1976 by the American Institute of Architects as "the proudest achievement of American architecture in the past 200 years," it became Jefferson's major retirement project in 1817.[89]

In that year he wrote a semiscolding note to Madison, who was still trying to disengage himself from the presidency, for missing the first meeting of the committee charged with planning what was then being called Central College: "A detention at Washington I presume prevented your attendance. . . . Circumstances which will be explained to you make us believe that a *full meeting* of *all* visitors, on the first occasion at least, will decide a great object in the State system of general education; and I have accordingly so pressed the subject on Colo. Monroe [the incumbent president replacing Madison] as I think will ensure his attendance, and I hope we shall not fail in yours." In case Madison had missed the point, Jefferson reiterated his annoyance at Madison's absence and his expectation that the next session would be "a *full meeting* of all. . . ." The episode illustrates Jefferson's total immersion in his new educational and architectural venture; it never occurred to him that the outgoing and incoming presidents of the United States might have more important things to do.[90]

He threw himself into the project with the same youthful enthusiasm he had earlier given to the renovations of Monticello. Indeed one can understand the architectural and construction challenges posed by the University of Virginia as convenient conduits for the same restless energies previously expended on his mansion on the mountain, which was now just about finished; it was the perfect building project to keep him busy. But it was also much more, since it involved cajoling the Virginia legislature for money, selecting a faculty, building a library, shaping a curriculum, in effect creating a model American university in his own image and likeness. Once Madison began attending the meetings of the Board of Visitors, he immediately recognized that the enterprise was intended to serve as a projection of Jefferson's personality. All members of the board understood they were appointed to follow Jefferson's lead, and all displayed "unaffected deference . . . for his judgment and experience." They were merely accomplices as he attempted, for what was obviously the last time, to institutionalize his dreams.[91]

His educational dreams went way back. First as governor of Virginia and then in his *Notes on Virginia* he had proposed a statewide system of public education designed to raise the Old Dominion out of its scandalously inadequate condition and place it on a par with the New England states. As president he had taken on George Washington's favorite scheme for a national university, presumably located in the nation's capital. But nothing came of the idea, and the academy established in New York with his blessing became an engineering school for army officers at West Point, not quite what he had in mind. Soon after his retirement from the presidency his broodings assumed the more tangible form of a master plan for Virginia. Each county would be divided into a series of local "hundreds" or "wards" modeled on the New England townships. Each ward would support a primary or elementary school funded out of public taxes, giving Virginia about twelve hundred local schools to teach basic literacy. Then each county would contain an academy or secondary school where the best graduates of the ward schools could learn their Latin and Greek and the rudiments of science, the poorer students at public expense. The capstone of the plan was a state university where the best graduates of the county academies would receive the best education available in America, again the poorest of the best on tax-supported scholarships.[92]

The scheme was pure Jefferson: magisterial in conception, admirable in intention, unworkable in practice. The Virginia legislature refused to provide the funds necessary for the comprehensive plan but did appoint a commission to meet at Rockfish Gap in 1818 and make recommendations for the site of a state university. Jefferson had himself and Madison appointed to the commission, dominated the deliberations and personally wrote the Rockfish Gap Report that advocated the creation of a state university in Charlottesville. Madison lent an editorial hand in his familiar way, suggesting that Jefferson's use of the term "monastic" to describe the preferred collegiate atmosphere, while graphic, "may not give umbrage," and that "the idea of seeking professors *abroad* may excite prejudices with some. . . ." Jefferson expressed his own apprehension that Virginia was deciding to place a capstone on an educational foundation that did not exist, but his enthusiasm for the project overwhelmed his reservations. He relished the prospect of reviving the Jefferson-Madison collaboration one final time, in yet another campaign to lead reluctant citizens toward truths that lay just beyond their vision. On the state commission, for example, Jefferson explained to Madison that "there is a floating body of doubtful and wavering men," so in his written report "I have therefore thrown in some leading ideas on the benefits of education . . . in the hope these might catch on some crotchets in their mind, and bring them over to us." It was like the old days.[93]

Several old and familiar Jeffersonian patterns also presented themselves, like characters in a play reappearing for a final encore. There was the meticulous master of detail, operating with a grand but clear vision to guide him, yet never quite able to perform successfully in that middle region where detail and vision intersect to create cost overruns. Jefferson surveyed the site for the Charlottesville campus himself, even personally laid out the stakes. For the Rotunda, which was to be the architectural centerpiece, he selected the Pantheon of Rome as his model and designed it to serve as both the library and a planetarium, with movable planets and stars on the interior of the dome manipulated by an ingenious and invisible set of pulleys and gadgets. (Control should never be visible.) He worked four hours each day for several months to assemble the catalog for the library of 6,860 volumes, which he estimated would cost $24,076. The false sense of mastery conveyed by such precise numbers kept being undermined by financial realities that always eroded Jefferson's most careful calculations. In 1820 the Virginia legislature, believing it was acting responsibly to meet the total costs, authorized the Board of Visitors to borrow $60,000. But the Rotunda proved more expensive than Jefferson had anticipated, and he revised the estimate upward—again the misleading precision—to $162,364. The following year, facing heavy criticism from the legislature for the Rotunda's cost, he predicted that $195,000 would completely cover all expenses. It did not, of course, but by then the pavilions were going up, the undeniable grandeur of Jefferson's architectural vision was becoming visible and the momentum of the enterprise had passed the point where anyone but a foolish spendthrift would demand a halt.[94]

The recruitment of the faculty exposed again his contradictory attitude toward Europe as both a den of political iniquity and the cradle of all learning. He insisted that only European scholars could provide the high level of intellectual distinction necessary for a truly first-rate university, so he persuaded a reluctant Board of Visitors to dispatch Francis Gilmer, a bright young Virginia lawyer, to recruit prospective faculty in England, France and Germany. When Adams learned that his old friend was scouring Europe for scholars, he poked fun at the unpatriotic scheme and jokingly reminded Jefferson of his most colorful condemnations of Europe as an intellectual swamp brimming with infectious political diseases. But Jefferson persisted in his quest for the best; that is, until Gilmer reported that none of the leading European scholars was interested in moving to an unfinished campus in the American wilderness. He tried to put the best face on this unexpected turn of events: "I consider that his [Gilmer's] return without any professors will completely quash every hope of the institution. . . . I think therefore he had better bring the best he can get. They will be preferable to secondaries of our country because the stature of these is known, whereas those he would bring would be unknown, and would be readily imagined to be the high grade we have calculated on." In short, the commitment to unalloyed excellence had to be abandoned in favor of at least the appearance of respectability. Poor Gilmer, whose health was destroyed by the trip, eventually returned to America in late 1824 with commitments from five youngish foreign scholars who agreed to come over shortly. Adams suggested mischievously to Jefferson that at least one of these foreigners should be charged with teaching about "the Limits of human knowledge already acquired . . . , though I suppose you will have doubts of the propriety of setting any limits . . . on human Wisdom, and human Virtue." Jefferson chose not to respond. At least, and at last, he had his faculty.[95]

Then there was the ardent defender of unbridled freedom of thought and inquiry who was equally ardent about the beneficiaries of such freedom reaching certain universal truths that all could then embrace as self-evident. Jefferson tended to associate restrictions on freedom of thought with religious creeds and doctrinal rules demanded by established churches. One of the most distinctive features of the University of Virginia was its disavowal of any religious affiliation—virtually all the major colleges in the nation up to this time had defined themselves as seminaries for particular denominations or religious sects—and Jefferson went so far as to prohibit the teaching of theology altogether. He was also extremely sensitive to the way boards of trustees at other American colleges, usually dominated by the clergy, imposed restrictions on what could be taught or what books could be read. He was absolutely insistent that his university not succumb to such forms of censorship.

And he meant it. But his acute sensitivity to religious creeds did not carry over to politics. As he explained to Madison, "there is one branch in which I think we are the best judges," an area of study so crucial "as to make it a duty in us to lay down the principles which are to be taught." That area was the study of government, where the Board of Visitors had an obligation to protect tender minds from the treasonable thoughts of "rank Federalists and consolidationists." Jefferson went on to prepare a list of standard texts to be required in the classes on law and government; his list included the Declaration of Independence, *The Federalist Papers,* the Virginia Resolutions of 1799, and George Washington's Inaugural and Farewell addresses. Although certain numbers of *The Federalist Papers* ought to have given Jefferson pause, the list represented his attempt to ensure that the rising generation imbibe the doctrines of republicanism according to Virginia's version of the American Revolution.[96]

Once again, Madison rescued him from his lapse in judgment and called him back to his own first principles. There were political creeds just as there were religious creeds, Madison observed, and Jefferson would not want to impose, albeit inadvertently, his political values in the manner of a priest or pope. Moreover, it was "not easy to find standard books that will be both guides and guards for the purpose." The Declaration of Independence, for example, could be read in different ways by different people (one of Madison's most telling and pointed acts of understatement), and Jefferson's selection of the Virginia Resolutions of 1799, though flattering to Madison himself, who had written them, left much "room for hesitation" because of their "narrow and local focus." (Madison already sensed danger in these earlier defenses of states' rights and wished to protect both Jefferson and himself from being appropriated by more militant southern spokesmen.) All in all, the very idea of a required list of readings, Madison concluded, was perhaps misguided. "I have, for your consideration, sketched a modification of the operative passage in your draught," he noted discreetly, "with a view to relax the absoluteness of its injunction. . . ." As usual, when Madison talked in this prudent way, Jefferson listened: "I concur with entire satisfaction in your amendment of my resolution." Despite the founder's initial instincts, there would be no tests of political faith at Jefferson's university.[97]

There remained, however, an unresolved tension between Jefferson's vision of the University of Virginia as America's premier national institution for higher education and the increasingly sectional character of his own thinking. What began as a suitable American alternative to Oxford or Cambridge, where America's natural aristocracy could be trained for the responsibilities of national leadership, became more provincial as Jefferson's obsession with a northern "conspiracy of consolidationists" grew more severe. As the buildings in Charlottesville were going up, his own optimistic version of a national university was going down, replaced by a more narrow and defensive sense of his school as a southern fortress where Virginia's young men could seek refuge from the poisonous environment of Harvard or Yale, which now specialized in producing "fanatics and tories." Here was yet another manifestation of his "Virginia-writ-large" version of patriotism toward the end.[98]

Two truly distinctive features of the university were very much a projection of Jefferson's personality. First, most of the traditional rules and curricular requirements that governed the operation of all other American colleges were completely abandoned. There were no distinctions among freshmen, sophomores or upperclassmen. Jefferson also wanted "to leave everyone free to attend whatever branches of instruction he wants, and to decline what he does not want." No specific courses or programs of study were required. It was a wholly elective system, indeed the rejection of any prescribed system at all. Nor was there any separate administration. The school was to be run by the faculty with the cooperation of the students, all overseen by the Board of Visitors. Jefferson was insistent that his university be devoted to the principle of "self government," which meant that proctors, provosts and even a president were superfluous. When the opportunity arose to attract William Wirt, the renowned biographer of Patrick Henry, as the first professor of law, Jefferson was enthusiastic—that is, until he learned that Wirt's acceptance was conditional upon his being named president. He blocked the appointment on the ground that his university did not require an executive presence. (In keeping with his wishes, the University of Virginia did not have a president until 1904.) In sum, the internal architecture of Jefferson's "academical village" was just as original as its physical exterior, and the guiding principle was not classical or Palladian, but rather the removal of all forms of external authority. There was no need for flying buttresses to order or stabilize the interior structure of his university; all meaningful discipline was internalized and invisible. It was the epitome of the Jeffersonian ideal— a society without government.[99]

The second distinctively personal feature of his plan for the university used architecture to institutionalize an educational version of domestic intimacy and harmony. At one level the campus plan was designed to replicate the idyllic New England village with its separate but proximate dwellings arranged around a common or green. This scheme maximized both independence and daily face-to-face encounters among neighbors. It almost certainly grew out of the thinking he had been doing about wards as the primal political and educational units in Virginia, where town meetings and schools were infused with those essential energies available only when participants knew one another in multiple contexts and civic trust, like a natural force, was simply taken for granted. The chief flaw in his ward scheme for education, apart from the legislature's rejection of the plan as wildly expensive, was that Virginia was demographically different from New England; the population was spread out rather than clustered in towns. Nevertheless, the intimacy and authenticity of social interactions in the village environment appealed to Jefferson enormously as the seminal source of what he was now willing to call "the democratic spirit," or the civilized version of political purity present in the tribal culture of Indians. Whatever the demographic problems might be in Virginia, his "academical village" would create its own demography. Unlike Oxford or Cambridge, which replicated the Gothic world of castles and drawbridges, or the preferred American collegiate scheme of a single large building, which suggested a fortress or prison, the Jeffersonian school would re-create the autonomous intimacies of the New England village.[100]

At yet another level the professors and students were clustered in conjugal units with each professorial house flanked by student dorm rooms along a colonnade. The intent was to create the semblance of a family environment with professors as quasi-parents or guardians. If the village was the idyllic essence of the harmonious society, the family was the essential component of the village, the place or space where mutual affection and familiarity came together and one learned, in all the invisible ways, to internalize discipline. The very design of the three-sided colonnade captured Jefferson's youthful ideal, which he cherished in his memories of William Small and George Wythe at William and Mary, of the teacher as mentor, friend, personal guardian. It aimed to close the distance, both physically and psychologically, between faculty and students and thereby make learning benefit from the interpersonal dynamics one normally associated with family life in its most affectionate and attractive forms.[101]

Though illustrative of Jefferson's deepest and fondest convictions, this was all pure theory. The more mundane and palpable realities struck with a vengeance in September 1825, when a group of fourteen drunken students rioted, broke windows up and down the colonnade and threatened two faculty members with physical injury. In an inverted version of the honor code, none of the students proved willing to confess his own guilt or testify against his peers. The incident required the calling of a special meeting of the Board of Visitors in October with the eighty-two-year-old Jefferson in the chair. It was quite a scene. The aging patriarch was flanked by Madison and Monroe—the flower of the Virginia dynasty and all former presidents—at a large table in the Rotunda, only recently completed. One of the students, Henry Tutwiler, described what happened. Jefferson rose to address the students. He began by declaring that it was one of the most painful events of his life, but he had not gone far before his feelings overcame him, and he sat down, saying that he would leave to abler hands the task of saying what he wished to say. His own world was falling apart just as he was about to leave it. Even the ideal world of perfect freedom, pure democracy and human affection he thought he had created in Charlottesville refused to cooperate with his expectations. He seemed destined by fate to end up a disappointed idealist.[102]

TRAGEDY

THE LAST FEW months were uniformly sad and grim, punctuated by one final effort to rescue at least a portion of his burdened estate for his heirs and one last and truly defiant display of the inimitable Jeffersonian style. The depth of his indebtedness now defied even his awesome powers of denial, and the looming character of his own death quashed the long-standing illusion that something would turn up before he headed for the hereafter. "To keep a Virginia estate together requires in the owner both skill and attention," he confided to Monroe, whose own financial prospects were also bleak, but "Skill I never had and attention I could not have, and really when I reflect on all the circumstances my wonder is that I should have been so long as 60 years in reaching the result to which I am now reduced." He was about $100,000 in debt; in modern equivalents, several million dollars.[103]

His one hope was a public lottery, which was officially against the law and therefore required a waiver from the Virginia legislature. If he could get the waiver, however, and if the lottery proved successful, he had some chance of selling off a portion of his estate and retaining Monticello, along with enough land to support his heirs and some fraction of his slave population. In February 1826 he drafted a lengthy petition to the legislature in which he reviewed the earlier history of lotteries in Virginia and—this must have been excruciatingly painful—provided an account of his lengthy public service on behalf of the state and the nation. For a man with Jefferson's sense of pride and personal honor, it was a truly desperate act justified only by his desperate circumstances. Then the legislature, in a fit of inexplicable ingratitude that also enhanced his embarrassment, denied his petition. "It is part of my mortification," he confessed to his equally bankrupt son-in-law, "to perceive that I had so far overvalued myself as to have counted on it [the lottery] with too much confidence. I see, in the failure of this hope, a deadly blast of all my peace of mind during my remaining days. You kindly encourage me to keep up my spirits; but, oppressed with disease, debility, age, and embarrassed affairs, this is difficult. For myself I should not regard a prostration of fortune, but I am overwhelmed at the prospect of the situation in which I may leave my family."[104]

A few weeks later, however, Jefferson's many friends and admirers successfully lobbied the legislature to reverse its decision. The approval of the lottery injected a last ray of hope into his final months of life. (This hope too proved illusory, but Jefferson was not around to face the facts.) He prepared his will in March with the expectation that

Monticello would be salvaged from his creditors and some of his land would pass to his heirs. Knowing that the auctioneers would claim many, if not most, of his slaves, he chose to free five members of the Hemings family: Burwell, his personal servant, immediately upon his death; John Hemings and Joe Fossett one year later; Madison and Eston Hemings, sons of Sally, who would be apprenticed to John Hemings until they were twenty-one, then freed. Sally herself was not freed or mentioned in the will.[105]

Perhaps buoyed by the false hope that the lottery would rescue him from total ruin, he managed one last burst of bravado in late June, just before his final illness confined him to bed. Officials planning the Independence Day celebrations in Washington invited him to attend the ceremonies honoring the fiftieth anniversary of the Declaration of Independence on July 4. Jefferson was in no condition to leave his mountaintop, but he agreed to send a written statement. He sensed that this would be his last public utterance, so he mustered up one final surge of energy, correcting and revising his statement with the same attention to detail that he had brought to the original draft of the Declaration and to his First Inaugural. After gracefully regretting his inability to rejoin in Washington "the small band, the remnant of that host of worthies who joined with us on that day, in the bold and doubtful election . . . between submission and the Sword," he then offered his distilled final rendering of just what the band of worthies had done:

> May it be to the world, what I believe it will be, (to some parts sooner, to others later, but finally to all,) the signal of arousing men to burst the chains under which monkish ignorance and superstition had persuaded them to bind themselves, and to assume the blessings and security of self-government. . . . All eyes are opened or opening to the rights of men. The general spread of the light of science has already laid open to every view the palpable truth, that the mass of mankind has not been born with saddles on their backs, nor a favored few, booted and spurred,

ready to ride them legitimately, by the grace of God. These are
grounds of hope for others; for ourselves, let the annual return of
this day forever refresh our recollections of these rights, and an
undiminished devotion to them.[106]

It was vintage Jefferson: the uplifting vision of the American Revolution as the opening chapter in the global struggle against the
entrenched prejudices of the past; the lyrical language, pitched at a
height that caused one to look up and feel the inspiration as the head
lifted to catch the verbal airbursts. As with his draft of the Declaration,
the core idea was not original and never intended to be; Jefferson had
been insisting on seeing the Revolution as a liberation movement, a
breaking away, for half a century. Again like the Declaration, the felicity of the style was also secondhand, borrowed from a famous speech
delivered by Colonel Richard Rumbold on the gallows in 1685 before
he was hanged for treason. Rumbold, a crusty Puritan soldier, had
coined the phrases about "saddles on their backs" and "a favored few,
booted and spurred, ready to ride them" just before he went to his
maker. Jefferson owned copies of several English histories that
reprinted the Rumbold speech. Perhaps certain phrases had lodged
themselves in his memory, then inadvertently leaped into his mind as
he wrote. Or perhaps the borrowing was done more consciously, justified on the ground that, like Rumbold, he was a dying man who
should be permitted the leeway to claim a favorite piece of eloquence
as his own. Whatever the truth, and no matter how personally despon-
dent he was about the prospective fate of his family and his beloved
Monticello, Jefferson sounded a triumphant final note that correctly
captured his optimistic message to posterity. About the core meaning
and the abiding significance of the American Revolution, he had no
doubts.[107]

Jefferson was also unable to attend another ceremony six months
later, on January 15, 1827, when the estate and slaves of Monticello were
put up for auction. Although his fear of living too long proved justified, his providential demise on July 4, 1826, spared him the ultimate

tragedy of watching all his worldly possessions, including "130 valuable negroes" sold to the highest bidders. All America was still talking about the simultaneous death of Adams and Jefferson, on the fiftieth anniversary to the day of their great collaboration of 1776, though in Virginia there were some expressions of resentment that Adams had edged his way into the dramatic departure scene with the great Virginian, even claims that reports of the date of Adams's death must be "a damn'd Yankee trick." But it was true. And Adams's last words— "Thomas Jefferson survives"—proved to be just as prophetically right in the long run as they were dead wrong at the time. Jefferson was fortunate in both senses, immortal for the ages but dead and gone on that cold January day when his surviving daughter and grandchildren saw Monticello dismembered and destroyed. His grandson Jeffy never forgot the sad scene, which he compared with "a captured village in ancient times when all were sold as slaves." The auction lasted five days, and when it was over, the proceeds covered only a portion of Jefferson's monumental debt, which was passed on to his descendants, and the slaves he had vowed to protect as a benevolent father were sold to the highest bidder. His life had always been about promise. And his enduring legacy became the most resonant version of the American promise in the national mythology. But in his life, if not in his legacy, there were some promises he could not keep. We do not know what promises he had made to Sally Hemings over the years. We do know she was not among the slaves he freed in his will.[108]

EPILOGUE

⊷ ❧ ⊶

THE FUTURE OF AN ILLUSION

The true Jefferson legacy is to be hostile to legacies.
—JOYCE APPLEBY (1993)

Jefferson's ideas had also this felicity, and also perhaps a little too much of it. They come to birth a little too easily, and rest a little precariously on the aspirations and ideals of good men, and not sufficiently on the brute concrete facts of the world as it is.
—CARL BECKER (1944)

W HAT, THEN, is the historically correct Jeffersonian legacy? What, if any, are the values that the real person who was Thomas Jefferson embodied in his life that remain vital and viable over two centuries after he declared American independence? More than half a century after the historian Carl Becker posed the question in its most familiar form, it seems appropriate and even timely to ask ourselves again, "What is still living in the political philosophy of Thomas Jefferson?"[1]

The question, it must be noted, would strike Jefferson himself and the majority of professional historians as bizarre. Jefferson certainly wanted to be remembered, but he had little patience with historical heritages, which he tended to regard as burdens imposed on the present by the past. Joyce Appleby, one of Jefferson's most astute modern-day admirers, has put it nicely: "The true Jeffersonian legacy is to be hostile to legacies." If he could make a miraculous appearance among us, it would be perfectly plausible for him to denounce the entire Jeffersonian enterprise as a massive waste of time. The present generation of Americans, he might well say, needs to liberate itself from the dead hand of ancestors and predecessors and seek its own fate and future. Indeed only by doing so will we remain faithful to the core Jeffersonian convictions.[2]

Most historians would chime in with a different version of the same message. As they see it, the past is a foreign country with its own distinctive mores and language. All efforts to wrench Jefferson out of his own time and place, therefore, are futile and misguided ventures that invariably compromise the integrity of the historical context that made him what he was. Lifting Jefferson out of that context and bringing him into the present is like trying to plant cut flowers. Granted, this means protecting the purity of the past at the expense of abandoning its relevance to the present. But most historians would rather run the risk of antiquarianism than commit the sin of presentism.

For better and for worse, however, Jefferson has long since broken through the barricades that historians set up between the present and the past. Different versions of him as both hero and villain are loose among us, and different claims on the Jeffersonian legacy have become a permanent feature of contemporary American culture. To be sure, Bill Clinton's calculated pilgrimage to Monticello and Ronald Reagan's uplifting recommendation that we "pluck a flower from Thomas Jefferson's life and wear it on our soul forever" represent the same transparent impulse to appropriate an icon for their own political purposes. Abraham Lincoln and Franklin Delano Roosevelt, now icons themselves, perfected this technique long ago. (In fact a good case can be made that Roosevelt championed the construction of the Jefferson Memorial primarily to provide the Democratic party with a symbolic counter to the Lincoln Memorial, which the Republican party claimed as its own.) Such public invocations and appropriations of the mythical Jefferson have only the faintest connection with the historical Jefferson, who is presumably resting comfortably in archival enclaves tended by vigilant but invisible scholars.[3]

While prominent public figures quote from Jefferson without fear and without embarrassment at their ignorance, there is also an ongoing conversation of equivalent superficiality occurring at all hours of the day and night on the Internet. When John Adams spoke his last and most prophetic words–"Thomas Jefferson survives"–he had no way of knowing about cyberspace. But there is now more "talk" about Jeffersonian topics (i.e., Tom and Sally, Jefferson and Newt [Gingrich], Monticello recipes, Jefferson and GOD) on America Online than any other historical figure. In February 1996 the Thomas Jefferson Memorial Foundation injected at least a semblance of informed opinion into these otherwise gossipy exchanges. "Monticello is pleased to announce its presence on the World-Wide Web," the foundation declared, offering access to "a typical day in Jefferson's life in the early 1800s" among other topics.[4]

In several senses cyberspace is the perfect Jeffersonian environment, an ethereal place where shifting images and impressions float freely and without any pretense of coherence. Likewise, the personal computer is the perfect Jeffersonian instrument; it allows ordinary individuals to communicate from the privacy of their solitary studies with laptop machines that a reincarnated Jefferson would surely regard as the modern analogue to his laptop desk. All this only reinforces the realization that maintaining scholarly control over Jefferson's memory and legacy is a long-lost cause.

To revisit Carl Becker's old question, then–"What is still living . . . ?" –is really to join an ongoing conversation that most scholars have simply chosen to avoid. Becker's formulation of the question also implicitly suggests that any answer with pretensions of historical accuracy must begin with the recognition that substantial portions of Jefferson's legacy are no longer alive; they have died a natural death somewhere between 1826 and now. Perhaps the best way to visualize that process is to imagine a series of sand castles on a beach, located different distances from the shoreline but all vulnerable to the tide of time.

The first major wave to strike was the Civil War, which destroyed slavery, the political primacy of the South and the doctrine that the states were sovereign agents in the federal compact. After 1865, Jefferson's "Virginia-writ-large" version of the United States was gone with the proverbial wind, and his convictions about the proper distribution of power between state and federal governments, if not completely washed away, were permanently put on the defensive.

The second wave, really a series of waves, struck between 1890 and 1920. In 1890 the census of the United States revealed that the frontier phase of American history was over. (Frederick Jackson Turner's influential essay "The Significance of the Frontier in American History" three years later announced that "the frontier is gone and with its going has closed the first period of American history.") Then the Census of 1920 reported that for the first time the majority of American citizens lived in urban as opposed to rural areas. And between these two dates the United States accepted a huge influx of European and Asian immigrants that permanently altered the previously Anglo-Saxon character of the American population. Taken together, these demographic changes transformed Jefferson's agrarian vision into a nostalgic memory, his belief in the resuscitative powers of the West into a democratic myth and his presumption of Anglo-Saxon hegemony into a racial relic.[5]

The third wave arrived in the 1930s with the New Deal. In hindsight, one could actually see it coming from the early years of the twentieth century, when the effects of urbanization, industrialization, the increased density of the population and the exponential growth of corporate power over the economy combined to generate a need for a more centralized government to regulate the inequities of the marketplace and discipline the boisterous energies of an industrial economy. Herbert Croly's *The Promise of American Life* (1909) had prophesied and championed these political changes, but it took Roosevelt's New Deal to implement and institutionalize them. Roosevelt's appropriation of Jefferson as a New Deal Democrat was one of the most inspired acts of political thievery in American history, since the growth of federal power during the New Deal represented the triumph, in Jeffersonian terms, of "consolidation" over "diffusion." The New Deal was in fact the death knell for Jefferson's idea of a minimalist government.[6]

The fourth and final wave came crashing down between 1950 and 1965. The onset of the Cold War in the late 1940s employed an essentially Jeffersonian moralism to mobilize public opinion against the Soviet Union. But with National Security Memorandum 68 in 1950, the United States committed itself to a massive military establishment to fight the Cold War that embodied precisely the kind of standing army (and navy and air force) that Jefferson abhorred. Meanwhile the Supreme Court decision in *Brown* v. *Board of Education,* then the civil rights legislation of the early 1960s, institutionalized the ideal of a biracial American society, making Jefferson's belief in the physical and legal separation of blacks and whites an anachronism. Lyndon Johnson's Great Society, with its entrenched military establishment, its dedication to the welfare state, its extension of full citizenship to blacks and women, represented the epitome of political corruption in the Jeffersonian scheme, as well as the repudiation of racial and gender differences that Jefferson regarded as rooted in fixed principles of nature.[7]

The mention of "fixed principles of nature" suggests an entirely different series of waves generated by the winds of change in the scientific as opposed to the political world. Chief among these are the discoveries associated with Charles Darwin, Sigmund Freud and Albert Einstein, which, taken together, completely shattered Jefferson's premodern assumptions about the physical principles that governed the natural world as well as the relationship between what he called "the heart and the head." The entire mental universe in which Jefferson did his thinking has changed so dramatically, modern science has so unmoored all the "fixed principles" that he took for granted, that any direct connection between then and now must be regarded as a highly questionable enterprise.[8]

It should now be abundantly clear that the ingrained reticence of historians to translate Jefferson across the ages is rooted in more than mere timidity; it is grounded in a fuller appreciation of the sea change that separates his world from our own. To extend the image of sand castles on the beach, it is not just that successive waves of change have swamped Jefferson's core convictions; it is also that the shape of the entire shoreline has been completely reconfigured. The decisive demographic and attitudinal changes that made the United States "post-Jeffersonian" occurred between 1890 and 1920. Ironically, one of the most discernible strands of Jeffersonian thought that remains very much alive is the steadfast reluctance, in some instances downright refusal, to accept the political implications of these changes.

The chief voice for this potent version of Jeffersonian nostalgia in the late twentieth century is the conservative wing of the Republican party. Starting with Barry Goldwater in the 1960s, then reaching a crescendo of national success with Ronald Reagan in the 1980s and continuing with Newt Gingrich's Contract with America in the 1990s, the conservative movement has campaigned against the encroaching character of the federal government, much as Jefferson campaigned against the consolidating tendencies of the English Parliament in the 1770s, the Hamiltonian financial program of the 1790s and federal efforts to block the expansion of slavery in the 1820s. It is not just that the Republican desire to shift power from the federal to the state governments echoes Jefferson's constitutional preference; more significantly the deeper echo is his profound hostility to government power per se. Indeed, since the end of the Cold War in 1989, the American government has replaced the Soviet Union as our domestic version of the Evil Empire.[9]

This is pure Jefferson, both in its congenital aversion to centralized authority located far from local communities and in its tendency to overlook the legitimate reasons why these political institutions at the federal level came into existence in the first place. Like Jefferson upon his ascendancy to the presidency in 1800, modern conservatives conceive their task as a dismantling operation designed to remove the accumulated political debris that has built up since the golden age. For Jefferson the clock needed to be turned back to 1776. For modern conservatives the target date is more elusive: 1963 (pre–Great Society); 1932 (pre–New Deal); even 1890 (pre-Progressivism). The underlying logic of conservative thought clearly regards the entire federal edifice that has developed in post-Jeffersonian America—that is, over the past century—as both dangerous and dispensable. One could argue that this is primarily a rhetorical posture, that no one seriously contemplates the elimination of Social Security or the Federal Reserve Board, that in fact the quadrennial assaults on the powers of the federal government have had little, if any, impact on the growth of federal spending or the size of the Washington bureaucracy. Nevertheless, the rhetorical prowess of Jefferson's antigovernment ethos should not be underestimated as an influence on the special character of political discourse. Unlike any other nation-state in the modern world, the very idea of government power is stigmatized in the United States. And it is the residual power of Jeffersonian rhetoric that keeps government on the defensive. This potent strand of Jeffersonian thought remains alive and well in the conservative wing of the Republican party.[10]

The persistent and even reinvigorated vitality of the antigovernment ethos cuts two ways, however, because its rhetorical relevance as a distinctly Jeffersonian way to frame questions about public policy means that on the most disturbing and controversial problems in contemporary American society—abortion, drugs, poverty, crime—the Jeffersonian legacy has little to say. The debate about such social problems is a debate about government's proper role, and from a Jeffersonian perspective, government should have no role at all. As Carl Becker put it, Jefferson believed that "the only thing to do with political power, since it is inherently dangerous, is to abate it."

Within that antigovernment context, Jefferson's most enduring legacy is the principle of religious freedom, defined as the complete separation of church and state, though he would be distressed to know that the chief defender of this negative principle in the last half of the twentieth century has been the Supreme Court, the branch of government he hated most. Nevertheless, the principle that the government has no business interfering with a person's religious beliefs or practices is the one specific Jeffersonian idea that has negotiated the passage from the late eighteenth to the late twentieth century without any significant change in character or coloration.[11]

His other enduring legacies are less specific and must be sought at more rarefied regions where the thinner intellectual atmosphere makes it much easier to mistake platitudes for ideas. Two examples of the dangers entailed in working at such altitudes might serve as object lessons that improve our prospects of avoiding the same vacuous fate. First, a host of otherwise intelligent commentators, following the lead of Gunnar Myrdal in *An American Dilemma* (1943), have claimed that the core ideas of what he called the American Creed, as first articulated by Jefferson in the natural rights section of the Declaration of Independence, constitute the intellectual common ground on which America's many different racial and ethnic groups can congregate. Jefferson's most eloquent words, and the ideas of freedom and equality they proclaim, thereby become the intellectual cement or glue holding multiracial America together.[12]

Not only is it rather preposterous to believe than an abstract idea can perform such a massive social function, but it also flies in the face of all that we know about the historical Jefferson to make him an advocate of racial equality or the modern-day multiracial ideal. He was a staunch believer in white Anglo-Saxon supremacy, as were several other leading figures in the revolutionary generation. Moreover, he went out of his way to identify the differences between the races as products of nature rather than nurture. Martin Luther King, Jr., was right to deliver his "I Have a Dream" speech on the steps of the Lincoln Memorial, for it was Lincoln's expansive revision of the original Jeffersonian version of the natural rights philosophy that broadened the message to include blacks. While it is plausible to cite Jefferson as an enemy of slavery, though even here the evidence of his life contradicts the logical imperatives of his thought, it is a wholesale distortion of both his life and his thought to describe him as a friend to racial integration.

Second, Jefferson has become the preeminent historical source for presidents and public officials eager to sound an optimistic note about the superiority of American political institutions and ideas and the foreordained character of their eventual triumph. A host of Jefferson quotations can in fact be gathered to support this most optimistic form of patriotism. The Cold War, for example, was waged within the intensely moralistic and dualistic Jeffersonian categories of thought. And it is neither implausible nor ahistorical to imagine Jefferson describing the collapse of the Soviet Union in 1989 as the culmination of the global struggle launched with the American and French revolutions, the long-term war of ideas fated to replace despotic regimes dependent upon coercion with representative governments and market economies based on popular consent and personal voluntarism.

On the other hand, it is misleading and in the end dead wrong to equate Jefferson's optimism about the outcome of the international struggle, often depicted in cosmic terms with providential guarantees, and his more specific vision of the United States as the eternal City on the Hill. Jefferson did not believe, as Ronald Reagan put it, that "it is always morning in America." Toward the end of his life especially, he was extremely pessimistic about the long-term viability of the American nation he had helped create. Although it is true that he was distinctive within the revolutionary generation for his way of describing America's limitless horizons, even Jefferson shared with his fellow founders the realistic realization that all nations, including the United States, had limited life spans.

Madison, writing in 1829, predicted that the American republic would last for another hundred years, a prediction that must have looked eerily prescient at the start of the Great Depression. Adams oscillated between apocalyptic warnings that the end was close and more sanguine projections ranging up to another century and a half. Even though one of the most seductive features of Jeffersonian thought was its capacity to levitate out of its specific historical context, Jefferson shared with other members of the revolutionary generation the belief that all rising nations must eventually fall, that America's political success depended on a favorable set of social, economic and demographic conditions, chiefly the existence of vast tracts of western land, that would eventually run out. As Drew McCoy has so succinctly put it, Jefferson hoped to delay the inevitable ravages of time by extending the American experiment through space. (John Kennedy's New Frontier represented the same Jeffersonian impulse projected into space itself.) As we have seen, those favorable conditions disappeared between 1890 and 1920, so that the entire political landscape of twentieth-century America would have struck Jefferson as alien, indeed symptomatic of American degeneration along what he regarded as the corrupt path of the British Empire. If, in other words, we wished to conjure up Jefferson standing atop the Berlin Wall and leading the cheers for its demolition, we must also realize that the victorious version of democratic politics and capitalistic economics triumphant at the end of the twentieth century was not at all what he had in mind.[13]

Virtually all commentators who ascend into the rarefied regions in pursuit of Jefferson's enduring legacy eventually end up discovering its essence in the natural rights section of the Declaration of Independence and the ideal of individual freedom it so eloquently celebrates. At the beginning of the twentieth century Woodrow Wilson, questing after what he called "The Spirit of Jefferson," found it in "the right of the individual to a free opportunity. . . ." At the end of the century Joyce Appleby, engaging in the same quest, also concluded that Jefferson's "most enduring legacy, entailed on us in the name of nature, has been a particular understanding of human freedom." In between these interpreters countless orators, statesmen and scholars have sounded a similar note, usually as part of a patriotic hymn in which Jefferson has proved a serviceable source for campaigns against foreign foes, such as Germany, Japan and the Soviet Union, or in domestic battles against such contradictory targets as labor unions and corporate power, welfare legislation and entrenched poverty, the death penalty and the right to die. Jeffersonian rhetoric lends itself naturally to this kind of benign dilution and functional promiscuity. Where the real Jeffersonian idea ends and the platitudinous cant begins has become an unanswerable question.[14]

Clearly, Jefferson's own conception of individual freedom was more restricted than modern-day notions. His vision was essentially negative: freedom from encroachments by either church or state. It was all a piece with his antigovernment ethos and therefore incompatible with our contemporary conviction about personal entitlements, whether it be for a decent standard of living, a comfortable retirement or adequate health care, all of which depend on precisely the kind of government sponsorship he would have found intrusive. His was the freedom to be left alone, which has more in common with twentieth-century claims to privacy rights than more aggressive claims to political or economic power. He really had little to say about the positive ways that Americans should use their individual freedom, though the nineteenth-century scramble for wealth, then the twentieth-century pursuit of unprecedented levels of consumption, would surely have left him disappointed in his fellowman.

For all those reasons modern-day invocations of Jefferson as "the apostle of freedom" are invariably misleading and problematic. Nevertheless, even though the content of the idea has changed in several expensive ways since Jefferson's time, what has not changed, and what remains a truly powerful Jeffersonian legacy, is the format within which all considerations of personal freedom are framed. Alone among the influential political thinkers of the revolutionary generation, Jefferson began with the assumption of individual sovereignty, then attempted to develop prescriptions for government that at best protected individual rights and at worst minimized the impact of government or the powers of the state on individual lives. Both Adams and Madison and, to an even greater extent, Hamilton, began with the assumption of society as a collective unit, which was embodied in the government, which itself should then be designed to maximize individual freedom within the larger context of public order. Jefferson did not worry about public order, believing as he did that individuals liberated from the last remnants of feudal oppression would interact freely to create a natural harmony of interests that was guided, like Adam Smith's marketplace, by invisible or veiled forms of discipline. This belief, as Adams tried to tell him in the correspondence of their twilight years, was always an illusion, but it was an extraordinarily attractive illusion that proved extremely efficacious during the rowdy "takeoff" years of the American economy in the nineteenth century, when geographic and economic growth generated its own topsy-turvy version of dynamic order. Not until the late nineteenth century, with the end of the frontier and the emergence of the massive economic inequalities of the Gilded Age, was it fully exposed as an illusion.

But by then the Jeffersonian formulation of individual freedom as the bedrock conviction and the privileged starting point in all political debates was firmly entrenched. Just as Jefferson himself was prepared to abandon the principle temporarily when great opportunities (i.e., the Louisiana Purchase) or great crises (the Embargo Act of 1807) required it, twentieth-century Americans have only been willing to adopt a more collectivistic mentality when threatened by the Great Depression or by foreign foes during World War II and then the Cold War. But individual sovereignty remains the seminal conviction and the ideological home-base for all mainstream political thinking after the threats recede. It continues to frame political conversations in ways that put all communal schemes and proposals for group rights, like affirmative action, on the defensive. At the end of his panoramic review of American democratic culture, Robert Wiebe has concluded that the Jeffersonian ideal of "self-government," though a contradiction in terms, remains the abiding belief of most Americans: "The substantial body of contemporary criticism that singles out individualism as the special curse of American democracy simply flies in the face of its history. Telling Americans to improve democracy by sinking comfortably into community, by losing themselves in a collective life, is calling into the wind. There never has been an American democracy without its powerful strand of individualism, and nothing suggests there will ever be."[15] For better and for worse, American political discourse is phrased in Jeffersonian terms as a conversation about sovereign individuals who only grudgingly and in special circumstances are prepared to compromise that sovereignty for larger social purposes.

Finally, Jefferson created a particular style of leadership adapted to the special requirements of American political culture that remains relevant two centuries later. It is a style based on the capacity to rest comfortably with contradictions. If you begin with the conviction that government is at best a necessary evil, then effective political leadership must be indirect and unthreatening. It must cloak the exercise of power from public view, appear to be a tamer and more innocuous activity than it really is. If there is also an inherent disjunction between the ideals on which the nation is founded (i.e., individual freedom, equality of opportunity and popular sovereignty) and the imperatives of effective government, imperatives which require the capacity to coerce and discipline the undecided and faint of heart, then effective leadership, especially at the executive level, must be capable of benign deception. And if the political culture claims to derive its authority from popular opinion, which is by definition divided over the contested questions of the day, then leadership must at least appear to be followship, and the knack of political survival requires the skill to use language in ways that permit different constituencies to hear what they are listening for.

Within the corporate world and the military profession, late-twentieth-century America does permit more direct, more conspicuous, less elusive styles of leadership. But in the political realm, authority remains severely circumscribed and must achieve its ends more covertly. Television has only intensified the manipulative milieu; instant, more accurate polling techniques have only amplified the influence of popular opinion. The exponential growth in the size of government over the course of the century, at the same time as the Jeffersonian hostility to government flourishes in the deepest corners of the culture, places an even greater premium on paradox by enhancing the attractiveness of political candidates who, like Jefferson in 1800, claim to despise the federal government they are campaigning to head.

Jefferson did not come to this style self-consciously, did not hone his personality to fit the requirements of popular leadership in a political culture inherently suspicious of government. The style came to him naturally. His protestations about public life were completely sincere. If he were reincarnated and invited to run for political office in our time, he would almost certainly decline in favor of the tranquillity of Monticello. But by temperament and disposition he possessed the internal agility to generate multiple versions of the truth, the rhetorical skills to propose policies that different audiences could hear favorably, the deep deviousness only possible in a dedicated idealist, the honest aversion to the very power he pursued so effectively. These remain invaluable political talents. And the bedrock moralistic simplicity of the Jeffersonian vision has only increased its political potency as the size of the American electorate has grown larger and more unwieldy. If we could ever persuade him to run, he would remain a formidable candidate for national office.

APPENDIX

A NOTE ON THE SALLY HEMINGS SCANDAL

Modern-day journalists and social commentators have frequently claimed that candidates for national office during the last third of the twentieth century have been exposed to unprecedented scrutiny into their personal, especially their sexual, lives. While the proliferation of talk shows and tabloids has certainly intensified the appetite for scandal by making such stories readily available to a mass market, the primal urge to know about the sexual secrets of the rich or famous is apparently as timeless as the primal urge itself. Long before we learned about the sexual escapades of Presidents Kennedy or Clinton or, before them, Harding and Franklin Roosevelt, there was the story of Jefferson and Sally. Indeed the alleged liaison between Thomas Jefferson and Sally Hemings may be described as the longest-running miniseries in American history.

The history of the story itself falls naturally, if not neatly, into three discernible phases. The first was the early nineteenth century, when James Callender published the initial accusations and the Federalist press spread them across the country. Callender's motives, all historians agree, were scurrilous and vengeful. He probably heard the rumors about miscegenation at Monticello while imprisoned in Richmond—it was a story that had been making the rounds in Virginia for several years—and felt no compunction about reporting the gossip as fact. His charges, while obviously motivated by the basest personal and political motives, derived a measure of credibility from three different factors. First, Callender had accurately reported on the adulterous affair between Alexander Hamilton and Maria Reynolds in 1797; while wildly irresponsible and blatantly smut-seeking, he tended to exaggerate rather than tell outright lies. Second, Sally Hemings did have several children who were obviously fathered by a white man and some of whom had features that resembled those of Jefferson. Third, Callender had correctly accused Jefferson of making unsolicited advances toward Elizabeth Walker, a married woman, when he was a young bachelor in 1768. Jefferson acknowledged the truth of this youthful indiscretion in 1805, made a public apology to her husband, John Walker, but claimed it was the only charge "founded on truth among all their allegations against me." Nevertheless, the accuracy of the Walker accusation lent a measure of credibility to the Sally story.

The next chapter in the story, which occurred in the middle decades of the nineteenth century, produced two new pieces of evidence, each important in its own right, but together contradicting each other. In 1873 Madison Hemings, Sally's next to last child (born in 1805), gave an interview to the *Pike County* (Ohio) *Republican* claiming that his mother had identified Thomas Jefferson as his father and, in fact, the father of all her children. This claim was verified by Israel Jefferson, another ex-slave from Monticello, also living in Ohio at the time and a longtime friend of Madison Hemings's. The following year, in 1874, James Parton published his *Life of Thomas Jefferson* and reported another story that had been circulating within the Jefferson and Randolph families for many years—to wit, that Jefferson's nephew Peter Carr had been the father of all or most of Sally's children and that he had admitted as much to Martha Jefferson when she had confronted him with the charge. Sally's children looked like Jefferson, then, because they were related, but through Carr rather than Jefferson himself. This version of miscegenation on the mountaintop received partial corroboration from Edmund Bacon, the former manager of Monticello, who claimed in his interview of 1862 that he had seen another man leaving Sally's quarters "many a morning." There were now two different versions of the Sally story placed before the public, one rooted in the oral tradition of the Hemings family and the other in the oral tradition of the white descendants of the Jefferson-Randolph family.

The third chapter of the story dates from the 1950s, when the scholarship on Jefferson, especially the massive publication project led by Julian Boyd and the authoritative six-volume biography by Dumas Malone, generated fresh evidence and a new and spirited debate about its meaning. Although the most dramatic episode occurred in 1974, with the publication of Fawn Brodie's *Thomas Jefferson: An Intimate History,* a national best-seller that argued in favor of the liaison and even claimed that Jefferson and Sally Hemings loved each other, the new evidence in fact came from Malone. Despite his own forcefully argued conclusion that the Sally story was a fictional creation of Callender and nothing more, Malone's research revealed that Jefferson was present at Monticello nine months prior to the birth of each of Sally's children. Since he was often away at Philadelphia or Washington, and since Sally never conceived in his absence, the timing of her pregnancies was compatible with his paternity. In 1993 the researchers at the Thomas Jefferson Memorial Foundation discovered a "missing" daughter, born in 1799, who had died soon thereafter. That birth was also compatible with Jefferson's residence at Monticello. Although Brodie's book ignited a raging debate within the scholarly world and then a proliferation of biographies, novels, films and popular magazine stories, it was in truth Malone's findings about the chronology of Sally's pregnancies that constituted the most tangible piece of new evidence to support the charge of a sexual liaison.

Where does that leave the matter? Well, unless the trustees of the Thomas Jefferson Memorial Foundation decide to exhume the remains and do DNA testing on Jefferson as well as some of his alleged progeny, it leaves the matter a mystery about which advocates on either side can freely speculate, and surely will. Within the scholarly world, especially within the community of Jefferson specialists, there seems to be a clear consensus that the story is almost certainly not true. Within the much murkier world of popular opinion, especially within the black community, the story appears to have achieved the status of a self-evident truth. If either side of this debate were to file for damages in a civil suit requiring a preponderance of evidence as the standard, it is difficult to imagine an impartial jury finding for either plaintiff. Jefferson's most ardent defenders still live under the influence of what might be called the Virginia gentleman ethos (i.e., this is not something that a Virginia gentleman would do), which increasingly has the quaint and charmingly naive sound of an honorable anachronism. Meanwhile those who wholeheartedly endorse the truth of the story, either in Callender's original version as a tale of lust and rape, or in Brodie's later rendering as a tragic romance between America's premier biracial couple, have also allowed their own racial, political or sexual agenda to take precedence over the evidence. On the basis of what we know now, we can never know.

That was then. In the original edition I went on to speculate that the likelihood of a Jefferson-Hemings liaison was remote, offering several plausible readings of the indirect evidence (i.e., Jefferson's voice in his letters to women; the reasons his enemies doubted the charges) to support my conjecture. No matter how plausible my interpretation, it turns out to have been dead wrong.

In the November 5, 1998, issue of *Nature*, the results of a DNA comparison between Jefferson's Y chromosome and the Y chromosome of several Hemings descendants demonstrated a match between Jefferson and Eston Hemings. Comparisons between the Y chromosome from the Carr line yielded negative results, as did comparisons between Jefferson and the first of Sally's children, Thomas Woodson. In effect, the interpretation offered by the white Jefferson descendants was discredited; the interpretation offered by the Hemings descendants was partially supported.

But the Eston match is the crucial new evidence and really all that matters, since it is virtually impossible to believe that a sixty-four-year-old Jefferson fathered a child by Sally Hemings six years after the Callender accusations surfaced in a Monticello version of the one-night stand. Sally gave birth to seven children between 1790 and 1808. Whether Jefferson fathered all of them will probably never be known. But the match with Eston shifts the burden of proof toward the presumption that Jefferson was the father of each. The likelihood of a long-standing sexual relationship between Jefferson and Hemings can never be proven absolutely, but it is now proven beyond a reasonable doubt.

November 1998

NOTES

ABBREVIATIONS

AHR *American Historical Review*

Boyd Julian P. Boyd et al., eds., The Papers of Thomas Jefferson, 25 vols. to date (Princeton, 1950–)

Cappon Lester G. Cappon, ed., *The Adams-Jefferson Letters: The Complete Correspondence Between Thomas Jefferson and Abigail and John Adams,* 2 vols. (Chapel Hill, 1959)

Domestic Life Sarah N. Randolph, *The Domestic Life of Thomas Jefferson* (Charlottesville, 1978). Originally published 1871

Family Letters Edwin Morris Betts and James A. Bear, eds., *The Family Letters of Thomas Jefferson* (Columbia, 1966)

Farm Book Edwin Morris Betts, ed., *Thomas Jefferson's Farm Book, with Commentary and Relevant Extracts from Other Writings* (Princeton, 1953)

Ford Paul Leicester Ford, ed., *The Writings of Thomas Jefferson,* 10 vols. (New York, 1892–99)

History	Henry Adams, *History of the United States of America During the Administrations of Thomas Jefferson*, 2 vols. (New York, 1986). Library of America edition. Originally published 1889–91
JAH	*Journal of American History*
JER	*Journal of the Early Republic*
JSH	*Journal of Southern History*
L&B	Andrew A. Lipscomb and Albert Ellery Bergh, eds., *The Writings of Thomas Jefferson*, 20 vols. (Washington, D.C., 1905)
LC	Library of Congress
Malone	Dumas Malone, *Jefferson and His Time*, 6 vols. (Boston, 1948–81)
Randall	Henry S. Randall, *The Life of Thomas Jefferson*, 3 vols. (New York, 1958)
Smith	James Morton Smith, ed., *The Republic of Letters: The Correspondence Between Thomas Jefferson and James Madison 1776–1826*, 3 vols. (New York, 1995)
VMHB	*Virginia Magazine of History and Biography*
WMQ	*William and Mary Quarterly*, 3d. Ser.

The notes that follow represent my attempt to adopt a commonsensical approach to the customary rules of scholarly citation. Jefferson presents a daunting challenge in this regard, in part because he himself left such a massive trail of literary evidence, in part because he subsequently attracted so many biographers and historians that the secondary literature on his life is truly imposing, and in part because his life crossed over virtually all the major political, social, cultural and intellectual developments of revolutionary America, each of which has generated substantial scholarly literatures in its own right. A full accounting of all the sources consulted, in short, would require another book as long as this one. This strikes me as silly, as well as a course vulnerable to the charge of conspicuous erudition. I have tried to cite all the primary sources from which I quote in the text. I have also tried to cite those secondary works and those titles that had a decided impact on my thinking. When it comes to Jefferson, the unspoken truth is that no mere mortal can read everything, and no sane reader would want an exhaustive account of all that has been consulted. In partial compensation for my sins of omission, I have littered the notes below with interpretive assessments of the sources cited, thereby giving the endnotes the occasional flavor of a bibliographic essay.

PROLOGUE. JEFFERSONIAN SURGE: AMERICA, 1992–93

1. Merrill Peterson, *The Jefferson Image in the American Mind* (New York, 1960), 395–420.

2. *Ibid.*, 375–76.

3. *Ibid.*, 377–78.

4. Information on the number of visitors to the Jefferson Memorial was provided by the National Park Service.

5. Jim Strupp, ed., *Revolution Song: Thomas Jefferson's Legacy* (Summit, N.J., 1992).

6. Mary Jo Salter to Joseph Ellis, February 5, 1993, author's personal correspondence.

7. Mary Jo Salter to Joseph Ellis, May 5, May 10, May 12, 1993.

8. Mary Jo Salter, *Sunday Skaters* (New York, 1994), 79–93.

9. Merrill Peterson, *Thomas Jefferson and the New Nation: A Biography* (New York, 1970), viii.

10. Susan R. Stein, *The Worlds of Thomas Jefferson* (New York, 1993).

11. See the review of the exhibit by Garry Wills, "The Aesthete," *New York Review of Books* (August 12, 1993), 6–10.

12. Douglas L. Wilson, "Thomas Jefferson and the Character Issue," *Atlantic Monthly,* CCLXX (November 1992), 62–64.

13. Frank Shuffleton, *Thomas Jefferson: A Comprehensive Annotated Bibliography of Writings About Him, 1826–1980* (New York, 1983) and, by the same author, *Thomas Jefferson, 1981–1990: An Annotated Bibliography* (New York, 1990).

14. Leonard Levy, *Jefferson and Civil Liberties: The Darker Side* (Cambridge, 1963); Winthrop Jordan, *White over Black: American Attitudes Toward the Negro, 1550–1812* (Chapel Hill, 1968).

15. Eric McKitrick, "The View from Jefferson's Camp," *New York Review of Books* (December 17, 1970), 35–38.

16. Paul Finkelman, "Jefferson and Slavery: 'Treason Against the Hopes of the World,' " in Peter S. Onuf, ed., *Jeffersonian Legacies* (Charlottesville, 1993), 181–221.

17. Scot A. French and Edward L. Ayers, "The Strange Career of Thomas Jefferson," in Onuf, ed., *Jeffersonian Legacies,* 449–50; *Washington Post,* October 17, 1992, D-1, D-4.

18. Peter S. Onuf, "The Scholars' Jefferson," *WMQ*, L (October 1993), 673–75.

19. *Ibid.*, 671–99.

20. Gordon Wood, "Jefferson at Home," *New York Review of Books* (May 13, 1993), 6–9.

21. *New York Times,* June 24, 1994, B-1, 3.

22. *Washington Post,* April 13, 1994, E-1.

23. E. A. Foster *et al.,* "Jefferson Fathered Slave's Last Child," *Nature,* November 5, 1998, 27–28; see also Eric S. Lander and Joseph J. Ellis, "DNA Analysis: Founding Father," *ibid.,* 13.

24. *U. S. News and World Report,* November 9, 1998, 58–69, which contains the fullest account of the DNA story as well as the popular response to it. My summary of the popular reaction is also based on the interviews that a group of my students at Mount Holyoke conducted with tourists at the Jefferson Memorial and Monticello as well as a reasonably thorough survey of the television talk shows the week following the *Nature* story.

I. PHILADELPHIA: 1775–76

1. *Boyd,* I, 169; *Randall,* I, 112; *Malone,* I, 202–03. The quotation about "haughty sultans" is from *Rivington's Gazette,* February 9, 1775.

2. On Jupiter, see *Farm Book,* 17; *Garden Book,* 269; *Family Letters,* 182–83.

3. For recollections of Jefferson's general appearance, see the comments by Isaac and Bacon in James A. Bear, ed., *Jefferson at Monticello* (Charlottesville, 1967), 4, 11, 83. The pen-and-ink drawing by du Simitière is reproduced as the frontpiece in Silvio A. Bedini, *Declaration of Independence Desk: Relic of Revolution* (Washington, D.C., 1981). Most leading authorities question the authenticity of this drawing, believing it to be of someone else.

4. Bear, ed., *Jefferson at Monticello,* 13, 18, 72–73, for the erect posture and "incessant singing." Other vivid firsthand descriptions are available in Margaret Bayard Smith, *The First Forty Years of Washington Society,* ed. Gaillard Hunt (New York, 1906), 69; Richard Beale Davis, ed., *Jeffersonian America* (San Marino, 1954), 10–12; E. S. Maclay, ed., *Journal of William Maclay, 1789–91* (New York, 1891), 113. The different portraits are gathered in Fiske Kimball, *The Life Portraits of Jefferson and Their Replicas* (Philadelphia, 1944) and Alfred L. Bush, *The Life Portraits of Thomas Jefferson* (Charlottesville, 1987). The best secondary accounts of Jefferson's physical appearance are

Malone, I, 48, and Garry Wills, *Inventing America: Jefferson's Declaration of Independence* (New York, 1978), 14–15. See also the files on "Jefferson's Physical Appearance" in the Research Department, Thomas Jefferson Memorial Foundation, Monticello. A nice summary of the contested character of Jefferson's appearance is in Peterson, *Jefferson Image,* 244–45.

5. This concise synthesis of the early years is drawn from the standard biographies. The best ones for this period are Marie Kimball, *Jefferson: The Road to Glory, 1743–1776* (New York, 1943); *Malone,* I, 3–112; Willard Sterne Randall, *Thomas Jefferson: A Life* (New York, 1993), 1–31, which engages in intriguing speculation about Jefferson's attitude toward his mother, all of it highly conjectural. The quotation about being carried by a slave to Tuckahoe is in *Randall,* I, 11. The matter of the Shadwell fire is nicely summed up in John Dos Passos, *The Head and Heart of Thomas Jefferson* (Garden City, 1954), 159.

6. Frank L. Dewey, *Thomas Jefferson, Lawyer* (Charlottesville, 1986).

7. On the decision to build Monticello and the earliest efforts at construction, see Jack McLaughlin, *Jefferson and Monticello: Biography of a Builder* (New York, 1988), 146–76; see also *Malone,* I, 143–52. For the political decision to enter the House of Burgesses, see *Malone,* I, 128–42. A concise summary of the political context in the Virginia House of Burgesses is in Jack P. Greene, "Foundations of Power in the Virginia House of Burgesses, 1720–1776," *WMQ,* X (1959), 485–506. Efforts to explain the reasons why the wealthy planters of Virginia were nearly unanimous in opposing British authority from 1765 to 1776 have moved past crudely economic explanations (i.e., indebtedness to English creditors). The most sophisticated overview of the political psychology within the Tidewater elite is T. H. Breen, *Tobacco Culture: The Mentality of the Great Tidewater Planters on the Eve of the Revolution* (Princeton, 1985). The best review of the issues is Herbert Sloan and Peter Onuf, "Politics, Culture and the Revolution in Virginia: A Review of Recent Work," *VMHB,* XCI (1983), 258–84.

8. *Malone,* I, 153–65; *Boyd,* I, 86–88. Douglas L. Wilson, "Thomas Jefferson's Early Notebooks," *WMQ,* XLII (1985), 433–52.

9. *Ford,* I, 6, for Jefferson's recollection of listening to Henry in his autobiography.

10. Jefferson to Thomas Adams, June 1, 1771, *Boyd,* I, 71–72, for the piano quotation; Jefferson to Archibald Cary and Benjamin Harrison, December 9, 1774, *ibid.,* I, 154–56, for the sashed windows.

11. This summary follows the general interpretive line of *Malone,* I, 182–96.

12. The quotations by Ward and Adams are most conveniently available in *Boyd*, I, 675–76, which is part of Boyd's note on *Summary View*.

13. For the best analysis of *Summary View*, see H. Trevor Colbourn, *The Lamp of Experience: Whig History and the Intellectual Origins of the American Revolution* (Chapel Hill, 1965), 158–64. The most recent appraisal, with an exhaustive account of the secondary literature, is Stephen A. Conrad, "Putting Rights Talk in Its Place: *The Summary View* Revisited," Onuf, ed., *Jeffersonian Legacies*, 254–80. The original draft of *Summary View* is in *Boyd*, I, 121–34.

14. *Boyd*, I, 125, for the quotations.

15. For the constitutional context of Jefferson's argument about parliamentary power, see Anthony Lewis, "Jefferson's *Summary View* as a Chart of Political Union," *WMQ*, V (1948), 34–51.

16. *Boyd*, I, 129–31.

17. *Ibid.*, I, 121–23.

18. On the "expatriation" theme, see Colbourn, *Lamp of Experience*, 158–64; there is also an excellent discussion in Wills, *Inventing*, 84–89. Jefferson's draft of the document designed to "prove" the purity of the original migration is in *Boyd*, I, 277–85.

19. *Ford*, I, 10, for Jefferson's autobiographical recollection.

20. The authoritative account of the episode is by Benjamin W. Labaree, *The Boston Tea Party* (New York, 1964); for a hilarious juxtaposition of Jefferson's version in *Summary View* with the real story, see Wills, *Inventing*, 27–28.

21. The quotation is from Jefferson to John Randolph, August 25, 1775, *Boyd*, I, 241; for Jefferson's childlike demeanor in building Monticello, see McLaughlin, *Monticello*, 373–74.

22. Jefferson to John Page, December 25, 1762, then again on January 20, 1763, *Boyd*, I, 3–8, for the anticipation of Rebecca's interest; then Jefferson to John Page, October 7, 1763, *ibid.*, I, 11–12, for the disillusionment with his rejection. On the stilted and adolescent prose style, see *ibid.*, I, 80–81. The best appraisal of Jefferson's sentimentalism is the excellent new book by Andrew Burstein, *The Inner Jefferson: Portrait of a Grieving Optimist* (Charlottesville, 1995).

23. One catches a provocative glimmering of these tendencies in Richard K. Matthews, *The Radical Politics of Thomas Jefferson: A Revisionist View* (Lawrence, 1984).

24. Lyman Butterfield, ed., *The Diary and Autobiography of John Adams* (4 vols., Cambridge, 1961), II, 121, 173, 182. My version of the Adams tem-

perament is more fully available in Joseph Ellis, *Passionate Sage: The Character and Legacy of John Adams* (New York, 1993).

25. On Pendleton, see David John Mays, *Edmund Pendleton, 1721–1803* (2
vols., Cambridge, 1952).

26. The best descriptions of Lee are in Edmund Randolph, *History of
Virginia,* ed. Arthur Shaffer (Charlottesville, 1970). See also Wills, *Inventing,* 3–4.

27. William Henry Wirt, *Patrick Henry: Life, Correspondence and Speeches*
(3 vols., New York, 1891) is the fullest account of Henry's life and career.
The best recent study is Richard R. Beeman, *Patrick Henry: A Biography*
(New York, 1974). The quotations from Randolph and Jefferson are reproduced in Beeman, *Patrick Henry,* 192, 133.

28. Butterfield, ed., *Diary and Autobiography,* III, 335.

29. Douglas L. Wilson, ed., *Jefferson's Commonplace Book* (Princeton,
1989), for specific entries and explicit examples of Jefferson's note-taking
habits.

30. The cost accounting of the war is in *Boyd,* I, 182–84; the prediction
of a short war is in Jefferson to John Randolph, November 29, 1775, *ibid.,* I,
269.

31. There is an excellent discussion of the awkward disjunction in the
Continental Congress by the summer of 1775 in Wills, *Inventing,* 48. The
quotations are from Jefferson to Francis Eppes, June 26, 1775, and Jefferson
to John Randolph, August 25, 1775, *Boyd,* I, 174–75, 242. The authoritative
modern study of the Continental Congress is Jack N. Rakove, *The Begin-
nings of National Politics: An Interpretive History of the Continental Congress*
(New York, 1979).

32. *Boyd,* I, 199–92. The quotations are taken from Jefferson's draft
rather than from the copy adopted by the Congress.

33. The full draft is in *ibid.,* I, 199–204. The earliest account of Jefferson's strong proclivity towards dichotomies is in Jordan, *White over Black,*
476–77.

34. Livingston's remarks are reproduced in *Boyd,* I, 189.

35. See the long note, containing all the quoted material, in *ibid.,* I,
187–92.

36. The final version of *Causes and Necessities* is in *ibid.,* I, 213–19.

37. *Ibid.,* I, 225–30, 276–77. The Adams quotation is from John Adams
to Timothy Pickering, April 11, 1822, Charles Francis Adams, ed., *The Works
of John Adams, Second President of the United States* (10 vols., 1850–56), II, 513.

38. On Jefferson's activities at Monticello, see *Malone*, I, 215–16. On the situation in Virginia, see Thad W. Tate, "The Coming of the Revolution in Virginia: Britain's Challenge to Virginia's Ruling Class, 1763–1776," *WMQ*, XIX (1962), 323–43.

39. The remark on his mother is from Jefferson to William Randolph, May–June, 1776, *Boyd*, I, 409.

40. Jefferson to Thomas Nelson, May 16, 1776, *ibid.*, I, 292.

41. *Jefferson*, I, 216–17; Bedini, *Declaration of Independence Desk*, 4–5. Jefferson eventually gave the desk to his granddaughter Ellen Randolph Colledge as a wedding present in 1825, predicting that "its imaginary value will increase with the years . . . , as the relics of the Saints are in those of the Church."

42. John Adams to Abigail Adams, March 17, 1776, Lyman Butterfield, ed., *Adams Family Correspondence* (3 vols., Cambridge, 1963), I, 410; John Adams to Abigail Adams, June 2, 1776, *ibid.*, II, 3.

43. Jefferson's three drafts of the Virginia constitution are reproduced in *Boyd*, I, 329–65.

44. *Ibid.*, I, 362–63, for the most progressive features in Jefferson's third and final draft.

45. *Ibid.*, I, 357.

46. *Ibid.*, I, 312–14, provides Jefferson's notes on the debate in the Continental Congress. The story told here has several contested features, the chief one being the reasons for selecting Jefferson over Lee. The fullest discussion of the controversy is in *Randall*, I, 145–62. Dumas Malone's synthesis in *Malone*, I, 217–19, is a model of fairness. Lee's resolution of June 7 is reproduced in *Boyd*, I, 298–99.

47. Butterfield, ed., *Diary and Autobiography*, III, 335–37, offers the classic Adams account, which mixes the truth with his own personal need to show posterity that he, not Jefferson, was in charge. For a discussion of Adams's persistent claim that the Declaration was no more than an elegant ornament to the crucial business in the Continental Congress, see Ellis, *Passionate Sage*, 64–65, 99–100.

48. The two authoritative studies of the chronology and different drafts of the Declaration are: Julian Boyd, *The Declaration of Independence: The Evolution of the Text* (Princeton, 1945) and John H. Hazelton, *The Declaration of Independence* (New York, 1906). Pauline Maier's forthcoming book, *Sacred Scriptures: Making the Declaration of Independence* (New York, 1997), which she graciously allowed me to read in draft form and which helped me in the

final stages of my own revisions, will unquestioningly become the new standard work. The Adams recollection is from Butterfield, ed., *Diary and Autobiography,* III, 336. Boyd attempts to hold open the possibility that the signing occurred on July 4, as Jefferson claimed, but the scholarly consensus is that Jefferson's memory was wrong. See *Papers,* I, 306–07. For a convenient summary of the many myths about the signing ceremony, see Charles Warren, "Fourth of July Myths," *WMQ,* II (1945), 242–48.

49. Jefferson's recollections are in Jefferson to James Madison, August 30, 1823, *Smith,* III, 223; Edmund Pendleton to Jefferson, July 22, 1776, *Papers,* 471.

50. Jefferson to Richard Henry Lee, July 8, 1776, *Boyd,* I, 455–56. Boyd's discussion of the revisions made by the Congress is the standard account, summarized in the long editorial note in *ibid.,* I, 413–17. But Boyd's account sometimes loses sight of the substantive issues at stake in ways that seem unnecessarily tedious. I found the account in Wills, *Inventing,* 306–17, most sensible.

51. *Boyd,* I, 314–15, 426.

52. Wills, *Inventing,* 72–73, provides a nice comparison of what Jefferson wrote in his drafts of the Virginia constitution and in the Declaration. It also provides reactions to this specific grievance by the British press, which did not fail to note the moral contradictions of slaveowners trumpeting liberty.

53. *Boyd,* I, 426.

54. *Ibid.,* I, 426–27; *Ford,* I, 21.

55. *Boyd,* I, 423; the most elegant version of the reverential interpretation is by Dumas Malone in *Jefferson,* I, 224–25. The Lincoln quotation, which dates from 1859, is cited in Wills, *Inventing,* xxi.

56. Jefferson to Richard Henry Lee, May 8, 1825, *Ford,* XVI, 118.

57. On Mason's role in the Virginia convention, see *Boyd,* I, 335.

58. For a convenient summary of the scholarly debate over the phrase "pursuit of happiness," see Wills, *Inventing,* 240–41. For the debate over Mason's language and its implications for slavery in Virginia, see Beeman, *Patrick Henry,* 100–02.

59. The classic statement of this liberal interpretation is Carl Becker, *The Declaration of Independence: A Study in the History of Political Ideas* (New York, 1922).

60. The seminal statement of this republican or collectivistic interpretation is Wills, *Inventing.* For a convincing critique of the Wills argument that

also reviews the evidence and implications of the Becker-Wills disagreement, see Ronald Hamowy, "Jefferson and the Scottish Enlightenment: A Critique of Garry Wills's Inventing America . . . ," *WMQ,* XXXVI (1979), 503–23.

61. Jay Fliegelman, *Declaring Independence: Jefferson, Natural Language, and the Culture of Performance* (Stanford, 1993). For the enthusiastic scholarly reaction to Fliegelman's novel thesis, see Peter Onuf, "The Scholars' Jefferson," *WMQ,* L (1993), 683–84.

62. *Boyd,* I, 78–81, for Jefferson's book list in 1771.

63. Jefferson to Edmund Pendleton, June 30, 1776; Jefferson to Francis Eppes, July 15, 1776; Jefferson to Richard Henry Lee, July 29, 1776, *Boyd,* I, 408, 458–59, 477.

64. *Ford,* I, 21–28, for his latter-day expression of disappointment in the Congress and reprinting of his own version alongside the official version.

65. Edmund Pendleton to Jefferson, August 10, 1776; Richard Henry Lee to Jefferson, July 21, 1776; John Page to Jefferson, July 20, 1776, *Boyd,* I, 488–89, 471, 470.

66. Jefferson to William Fleming, July 1, 1776; Jefferson to Edmund Pendleton, August 26, 1776, *ibid.,* I, 411–12, 503–07.

67. Jefferson to John Page, August 5, 1776, *ibid.,* I, 485–86.

68. Butterfield, ed., *Diary and Autobiography,* III, 336, for Adams's remarks on the political efficacy of silence. This was a popular Adams theme in old age; Jefferson was linked with Franklin and Washington as the "silent trinity." See John Adams to John Quincy Adams, July 15, 1813, *The Microfilm Edition of the Adams Papers* (608 reels, Boston, 1954–59), Reel 95.

69. Jefferson to John Hancock, October 11, 1776, *Boyd,* I, 524.

2. PARIS: 1784–89

1. Marie Kimball, *Jefferson: The Scene of Europe, 1784–1789* (New York, 1950), 5–9, offers the best descriptions of Jefferson's arrival in France and, more generally, the fullest coverage of the Paris years. See also *Malone,* II, 3–6. The forthcoming book by Howard Adams on Jefferson's years in Paris, which he has graciously allowed me to see in manuscript, promises to become the authoritative account.

2. Jefferson to William Templeton Franklin, August 18, 1784, *Boyd,* VII, 400. Howard C. Rice, *Thomas Jefferson's Paris* (Princeton, 1976) is splendid on the city as it looked when Jefferson arrived.

3. Kimball, *Scene of Europe,* 17–18.

4. *Malone,* I, 301–69, for the best narrative of Jefferson's years as governor, which at times takes on the tone of a defense attorney's brief for the accused.

5. Jefferson to James Monroe, May 20, 1782, *Boyd,* VI, 184–86.

6. The story of the deathbed promise first appeared in print in George Tucker, *The Life of Thomas Jefferson* (2 vols., Philadelphia, 1837), I, 158.

7. Edmund Randolph to James Madison, September 20, 1782, *Boyd,* VI, 199; *Family Letters,* 63.

8. For the best accounts of his reform efforts in Virginia, see *Malone,* I, 261–73; Peterson, *New Nation,* 79–107; John E. Selby, *The Revolution in Virginia* (Williamsburg, 1988), 14–99.

9. Jefferson to Jean Nicholas Démeunier, June 1786, *Boyd,* X, 63. For an overview of his work in the Congress, see *Malone,* I, 373–423; Peterson, *New Nation,* 241–96.

10. For Jefferson's views on the proper powers of the federal government over foreign affairs, see the long note by Julian Boyd in *Boyd,* VII, 463–70; Jefferson to James Monroe, June 17, 1785, *ibid.,* VIII, 230–31.

11. Jefferson to James Monroe, March 18, 1785, *Boyd,* VIII, 43.

12. The remark by John Quincy Adams is from his *Memoirs* and refers to a dinner party conversation in 1804. It is reproduced in *Boyd,* VII, 383.

13. Howard C. Rice, *L'Hôtel de Langeac, Jefferson's Paris Residence* (Charlottesville, 1947); for the map of Jefferson's various residences in Paris, see *Boyd,* VII, 453; for the cost, see *ibid.,* VIII, 485–88. A convenient summary is available in Kimball, *Scene of Europe,* 110–13.

14. Kimball, *Scene of Europe,* 11–15, for the most succinct treatment of the entourage. Jefferson to William Short, September 24, 1785, *Boyd,* VIII, 547, for the terms of Short's appointment. For Humphreys, see Francis L. Humphreys, *Life and Times of David Humphreys* (2 vols., New York, 1917), I, 2–9. For Patsy at Panthemont, see Jefferson to John Lowell, December 18, 1784, *Boyd,* VII, 576–77.

15. The quotation is from Jefferson to James Madison, December 8, 1784, *Boyd,* VII, 558–59. Good examples of the "listening post" syndrome as it was established are: James Madison to Jefferson, September 7, 1784, and Jefferson to William Short, April 2, 1785, *Boyd,* VII, 416–17; VIII, 68. On the friendship between Jefferson and Madison, see Adrienne Koch, *Jefferson and Madison: The Great Collaboration* (New York, 1950). See also the splendid introduction in *Smith,* I, 1–36.

16. Adams's observations on Jefferson are reproduced in *Boyd,* VII, 382–83. See also the editorial remarks in *Cappon,* I, xxxix–xl.

17. John Adams to Jefferson, January 22, 1825, *Cappon,* II, 606.

18. Jefferson to Abigail Adams, September 25, 1785, and Abigail Adams to Jefferson, February 11, 1786, *ibid.,* I, 69–70, 119–20. The best recent study of Abigail's career and character is Edith B. Gelles, *Portia: The World of Abigail Adams* (Bloomington, 1992).

19. Jefferson to Abigail Adams, August 9, 1786; Abigail Adams to Jefferson, October 19, 1785, November 24, 1785, October 7, 1785; Jefferson to Abigail Adams, October 11, 1785, July 9, 1786, *Cappon,* I, 148–49, 84, 79–80, 84–85, 141.

20. Elizabeth Wayles Eppes to Jefferson, October 13, 1784; Jefferson to Francis Eppes, February 5, 1785, *Boyd,* VII, 441, 635; Abigail Adams to Jefferson, July 23, 1786, *Cappon,* I, 146.

21. Abigail Adams to Jefferson, June 26, 1787, July 10, 1787; Jefferson to Abigail Adams, July 1, 1787, July 16, 1787; Abigail Adams to Jefferson, July 6, 1787, *Cappon,* I, 178–79, 183–85, 188.

22. Abigail Adams to Jefferson, September 10, 1787, *ibid.,* I, 197.

23. Abigail Adams to Jefferson, June 6, 1785, *ibid.,* I, 28. For Adams and Jefferson as America's "odd couple," see Ellis, *Passionate Sage,* 113–42.

24. Jefferson to William Stephens Smith, June 28, 1785, *Boyd,* VIII, 249; John Adams to Jefferson, March 1, 1787, *Cappon,* I, 175–76. Precisely what happened when the two men were introduced at the Court of St. James's is the subject of some disagreement, though their respective autobiographies tell the same story of George III's ostentatious gesture of disrespect. See Charles R. Ritcheson, "The Fragile Memory: Thomas Jefferson at the Court of George III," *Eighteenth Century Life,* VI (1981), 1–16.

25. Jefferson to John Adams, July 28, 1785; John Adams to Jefferson, September 4, 1785, *Cappon,* I, 46, 61.

26. Jefferson and John Adams to American Commissioners, March 28, 1786, *Boyd,* IX, 357–59.

27. See Julian Boyd's note on "Jefferson's Proposed Concert of Powers Against the Barbary Pirates," *Boyd,* X, 560–66.

28. John Adams to Jefferson, November 4, 1785, June 6, 1786, July 3, 1786, July 11, 1786, July 31, 1786; Jefferson to John Adams, July 11, 1786, *Cappon,* I, 89, 133–34, 139, 146, 142–43.

29. Commissioners of the Treasury to Jefferson, May 9, 1786, *Boyd,* IX, 479–81; Jefferson to Abigail Adams, September 25, 1785, *Cappon,* I, 70.

30. Claude Ann Lopez, *Mon Cher Papa: Franklin and the Ladies of Paris* (New Haven, 1990). For Jefferson's ranking of Franklin as next to Washing-

ton, and all others "on the second line," see Jefferson to William Carmichael, August 12, 1788, *Boyd*, XIII, 502.

31. See Boyd's note on Jefferson's introduction to Vergennes, *Boyd*, VIII, 157–58; the Franklin quotation on Adams is repeated, with a slight alteration, in Jefferson to James Madison, July 29, 1789, *ibid.*, XV, 316.

32. John Jay to Jefferson, August 18, 1786; Jefferson to James Monroe, August 11, 1786; James Madison to Jefferson, March 18, 1786, *ibid.*, X, 271–72, 223–25; IX, 334.

33. David Hartley to Jefferson, October 5, 1785; Jefferson to James Madison, April 25, 1786; Jefferson to Benjamin Franklin, October 5, 1785, *ibid.*, VIII, 587; IX, 433–34.

34. On Jefferson's belief in free markets, see Jefferson to Vergennes, November 20, 1785, and December 20, 1785, *ibid.*, IX, 51, 112. See also Jefferson to Louis Guillaume Otto, May 7, 1786, *ibid.*, IX, 470–71. The quotation is from Jefferson to John Bonfield, December 18, 1787, *ibid.*, XII, 434.

35. Jefferson to James Madison, December 20, 1784; John Jay to Jefferson, June 16, 1786, *ibid.*, VII, 563; IX, 650–51.

36. Jefferson to Calonne, January 7, 1787; Jefferson to John Jay, January 9, 1787; "Documents Concerning the Whale Industry," 1788, *ibid.*, XI, 25, 30; XIV, 217–72.

37. The most recent scholarly assessment of the Dutch loan is in John Ferling, "John Adams, Diplomat," *WMQ*, LI (1994), 227–52. See also Jefferson to John Adams, March 2, 1788, *Boyd*, XII, 637–38; Jefferson to John Adams, December 12, 1787, *Cappon*, I, 216.

38. Jefferson to John Adams, February 6, 1788; John Adams to Jefferson, February 12, 1788, *Cappon*, I, 224–25.

39. The selection from Chastellux's *Travels in America* is conveniently available in *Boyd*, VII, 585–86, along with a note by Julian Boyd on Chastellux, who had served as an officer in the French Army at Yorktown. The appointment to the American Philosophical Society is conveyed in Benjamin Franklin to Jefferson, October 8, 1786, *ibid.*, X, 437, and the Yale honorary degree in Ezra Stiles to Jefferson, September 14, 1786, *ibid.*, X, 385–86. For a picture of Jefferson at court, see Thomas Shippen's letters, reproduced in *ibid.*, XII, 502–04.

40. Jefferson to Antonio Giannini, February 5, 1786; Jefferson to James Monroe, June 17, 1785; Jefferson to Francis Hopkinson, September 25, 1785, and January 13, 1785; Jefferson to G. K. Hogendorp, August 25, 1786, *ibid.*, IX, 252–55; VIII, 233, 550–51; VII, 602; X, 297–99. His editorial revisions of

Jean Nicolas Démeunier's *Encyclopédie* are in *ibid.*, X, 3–63. Similar revisions of François Soulés, *Historie* (1785) are in *ibid.*, X, 364–65.

41. The correspondence on the Capitol building at Richmond is too extensive to identify in full. See Jefferson to Madison, September 1, 1785; Jefferson to William Buchanan and James Hay, January 26, 1786. The quotation is from Jefferson to James Currie, January 28, 1786, *ibid.*, VIII, 534–35; IX, 220–23, 240.

42. Jefferson's somewhat comic (except for the moose) quest can be found in Jefferson to John Sullivan, January 7, 1786; Jefferson to Archibald Cary, January 7, 1786; Jefferson to John Sullivan, October 5, 1787, January 26, 1787, April 16, 1787; Jefferson to William Stephens Smith, September 28, 1787, *ibid.*, IX, 158, 160; XI, 68, 295–97; XII, 192–93, 208–09.

43. Jefferson to Eliza House Trist, August 18, 1785, *ibid.*, VIII, 404.

44. Jefferson to Joseph Jones, August 14, 1787; Jefferson to George Wythe, August 13, 1786; Jefferson to David Ramsay, August 4, 1787; Jefferson to John Rutledge, August 6, 1787, *ibid.*, XII, 34; X, 244; XI, 687, 701.

45. "Hints to Americans Travelling in Europe," June 19, 1788; Jefferson to John Bannister, October 15, 1785; Jefferson to Thomas Mann Randolph, July 6, 1787, *ibid.*, XIII, 264–77; VIII, 636–37; XI, 556–59.

46. William H. Peden, ed., *Notes on the State of Virginia* (Chapel Hill, 1954) is the standard and most accessible edition that also contains an introductory essay on the complicated publishing history of the book. The two best secondary accounts of *Notes* are Fawn M. Brodie, *Thomas Jefferson: An Intimate History* (New York, 1974), 150–61, and Jordan, *White over Black*, 238–85, 481–96. John Adams to Jefferson, May 22, 1785, *Cappon*, I, 21.

47. Jefferson to James Madison, May 11, 1785; James Madison to Jefferson, November 15, 1785, *Boyd*, VIII, 147–48; IX, 38–39.

48. Peden, ed., *Notes*, 138, 163. The literature on Jefferson and slavery is enormous, and a fuller treatment of the subject will be forthcoming in chapters 3 and 4. For now, three basic accounts must suffice: Jordan, *White over Black*; Robert McColley, *Slavery and Jeffersonian Virginia* (Urbana, 1964); and John Chester Miller, *The Wolf by the Ears: Thomas Jefferson and Slavery* (New York, 1977).

49. David Ramsay to Jefferson, May 3, 1786; Reverend James Madison to Jefferson, December 28, 1786, *Boyd*, IX, 441; X, 138. The letters Jefferson received on *Notes* were uniformly encouraging on the slavery issue, congratulating Jefferson on his forthright denunciation. "This is a cancer that we must get rid of," wrote Charles Thomson from Philadelphia. "It is a blot

on our character that must be wiped out. If it cannot be done by religion, reason and philosophy, confident I am that it will one day be by blood." Charles Thomson to Jefferson, November 2, 1785, *ibid.*, IX, 9–10.

50. Jefferson to Brissot de Warville, February 11, 1788; Jefferson to Richard Price, August 7, 1785, *ibid.*, XII, 577–78; VIII, 356–57. The best secondary account of Jefferson's more procrastinating posture is William Freehling, *The Road to Disunion: Secessionists at Bay, 1776–1854* (New York, 1990), 122–31.

51. Jefferson to Paul Bentalou, August 25, 1786, *Boyd*, X, 296. Jefferson eventually freed James Hemings in 1796.

52. John Adams to Francis Vanderkemp, April 8, 1815, *The Microfilm Edition of the Adams Papers* (608 reels, Boston, 1954–59), Reel 122.

53. Jefferson to George Washington, December 4, 1788; Jefferson to Anne Willing Bingham, May 11, 1788, *Boyd*, XIV, 330; XIII, 151–52.

54. Jefferson to Mary Jefferson Bolling, July 23, 1787; also Jefferson to James Maury, December 24, 1786, *ibid.*, XI, 612; X, 628.

55. Martha Jefferson to Jefferson, May 27, 1787; Martha Jefferson to Jefferson, March 8, 1787; Martha Jefferson to Jefferson, April 9, 1787, *ibid.*, XI, 203–04, 380–81, 282. The story of Jefferson's removal of Patsy from Panthemont is in *Randall*, I, 538–39.

56. On Jefferson's idealization of domestic life, see Jan Lewis, *The Pursuit of Happiness: Family and Values in Jefferson's Virginia* (New York, 1983).

57. Jefferson to Martha Jefferson, May 5, 1787; Jefferson to Martha Jefferson, March 28, 1787; Jefferson to Mary Jefferson, September 20, 1785, *Boyd*, XI, 348–49, 250–51; VIII, 532–33.

58. Jefferson to Angelica Schuyler Church, February 17, 1788; Jefferson to Madame de Tessé, March 20, 1787, *ibid.*, XII, 600–01; XI, 226.

59. Helen D. Bullock, *My Head and My Heart: A Little Chronicle of Thomas Jefferson and Maria Cosway* (New York, 1945) remains the fullest telling of the story. Though excessively psychiatric, Brodie's *Intimate History*, 109–215, is a full rendering.

60. Jefferson to William Stephens Smith, October 20, 1786, *Boyd*, X, 478–79; Lyman Butterfield and Howard C. Rice, "Jefferson's Earliest Note to Maria Cosway and Some New Facts and Conjectures on His Broken Wrist," *WMQ*, II (1948), 26–33. Jefferson to Maria Cosway [October 5, 1786], *Boyd*, X, 431–32.

61. Jefferson to Elizabeth House Trist, December 15, 1786, *Boyd*, X, 600.

62. Jefferson to Maria Cosway, October 12, 1786, *ibid.*, X, 443–55.

63. Jefferson to Maria Cosway, December 24, 1786, *ibid.*, X, 627–28.

64. Maria Cosway to Jefferson, February 15, 1787, *ibid.*, XI, 148–51.

65. Jefferson to Maria Cosway, July 1, 1787; Maria Cosway to Jefferson, March 7, 1788, *ibid.*, XI, 519–20; XII, 645.

66. Jefferson to Maria Cosway, April 24, 1788; Maria Cosway to Jefferson, April 29, 1788, *ibid.*, XIII, 103–04, 114–16.

67. Maria Cosway to Jefferson, August 19, 1789; Jefferson to Maria Cosway, May 21, 1789, *ibid.*, XV, 351, 142–43. This is only a small sampling of the extensive correspondence between Jefferson and Cosway, which is rich enough to merit a fuller treatment than space allows here.

68. Jefferson to James Madison, February 8, 1786; Jefferson to James Madison, December 16, 1786, *ibid.*, IX, 264; X, 603.

69. Douglass Adair, " 'That Politics May Be Reduced to a Science': David Hume, James Madison and the Tenth Federalist," in Trevor Colbourn, ed., *Fame and the Founding Fathers* (New York, 1974), 3–26; the arrival of the load of books is reported in James Madison to Jefferson, January 22, 1786, *Boyd*, IX, 194. The quotation is from Jefferson to James Monroe, June 17, 1785, *ibid.*, VIII, 227–28. Two recent books on Madison's political thought offer different interpretations of his legacy: Lance Banning, *The Sacred Fire of Liberty: James Madison and the Creation of the Federal Republic* (Madison, 1995) and Richard K. Matthews, *If Men Were Angels: James Madison and the Heartless Empire of Reason* (Lawrence, 1995).

70. John Jay to Jefferson, October 27, 1786, *Boyd*, X, 488–89; Abigail Adams to Jefferson, January 29, 1787, *Cappon*, I, 168–69. On Shays's Rebellion, see David P. Szatmary, *Shays's Rebellion: The Making of an Agrarian Insurrection* (Amherst, 1980) and Robert Gross, ed., *In Debt to Shays: The Bicentennial of an Agrarian Rebellion* (Charlottesville, 1993).

71. Jefferson to Abigail Adams, February 22, 1787, *Cappon*, I, 173; Jefferson to Ezra Stiles, December 24, 1786; Jefferson to James Madison, January 30, 1787; Jefferson to William Stephens Smith, November 13, 1787, *Boyd*, X, 629; XI, 92–93; XII, 356–57.

72. Jefferson to James Madison, January 30, 1787; Jefferson to Edward Carrington, January 16, 1787, *Boyd*, XI, 92–93, 48–50.

73. James Madison to Jefferson, March 19, 1787; Jefferson to James Madison, June 20, 1787; Edward Carrington to Jefferson, June 9, 1787, *ibid.*, XI, 219–20, 480, 407–11. Jefferson to John Adams, November 13, 1787, *Cappon* I, 212.

74. Jefferson to C. W. F. Dumas, September 10, 1787; James Madison to Jefferson, July 18, 1787, *Boyd*, XII, 113; XI, 600.

75. James Madison to Jefferson, October 24, 1787; Jefferson to James Madison, December 20, 1787, *ibid.*, XII, 270–86, 438–43.

76. Jefferson to Edward Carrington, December 21, 1787, *ibid.*, XII, 446.

77. Jefferson to George Washington, May 2, 1788, *ibid.*, XIII, 128.

78. Francis Hopkinson to Jefferson, December 1, 1788; James Madison to Jefferson, July 24, 1788, *ibid.*, XIV, 324; XIII, 412.

79. Jefferson to William Stephens Smith, February 2, 1788; Jefferson to John Brown, May 28, 1788; Edward Carrington to Jefferson, May 14, 1788; Jefferson to James Madison, November 18, 1787; Jefferson to James Madison, July 31, 1788; Jefferson to Francis Hopkinson, March 13, 1789, *ibid.*, XII, 557–58; XIII, 212–13, 157; XIV, 188; XIII, 443; XIV, 650.

80. The secondary literature on the French Revolution defies succinct summary. The classic general accounts are George Lefebvre, *The Coming of the French Revolution* (Princeton, 1947) and R. R. Palmer, *The Age of the Democratic Revolution: A Political History of Europe and America, 1760–1800* (2 vols., Princeton, 1959–64). A more recent account that emphasizes the violent and catastrophic character of the events is Simon Schama, *Citizens: A Chronicle of the French Revolution* (New York, 1988).

81. Jefferson to Lafayette, February 28, 1787; Jefferson to James Monroe, August 5, 1787, *Boyd*, XI, 186, 687–88; Jefferson to John Adams, December 10, 1787, *Cappon*, I, 214.

82. Jefferson to John Jay, October 8, 1787; Jefferson to James Madison, August 2, 1787, *Boyd*, XII, 218; XI, 664.

83. Jefferson to John Jay, June 21, 1787, *ibid.*, XI, 489–90.

84. Jefferson to James Monroe, August 9, 1788; Jefferson to George Washington, November 4, 1788; Jefferson to James Madison, November 18, 1788; Jefferson to Francis Hopkinson, December 21, 1788, *ibid.*, XIII, 489; XIV, 330, 188–89, 369–70; Jefferson to John Adams, August 2, 1788, *Cappon*, I, 230.

85. Jefferson to Madame de Tessé, March 20, 1787, *Boyd*, XI, 228. In his note Boyd dates the insertion as made between 1809 and 1826, on the basis of the watermark on the paper. Representative expressions of his confidence can be found in Jefferson to John Jay, November 19, 1788; Jefferson to James Madison, January 12, 1789, *ibid.*, XIV, 211–17, 436–40.

86. Jefferson's fullest account of his faith in the Patriot Party can be

found in Jefferson to John Jay, May 9, 1789; Jefferson to Richard Price, January 8, 1789, *ibid.*, XV, 110–13; XIV, 420–24. For his faith in Lafayette, see Jefferson to Lafayette, May 6, 1789, *ibid.*, XV, 97–98. For a full account of Lafayette's role in the French Revolution, see Louis Gottschalk, *Lafayette Between the French and the American Revolution, 1783–89* (Chicago, 1950) and Louis Gottschalk and Margaret Maddox, *Lafayette in the French Revolution* (Chicago, 1969).

87. Jefferson to John Jay, May 23, 1788; Jefferson to David Ramsay, May 7, 1788; Jefferson to Ralph Izard, July 17, 1788; Jefferson to John Jay, June 17, 1789; Jefferson to Tom Paine, May 19, 1789, *Boyd*, XIII, 188–97, 140, 373; XV, 188–91, 136–37. For Jefferson's draft of a Charter of Rights, *ibid.*, XV, 167–68 and 230–33 for Lafayette's version of same.

88. Jefferson to John Jay, June 29, 1789; Jefferson to Tom Paine, July 11, 1789, *ibid.*, XV, 221–23, 268.

89. Jefferson to John Jay, July 19, 1789; Jefferson to James Madison, July 22, 1789, *ibid.*, XV, 284–91, 299–301.

90. Jefferson to Edward Bancroft, August 5, 1789, *ibid.*, XV, 333.

91. Jefferson to James Madison, September 6, 1789, *ibid.*, XV, 392–98. All previous work on the issues raised by Jefferson's letter has been synthesized and then superseded by Herbert E. Sloan, *Principle and Interest: Thomas Jefferson and the Problem of Debt* (New York, 1995), which is one of those truly pathbreaking books that comes along, excuse the pun, about every generation.

92. James Madison to Jefferson, February 4, 1790, *Boyd*, XVI, 131–34.

93. Drew R. McCoy, *The Last of the Fathers: James Madison and the Republican Legacy* (Cambridge, 1989), 45–61; Sloan, *Principle and Interest,* 140.

94. Jefferson to James Madison, October 28, 1785, *Boyd*, VIII, 682.

95. Gottschalk and Maddox, *Lafayette in the French Revolution,* 72–99; Sloan, *Principle and Interest,* 63–67.

96. Thomas Paine to Jefferson, (no date), *Boyd*, XIII, 4–8; for Julian Boyd's note on the August 26 meeting in Jefferson's residence, see *ibid.*, XV, 354–55, and for his note on the generational idea, 384–91. The proposition by Richard Gem is in *ibid.*, XV, 391–92.

97. Jefferson to Nicholas Lewis, July 29, 1787, *ibid.*, XI, 639–42. Additional expressions of deepening concern about his indebtedness can be found in Jefferson to Nicholas Lewis, December 19, 1786; Jefferson to Nicholas Lewis, September 17, 1787; Jefferson to James Madison, May 25, 1788; Jefferson to Nicholas Lewis, July 11, 1788, *ibid.*, X, 614–16; XII, 134–36,

201–03, 339–44. This emphasis on Jefferson's personal indebtedness as the major source of his motivation is a central argument in Sloan, *Principle and Interest.*

98. James Madison to Jefferson, May 27, 1789; Jefferson to James Madison, August 28, 1789, *Boyd,* XV, 153–54, 369.

99. Jefferson to Lucy Ludwell Paradise, September 10, 1789; Jefferson to Richard Price, September 13, 1789, *ibid.,* XV, 412, 425.

100. Jefferson to David Ramsay, September 18, 1789; Jefferson to John Jay, September 19, 1789, *ibid.,* XV, 450, 454–61.

101. William Short to Jefferson, October 8, 1789; Maria Cosway to Jefferson, October 8, 1789; George Washington to Jefferson, October 13, 1789, *ibid.,* XV, 510–12, 513, 519–20.

3. MONTICELLO: 1794–97

1. Jefferson to Enoch Edwards, December 30, 1793, *Ford,* VI, 495; Jefferson to George Washington, July 31, 1793, *Domestic Life,* 218.

2. John Adams to Abigail Adams, January 14, 1797, quoted in *Smith,* II, 895, where Adams is in fact referring to Madison's retirement. On the influence of the classical tradition and its enshrinement of agrarian solitude, see Douglass Adair, "Fame and the Founding Fathers," in Colbourn, ed., *Fame and the Founding Fathers,* 3–26.

3. Jefferson to James Madison, April 27, 1795, *Smith,* II, 897–98; Jefferson to Angelica Church, November 27, 1793, *Ford,* VI, 455; Jefferson to Horatio Gates, February 3, 1794, quoted in *Malone,* III, 168; Jefferson to John Adams, April 25, 1794, *Cappon,* I, 254.

4. For Isaac Jefferson's recollections of the rheumatism, see Bear, *Jefferson at Monticello,* 19; Jefferson to Edmund Randolph, September 7, 1794, *Domestic Life,* 231, and *ibid.,* 233, for "the effects of age" quotation.

5. Jefferson to James Madison, June 9, 1793, *Smith,* II, 781. The secondary literature on the hyperbolic character of politics in the 1790s is vast. Jefferson's own role is discussed in loving detail in *Malone,* II, 281–488, and III, 3–166. See also Dumas Malone, *Thomas Jefferson as a Political Leader* (Westport, 1979), in which Malone summarizes his interpretive conclusions and acknowledges that "after living intimately with Jefferson in earlier periods of his life, I found him a rather different man in parts of this one." The standard work on Jefferson's ideological posture in the 1790s is Lance Banning, *The Jeffersonian Persuasion: Evolution of a Party Ideology*

(Ithaca, 1978). The best general overview of the intellectual frenzy is Richard Buel, Jr., *Securing the Revolution: Ideology in American Politics, 1789–1815* (Ithaca, 1972). Two seminal articles are quite suggestive: Marshall Smelser, "The Federalist Period as an Age of Passion," *American Quarterly,* X (1958), 391–419, and John R. Howe, Jr., "Republican Thought and the Political Violence of the 1790s," *American Quarterly,* XIX (1967), 147–65. The most authoritative account of the political history of the period is Stanley Elkins and Eric McKitrick, *The Age of Federalism: The Early American Republic, 1788–1800* (New York, 1993).

6. The scholarly literature on the intellectual issues at stake is both vast and contentious. Perhaps the best place to begin is with Banning, *Jeffersonian Persuasion,* then proceed to Joyce O. Appleby, *Capitalism and a New Social Order: The Republican Vision of the 1790s* (New York, 1984) along with the relevant essays in her collection, *Liberalism and Republicanism in the Historical Imagination* (Cambridge, 1992). At this point one begins to realize that the term "republicanism" has created an electromagnetic field within the scholarly world. Gordon Wood, *The Radicalism of the American Revolution* (New York, 1992) offers the most comprehensive synthesis of the interpretive trends. The terms of the ongoing debate are best reviewed in the Banning-Appleby exchange: "Jeffersonian Ideology Revisited: Liberal and Classical Ideas in the New American Republic" and "Republicanism in Old and New Context," *WMQ,* XLIII (1986), 3–34. An elegant synthesis is available in Elkins and McKitrick, *Age of Federalism,* 3–29. The best summary of the inconclusive character of the current debate as it relates to Jeffersonian scholarship is in Onuf, "The Scholar's Jefferson," *WMQ,* L (1993), 675–84.

7. Once again, the literature on the emergence of political parties defies easy summary. Three old but still-useful books are: Charles Beard, *Economic Origins of Jeffersonian Democracy* (New York, 1915), Joseph Charles, *The Origins of the American Party System* (New York, 1961) and Noble Cunningham, Jr., *The Jeffersonian Republicans: The Formation of Party Organization, 1789–1801* (Chapel Hill, 1957). More recent studies that emphasize the nascent character of the "party" idea are: Richard Hofstadter, *The Idea of a Party System: The Rise of Legitimate Opposition in the United States, 1780–1840* (Berkeley, 1969), Buel, *Securing the Revolution* and Elkins and McKitrick, *Age of Federalism.*

8. The classic account is Koch, *Jefferson and Madison.* The new edition of the correspondence between Jefferson and Madison, edited by James

Morton Smith, provides the most up-to-date account of their relationship in the introductory essay that precedes each section of the correspondence. If read as a series of chapters, they offer the most comprehensive version of the story available. They deserve to be published as a separate volume. The quotation from John Quincy Adams is in *Smith*, I, 1–2.

9. *Malone*, II, 370, III, 109; Adams, ed., *The Works of John Adams*, I, 616.

10. James Monroe to Jefferson, March 3, 1794, quoted in *Malone*, III, 162–63.

11. Pierre Adet to minister of foreign affairs, December 31, 1796, *Smith*, II, 942. The standard account of Jefferson's years as secretary of state is *Malone*, II, 256–88, III, 3–166. The most recent and revisionist account is Elkins and McKitrick, *Age of Federalism*, 209–56. The best overview of Jefferson's foreign policy views is Robert W. Tucker and David C. Hendrickson, *Empire of Liberty: The Statecraft of Thomas Jefferson* (New York, 1990).

12. This is a highly telescoped account most influenced by Elkins and McKitrick, *Age of Federalism*, 209–56, and Charles R. Ritcheson, *Aftermath of Revolution: British Policy Toward the United States, 1783–95* (Dallas, 1969). See also Walter La Feber, "Jefferson and American Foreign Policy," in Onuf, ed., *Jeffersonian Legacies*, 370–91.

13. For the linkage between his personal debt and his Anglophobia, see Sloan, *Principle and Interest*, 86–124.

14. Jefferson to James Madison, August 11, 1793, *Smith*, II, 803. On Genêt's disastrous career in America, see Harry Ammon, *The Genêt Mission* (New York, 1973).

15. Jefferson to William Short, January 3, 1793, *Ford*, VI, 153–57.

16. Jefferson to Trench Coxe, June 1, 1795, *Ford*, VII, 22. The classic comparative account of the American and French experience with Revolution is Palmer, *The Age of the Democratic Revolution*. For Paine's career in France, see John Keane, *Tom Paine: A Political Life* (Boston, 1995), 267–452. For the best and most recent edition of *The Rights of Man*, see Eric Foner, ed., *Paine: Collected Writings* (2 vols., New York, 1995).

17. John Adams to Abigail Adams, December 19, 1793, Adams, ed., *Works*, I, 460; Jefferson to George Washington, September 9, 1792, *Boyd*, XXIV, 352. On the dinner table bargain, see Norman Risjord, *Chesapeake Politics, 1781–1800* (New York, 1978) and also his "The Compromise of 1790: New Evidence on the Dinner Table Bargain," *WMQ*, XXXIII (1976), 309–14.

18. The Adams epithet is from John Adams to Francis Vanderkemp, Jan-

uary 25, 1806, *The Microfilm Edition of the Adams Papers,* Reel 118. This brief sketch of Hamilton makes no effort to comprehend the whole man. The best biographies are: John C. Miller, *Alexander Hamilton: Portrait in Paradox* (New York, 1959) and Gerald Stourz, *Alexander Hamilton and the Idea of Republican Government* (Stanford, 1970). See also the first chapter of Clinton Rossiter, *Alexander Hamilton and the Constitution* (New York, 1964) for the differing views of his character. There is also a brilliant profile of the man and his ideas in Elkins and McKitrick, *Age of Federalism,* 90–131.

19. For the Hamiltonian attacks on Jefferson's character, see Harold Syrett, ed., *The Papers of Alexander Hamilton* (26 vols., New York, 1974–92), XXI, 432, 504.

20. All previous discussions of Jefferson's role in the creation of the Giles Resolutions have been superseded by the brilliant detective work in Eugene R. Sheridan, "Thomas Jefferson and the Giles Resolutions," *WMQ,* XLIV (1992), 589–608.

21. Jefferson to George Washington, September 9, 1792, *Boyd,* XXIV, 358–59.

22. The leading spokesman for the "Country" interpretation is Banning, *Jeffersonian Persuasion.* See also David N. Mayer, *The Constitutional Thought of Thomas Jefferson* (Charlottesville, 1994) for a similar argument.

23. The standard work on the subject is Richard Hofstadter, *The Paranoid Style in American Politics and Other Essays* (New York, 1965). On the integrity of conspiratorial thinking in the revolutionary era, see Gordon S. Wood, "Conspiracy and the Paranoid Style: Causality and Deceit in the Eighteenth Century," *WMQ,* XXXIX (1982), 401–41.

24. Matthews, *The Radical Politics of Thomas Jefferson,* makes the clearest case for Jefferson's credentials as a radical utopian. While not landing squarely in the middle of his position, I am prepared to cozy up to it, though Matthews seems to endorse the utopianism while I consider it inherently illusory. If I land squarely anywhere, it is on Jefferson's multiple personae and ideological versatility, which makes him capable of sounding like a republican of the Old Whig sort in certain contexts (i.e., the party wars of the 1790s), a liberal in other contexts (i.e., the defender of the French Revolution in the Thomas Paine mode) and a radical on yet other occasions (i.e., his generational argument and deeply felt hostility to any source of authority outside the self). This latter persona has more in common with the American radicalism of the New Left in the 1960s than with any Marxist tradition, although its antigovernment ethos also can blend

easily with the conservatism of Barry Goldwater and Ronald Reagan. The core conviction, as I see it, is individual sovereignty.

25. Notes on Professor Eberling's letter of July 30, 1795, *Ford*, VII, 44–49.

26. On the concept of "the people" as an invention or, if you will, a fiction, see Edmund S. Morgan, *Inventing the People: The Rise of Popular Sovereignty in England and America* (New York, 1988).

27. Jefferson to George Washington, May 14, 1794, *Ford*, VI, 509–10; Jefferson to James Monroe, May 26, 1795, *Ford*, VII, 15–22; Jefferson to Maria Cosway, September 8, 1795, quoted in Bullock, *My Head and My Heart*, 142–43; Jefferson to Edward Rutledge, November 30, 1795, *Ford*, VII, 39–40.

28. Jefferson to François de Barbé-Marbois, December 5, 1783, *Boyd*, VI, 373–74; for Randolph's character, see William H. Gaines, Jr., *Thomas Mann Randolph: Jefferson's Son-in-Law* (Baton Rouge, 1966). On the domestic situation at Monticello, see Donald Jackson, *A Year at Monticello* (Golden, 1989) and Lewis, *The Pursuit of Happiness*, as well as her " 'The Blessings of Domestic Society': Thomas Jefferson's Family and the Transformation of American Politics," Onuf, ed., *Jeffersonian Legacies*, 109–46.

29. The La Rochefoucauld-Liancourt court quotations are from Merrill D. Peterson, *Visitors to Monticello* (Charlottesville, 1989), 29; Jefferson to Martha Jefferson Randolph, June 8, 1797, *Domestic Life*, 245.

30. Gaines, *Thomas Mann Randolph*, 46–48; Jefferson to James Monroe, May 26, 1795, *Ford*, VII, 20–21, for the report that Randolph "is very frail indeed . . . , the more discouraging as there seems too have been no founded conjecture what is the matter with him." For additional reflections, see Robert P. Sutton, "Nostalgia, Pessimism, and Malaise: The Doomed Aristocrat in Late-Jeffersonian Virginia," *VMHB*, LXXVI (1968), 41–55. On the imaginative response to the decay of Virginia's gentry in the Randolph mode, see William R. Taylor, *Cavalier and Yankee: The Old South and the American National Character* (New York, 1961), 67–94.

31. Martha Jefferson Randolph to Jefferson, July 1, 1798, *Family Letters*, 166. Although I cannot accept the central premise of her book, Fawn Brodie's treatment of Martha provides one of the fullest renderings of the father-daughter relationship after Martha's marriage. See especially Brodie, *Intimate History*, 287–300. Martha still awaits a biographer who can see her as the most important woman in Jefferson's life and not just as a footnote to Sally Hemings.

32. Jefferson to Maria Jefferson Eppes, January 7, 1798, *Domestic Life*,

246–48. One can see the same internal mechanisms at work in several emotionally charged domestic conflicts that Jefferson preferred to relegate to some sealed inner chamber, to include a highly publicized infanticide case involving the Randolph family in 1793 and the death by poisoning of his old mentor George Wythe in 1806, a scandal that also included the not-to-be-mentioned fact that Wythe's mulatto housekeeper was his mistress and mother of two of his children.

33. Peden, ed., *Notes*, 164–65. The scholar-farmer referred to here is Douglas L. Wilson, currently the director of the International Center for Jefferson Studies at Monticello. A nice review of the issues is available in Joyce Appleby, "The 'Agrarian Myth' in the Early Republic," *Liberalism and Republicanism*, 253–76.

34. Until recently the most succinct and accessible assessment of Jefferson's indebtedness has been *Malone*, III, 528–30. But the new authoritative source for our understanding of both the economic and psychological dimensions of Jefferson's debt problem is Sloan, *Principle and Interest*, especially 13–49. Jefferson to George Washington, [April] 1794, *Domestic Life*, 229–30. The most recent study of the planter class in revolutionary Virginia is Bruce A. Ragsdale, *A Planters' Republic: The Search for Economic Independence in Revolutionary Virginia* (Madison, 1994).

35. Answers to [Jean] Démeunier's Additional Queries, [January–February 1786], *Boyd*, X, 27; Jefferson to Mary Jefferson Eppes, January 7, 1798, *Domestic Life*, 247–48. For the economic condition of postrevolutionary Virginia, see Risjord, *Chesapeake Politics*, 96–116; Breen, *Tobacco Culture*, 84–123; Sloan, *Principle and Interest*, 86–124; Lorena S. Walsh, "Slave Life, Slave Society, and Tobacco Production in the Tidewater Chesapeake, 1620–1820," in Ira Berlin and Philip D. Morgan, eds., *Cultivation and Culture: Labor and the Shaping of Slave Life in the Americas* (Charlottesville, 1993).

36. *Farm Book*, viii–x, 201–02, 325–36. The Research Department of the Thomas Jefferson Memorial Foundation at Monticello prepared a packet of materials entitled "My Family, My Farm, and My Books" for its winter tour of 1990–91 that includes a great deal of information on Jefferson's lands and his efforts to improve them in the 1794–97 years.

37. *Farm Book*, 257–310; Jefferson to Francis Willis, July 15, 1796, *ibid.*, 255–57.

38. *Ibid.*, 310–11, 316–17, for the nagging problems with the crop rotation system and the elements. See also La Rochefoucauld-Liancourt's appraisal

of the predicament in Peterson, *Visitors to Monticello*, 24–26, and *Malone*, III, 198–206, for a nice summary of the clash between weather and hope.

39. *Farm Book*, 335–36, 227–28, 238–39.

40. The classic analysis of Virginia's soil problems is Avery O. Craven, *Soil Exhaustion as a Factor in the Agricultural History of Virginia and Maryland, 1606–1860* (Urbana, 1925). See also Jack Temple Kirby, "Virginia's Environmental History: A Prospectus," *VMHB*, IC (1991), 464–67.

41. Jefferson to Jean Démeunier, April 29, 1795, *Ford*, VII, 14; Jefferson to James Lyle, July 10, 1795, *Farm Book*, 430; Jefferson to Henry Remsen, October 30, 1794, *ibid.*, 428. See also Jefferson to Archibauld Stuart, January 3, 1796, *Ford*, VII, 49–51, and Jefferson to James Madison, March 6, 1796, *Smith*, II, 923. For Isaac Jefferson's recollection, see Bear, ed., *Jefferson at Monticello*, 23.

42. To my knowledge, the only book that has recognized the imaginative implications of Jefferson's nailery is McLaughlin, *Jefferson and Monticello*, 110–11.

43. "Reminiscences of Madison Hemings," in Brodie, *Intimate History*, 474; Edmund Bacon, in Bear, ed., *Jefferson at Monticello*, 71–82. For the interest in the other mechanical or construction projects, see *Farm Book*, 72–73, 341–46, 363–64.

44. For the architectural and construction story of Monticello, the best book is McLaughlin, *Jefferson and Monticello*. For the aesthetic and interior story, Susan R. Stein, *The Worlds of Thomas Jefferson at Monticello* (New York, 1993) is incomparable. For a convenient review of the story of the family and the mansion, see Elizabeth Langhorne, *Monticello: A Family Story* (Chapel Hill, 1987).

45. Jefferson to George Wythe, October, 1794, quoted in McLaughlin, *Jefferson and Monticello*, 258; Jefferson to Steven Willis, November 12, 1792, *Farm Book*, 173, for the estimate of the bricks required; Jefferson to William Giles, March 19, 1796, *Ford*, VII, 67; Peterson, *Visitors to Monticello*, 18–19, 21–22; Jefferson to Count Constantin François de Volney, April 10, 1796, quoted in McLaughlin, *Jefferson at Monticello*, 259–60. and ?

46. Lucia Stanton, " 'Those Who Labor for My Happiness': Thomas Jefferson and His Slaves," Onuf, ed., *Jeffersonian Legacies*, 147–80, displaces all previous scholarly studies of the slave population at Monticello and draws extensively on the ongoing work of the Monticello Research Department.

47. More has been written on Jefferson and slavery than any other subject in the Jefferson corpus. And here there is nothing like a scholarly consensus. The best defense of Jefferson's record is Douglas L. Wilson, "Thomas Jefferson and the Character Issue," *Atlantic Monthly*, CCLXX (1992), 61–78. The most sustained scholarly attack of Jefferson's record is Paul Finkelman, "Jefferson and Slavery: 'Treason Against the Hopes of the World,' " Onuf, ed., *Jeffersonian Legacies*, 181–221. The standard survey of the subject is Miller, *The Wolf by the Ears*. The deepest probe into the psychological issues at stake is Jordan, *White over Black*, 429–81. The best look at the Virginia context is McColley, *Slavery and Jeffersonian Virginia*. The most extensive effort to understand his latter-day procrastinations is Freehling, *The Road to Disunion*, 122–57. And this merely scratches the proverbial surface. What I am attempting to argue here is that our understanding of this controversial subject will be enhanced if we do two things: First, try to relate Jefferson's position on slavery as a social problem with his own predicament as an owner of slaves and, second, recognize the shift that occurs in his thinking somewhere between 1783 and 1794, a shift toward passivity and procrastination.

48. Jefferson to William A. Burwell, January 28, 1805, *Farm Book*, 20. One of the few ironies of Jefferson's relation to slavery that has escaped the notice of historians involves the cotton gin. Jefferson's oft-stated confidence that slavery was doomed in America was based on his belief that it would simply fail as a labor system. The development of the cotton gin was a crucial factor in vitalizing the slave economy, especially in the Deep South, thereby making him a poor prophet. When he was secretary of state, one of Jefferson's responsibilities was the approval of patents, including Eli Whitney's request for the cotton gin. See Jefferson to Eli Whitney, November 16, 1793, *Ford*, VI, 448.

49. The fullest statement of his mature position on slavery was made in a letter to Edward Coles, a member of the younger generation that Jefferson regarded as the proper source of leadership. See Jefferson to Edward Coles, August 25, 1814, *Farm Book*, 37–39. For the short-lived scheme to import German peasants to "intermingle" with blacks, see Jefferson to Edward Bancroft, January 26, [1789], *Boyd*, XIV, 492–94.

50. The following letters from Jefferson to his overseer at Monticello, Nicholas Lewis, discuss the sale of slaves, or the leasing of their labor, to meet the problem of rising debt: December 19, 1786, *Boyd*, X, 614–16; July 29, 1787, *ibid.*, XI, 639–42; July 11, 1788, *ibid.*, XIII, 339–44; Sloan, *Principle*

and Interest, 22–23, also sees the late 1780s as the crucial moment when debt begins to become an integral part of all his thinking.

51. Stanton, "Thomas Jefferson and His Slaves," 174. Interestingly, this assiduous assessment of Jefferson's position on slavery, which is unquestionably the most significant statement in the entire memoir that La Rochefoucauld-Liancourt wrote of his visit to Monticello, did not make it into any of the published editions produced by modern scholars until Stanton generated her own translation from the microfilm version at the Library of Congress.

52. *Farm Book,* 18.

53. *Domestic Life,* 152–53, for the description of Jefferson's return to Monticello in 1789, when the slaves disengaged the horses and pulled the carriage up the mountain, then crowded around the returning master, laughing and crying with joy. Jefferson to Bowling Clarke, September 21, 1792, *Farm Book,* 13; Jefferson to Nicholas Lewis, April 12, 1792, *ibid.,* 12. For his policy on runaways, see Jefferson to Reuben Perry, April 16, 1812, *ibid.,* 34–35; and Jefferson to Randolph Lewis, April 23, 1807, *ibid.,* 26, for his view on preserving slave families. All of this is carefully presented in Stanton, "Thomas Jefferson and His Slaves," 158–59.

54. *Farm Book,* 7.

55. Thomas Mann Randolph to Jefferson, April 22, 1798, *ibid.,* 436. The genealogy of the Hemings family is conveniently provided in Bear, ed., *Jefferson at Monticello,* insert after page 24. The terms governing the emancipation of Robert and James Hemings are set forth in *Farm Book,* 15–16. This La Rochefoucauld-Liancourt quotation is available in Peterson, *Visitors to Monticello,* 30.

56. Judith P. Justus, *Down from the Mountain: The Oral History of the Hemings Family* (Perrysburg, Ohio, 1990), while not wholly reliable, gathers much evidence about many branches of the Hemings family. The Research Department of the Thomas Jefferson Memorial Foundation is currently involved in a major project to interview the descendants of the Hemings family, many of whom regard themselves as descendants of Jefferson via Sally Hemings.

57. James Madison to Jefferson, October 5, 1794, *Smith,* II, 857.

58. James Madison to Jefferson, November 16, 1794; Jefferson to James Madison, December 28, 1794, *Smith,* II, 859–60, 866–68; Jefferson to Edmund Randolph, September 7, 1794, *Ford,* VI, 512.

59. On the Whiskey Rebellion, the most recent study is Thomas P.

Slaughter, *The Whiskey Rebellion* (New York, 1986). An older but still-valuable account is Leland D. Baldwin, *Whiskey Rebels: The Story of a Frontier Uprising* (Pittsburgh, 1939). On the politics of the Federalists arguing for a massive show of military force, see Richard H. Kohn, "The Washington Administration's Decision to Crush the Whiskey Rebellion," *JAH,* LIX (1972), 567–74.

60. James Madison to Jefferson, November 30, 1794, and December 21, 1794, *Smith,* II, 861–62, 865–66. See also Philip S. Foner, ed., *The Democratic-Republican Societies, 1790–1800: A Documentary Sourcebook* (Westport, 1976).

61. Jefferson to Madison, December 28, 1794, *Smith,* II, 866–68. See also Jefferson to William Branch Giles, December 17, 1794, *Ford,* VI, 515–16.

62. Jefferson to James Madison, February 5, 1795, February 23, 1795, March 5, 1795, *Smith,* II, 871–75. See also Jefferson to James Monroe, May 26, 1795, *Ford,* VII, 16–17.

63. For the decision to subscribe to the *Aurora,* see Jackson, *A Year at Monticello,* 104.

64. Jefferson to James Madison, March 6, 1796, *Smith,* II, 922.

65. Perhaps my own lack of conviction toward most efforts at psychohistory requires me to offer an aside to the skeptical reader here. The problem with most Freudian, neo-Freudian or Eriksonian explanations of human motivation is that they employ a methodology that does not meet the traditional canons of evidence employed by historians and biographers. They essentially posit a hypothetical cause deep in the subconscious and usually deep in the childhood experience of the subject that "explains" the pattern of behavior by the adult but that lies beyond our retrieval except by reference to the particular theory posited at the start. The adult behavior sanctions or confirms the theory, which then achieves the status of a "fact," and a circular process has begun that can generate some notorious conclusions. This is the method of Fawn Brodie in *Intimate History* and Erik Erikson in *Dimensions of a New Identity: The 1973 Jefferson Lectures in the Humanities* (New York, 1974). My intention here is not to attempt an exhaustive discussion of the clinical literature, which is vast, but rather to record my own inability to accept such circular reasoning and to note the central flaw of this interpretive tradition as I see it—namely, its capacity to "create" its own evidence based on a purely hypothetical model.

That said, any historian or biographer worth his or her salt is intellectu-ally obliged to make some occasional effort at explaining a decision or act without possessing all the direct evidence one would like. The explanation offered here for Jefferson's obsessive hatred of the Hamiltonian fiscal program does not depend on any specific theory of human personality. It depends only on establishing a connection between Jefferson's private problems with debt and his public position on the enlargement of the national debt. Since the private and public Jefferson were the same person, it is a connection made by common sense rather than theory. It represents an effort to unite that which Jefferson wished to keep separate in his own mind. The credibility of the connection also depends on the massive evidence about Jefferson's indebtedness gathered in Herbert Sloan's *Principle and Interest.*

66. The two authoritative books on the Jay Treaty are Samuel Flagg Bemis, *Jay's Treaty: A Study in Commerce and Diplomacy* (New Haven, 1962) and Jerald A. Combs, *The Jay Treaty: Political Background of the Founding Fathers* (Berkeley, 1970).

67. James Madison to Jefferson, February 15, 1795; Jefferson to James Madison, February 23, 1795; Jefferson to James Madison, March 5, 1795, *Smith*, II, 872–74.

68. James Madison to Jefferson, June 14, 1795, *ibid.*, 879–80. The references to Hamilton and the mock toast are conveniently summarized in *ibid.*, 882–85.

69. Jefferson to James Madison, September 21, 1795, November 26, 1795, James Madison to Jefferson, December 13, 1795, *ibid.*, 897–98, 900–01, 903–04; Jefferson to James Madison, November 30, 1795, *ibid.*, 888–89.

70. These are essentially the conclusions of Bemis and Combs, cited above, as well as the most recent scholarly treatment by Elkins and McKitrick, *Age of Federalism,* 375–450. Concerning Jefferson's rock-ribbed belief that England was a nation on the decline, it would be fascinating to give him a copy of Linda Colley's *Britons: Forging the Nation, 1707–1837* (New Haven, 1992), a truly elegant appraisal of the various sources of extraordinary allegiance the emerging British nation was able to draw upon from all sectors of its populace.

71. James Madison to Jefferson, March 23, 1795, *Smith*, II, 875–76; James Madison to James Monroe, February 26, 1796, quoted in *ibid.*, 940.

72. *Ibid.*, 940–41.

73. Jefferson to Philip Mazzei, April 24, 1796, *Ford*, VII, 72–76. The infamous "Mazzei Letter" was picked up by an Italian newspaper in Florence and then translated back into English by Noah Webster's Federalist

newspaper the *Minerva,* on May 14, 1797. Washington ceased all correspondence with Jefferson as of this date. See *Malone,* III, 267–68, 302–07, for a heroic but futile effort to rescue Jefferson from his own denials of authorship.

74. Jefferson to William Branch Giles, December 31, 1795; Jefferson to James Monroe, March 21, 1796, *Ford,* VII, 41–42, 67–68; Jefferson to James Madison, March 27, 1796, *Smith,* II, 928.

75. Madison's explanation of his constitutional strategy is most readily available in his many letters to Jefferson during the spring of 1796. See especially James Madison to Jefferson, March 6, 1796, and March 13, 1796, *Smith,* II, 925–26.

76. John Adams to Abigail Adams, April 28, 1796, cited in *ibid.,* 894; James Madison to Jefferson, May 1, 1796, April 18, 1796, April 23, 1796, May 22, 1796, *ibid.,* 933–34, 936–38. A major contributing factor to the switch of western interests was the announcement of Pinckney's Treaty with Spain, which guaranteed navigation rights on the Mississippi River and, when linked with the removal of British troops guaranteed by the Jay Treaty, allowed for unimpeded expansion into and beyond the Mississippi Valley. See Samuel Flagg Bemis, *Pinckney's Treaty: America's Advantage from Europe's Distresses* (rev. ed., New Haven, 1960).

77. Jefferson to James Monroe, June 12, 1796, and July 10, 1796, *Ford,* VII, 80, 89.

78. For an extended discussion of this more democratic brand of politics and its implications for the Federalists, see Elkins and McKitrick, *Age of Federalism,* 431, 451–88.

79. Fisher Ames to Oliver Wolcott, September 16, 1796, quoted in *Smith,* II, 940; James Madison to James Monroe, May 14, 1796, *ibid.*

80. James Madison to Jefferson, December 5, 1796, *ibid.,* II, 948. On Adams's political position vis-à-vis Hamilton at this stage, see Stephen G. Kurtz, *The Presidency of John Adams: The Collapse of Federalism, 1795–1800* (Philadelphia, 1957), 96–113. See also Manning Dauer, *The Adams Federalists* (Baltimore, 1953).

81. Jefferson to James Madison, December 17, 1796, *Smith,* II, 949–50.

82. Jefferson to John Adams, December 28, 1796, *Cappon,* I, 262–63; Jefferson to Archibauld Stuart, January 4, 1797, *Ford,* VII, 102–03; Jefferson to James Madison, January 1, 1797, *Smith,* II, 952–55; Jefferson to John Langdon, January 22, 1797, *Ford,* VII, 111–12; Jefferson to Benjamin Rush, January 22, 1797, *ibid.,* VII, 114.

83. Jefferson to Elbridge Gerry, May 13, 1797, Jefferson to Edward Rutledge, December 27, 1796, *Ford,* VII, 119–20, 93–95; Jefferson to James Madison, January 8, 1797, *Smith,* II, 955.

84. Jefferson to John Adams, December 28, 1796, enclosure with letter of January 1, 1797, *Smith,* II, 954–55.

85. James Madison to Jefferson, January 15, 1797, *ibid.,* II, 956–58.

86. Jefferson to James Madison, January 30, 1797, *ibid.,* 962–63.

87. Jefferson's recollection in "The Anas," *Ford,* I, 273; Adams had a corresponding sense of the poignancy of the separation, though he tended to regard both Jefferson and his Federalist colleagues in the cabinet as misguided and motivated by party considerations. See Charles Francis Adams, ed., *Works,* IX, 285.

88. *Malone,* III, 296–301.

4. WASHINGTON, D.C.: 1801–04

1. *Domestic Life,* 275–76, for the legendary account.

2. Jefferson to Spencer Roane, September 6, 1819, *L&B,* XV, 212.

3. My effort at a realistic rendering of the inauguration draws upon multiple accounts. See especially Smith, *The First Forty Years of Washington Society, History,* I, 126–48; Noble Cunningham, Jr., *The Process of Government Under Jefferson* (Princeton, 1978). The quotation is from Jefferson to Maria Jefferson Eppes, February 15, 1801, *Domestic Life,* 274–75. The chief secondary work on the revolution theme is Daniel Sisson, *The American Revolution of 1800* (New York, 1974).

4. Constance McLaughlin Green, *Washington: A History of the Capital, 1800–1850* (Princeton, 1962), I, 3–20; James Sterling Young, *The Washington Community, 1800–1828* (New York, 1966). There is also a splendid summary in Martin Smelser, *The Democratic Republic, 1801–1815* (New York, 1968), 2–5.

5. Bob Arnbeck, *Through a Fiery Trial: Building Washington, 1790–1800* (Lanham, 1991); Charles Janson, *The Stranger in America* (London, 1807). For an excellent collection of travelers' accounts and early maps, see John W. Reps, *Washington on View: The Nation's Capital Since 1790* (Chapel Hill, 1991), 50–85.

6. Smith, *Forty Years,* 10–13; George Waterston, *The L . . . Family at Washington, or A Winter in the Metropolis* (Washington, 1822), 21–22; Reps, *Washington on View,* 51.

7. See, for example, the description of the Capitol in *History,* I, 135.

8. For a convenient review of the scholarly literature on Burr, see J. C. A. Stagg, "The Enigma of Aaron Burr," *Reviews in American History,* XII (1984), 378–82. The standard biographies are Nathan Schachner, *Aaron Burr: A Biography* (New York, 1937) and Milton Lomastz, *Aaron Burr* (2 vols., New York, 1979–83). Though obviously not reliable as history, Gore Vidal's *Burr* (New York, 1973) is a fictional treatment of considerable erudition and even greater wit.

9. Sisson, *Revolution of 1800,* 13–58, offers the fullest secondary account of the election.

10. On the election in the House, see Morton Borden, *The Federalism of James A. Bayard* (New York, 1955), 73–95.

11. There is no first-rate modern biography of Marshall. Leonard Baker, *John Marshall: A Life in Law* (New York, 1974) falls short. The best biography remains Albert J. Beveridge, *Life of John Marshall* (4 vols., Boston, 1916–19).

12. The "twistifications" reference is from Jefferson to James Madison, May 25, 1810, *Smith,* III, 1632. John Marshall to Alexander Hamilton, January 1, 1800, Charles F. Hobson, ed., *The Papers of John Marshall* (7 vols., Chapel Hill, 1974–), VI, 46–47.

13. For the midnight judges story and Adams's view of the political context, see Ellis, *Passionate Sage,* 19–26.

14. John Marshall to Charles Cotesworth Pinckney, March 4, 1801; Jefferson to John Marshall, March 4, 1801; Marshall to Jefferson, March 4, 1801, Hobson, ed., *Marshall Papers,* VI, 88–89.

15. Sisson, *Revolution of 1800,* 41–58; Elkins and McKitrick, *Age of Federalism,* 726–42.

16. Smith, *Forty Years,* 25–26; Jefferson to James Monroe, February 18, 1801, *Ford,* VII, 490–91; *Malone,* IV, 10–14.

17. My interpretation of Jefferson's political ideology in 1800 draws upon my reading in the vast scholarly literature on republicanism that has appeared over the last thirty years. For a succinct summary of the "oppositional" argument, see Banning, *Jeffersonian Persuasion,* 273–302. For the Federalists' fears of Jefferson, see Elkins and McKitrick, *Age of Federalism,* 746–50. The quotation is from Charles Lee to Leven Powell, February 11, 1802, cited in Cunningham, *Jeffersonian Republicans,* 316.

18. Jefferson to Gideon Granger, August 13, 1800, *LC;* in the same vein, see Jefferson to Thomas Lomax, February 25, 1801, *Ford,* VII, 500. The clas-

sic secondary account of what was in Jefferson's mind as he assumed the presidency is *History*, I, 145–47.

19. Alexander Hamilton to James A. Bayard, January 16, 1801, Harold Syrett, ed., *The Papers of Alexander Hamilton* (27 vols., New York, 1961–81), XXV, 319–20.

20. The Inaugural Address is printed in a somewhat muddled fashion in *Ford*, VIII, 1–6. I am indebted to Andrew Burstein, who provided me with copies of Jefferson's final draft from the Jefferson Papers in the Library of Congress.

21. *Ford*, VIII, 5.

22. *Ibid.*, 3, 4.

23. Compare the handwritten version in the Library of Congress with the printed version that appeared in the *National Intelligencer*, March 4, 1801. Alexander Hamilton, "An Address to the Electors of the State of New York," March 21, 1801, Syrett, ed., *Hamilton Papers*, XXV, 365. See also Elkins and McKitrick on the reconciliation theme in *Age of Federalism*, 750–54.

24. John Marshall to Charles Cotesworth Pinckney, March 4, 1801, Hobson, ed., *Marshall Papers*, VI, 89.

25. *Ford*, VIII, 4.

26. *Ibid.*, 3.

27. Jefferson to John Dickinson, March 6, 1801; Jefferson to Nathaniel Niles, March 22, 1801; Jefferson to Benjamin Rush, March 24, 1801; Jefferson to Samuel Adams, March 29, 1801, *Ford*, VIII, 7–8, 24–25, 35–37, 38–40.

28. Jefferson to John Dickinson, March 6, 1801, *Ford*, VIII, 7.

29. The classic account, and it truly is, of the domestic and international situation on the eve of Jefferson's presidency, is *History*, I, 5–125.

30. A concise summary of the scholarly overview is available in Smelser, *Democratic Republic*, 20–44. Jefferson's own sense of the favorable conditions can be seen in Jefferson to Joseph Priestley, March 21, 1801; Jefferson to George Logan, March 21, 1801, *Ford*, VII, 21–23. The "noiseless course" remark is from Jefferson to Thomas Cooper, November 29, 1802, *ibid.*, VIII, 178.

31. Jefferson to Gideon Granger, October 31, 1801, *LC*. The reference to Adams's tantrums is in Jefferson to William Short, June 12, 1807, *Ford*, X, 414–15. For an excellent appraisal of Jefferson's cabinet by a shrewd contemporary, see John Quincy Adams to Abigail Adams, November 1804, *Microfilm Edition of Adams Papers*, Reel 437.

32. Cunningham, *Process of Government*, 14–15. Koch, *Jefferson and Madison*, 212–59, for Madison's role, as well as the more recent treatment in *Smith*, II, 1164–68. Gallatin still awaits a modern biographer who is up to the subject. On his administrative skill, see Jay C. Henlein, "Albert Gallatin: A Pioneer in Public Administration," *WMQ*, VII (1950), 64–94 and Leonard D. White, *The Jeffersonians: A Study in Administrative History, 1801–1829* (New York, 1951), 71–74.

33. Once again, the subject has been treated by scores of political historians, but none has surpassed the version in *History* I, 148–68.

34. See Jefferson's original statement of his administrative style in his "Circular to the Heads of Departments," November 6, 1801, *Smith*, II, 1201–02, which is also available in *Ford*, VIII, 99–101. A modern appraisal of Jefferson as moderator of cabinet sessions is Robert M. Johnstone, Jr., *Jefferson and the Presidency: Leadership in the Young Republic* (Ithaca, 1978), 80–113.

35. Jefferson to Destutt de Tracy, January 26, 1811, and Jefferson to Joel Barlow, January 24, 1810, *Ford*, X, 184; IX, 269. Cunningham, *Process of Government*, 60–71; Jefferson to Madison, April 9, 1804, *Smith*, II, 1304.

36. Smith, *Forty Years*, 28, 34–35, 46–47, 80; Louisa Catherine Adams, November 1803, *Microfilm Edition of Adams Papers*, Reel 269; William Plumer, *Memorandum of Proceedings in the United States Senate, 1803–1807*, ed. E. S. Brown (New York, 1923), 455. On the Merry Affair, see "Rules of Etiquette" [November ? 1803], *Ford*, VIII, 276–77; Jefferson to James Monroe, January 8, 1804, *ibid.*, 290–91; Jefferson to William Short, January 23, 1804, *LC; History*, I, 546–67.

37. Cunningham, *Process of Government*, 42–43; Johnstone, *Jefferson Presidency*, 33–34.

38. Cunningham, *Process of Government*, 25–26. See also Jeffrey K. Tules, *The Rhetorical Presidency* (Princeton, 1987), 70–71.

39. Jefferson to Thomas Mann Randolph, November 16, 1801, *LC;* Jefferson to William Thornton, February 14, 1802, *LC;* Jefferson to James Madison, December 29, 1801, *Smith*, II, 1211–12. Cunningham, *Process of Government*, 35–41.

40. Jefferson to Madison, November 12, 1801, *Smith*, II, 1203; Albert Gallatin to Jefferson, November 21, 1802, quoted in Cunningham, *Process of Government*, 82.

41. Jefferson to Albert Gallatin, October 11, 1809, *Ford*, IX, 264; Jefferson to James Madison, December 29, 1801, *Smith*, II, 1212–13.

42. One of the clearest and most concise summaries of the debt issue is

in Norman Risjord, *Thomas Jefferson* (Madison, 1994), 130–34. See also *History*, II, 158–63, and Albert Gallatin to Jefferson, November 16, 1801, *Ford*, VIII, 109–17.

43. Cunningham, *Process of Government*, Appendix I, 325–26, lists all the employees of the federal government in 1801 and 1808.

44. On Adams's worries about the reduction in the size of the navy and the likelihood of war with England, see Ellis, *Passionate Sage*, 106–12.

45. Sloan, *Principle and Interest*, 197–201.

46. First Annual Message, December 8, 1801, *Ford*, VIII, 108–25. The final quotation is from the Second Inaugural Address, March 4, 1805, *ibid.*, 343.

47. Jefferson to Thomas Mann Randolph, June 18, 1801, *LC;* Jefferson to William Short, October 3, 1801, *Ford*, VIII, 97–99; Jefferson to Gallatin, April 1, 1802, *ibid.*, 139–41; Jefferson to du Pont de Nemours, January 18, 1802, *ibid.*, 127.

48. Jefferson to Dr. Benjamin Smith Barton, February 14, 1801; Jefferson to James Monroe, March 7, 1801; Jefferson to Horatio Gates, March 8, 1801; Jefferson to Elias Shipman, July 12, 1801, *Ford*, VII, 489–90; VIII, 8–10, 11–12; IX, 270–74. The fullest treatment of the patronage problem is in Cunningham, *Jeffersonian Republicans*, 30–70. The most incisive analysis is in Carl Prince, "The Passing of the Aristocracy: Jefferson's Removal of the Federalists, 1801–1805," *JAH*, LVII (1970), 563–75.

49. *History*, I, 201. This of course was just the kind of ironic predicament that Adams found most worthy of extended treatment.

50. Jefferson to William Branch Giles, March 23, 1801; Jefferson to Levi Lincoln, July 11, 1801; Jefferson to John Dickinson, July 23, 1801; Jefferson to Thomas McKean, July 24, 1801; Jefferson to Joel Barlow, May 3, 1802; Jefferson to Elbridge Gerry, August 28, 1802, *Ford*, VIII, 25–26, 67, 75–77, 79–80, 149–50, 170.

51. *New York Evening Post*, June 29, 1802, quoted in *Malone*, IV, 83–84.

52. Jefferson's most famous celebration of Indian nobility occurred in his *Notes on Virginia*. See Peden, *Notes*, 159–60. The fullest discussion of Jefferson's mentality in this racial area remains Jordan, *White over Black*, 429–81. The quotation comes from the Second Inaugural Address, March 4, 1804, *Ford*, VIII, 344–45. The fullest presentation of his benevolent intentions toward the Indian population during his first term is in Jefferson to Benjamin Hawkins, February 18, 1803, *ibid.*, 213–14.

53. Jefferson to Governor William Henry Harrison, February 27, 1803, *L&B*, X, 368–73.

54. See Jefferson's welcoming remarks to Indian delegates on January 7, 1802, *ibid.*, 391–400. Also Jefferson to Henry Dearborn, December 29, 1802, *LC*, where he suggests that policies that force Indians to go into debt were justified on the ground that this would hasten the inevitable by leading to their removal west of the Mississippi. The seminal study of this entire question is Bernard W. Sheehan, *Seeds of Extinction: Jeffersonian Philanthropy and the American Indian* (Chapel Hill, 1973).

55. Second Inaugural Address, March 4, 1805, *Ford*, VIII, 345; Jefferson to James Monroe, November 24, 1801, *ibid.*, 103–06.

56. The best book-length treatment of Jefferson's foreign policy is Robert W. Tucker and David C. Hendrickson, *Empire of Liberty: The Statecraft of Thomas Jefferson* (New York, 1990). The best brief overview is Walter La Faber, "Jefferson and an American Foreign Policy," Onuf, ed., *Jeffersonian Legacies*, 370–91.

57. Jefferson to James Madison, August 28, 1801, July 30, 1802, August 23, 1802, *Smith*, II, 1193, 1231–32, 1239; Jefferson to Wilson Carey Nicholas, June 11, 1801, *Ford*, X, 264–65. A convenient synthesis of Jefferson's views on the Barbary pirates is available in Reginald C. Stuart, *The Half-Way Pacifist: Thomas Jefferson's View of War* (Toronto, 1978), 35–51. The standard history of the naval war in the Mediterranean is William M. Fowler, Jr., *Jack Tars and Commodores: The American Navy, 1783–1815* (Boston, 1984), 82–105.

58. Robert J. Allison, *The Crescent Obscured: The United States and the Muslim World, 1776–1815* (New York, 1995), 187–206, is excellent on the popular response to Decatur's exploits.

59. The decision to build a small fleet of gunboats rather than the more expensive frigates was the Jefferson answer to the budget demands. See Spencer C. Tucker, *The Jeffersonian Gunboat Navy* (Columbia, 1993).

60. The standard account is Alexander DeConde, *The Affair of Louisiana* (New York, 1976). Recent and briefer scholarly treatments of the subject include Reginald Horsman, "The Dimensions of an 'Empire for Liberty': Expansionism and Republicanism, 1775–1825," *JER*, IX (1985), 1–20; and John M. Belolavek, "Politics, Principle, and Pragmatism in the Early Republic: Thomas Jefferson and the Quest for American Empire," *Diplomatic History*, XV (1991), 599–606.

61. The reference to Napoleon's decision to "throw the province" is from the historian Edward Channing, cited in *Malone*, IV, 285, which also contains the quotation from the *New York Evening Post*. Even such a loyal

Jeffersonian as Margaret Bayard Smith attributed "little or no agency" to Jefferson. See Smith, *Forty Years*, 40.

62. James Madison to Robert R. Livingston, May 1, 1802, quoted in *Malone*, IV, 258; for Jefferson's view of Spain as a mere stalking-horse for eventual American occupation, see Jefferson to William C. Clarborne, July 13, 1801, *Ford*, VIII, 71–72; the Rufus King quotation is from Rufus King to James Madison, June 1, 1801, cited in *Malone*, IV, 249. The narrative of these heady times and the silent collaboration between Jefferson and Madison is handled with a truly deft touch in *Smith*, II, 1254–57.

63. Jefferson to Robert R. Livingston, April 18, 1802, *Ford*, VIII, 143–47. The French side of this diplomatic equation is best covered in George Dangerfield, *Chancellor Robert Livingston of New York, 1746–1813* (New York, 1960), 309–94.

64. Jefferson to James Monroe, January 13, 1803, *Ford*, VIII, 190–92; see also Jefferson to James Monroe, January 10, 1803, *ibid.*, 188.

65. Jefferson to du Pont de Nemours, February 1, 1803, *Ford*, VIII, 204; Jefferson to James Madison, February 22, 1803, *Smith*, II, 1262; Hamilton quotation in *Malone*, IV, 277–78; Jefferson to John Bacon, April 30, 1803, *Ford*, VIII, 228–29.

66. Livingston quoted in *Malone*, IV, 258. The matter of Napoleon's unfathomable character was discussed in Jefferson to James Madison, August 18, 1803, *Smith*, II, 1279.

67. Jefferson to L. A. Pichon, July 1802, *LC*. The American posture toward the insurrection in Santo Domingo was discussed in Jefferson to James Madison, November 22, 1801, *Smith*, II, 1204, and Jefferson to James Monroe, June 2, 1802, *Ford*, VIII, 152–54. The best scholarly account of Jefferson's posture toward Toussaint is Douglas R. Egerton, *Gabriel's Rebellion: The Virginia Slave Conspiracies of 1800 and 1802* (Chapel Hill, 1993), 45–48, 160–61, 168–72.

68. The Talleyrand quotation is in *Malone*, IV, 306; Jefferson to John Colvin, September 20, 1810, *Ford*, X, 146.

69. Jefferson to Meriwether Lewis, April 27, 1803, and July 15, 1803, *Ford*, VIII, 193–97, 199–200; also Confidential Message on Expedition to the Pacific, January 18, 1803, *ibid.*, 202.

70. For Jefferson's somewhat expansive interpretation of the maps, see Jefferson to James Madison, August 24, 1803, *Smith*, II, 1282. This is the kind of collaboration with Madison that is usually invisible to historians, but

because Jefferson had retreated to Monticello to avoid Washington's heat and humidity he was forced to correspond with Madison.

71. Jefferson to James Monroe, January 8, 1804, *Ford*, VIII, 289; Jefferson to John Breckinridge, August 12, 1803, *ibid.*, 243; Jefferson to William Dunbar, September 21, 1803, *ibid.*, 256. See also Jefferson to James Madison, July 17, 1803, September 12, 1803, September 14, 1803, *Smith*, II, 1272–73, 1285–86.

72. Draft of an amendment to the Constitution, [July, 1803], *Ford*, VIII, 241–49; Jefferson to Albert Gallatin, January 1803, *ibid.*, 242; Jefferson to John Breckinridge, August 12, 1803, *ibid.*, 244; Jefferson to John Dickinson, August 9, 1803, *ibid.*, 262.

73. Jefferson to Levi Lincoln, August 30, 1803, *ibid.*, 246; also Jefferson to Thomas Paine, August 18, 1803, *ibid.*, 245; Jefferson to Wilson Cary Nicholas, September 7, 1803, *ibid.*, 247–48.

74. The senator was William Plumer, quoted in Plumer, *Memorandum of Proceedings*, 13–14. The remark by John Quincy Adams is cited in *Malone*, IV, 331–32.

75. Jefferson to John Breckinridge, November 24, 1803, *Ford*, VIII, 279–81.

76. James Madison to Robert R. Livingston, January 31, 1804, cited in *Malone*, IV, 353.

77. Jefferson felt uneasy about his posture, but mostly because of the opening it created for his Federalist critics. See Jefferson to De Witt Clinton, December 2, 1803, and Jefferson to James Monroe, January 8, 1804, *Ford*, VIII, 282–83, 287–88. For the remonstrance, see *Malone*, IV, 359–60.

78. On his insistence that the suspension of republican principles would only be temporary, see Jefferson to James Madison, August 7, 1804, *Smith*, II, 1332.

79. The best discussion of Jefferson's belief that the life span of the American republic could be extended only by territorial expansion is Drew R. McCoy, *The Elusive Republic: Political Economy in Jeffersonian America* (New York, 1980).

80. Jefferson to Joseph Priestley, January 29, 1804, *Ford*, VIII, 295.

81. The standard work on Federalist criticisms of Jeffersonian values is Linda Kerber, *Federalists in Dissent: Imagery and Ideology in Jeffersonian America* (Ithaca, 1970). On the politics, see David Hackett Fischer, *The Revolution of American Conservatism: The Federalist Party in the Era of Jeffersonian Democracy* (New York, 1965).

82. Hamilton's pamphlet vilifying Adams is reprinted in Syrett, ed., *Hamilton Papers*, XXV, 186–209. The charges against Hamilton, along with his response, are also available in *ibid.*, XXI, 238–85. The charges against Washington are conveniently gathered in John C. Fitzpatrick, *The George Washington Scandals* (Alexandria, 1929). Jefferson to Robert R. Livingston, October 10, 1802, *Ford*, VIII, 174–75.

83. Henry Adams, ed., *Documents Relating to New England Federalism* (Boston, 1877), 230–32, 321–22. For the obsession with the mammoth metaphor, see Kerber, *Federalists in Dissent*, 69–70. For the mammoth cheese, see *Malone*, IV, 106–07.

84. Peden, ed., *Notes*, 159; "Syllabus of an Estimate of the Merit of the Doctrines of Jesus, Compared with Those of Others," which was enclosed with his letter to Rush, April 21, 1803, *Ford*, VIII, 223–28. The most recent and comprehensive discussion of Jefferson's religious views is Edwin S. Gaustad, *Sworn on the Altar of God: A Religious Biography of Thomas Jefferson* (Grand Rapids, 1995).

85. Jefferson to Tom Paine, March 18, 1801, *Ford*, VIII, 19.

86. The flood of newspaper attacks on Paine and Jefferson is conveniently available in Keane, *Tom Paine*, 455–75; see also *Malone*, IV, 192–200. The Adams quotation is from *History*, II, 215–16. Jefferson's loyalty to Paine is nicely on display in Jefferson to Tom Paine, January 13, 1803. John Adams, on permanent sentry duty in Quincy, was willing to forgive Paine his atheism, but not his politics. Adams described Paine as "a mongrel between Pig and Puppy, begotten by a wild Boar on A Bitch Wolf. . . ." John Adams to Benjamin Waterhouse, October 29, 1805, Worthington C. Ford, ed., *Statesman and Friend: Correspondence of John Adams and Benjamin Waterhouse, 1784–1822* (Boston, 1927), 31.

87. A good sampling of the newspaper coverage can be gleaned from three sources: Douglass Adair, "The Jefferson Scandals," in Colbourn, ed. *Fame and the Founding Fathers;* Virginius Dabney, *The Jefferson Scandals: A Rebuttal* (New York, 1981) and Brodie, *Intimate History*, 339–75. A much more comprehensive sampling of the press reports deriving from Callender's initial story was made available to me by Robert McDonald, a graduate student at the University of North Carolina at Chapel Hill.

88. The most psychologically perceptive and historically balanced treatment of the Sally Hemings charge remains Jordan, *White over Black*, 461–69. For the Adams reaction, see John Adams to Colonel Ward, January 8, 1810, *Microfilm Edition of Adams Papers*, Reel 118.

89. For Callender's career, see Michael Durey, *With the Hammer of Truth: James Thomas Callender and America's Early National Heroes* (Charlottesville, 1990). Jefferson to James Monroe, May 26, 1801, and July 15, 1802, *Ford,* VIII, 57–58, 164–68, for Jefferson's efforts to conceal his past dealings with Callender. Given Henry Adams's highly nuanced understanding of Jefferson's character, his conclusions about the Callender charges are worthy of special attention. See *History,* II, 219–23, where Adams finds Jefferson guilty of lying about his complicity with Callender but innocent of the sexual charges.

90. John Quincy Adams to Rufus King, October 8, 1802, quoted in *Malone,* IV, 139.

91. Jefferson to M. Pictet, February 5, 1803, *L&B,* X, 356–57. For the newspaper explosion during the first decade of the nineteenth century, see Fischer, *Revolution of American Conservatism,* appendix III.

92. Jefferson to Thomas McKean, February 19, 1803, *Ford,* VIII, 216–19. Malone sees these prosecutions as "a temporary aberration." See *Malone,* IV, 235. The strongest case on the other side, seeing these incidents as representative, is by Leonard Levy, *Jefferson and Civil Liberties: The Darker Side* (Cambridge, 1963).

93. Jefferson to Levi Lincoln, August 26, 1801, *L&B,* X, 276; Richard Branch Giles to Jefferson, June 1, 1801, *LC.* The authoritative scholarly work on the subject is Richard E. Ellis, *The Jeffersonian Crisis: Courts and Politics in the Young Republic* (New York, 1971).

94. Jefferson to Abigail Adams, June 13, 1804, *Cappon,* I, 270. Charles Warren, *The Supreme Court in United States History* (3 vols., Boston, 1923), I, 179–81, for the anecdote about Marshall. On the relationship between Jefferson and Marshall, see Julian Boyd, "The Chasm That Separated Thomas Jefferson and John Marshall," in Gottfried Dietze, ed., *Essays on American Constitutionalism* (Englewood Cliffs, 1964), 3–20.

95. Jefferson to Spencer Roane, September 6, 1819, *L&B,* XV, 135–36, where Jefferson recalls the advice from Madison and Gallatin in 1801.

96. Ellis, *Jeffersonian Crisis,* 3–16, offers an elegant synthesis of the judicial ambiguities in the wake of the American Revolution. A more recent and exhaustive treatment of judicial review is J. M. Sosin, *The Aristocracy of the Long Robe: The Origins of Judicial Review in America* (New York, 1989).

97. This interpretation of Jefferson's attitude toward the federal judiciary reverses the conventional view, best presented by Richard Ellis in *Jeffersonian Crisis,* that sees Jefferson as a moderate Republican trying to keep

radicals like Giles under control. Jefferson's view of the federal courts, I am arguing, was much like Jackson's view of the national bank, a deeply felt and vitriolic hatred that went beyond the personalities on the federal bench to the very character of the institution itself.

98. Kathryn Turner, "Federalist Policy and the Judiciary Act of 1801," *WMQ*, XXII (1965), 9–14; Ellis, *Jeffersonian Crisis*, 36–52; First Annual Message, December 8, 1801, *Ford*, VIII, 123. The report Jefferson prepared for the Congress, allegedly showing that circuit courts were unnecessary because the number of cases was small, proved an embarrassment when Federalists demonstrated that the report was riddled with errors.

99. Hobson, ed., *Marshall Papers*, VI, 160–83, provides the opinion itself along with an excellent editorial note that conveniently summarizes the massive scholarship on the landmark decision. The discussion in *Malone*, IV, 135–56, is also excellent in rescuing the historical context of Marshall's opinion from the constitutional lawyers, who are invariably more disposed to view the matter in the context of judicial review. See also Ellis, *Jeffersonian Crisis*, 53–68. The most recent historical assessment is Robert L. Clinton, *Marbury v. Madison and Judicial Review* (Lawrence, 1989).

100. Jefferson to J. H. Nicholson, May 13, 1803, *L&B*, X, 390. Ellis, *Jeffersonian Crisis*, 76–82, and *Malone*, IV, 464–80, for the story of Chase's impeachment.

101. See Jefferson Papers, February 1805, *LC*, for Jefferson's longhand record of the votes on the five separate charges against Chase and the senators who voted each way. The most telling criticism of the Republican campaign against Chase came from John Quincy Adams, who argued that the prosecution was a political affair devoid of any pretense of principle. See Charles Francis Adams, ed., *Memoirs of John Quincy Adams* (12 vols., Philadelphia, 1874), I, 318–23.

102. Jefferson to Thomas Ritchie, December 25, 1820, *Ford*, X, 170–71.

103. Jefferson to Spencer Roane, September 6, 1819, *L&B*, XV, 135–36; *History*, I, 188.

104. Services of Jefferson, [1800?], *Ford*, VII, 475–77. Lucia Stanton has called my attention to the term "Memorandum of Services" in the manuscript version of the Jefferson Papers in the Library of Congress. The title "Services of Jefferson" in *Ford* is obviously a silent revision.

105. Jefferson to Elbridge Gerry, March 3, 1804, *Ford*, VIII, 297–98.

106. Jefferson to John Page, June 25, 1804, *Domestic Life*, 302–04. See also Jefferson to James Madison, April 23, 1804, *Smith*, II, 1323, for an equally

poignant reflection on Maria's death and what it meant to him. In the election of 1804 Jefferson and George Clinton received 162 electoral votes to 14 for Charles Cotesworth Pinckney and Rufus King. Jefferson swept every state except Connecticut and Delaware, plus two electors in Maryland.

5. MONTICELLO: 1816–26

1. *Domestic Life,* 381–83, for the Old Eagle story and the various injuries suffered in falls. *Malone,* VI, is the final volume in the authoritative biography covering these years, but the affection for Jefferson, the endearing hallmark of Malone's approach throughout his six-volume masterpiece, becomes a problem in these latter years of the story. I have found Peterson, *New Nation,* 922–1099, more reliable for this period. On the problem of Jefferson's latter-day sense of despondency, see Gordon Wood, "The Trials and Tribulations of Thomas Jefferson," Onuf, ed., *Jeffersonian Legacies,* 410–15.

2. Jefferson to Benjamin Waterhouse, January 8, 1825, *Ford,* X, 335–36, for Jefferson's own summary of his physical condition. *Domestic Life,* 394–95, for his remark on physicians. Jefferson to John Adams, July 5, 1814, *Cappon,* II, 430.

3. *Domestic Life,* 331, 337; for a running account of his physical appearance and condition, see the multiple letters to James Madison in *Smith,* III, 1795, 1807, 1815, 1822, 1824, 1841, 1852; see also Jefferson to Frances Wright, August 7, 1825, Jefferson to William Gordon, January 1, 1826, Jefferson to Thomas Jefferson Randolph, February 8, 1826, *Ford,* X, 344, 358, 374–75.

4. Peterson, ed., *Visitors to Monticello,* 95–99, 104–06.

5. Jefferson to Dr. Vine Utley, March 21, 1819, *Domestic Life,* 370–72, for his diet, regimen, eyesight; see also Jefferson to Benjamin Rush, February 28, 1803, *Ford,* VIII, 220, for the lengthiest description of matters intestinal.

6. *Domestic Life,* 341–43, 346, 361; Peterson, ed., *Visitors to Monticello,* 53–54, for Margaret Bayard Smith's reminiscence of his grandfatherly games.

7. Peterson, ed., *Visitors to Monticello,* 73, for George Ticknor's remark about Monticello as "Mecca"; *Domestic Life,* 401–02, for the number of visitors and guests.

8. Jefferson to John Adams, June 27, 1822, John Adams to Jefferson, July 12, 1822, *Cappon,* II, 581–82.

9. Jefferson to James Madison, May 3, 1826, James Madison to Jefferson, May 6, 1826, *Smith,* III, 1970–71.

10. Jefferson to John Adams, June 1, 1822, John Adams to Jefferson, June 11, 1822, *Cappon,* II, 578–79; Jefferson to Maria Cosway, December 27, 1820, *Domestic Life,* 374; Jefferson to Francis Vanderkemp, January 11, 1825, *Ford,* X, 336–38.

11. *Domestic Life,* 390–91; J. Bennett Nolan, ed., *Lafayette in America: Day by Day* (Baltimore, 1934), 257. See the account of the visit, with Madison's remarks on Lafayette, in *Smith,* III, 1889.

12. Jefferson to James Madison, October 18, 1825, *Smith,* III, 1942. See also Alfred L. Bush, *The Life Portraits of Thomas Jefferson* (Charlottesville, 1987), 95.

13. Peterson, ed., *Visitors to Monticello,* 109, for Henry Lee's observations of the dying Jefferson. *Domestic Life,* 422–32.

14. John Adams to Thomas Jefferson, July 15, 1813, *Cappon,* II, 358; John Adams to Benjamin Rush, April 18, 1808, John A. Schutz and Douglass Adair, eds., *The Spur of Fame: Dialogues of John Adams and Benjamin Rush, 1805–1813* (San Marino, 1966), 107–08.

15. Jefferson to Abigail Adams, June 13 and July 22, 1804, Abigail Adams to Jefferson, July 1 and August 18, 1804, *Cappon,* I, 268–74. The appended note by John Adams, dated November 19, 1804, is in *ibid.,* 282.

16. This very succinct summary is based on a score of specialized studies, but two accounts of Jefferson's second term stand out: Henry Adams, *History,* I, 603–1232; *Malone,* V, entitled *Jefferson the President: Second Term, 1805–1809.*

17. The standard account of the embargo and the Anglo-American diplomacy of the era is Bradford Perkins, *Prologue to War: England and the United States* (Berkeley, 1961). My interpretation tends to follow the line best traced by Tucker and Hendrickson, *Empire of Liberty.* For a succinct summary of the way Jefferson thought about the choices of war and peace in 1807, see Reginald C. Stuart, "Thomas Jefferson and the Function of War: Policy or Principle," *Canadian Journal of History,* XI (1976), 160–71. The most recent scholarly appraisal is Walter La Feber, "Jefferson and an American Foreign Policy," Onuf, ed., *Jeffersonian Legacies,* 382–86. When all is said, however, and a great deal has been said, the account by Henry Adams, *History,* I, 1031–48, has never been surpassed.

18. *History,* I, 1239–52, for the political mood surrounding Jefferson's retirement; an elegant summary is also available in *Smith,* III, 1551–54; Jef-

ferson to Pierre Samuel du Pont de Nemours, March 2, 1809, *L&B*, XII, 259–60.

19. John Adams to Benjamin Rush, March 4, 1809, *Microfilm Edition of Adams Papers*, Reel 118.

20. Benjamin Rush to John Adams, February 17, 1812, Schutz and Adair, eds., *Spur of Fame*, 211; John Adams to Benjamin Rush, August 31, 1809, and July 12, 1812, in Alexander Biddle, ed., *Old Family Letters . . .* (Philadelphia, 1892), 246, 297–98. See also Lyman H. Butterfield, "The Dream of Benjamin Rush: The Reconciliation of John Adams and Thomas Jefferson," *Yale Review*, 40 (1950–51), 297–319.

21. John Adams to Benjamin Rush, August 31 and December 21, 1809, July 3 and February 10, 1812, Biddle, ed., *Old Family Letters*, 246, 249, 297, 313.

22. John Adams to Jefferson, January 1, 1812, *Cappon*, II, 290. Donald Stewart and George Clark, "Misanthrope or Humanitarian? John Adams in Retirement," *New England Quarterly*, XXVIII (1955), 216–36, for the "brother sailor" reference. I have also devoted a chapter to the Adams-Jefferson correspondence in *Passionate Sage*, 113–42.

23. Jefferson to John Adams, January 21, 1812, John Adams to Jefferson, February 3, 1812, Jefferson to John Adams, April 8, 1816, John Adams to Jefferson, May 3, 1816, *Cappon*, II, 291–92, 295, 467, 471.

24. John Adams to Benjamin Rush, February 10, 1812, *Microfilm Edition of Adams Papers*, Reel 118; Jefferson to John Adams, August 15, 1820, and September 12, 1821, John Adams to Jefferson, September 24, 1821, *Cappon*, II, 566–67, 574, 576.

25. The troublesome letter that Adams worried about referred to Jefferson as a congenital liar whose presidency was likely to produce "only calamities." See John Adams to William Cunningham, January 16, 1804, *Microfilm Edition of Adams Papers,* Reel 118. Jefferson to John Adams, October 12, 1823, John Adams to Jefferson, November 10, 1823, *Cappon*, II, 599–601, 601–02.

26. Jefferson to Benjamin Rush, December 5, 1811, *Ford*, IX, 300; for Jefferson's "Adams Problem," see Ellis, *Passionate Sage*, 143–45.

27. Philip F. Detweiler, "The Changing Reputation of the Declaration of Independence: The First Fifty Years," *WMQ*, XIX (1962), 551–73. I am also indebted to Robert S. McDonald, a graduate student at the University of North Carolina at Chapel Hill, who shared a draft chapter from his dissertation on Jefferson's early anonymity as author of the Declaration. On

Madison's conference with John Trumbull about the Rotunda paintings, see *Smith*, III, 1774–75.

28. John Adams to Jefferson, June 22, 1819, Jefferson to John Adams, July 9, 1819, John Adams to Jefferson, July 21, 1819, *Cappon*, II, 542–46. John Adams to Francis Vanderkemp, August 21, 1819, *Microfilm Edition of Adams Papers*, Reel 124.

29. For the account in Adams's autobiography, see L. Butterfield, ed., *Diary and Autobiography*, III, 335–38. For Jefferson's account in his autobiography, see *Ford*, I, 30–38. Jefferson to James Madison, August 30, 1823, *Smith*, III, 1875–76; James Madison to Jefferson, September 6, 1823, *ibid.*, 1877–78.

30. John Adams to Benjamin Rush, September 30, 1805, and June 21, 1811, *Microfilm Edition of Adams Papers*, Reel 118; John Adams to Jefferson, November 12, 1813, *Cappon*, II, 392–93.

31. John Adams to Jefferson, July 30, 1815, Jefferson to John Adams, August 10–11, 1815, *Cappon*, II, 451–53.

32. Butterfield, ed., *Diary and Autobiography*, III, 335–36.

33. John Adams to Jefferson, July 13, 1813, and December 16, 1816, *Cappon*, II, 355–56, 500–01.

34. John Adams to Jefferson, May 6, 1816, *ibid.*, 472.

35. Jefferson to John Adams, August 1, 1816, and October 14, 1816, *ibid.*, 483, 490; John Adams to Jefferson, February 2, 1816, *ibid.*, 461.

36. Jefferson to John Adams, June 27, 1813, *ibid.*, 335.

37. John Adams to Jefferson, July 9, 1813, and November 13, 1813, *ibid.*, 351, 456.

38. John Adams to Jefferson, July 9, 1813, August [14], 1813, December 19, 1813, *ibid.*, 351, 365, 409.

39. Jefferson to John Adams, October 28, 1813, *ibid.*, 387–92.

40. John Adams to Jefferson, September 2, 1813, September 15, 1813, November 15, 1813, *ibid.*, 371, 376, 400.

41. Jefferson to John Adams, March 25, 1826, *ibid.*, 613–14.

42. The Whitehead reference and the larger point about the influence that posterity's judgment had on the revolutionary generation are elegantly suggested in Adair, "Fame and the Founding Fathers," Colbourn, ed., *Fame and the Founding Fathers*, 3–26.

43. Jefferson to William Wirt, September 4, 1816, Jefferson to Benjamin Waterhouse, March 3, 1818, *Ford*, X, 59–60, 102–04.

44. Jefferson to Benjamin Waterhouse, January 31, 1819, Jefferson to Samuel Adams Wells, May 12, 1819, *ibid.*, 124, 129.

45. Jefferson to James Madison, June 22, 1817, *Smith*, III, 1786. When Marshall's biography first appeared, Jefferson tried to get Joel Barlow to write a rebuttal. See Jefferson to Joel Barlow, May 3, 1802, *Ford*, VIII, 148–51.

46. Jefferson to William Johnson, March 4, 1823, *Ford*, X, 246–49.

47. John Adams to Jefferson, July [3], 1813, *Cappon*, II, 349; John Marshall, *The Life of George Washington* (5 vols., Philadelphia, 1804–07), V, 33; Franklin B. Sawvel, ed., *The Complete Anas of Thomas Jefferson* (New York, 1903), 43.

48. *Boyd*, XXV, 33–38, for the editorial note on the rather odd history of these materials, whatever we wish to call them. The note is by Charles Cullen and includes Jefferson's comment quoted here.

49. The most accessible version of the "Anas" is in *Ford*, I, 154–339. As we now know, Jefferson did not intend to include material after 1792, and most of the earlier editions of his papers violated that intention by adding material up to and through his presidency. Keeping that editorial fact in mind, I have chosen to quote from the Ford edition of the "Anas" for reasons of convenience. *Ibid.*, 156, 165, 166–67.

50. The appraisal of Washington is in Jefferson to Dr. Walter Jones, January 2, 1814, *Domestic Life*, 356–57. The many conversations between Jefferson and Washington constitute the largest section of the "Anas" and are reproduced in *Ford*, I, 168–278. Jefferson also repeated these stories in several letters in the years after compiling the material. See especially Jefferson to Martin Van Buren, June 29, 1824, and Jefferson to William Short, January 8, 1825, *Ford*, X, 305–16, 328–35.

51. Joanne B. Freeman, "Slander, Poison, Whispers, and Fame: Jefferson's 'Anas' and Political Gossip in the Early Republic," *JER*, XV (1995), 25–59.

52. *Ford*, I, 20–47, for the autobiographical version of the drafting of the Declaration and the debate in the Continental Congress.

53. *Ibid.*, 118–47, for the story of the coming of the French Revolution; *ibid.*, 140, for the quotation on the culpability of the queen.

54. Jefferson to Benjamin Austin, January 9, 1816, and February 9, 1816, *Ford*, X, 7–11.

55. Jefferson to William H. Crawford, June 20, 1816, *ibid.*, 36. The best discussion of Jefferson's evolution on this subject is in McCoy, *The Elusive Republic*, 34–57.

56. O. I. A. Roche, ed., *The Jefferson Bible: The Life and Morals of Jesus of Nazareth* (New York, 1964). The earlier version, "Syllabus of an Estimate of the Merit of the Doctrines of Jesus, Compared with Those of Others," is in *Ford*, VIII, 223–28. The quotations come from his many letters on this subject: Jefferson to Charles Thomson, January 9, 1816, Jefferson to Horatio Gates Spafford, January 10, 1816, Jefferson to William Short, October 31, 1819, Jefferson to Benjamin Waterhouse, June 26, 1822, Jefferson to John Davis, January 18, 1824, *Ford*, X, 5–7, 12–15, 144, 219–20, 287–88.

57. Jefferson to Judge Spencer Roane, September 6, 1819, *ibid.*, 140–43. The classic Jeffersonian interpretation of the era, indeed of all American history, is Vernon L. Parrington, *Main Currents in American Thought* (3 vols., New York, 1927–30).

58. Jefferson to Samuel Kercheval, July 12, 1816, Jefferson to John Taylor, May 28, 1816, *Ford*, X, 37–39, 27–31.

59. Jefferson to Samuel Kercheval, July 12, 1816, and September 5, 1816, *ibid.*, 40–43, 45–46. The issue was on his mind at this time, as can be seen in other letters in which it comes up. See especially Jefferson to du Pont de Nemours, April 24, 1816, and Jefferson to Francis W. Gilmer, June 7, 1816, *ibid.*, 22–25, 31–33. The most recent revisionist interpretation of the American Revolution is Wood, *The Radicalism of the American Revolution*, which argues that there were incipient democratic implications embedded within the independence movement, which most of the revolutionary generation did not fully appreciate at the time and which seeped out slowly over the next fifty years, becoming fully discernible only in the Age of Jackson. On the one hand, Jefferson is an almost perfect illustration of the argument, and his own revisionist views of 1816–19 document Wood's interpretation handsomely. On the other hand, as Wood himself has often noted, Jefferson had only a partial grasp of the leveling implications inherent in democratic culture and was never comfortable in the world that Andrew Jackson symbolized and Alexis de Tocqueville described.

60. Jefferson to Samuel Kercheval, September 5, 1816, *Ford*, X, 45–46.

61. Jefferson to John Hambden Pleasants, April 19, 1824, *ibid.*, 302–04.

62. Jefferson to James Madison, February 25, 1822, *Smith*, III, 1837–38.

63. *Ford*, I, 77.

64. Jefferson to George Logan, May 11, 1805, Jefferson to Dr. Thomas Humphreys, February 8, 1817, *Ford*, IX, 141, X, 76–77. In the same vein, see Jefferson to Fanny Wright, August 7, 1825, and Jefferson to William Short, January 18, 1826, *ibid.*, 343–45, 361–62. The best discussion of Jeffer-

son's procrastinating tendencies is in Freehling, *Road to Disunion*, 122–31, 152–57.

65. Jefferson to John Adams, December 10, 1819, *Cappon*, II, 548–49; Jefferson to Hugh Nelson, February 7, 1820, and March 12, 1820, *Ford*, X, 156–57; Peterson, ed., *Visitors to Monticello*, 90–91. I am much indebted to Peter Onuf, who shared an early draft of his lengthy essay "Thomas Jefferson, Missouri and the 'Empire of Liberty,'" which focuses in a fresh way on these years as a culmination of Jefferson's somewhat tortured thinking on the slavery question.

66. Jefferson to John Holmes, April 22, 1820, *Ford*, X, 157–58. Good discussions of this important letter are readily available in: Miller, *Wolf by the Ears*, 221–52; *Malone*, VI, 328–44; and Donald E. Fehrenbacher, "The Missouri Controversy and the Sources of Southern Separatism," *Southern Review*, XIV (1978), 653–67.

67. For the Adams view, see John Adams to Robert Walsh, January 19, 1820, and John Adams to Joshua Cushman, March 16, 1820, *Microfilm Edition of Adams Papers*, Reel 124.

68. John Adams to Louisa Catherine Adams, January 29, 1820, and John Adams to William Tudor, November 20, 1819, *ibid.*

69. John Adams to Jefferson, February 3, 1821, *Cappon*, II, 571; Jefferson to Charles Pinckney, September 30, 1820, *Ford*, X, 162–63.

70. Jefferson to David Bailey Warden, December 26, 1820, and Jefferson to Jared Sparks, February 4, 1824, *Ford*, 173, 289–93.

71. Jefferson to Fanny Wright, August 7, 1825, and Jefferson to William Short, January 18, 1826, *ibid.*, 343–45, 361–62.

72. Jefferson to Albert Gallatin, December 26, 1820, and Jefferson to Henry Dearborn, August 17, 1821, *ibid.*, 175–78, 191–92.

73. John Adams to Louisa Catherine Adams, January 29, 1820, John Adams to John Quincy Adams, December 23, 1819, *Microfilm Edition of Adams Papers*, Reel 124. On the large question of what the revolutionary generation intended concerning slavery, see Gary Nash, *Race and Revolution* (Madison, 1990).

74. Jefferson to Charles Pinckney, September 30, 1820, *Ford*, X, 161–62.

75. Jefferson to Marquis de Lafayette, October 28, 1822, *ibid.*, 233; Jefferson to Albert Gallatin, October 29, 1822, *ibid.*, 235–36.

76. On this phase of Jefferson's superheated response to national events, especially the vilification of those endorsing internal improve-

ments, see the following: Joseph H. Harrison, Jr., *"Sic et Non:* Thomas Jefferson and Internal Improvements," *JER,* VII (1987), 335–49; John Lauritz Larson, "Jefferson's Union and the Problems of Internal Improvements," Onuf, ed., *Jeffersonian Legacies,* 340–69; Robert Shalhope, "Thomas Jefferson's Republicanism and Antebellum Southern Thought," *JSH,* XLII (1976), 529–56.

77. Jefferson to Albert Gallatin, December 26, 1820, *Ford,* X, 177; Jefferson to Marquis de Lafayette, November 4, 1823, *ibid.,* 279–83; Jefferson to William Branch Giles, December 26, 1825, *ibid.,* 355–56.

78. The best account of the panic is in George Dangerfield, *The Awakening of American Nationalism, 1815–1828* (New York, 1965), 108–41. This is the implicit defense of Jefferson's mentality offered by his descendants in *Domestic Life,* 405–11 and, more explicitly, in Peterson, *New Nation,* 991–94. For the *"coup de grace"* reference, see Jefferson to James Madison, February 17, 1826, *Smith,* III, 1966.

79. Jefferson to Nathaniel Bacon, January 12, 1819, *Ford,* X, 121–22. For Taylor's agrarian philosophy, see Robert Shalhope, *John Taylor of Caroline: Pastoral Republican* (Columbia, 1980). For Johnson's judicial career, see Donald G. Morgan, *Justice William Johnson, the First Dissenter: The Career and Constitutional Philosophy of a Jeffersonian Judge* (Columbia, 1954).

80. Jefferson to James Madison, February 17, 1826, *Smith,* III, 1967; James Madison to Nicholas P. Trist, May 29, 1832, *ibid.,* 1993. See the splendid account of this phase of the Jefferson-Madison partnership in McCoy, *Last of the Fathers,* 39–83. See also the earlier account in Koch, *Jefferson and Madison,* 283–90.

81. McCoy, *Last of the Fathers,* 9–170, is excellent on all these issues.

82. Jefferson to William Johnson, June 12, 1823, *Smith,* III, 1865; Jefferson to Robert J. Garnett, February 14, 1824, *Ford,* X, 295; James Madison to Jefferson, June 27, 1823, *Smith,* III, 1870–75; the Dolley Madison quotation, which dates from 1836, is in *ibid.,* 1850.

83. Jefferson to Judge Spencer Roane, March 9, 1821, *Ford,* X, 189; Jefferson to Thomas Ritchie, December 25, 1820, *ibid.,* 169–71; the "sappers and miners" comment is repeated in his autobiography, *ibid.,* I, 113; see also Jefferson to Nathaniel Bacon, August 19, 1821, and Jefferson to William Johnson, October 27, 1822, *ibid.,* X, 192–93, 222–26.

84. Jefferson to William Johnson, June 12, 1823, *Smith,* III, 1866.

85. James Madison to Jefferson, June 27, 1823, *ibid.,* 1868–70.

86. *Ibid.*, 1944–46, for Jefferson's draft proposal; Jefferson to James Madison, December 24, 1825, 1943, for the quotation about Madison's opinion.

87. James Madison to Jefferson, December 28, 1825, *ibid.*, 1948–51, which includes Madison's letter to Thomas Ritchie on the same subject, an enclosure Madison sent along to Jefferson in order to make his disagreement less direct; Jefferson to James Madison, January 2, 1826, *ibid.*, 1961–62.

88. From Thomas Jefferson Randolph's account of the final hours in *Domestic Life,* 427.

89. The secondary literature on Jefferson and the University of Virginia defies accurate or easy summary. The standard work on Jefferson and education is Roy J. Honeywell, *The Educational Work of Thomas Jefferson* (New York, 1964). The most recent revisionist account is Harold Hellenbrand, *The Unfinished Revolution: Education and Politics in the Thought of Thomas Jefferson* (Newark, 1990). Since this is the most attractive aspect of Jefferson's tortured final phase, Dumas Malone makes it the centerpiece of *Malone,* VI, 232–425. Because Madison was such a close partner in the enterprise, the narrative sections of *Smith* are helpful as guides. American Institute of Architects, *Journal,* LXV (1976), 91.

90. Jefferson to James Madison, April 13, 1817, *Smith,* III, 1784–85.

91. *Ibid.*, 1796.

92. A conveniently concise account is in Hellenbrand, *Unfinished Revolution,* 68–140.

93. *Smith,* III, 1776–94; *Malone,* VI, 240–44; James Madison to Jefferson, January 1, 1818, *Smith,* III, 1801; Jefferson to James Madison, June 28, 1818, *ibid.*, 1804–05.

94. Dumas Malone, *The Public Life of Thomas Cooper, 1783–1839* (New Haven, 1922), 234–46, contains information on the difficulties with the Virginia legislature, as does *Smith,* III, 1817–18. Jefferson to James Madison, September 24, 1824, *ibid.*, 1902; Jefferson to Joseph C. Cabell, November 28, 1820, *Ford,* X, 165–68; Jefferson to James Madison, September 30, 1821, *Smith,* III, 1833.

95. Richard Beale Davis, *Francis Walker Gilmer: Life and Learning in Jefferson's Virginia* (Richmond, 1939); Jefferson to James Madison, October 6, 1824, and December 10, 1824, *Smith,* III, 1903, 1910–11; John Adams to Jefferson, February 21, 1820, and January 22, 1825, *Cappon,* II, 561, 607.

96. Jefferson to James Madison, February 1, 1825, *Smith,* III, 1923–34.

97. James Madison to Jefferson, February 8, 1825, *ibid.*, 1026.

98. Peterson, *New Nation,* 980–82, is excellent and forthright about this unattractive development.

99. Jefferson to James Madison and Board of Visitors, April 3–4, 1826, *Smith,* III, 1968–69.

100. Hellenbrand, *Unfinished Revolution,* 143–46, is good on this issue, but the full implications for Jefferson's core political values are best discussed in Matthews, *Radical Politics,* 15–16, 81–89. This is also the focus of Hannah Arendt's appraisal of Jefferson as a truly radical political thinker in her *On Revolution* (New York, 1963), 217–85. My own view is that Matthews and Arendt are right about this seminal aspect of Jefferson's thinking on politics, but I would argue that he does not reach a conscious realization of the ward as his ideal republic until late in life (it was there in embryo from the start, however) and that it is a romantic fantasy more than a cogent political idea.

101. Hellenbrand, *Unfinished Revolution,* 146–50, for the most concise descriptive account of the spatial arrangements at the University of Virginia. At the deeper level of Jefferson's character, one can see this as an attempt to institutionalize his most sentimental attitudes about the affectionate bonds among friends and within families. Here the best source is Burstein, *Inner Jefferson,* which does the most insightful job of exploring the sentimental core of Jefferson's personality.

102. *Malone,* VI, 463–68, tells the story more positively. For the Tutwiler quotation, see *Smith,* III, 1920.

103. Jefferson to James Monroe, March 8, 1826, *Ford,* X, 383. On the debt question see *Malone,* VI, 505–07, and the incomparable account of the nexus of financial and ideological issues in Sloan, *Principle and Interest,* 221–37.

104. Jefferson's "Thoughts on Lotteries," February 1826, *Ford,* X, 362–72; Jefferson to Thomas Jefferson Randolph, February 8, 1826, *ibid.,* 374–75.

105. Jefferson's will is in *ibid.,* 392–96; on the false hope, see Jefferson to George Loyall, February 22, 1826, *ibid.,* 379–80.

106. Jefferson to Roger C. Weightman, June 24, 1826, *ibid.,* 390–92. The handwritten draft, with its multiple cross-outs and revisions, is reproduced in Ellis, *Passionate Sage,* 207.

107. Douglass Adair, "Rumbold's Dying Speech, 1685, and Jefferson's Last Words on Democracy, 1826," in Colbourn, ed., *Fame and the Founding Fathers,* 192–202.

108. The auction scene has been recovered from many fragmentary

sources in Lucia Stanton, " 'Those Who Labor for My Happiness': Thomas Jefferson and His Slaves," Onuf, ed., *Jeffersonian Legacies*, 147–48. The reference to Adams's death as a "Yankee trick" is in *Domestic Life*, 421.

EPILOGUE: THE FUTURE OF AN ILLUSION

1. Carl Becker, "What Is Still Living in the Political Philosophy of Thomas Jefferson?" *Proceedings of the American Philosophical Society*, LXXXVII (1944), 201–10.

2. Joyce Appleby, "Jefferson and His Complex Legacy," Onuf, ed., *Jeffersonian Image*, 2.

3. *Ibid.*, 1; Peterson, *Jefferson Image*, 420–32.

4. The Thomas Jefferson Memorial Foundation publicized its access code in the World Wide Web as http://www.monticello.org.

5. The classic essay by Frederick Jackson Turner is reprinted in his *The Frontier in American History* (Tucson, 1986), 37–38 for the quotation. For a brilliant and bracing reappraisal of what he calls "Anglo-America," with Jefferson playing a major role as America's premier racist, see Michael Lind, *The Next American Nation: The New Nationalism and the Fourth American Revolution* (New York, 1995), 17–96.

6. Herbert D. Croly, *The Promise of American Life* (New York, 1909), perhaps the most influential book about American politics ever written by a practicing journalist.

7. The most recent and panoramic review of these events, all considered within the broad sweep of American cultural history, is Robert H. Wiebe, *Self-Rule: A Cultural History of American Democracy* (Chicago, 1995), 181–246.

8. The classic account of Jefferson's "pastness" is Daniel J. Boorstin, *The Lost World of Thomas Jefferson* (New York, 1948).

9. Dan Balz and Ronald Brownstein, *Storming the Gates: Political Protest and the Republican Revival* (Boston, 1996).

10. An earlier and profound assessment of the enduring role of the antigovernment ethos in American political history is Samuel P. Huntington, *American Politics: The Promise of Disharmony* (Cambridge, 1981), 13–30. In the concluding chapter of *Self-Rule*, 247–66, Robert Wiebe calls for "guerrilla politics" to recover the Jeffersonian essence that has been missing from American democracy for about a century. This is pure nostalgia,

but when embraced by a historian of Wiebe's stature, it illustrates the persistent allure of the Jeffersonian vision.

11. See, for example, Isaac Kramnick and Laurence Moore, *The Godless Constitution: The Case Against Religious Correctness* (New York, 1996).

12. Gunnar Myrdal, *An American Dilemma* (New York, 1943), was the pathbreaking study of race as the central problem facing modern America, which also emphasized its cultural and historical origins rather than its biological character.

13. For the pervasive sense of social "aging" that the revolutionary generation presumed unavoidable, see McCoy, *Last of the Fathers*, 39–84, 171–216; and Ellis, *Passionate Sage*, 237–40.

14. The Wilson quotation is from Peterson, *Jefferson Image*, 343–44. The Appleby quote is from "Jefferson and His Complex Legacy," Onuf, ed., *Jeffersonian Legacies*, 3.

15. Wiebe, *Self-Rule*, 264.

INDEX

abolitionists, 8
Adair, Douglass, 116
Adams, Abigail, 55, 84–7, 101,
　106, 107, 117–18, 140, 264,
　282
Adams, Charles Francis, 146
Adams, Henry, 139, 167, 226, 235,
　257, 270, 366
Adams, John, 7, 12, 16, 35, 47, 73,
　142, 232, 312, 357, 359–60,
　378n68
　on Burr, 206
　and Constitution, 120–3

in Continental Congress, 33,
　42–4, 46, 52–5
correspondence with Jefferson,
　in old age, 6, 14, 254, 274,
　277–8, 281, 285–301, 307, 311,
　327, 333
death of, 14, 346–7, 351
and Declaration of
　Independence, 57, 59, 290–3,
　376n47
election of, 195–6
in England, 88–9, 90, 93, 95–6,
　101, 148, 380n24

From the author of the Pulitzer Prize-winning
best-seller *Founding Brothers* and the National Book
Award-winning best-seller *American Sphinx*—a
landmark biography that brings to life in all his
complexity the most important and perhaps
least understood figure in American history.

His Excellency

GEORGE WASHINGTON

BY JOSEPH J. ELLIS

Available October 2004 in hardcover from Knopf
$26.95 (Canada: $37.95) • 1-4000-4031-0

PLEASE VISIT www.aaknopf.com

Available in Vintage paperback:

American Sphinx • 0-679-76441-0
Founding Brothers • 0-375-70524-4

213 Hamilton on Jefferson